EATING PROBLEMS

EATING PROBLEMS

A Feminist Psychoanalytic Treatment Model

THE WOMEN'S
THERAPY CENTRE INSTITUTE

Carol Bloom
Andrea Gitter
Susan Gutwill
Laura Kogel
Lela Zaphiropoulos

BasicBooks
A Subsidiary of Perseus Books, L.L.C.

Designed by Ellen Levine

LIBRARY OF CONGRESS CATALOGING-IN-PUBLICATION DATA
Eating problems : a feminist psychoanalytic treatment model / by
Women's Therapy Centre Institute ; Carol Bloom . . . [et al.].
        p.   cm.
    Includes bibliographical references and index.
    ISBN 0–465–08876–7
    1. Eating disorders—Treatment. 2. Feminist therapy. 3. Eating dis-
orders—Social aspects. I. Bloom, Carol, 1948– . II. Women's Therapy
Centre Institute.
RC552.E18E294 1994
616.85'260651—dc20   94–12502
                                                                  CIP

01 00 99 98 ❖/RRD 9 8 7 6 5 4

*To our clients and to all women and men who suffer from eating and
body image problems of all kinds, may we dignify these problems.
And to Laurie Phillips, whose life and work are a gift to us all.*

Contents

Foreword by Susie Orbach   ix

Preface   xi

Acknowledgments   xvii

CHAPTER 1   Women's Eating Problems: Social Context and
              the Internalization of Culture
      Susan Gutwill 1

CHAPTER 2   The Diet: Personal Experience, Social Condition,
              and Industrial Empire
      Susan Gutwill 28

CHAPTER 3   Tracing Development: The Feeding Experience
              and the Body
      Carol Bloom and Laura Kogel 40

CHAPTER 4   Symbolic Meanings of Food and Body
      Carol Bloom and Laura Kogel 57

CHAPTER 5   Beginning the Eating and Body Work:
              Stance and Tools
      Carol Bloom, Laura Kogel, and Lela Zaphiropoulos 67

CHAPTER 6   Learning to Feed Oneself:
              A Psychodynamic Model
      Carol Bloom, Laura Kogel, and Lela Zaphiropoulos 83

CHAPTER 7   Working Toward Body/Self Integration
Carol Bloom, Laura Kogel, and Lela Zaphiropoulos 116

CHAPTER 8   Transference and Countertransference Issues:
The Impact of Social Pressures on Body Image and
Consciousness
Susan Gutwill 144

CHAPTER 9   Transference and Countertransference Issues:
The Diet Mentality versus Attuned Eating
Susan Gutwill 172

CHAPTER 10   Eating Problems and Sexual Abuse:
Theoretical Considerations
Susan Gutwill and Andrea Gitter 184

CHAPTER 11   Eating Problems and Sexual Abuse:
Treatment Considerations
Susan Gutwill and Andrea Gitter 205

CHAPTER 12   Eating Problems in Patients with Multiple
Personality Disorder
Susan Gutwill 227

Epilogue   243
Women's Therapy Centre Institute Resources   245
References   247
Index   271

Foreword

THE BODY of the woman with an eating problem is not the passive sponge of society's projections. Rather, it is a mouthpiece through which woman's language is extended. To take but one example, when encountering a woman suffering with anorexia we are forced into the recognition that her sense of her own authority is limited by psychic and social girdles. She feels constrained to act in a very small space, but she has a fury about the cell she has created.

She has understood that while food is love when she gives it to others, it is dangerous when she eats it. She has understood that while processing or soothing the emotional lives of others is valued, her own needs are taboo. In many different ways, from creating a body that mimics, defies, and conforms to our current aesthetic to feeding others and keeping her antennae alert for their needs, she creates a femininity she can somehow live with. This bargain, her protest and defiance, her surrender and complicity carry the pressure of trying to solve the dilemmas she experiences by transforming the self and the body. She says with her body what dare not be heard and daren't be said both personally and in the wider body politic.

Part of what she tells us, as do women with bulimia or with a compulsive eating problem, is that at bottom she does not feel entitled to eat, to take food for granted, to respond to hunger that arises from within, or to a body that is stable, knowable.

This book explores and extends with compassion and deep intelligence the theory that situates women's eating problems in the context of late-twentieth-century consumer society. It looks at how the body is for woman the place in which are inscribed the rules of culture and how the body is the site of woman's expression, of her social position, and of her agency. By reading eating problems and body transformations as text, we can decode our culture's values, assignations, power relations, and symbolic representations as well as the inter- and intrapsychic meanings that the individual is embodying or attempting to dis-embody. We begin to understand the body as the personification of culture; as the place in which the individual writes out her understanding of the meaning and possibilities that exist for her; as the place she tells of her standing in the world—the world of the family, the sexual world, the school, the wider public sphere, the gendered world, the world of class, of consuming, of possibility and impossibility.

These painful adaptations that women make are well described, understood, and theorized in this book. By extending psychoanalytic and feminist social theory, the authors present us with a comprehensive look at women's eating problems. The subject matter of the book is dreadfully painful. The authors have chosen to explore their own countertransferential responses to their patients' eating dilemmas in a way that allows us to contain and tolerate the pain that needs to infuse the consulting room if the problems are to shift. It gives the clinician the tools to invite that pain into the therapeutic space. Once enabled, the clinician can provide for the client an experience of digestion—digestion that goes to the heart of transforming eating problems.

Clinicians in psychiatry—psychotherapists, psychoanalysts, social workers, as well as physicians spanning every specialty from general practice, adolescent medicine, gastroenterology to geriatric medicine—are faced with an ever-increasing number of clients and patients whose eating problems bewilder and alarm them. The task of the clinician demands an understanding of the social and psychological meanings of disordered eating. The clinician needs a text that can illuminate the range of possible meanings that eating problems and body image distortions hold. Beyond this, they need treatment protocols that can guide them through not just the generalities but also offer useful interventions. *Eating Problems* does this through the explication of theory which is now well advanced in this area and the use of brief clinical vignettes that covers the spectrum of problems encountered.

Although this is not a textbook per se, after reading *Eating Problems*, the reader will feel, "Yes. Now I see what I might be able to do." By linking examples with different aspects of theory developed and elaborated since the 1970s, clinicians are left with a rich palate from which to select openings that will help them to reach their patients.

This book, which translates to the written page the innovative work of practitioners at The Women's Therapy Centre Institute in New York, is at once inspiring, thoughtful, and practical. Women patients will greatly benefit from visiting clinicians who have digested its contents.

SUSIE ORBACH

Preface

IN OUR TITLE we intentionally used the phrase "eating problems" rather than the more common term "eating disorders." Disorder connotes personal pathology and medicalizes the etiology of eating and body image problems. But when 85% of American women diet chronically and 75% feel humiliated by their body size and shape, as current estimates suggest, it is important first to identify the cultural pressures as pathological.

Although difficulties with food, eating, and body image are recognized as pervasive, why is it that only anorexia, bulimia, and obesity are considered serious problems? This book argues that compulsive eating and its corollary "going on a diet" are so common that they are experienced as normal by all, including those of us in the mental health professions. In fact, these experiences are so much a part of ordinary daily life, a lived ideology, that it is hard to imagine a world in which people did not worry constantly about their size and appetite. Ideology, be it scientific, medical, social, or political, is powerful and particularly so when these establishments reinforce and buttress each other. To see the rules and to see through the rules, we must detach ourselves enough to use an anthropologist's vision. Only then, we contend, can we see the madness, the tremendous insecurity, and need for control that have gripped us in the twentieth century, playing itself out through the female body.

While the current literature focuses primarily on anorexia and bulimia, we argue that understanding the dynamics of compulsive eating and compulsive dieting is the basis for working with all eating problems. The state of internal need and want manifested in compulsive eating and the chronic restraint of that need and want inherent in the diet are central to all eating problems. Eating or restricting food without reference to hunger and satiation, berating oneself for eating and for needing to eat, being obsessively

concerned about food, and devaluing one's body are the common characteristics of all eating problems. Body insecurity leads to dieting, which leads to
bingeing (mentally and/or behaviorally), which leads to further starving,
purging, dieting, or overexercising in an endless cycle. These dynamics
apply to women in hospitals on the verge of death, to "ordinary" women
who diet several times a year, and to all who never actually diet but declare
their need to do so many times a day.

All these women experience pain about themselves, their food consumption, and their bodies on a daily basis. Yet this pain is seen as trivial, superfi-
cial, and normal in all but the extreme cases. Far from being superficial or
trivial, we see all eating problems as ways women use their bodies to negotiate the socially created, psychological circumstances of their role in today's
world.

Contemporary discourses read the female body as the medium of culture,
the arena for social control, the emblem of consumer culture, the site of both
protest and compliance regarding gender socialization and inequities, the
flesh and blood container of urges, sensations, needs, passions, and memories. The multiplicity of texts requires clinicians to make multiple clinical
transcriptions rather than one singular explanatory exposition. Working
with women (and increasingly with men) with eating problems reveals that
the body is not used as a place to live in, but rather is reified as an object
needing to be controlled. In this way, people are alienated from their bodies
and from the disavowed parts of self and self experience that the body holds.

We hope to contribute to the literature in two primary ways. The first is to
provide the practitioner with clinically useful theorizing about the internalization of culture. Psychological thinking, including most psychoanalytic
thinking, not only does not integrate social and cultural phenomena, it tends
to split them off entirely. In the medical model of treatment, and in many
psychoanalytic theories, the culture is either not seen or is reduced to one
isolated factor rather than a force that is continuously shaping and interact-
ing with the individual. In developing and applying psychoanalytic theory
to the culture, and in offering clinical ways to use that theory, we draw on
contemporary dialogues in psychoanalytic thinking, feminist cultural criticism, and psychological trauma theory pertaining to sexual abuse. We speak
to an audience broader than therapists—one that includes people interested
in unifying cultural, political, and economic criticism with current psychoanalytic thinking, and feminist thinkers and researchers from all disciplines.

The second purpose of this book is to help the clinician learn to work with
people with eating problems within a general treatment. We explain why it
is that many, many people leave otherwise successful therapies with their
eating problem still intact. With the increase in the incidence and recognition
of eating problems, treatments have proliferated. Many of these seek to con-

trol the symptom, seeing control as a goal rather than as the problem. Others deny and ignore the eating problem itself in an effort to get at the "root" of the "real" psychological problem. But it is the symptom itself that contains and reveals internal life. We discuss how to understand this symptom as expressing the convergence of intrapsychic, interpersonal, and cultural experience. We use an integrative approach that addresses the psychological, physiological, behavioral, and cognitive aspects of the dieting mentality, hunger, satiation, food, and the body.

The ideas in chapter 1 developed from our efforts to answer the question: How do the social symbols that represent the ideal of the "perfect" female body enter emotional life? While all intelligent thinking about eating problems mentions the impact of culture, only feminist thinkers have tried to analyze it in depth. In the tradition of Orbach, Chernin, Wooley, and Steiner-Adair, we extend object relations theory and explore the internalization of cultural symbols. Blending cultural criticism, history, and psychoanalysis, this chapter not only explicates social history, but also proposes a psychodynamic theory of our relationship to cultural symbols. We argue that public culture functions as a relational matrix, a form of "maternal" matrix to which individuals consciously and unconsciously attach. Fairbairn's thesis that the subject is object seeking does not apply only to individuals in their early families. In mass consumer culture, individuals seek object relationships with the dominant cultural symbols—from Ninja turtles to Barbie dolls to Calvin Klein clothes. In this book we limit our discussion to the specific case of how women relate to the visual symbols of the female body and appetite created by advertising. These symbols are monolithic—images of a hard, thin, young, restrained female body, that become the objects of transitional experience. But unlike Winnicott's benign transitional phenomena— the child's teddy bear and blanket or the adult's music and painting—these symbols and images of the female body are meant to control those who symbolically attach to them. We argue that the line between the creativity of transitional experiencing, in which the individual works and plays at connection, differentiation, self-soothing, and mastery, is not always clearly distinguished from attachment to internalized unsatisfying objects when applied to the images of women in mass consumer society. A critical rereading as well as an extension of Winnicott's theory lies at the heart of chapter 1. Chapter 2 then develops and explores this theory in relation to the diet as industry, as personal experience, and as social practice.

In chapter 3, we propose that learning to feed oneself and to live at peace in one's body are developmental achievements. This developmental process has its own imperatives, and though rarely theorized about, is essential to understanding the complexity of eating problems. Extending Orbach's work (1978, 1986) on the early feeding situation and the mother's role as nurturer, we trace what we believe to be the developmental path of learning to feed oneself. How the culture impacts directly on the individual as well as through the family is seen in interaction with the development of body/self experience. Chapter 4 then describes the various symbolic uses of food and body by people with anorexic, bulimic, and compulsive eating problems. We discuss eating problems as psychosomatic and metaphorical formulations of psychic states that cannot be verbally expressed because of personal and social repression and dissociation.

The middle section of the book details the conceptualization and practice of working with eating problems that holds us as therapists throughout the duration of treatment. Chapters 5, 6, and 7 explore the heart of our method: how we work with the symptom, and the specific tools from an integrative approach that we use in the context of a feminist, psychoanalytic, relational psychotherapy. We demonstrate how to use an anti-diet, anti-deprivation approach, that is, a model of what we call attuned eating and body acceptance. We present a psychodynamic understanding of hunger, satiation, food, and the body, which reflects and reveals the essential dynamics of the person.

In chapters 8 and 9, we describe transference and countertransference conundrums and issues. Our emphasis here is on how psychoanalytic ideas about "embeddedness" and the interactional field of treatment must be extended when working with people with eating problems to include the symbolic impact of consumer culture on the inner object worlds of therapist and client, as well as on their relationship.

The last three chapters of this book extend our theory and practice to those women who endured sexual abuse only to then suffer with eating problems. As women and men have come forward to recount their sexual abuse as children, many practitioners have found a significant number of clients with both eating problems and a history of sexual abuse. With a growing interest in the convergence of sexual abuse and eating problems, the time has come to explore what a feminist psychoanalytic, anti-diet, attuned eating approach might mean for this population. Therefore, we extended the scope of this book by adding three chapters demonstrating the specific value of our basic principles for trauma survivors.

In so doing we had the opportunity to expand the theoretical foundation of our treatment principles. We propose that the female survivor of sexual abuse is revictimized in the symbolic landscape of consumer culture. This symbolic violation has dynamics that are homologous with sexual abuse. We further propose that the attuned-eating method is a healing tool for the trauma survivor, and that the principles of feminist analytic treatment for eating problems dovetail with many of the standard principles for treating people with posttraumatic stress, including its most extreme form, multiple personality disorder (MPD).

A few specific notes to the reader:

Although this book is divided into chapters by different authors, the book was conceived as a whole by the authors and the chapters are meant to be read consecutively. Each chapter builds upon and assumes the material presented in the chapters prior to it.

We chose to use the pronouns "she" and "her" throughout the book because the theory and practice were developed by female therapists listening to women speak. As with most feminist thought, our contribution to understanding the real gendered base of life is relevant to men's experience as well as to women's. Indeed we have found this method to be of tremendous value to men. Male therapists also can use this approach successfully, especially as they grapple with the impact of gendered social realities on themselves, their clients, and the therapy dyad. Our approach can be used whether the therapist is a generalist or a specialist in working with eating problems and whether the patient enters treatment naming her problem or it is discovered later in the treatment. We hope that the book also helps therapists in their understanding of compulsive behaviors in general, such as compulsive drug usage, compulsive sex, compulsive shopping.

We have provided many illustrations to teach technique. In the short examples, we tend to give only one identifying characteristic, that of age. We wanted to provide the reader with at least one attribute to place the person in the life cycle. For the most part we leave out race, sexual orientation, and class, which we realize is a loss. When people talk, they convey their history, fantasies, dreams, values, and social circumstances. But it is our purpose in the short vignettes to focus on food and body image dynamics, emphasizing the variety of meanings for different individuals and for each individual. It is also, of course, a way to maintain confidentiality for our patients.

We use the terms *patient* and *client* interchangeably because both are problematic. Jo Ryan and Noreen O'Connor in *Wild Desires and Mistaken Identities* eloquently articulate our own dilemma with these terms. *Patient* connotes a medical model, the model of pathology in which a "healthy" practitioner "cures" a "sick" patient. Although *client* redresses this imbalance, it doesn't represent the kind of intense and intimate relationship that is true of the therapeutic dyad, nor does it speak to the suffering that one brings to another within this relationship.

Our priority in this book is to put this theory and method into the context of psychoanalytic psychotherapy. Unfortunately space constraints did not allow us a comprehensive discussion of therapy in groups. But we do, indeed, apply our approach to group psychotherapy. Groups are an excellent modality for clients to lessen their shame and isolation while learning to work with their eating problems and body image distortions in a new supportive holding environment. Our long-standing method of group treatment, a theme-centered group, focuses on symptoms. The purpose is to understand the dynamic issues embedded in the eating problem while teaching a new way to eat and live in the body based on responding to internal cues, rather than external criteria (Bloom, 1976; Gitter, 1986; Orbach, 1982).

It has been our good fortune, with our colleagues at The Women's Therapy Centre Institute, Luise Eichenbaum, Anne Leiner, Susie Orbach, and Laurie Phillips, to live and work in a period of invigorating social possibilities, both in feminism and psychoanalysis, which brought us together and encouraged us over the years. Our collaboration began with a shared commitment to understanding gendered psychology and social life as well as to navigating the vicissitudes of daily life with our clients burdened with eating problems. We have always tried to balance our commitments to the politics of gender, women's rights and struggles, and to the psychoanalytic and psychotherapy community with its growing field of feminist psychoanalytic theory and practice. We hope that this body of work, which represents our years of study, practice, and community involvement, will be of use to the psychotherapeutic community, to feminists, and to supporters of the women's movement.

Acknowledgments

W̲E WOULD like to thank the following people who read early and later drafts of these chapters and who offered intellectual and emotional support throughout this project. We are very grateful for the time, care, inspiration, and encouragement these colleagues, advisers, and dear friends provided to us in all their different ways. Carol Barko, Dori Bender, Susan Bordo, Marti Burt, Dierdre Cole-McMannes, Marcia Craden, Carol Davis, Jackie DiSalvo, Mark Epstein, Bonnie Gitlin, Miriam Habib, Marg Hainer, Karen Hoppenwasser, Maria Katonak, Susan Kavaler-Adler, Jay Kwawer, Anne and Marvin Leiner, Debbie Liner, Sheree Neese-Todd, Marcia Pollak, Judith Riven, Wendy Saiff, Ellen Saraisky, Tanya Sholsberg (for research about inpatient care), Juliet Ucelli, Tina Weishaus, Ann Wexler, and Vicki Wurman.

We especially thank Jo Ann Miller, our editor, for proposing and encouraging this project. We thank both Jo Ann Miller and Stephen Francoeur for their professional support.

We thank our typist, Linda Phillips, for her intelligence, endurance, and reliability, as well as her good humor.

We thank David Stone for his persistent encouragement, support, commitment to the ideas of this project, and most especially for his astute and rigorous editing of the entire book.

We thank all our mothers, Estelle Bloom, Corinne Gitter, Mollie Ramer Gutwill, Isabel Kogel, and Augusta Zaphiropoulos Barnet for the love that sustained us in the arduous process of growing up and growing up female.

We thank Susie Orbach for her creative and groundbreaking work in the area of eating problems and women's psychology, work that provided foundation and inspiration.

Our special thanks to our colleagues at the Women's Therapy Centre Institute—Luise Eichenbaum, Anne Leiner, Laurie Phillips, and Margery

Rosenthal—for their belief in and support of this project, which sometimes meant doing more than their share. We are grateful for a shared intellectual and political life that grows from our collective thought and work and our commitment to feminism and to each other.

From Carol Bloom

I thank Peter Scaglione and Nick Bloom-Scaglione for making sacrifices great and small as I did my disappearing act. Throughout, we held on to the fact that I would come back a changed woman and we would all move forward. I am grateful for a life shared.

Thank you to Sara Baerwald, Luise Eichenbaum, Susie Orbach, and Kathleen Sexton, whose love and fantastically rich friendship live deep in my heart and who always encourage me to speak my mind.

Thank you to Robert Bloom, Barbara Bloom, Tessie Bloom, Marcia Craden, Cari Craden, Abby Craden, Fred Craden, and Cecil Stavin for allowing the ideas in this book to touch you personally and politically for as long as they have been a part of me.

From Andrea Gitter

I would like to thank Corinne and Harvey Gitter for their belief in me always—and for so much more. I am truly lucky.

Thank you to Jeffry and Ashley Gitter for providing a haven for me to spend some very precious moments.

To Debbie Cohn, with whom I originally learned to work collaboratively, for putting up with my continually postponing visits. I treasure your friendship.

Thank you to Anne Leiner for her support, friendship, and the most comfortable and loving atmosphere in which to share ideas about theory, practice, and life. Our Friday mornings have sustained me.

I am grateful to Stephan Fox, my partner in life, for life—for his enormous tolerance, unending encouragement, generous spirit, humor, and the love I can always count on.

From Susan Gutwill

I am grateful to Nancy Caro Hollander for our exciting intellectual partnership and her profound emotional support, which works on a daily basis even though it reaches across 3,000 miles. Thank you also for nitty-gritty, careful editorial help.

I thank David Stone for his dedication to me, to my work, and to this project. His support for this book remained lively, loving, and intelligent through all the different relationships I myself had to the book. As editor, encourager, coach, and appreciator, David was there from the most inchoate to the more coherent forms of this thinking and writing. I am deeply grateful for David's love, heart, imagination, and pencil—all of which held me in this work. In the process of birthing this project we gave birth to another, and as this book goes to the publisher, we go overseas to adopt our daughter. I am, indeed, deeply grateful.

From Laura Kogel

I thank Tom Smucker for his enduring love, for the complexity and integrity of his thinking and being that have so nurtured me, for his humor, passion, and maturity throughout all the joyous and hard times we've shared together for a quarter of a century. And specifically, I thank him for his many sacrifices for this project, for his editorial assistance, for always remembering to buy the raisin bran, oversee the kids, and keep the hearth going while putting in 40 hours a week at work.

Also for a quarter of a century I have been supported by Laurie Phillips through big life events and the small day-to-day ones. I am grateful for her consistent and rich and loving emotional and intellectual companionship, which has sustained and expanded me as a person. Her depth, smarts, vision, and integrity in health and sickness, are an inspiration to me, and to us all. Thanks from Carol, Lela, and me for coming through just in time to provide a wonderful last edit.

I appreciate Sarah Kogel Smucker and Aaron Kogel Smucker for being exactly who they are—lively, understanding, funny, smart, full people whom I love and adore and who make home a great place to be. Thank you for waiting for me and putting up with my nose in the manuscript for so long.

In addition to group appreciation for editorial input, I want to express love and appreciation to Bonnie Gitlin for collegial and personal friendship since graduate school.

From Lela Zaphiropoulos

To Miltiades L. Zaphiropoulos, Doris Zaphiropoulos, Leigh Zaphiropoulos, Bryn McCornack, Renn Zaphiropoulos, and Marie Zaphiropoulos, my thanks for sharing warmth, wit, wisdom, history, and havens, past and present.

My enduring gratitude to Arlene Demirjian, Lucy Gilbert, Jean Golden, Virginia Lehman, Adeline Levine, Ronnie Littenberg, Harry Lutrin, Carole Morgan, Vivian Ubell: a wonderful and sustaining circle of friends.

To Jan Van Assen, my greatest and unwavering appreciation for his original perspective, depth of insight and integrity, irreplaceable generosity of time, spirit, space, and steadfast love that were enlivening and inspiring throughout the years of this project.

From Andrea, Carol, Laura, and Lela

We thank Susan Gutwill, our colleague and co-author, for her passionate commitment, intellectual rigor, and persistent pushing that kept this project moving to its completion.

Lastly, we would like to acknowledge each other for an enriching, challenging, sometimes bumpy but mostly fun experience. This project provided an opportunity to think and create individually and collectively in a mutually responsive and respectful environment. This has been a great gift.

EATING PROBLEMS

CHAPTER 1

Women's Eating Problems: Social Context and the Internalization of Culture

SUSAN GUTWILL

W HY IS IT that the more women are able to have—the ideal super-woman life of home, children, *and* careers—the less they are "allowed" to be? Why is it that the greater are their opportunities, the fewer pounds there are on the scale to represent them? The greater the number of life choices they are offered in a man's world, the smaller their waists are required to become. The looser the restrictions on what a woman may be professionally—doctor, lawyer, or computer expert—the tighter the muscles in her buttocks, thighs, and arms must be. Why are women literally dying to be thin, hard, and totally in control in order to be "free" to live "the good life"? Although biological explanations may have relevance to body size, they do not begin to address the question of the etiology of the widespread contemporary epidemic of eating problems.[*]

According to some social scientists quoted in a recent *New York Times* article, the answer to these questions is that "Mothers Pass Along Eating Problems" (*New York Times*, 1991). Another answer given by prominent family therapists holds that psychosomatic family systems are at fault—families that cannot express conflict, are unable to communicate, or have no boundaries (e.g., Fishman, 1990; Minuchin, 1974). The mother, families, and "toxic parents" certainly play their part, but they too are victims and agents of the real culprit.

---

[*]The medical literature claims that there is a chemical basis underlying and causing eating problems, a socially determined epidemic, and it proposes psychopharmacological solutions. Although drugs can sometimes be helpful to people in treatment, it is absurd to consider the biological model to be the dominant explanatory model for eating problems.

The real culprit is a social phenomenon, far wider than the family, but that, like the family has found a way into the innermost recesses of the self. In our society the pursuit and adoration of thinness is more than a shared goal, it is a socially constructed, desperately held imperative, whose status is that of a god. This imperative is the context in which mothers, fathers, and children look to thinness as a truly magical solution to a myriad of felt problems. The present chapter explores the enormous complexity of the contemporary discourse of thinness.

The first half of this chapter focuses on three main factors contributing to the current epidemic of women's body distortions and eating problems: (1) women; (2) their environment—the consumer culture; and (3) the ideal—extreme thinness.

Women in the Social Division of Labor

Before all else, women's social position requires that they be nurturers of others, fulfilling needs for food and attachment and thus making life possible. As infants come into this world, food and mother are indistinguishable to them: Women, themselves, are synonymous with their first food. Later, as children's personal needs become more complex, women provide emotional nurturance; they provide the metaphorical food of emotional sustenance. According to myth and art the world over, the very image of the female body has come to signify care, nurture, and essential desire. Everyone carries an elemental knowledge that without mother one could die. Mother's presence brings a sense of joyful relief; her absence, annihilation. One's body remembers the hair on her face and the feel of her skin.

As nurturers, women have developed life-sustaining abilities in and commitment to making relationships by noting the needs of others and caring for them. Along with many other feminist theorists, we believe that the world would benefit greatly by integrating these developed capacities to nurture into a shared social image of respected and valued, socially necessary labor (Gilligan, 1983; Miller, 1976; Ruddick, 1989; Stone Center, 1991). Unfortunately, however, women do not care for others from a position that is valued, dignified, acknowledged, or even recognized with pay. Instead, this very real and socially necessary job of providing nurturance is seen and experienced as if it were not a job at all. In fact, according to patriarchal ideology, women's work as wives—especially as mothers—seems natural, second nature, a fact of sociobiology. In this way an abstraction called "woman" is idealized even while women's actual work and contribution are denigrated. To understand this gendered division of labor and how it affects women requires an examination of the origins of the split between public and private life.

THE HISTORICAL DENIGRATION OF THE LABOR OF NURTURANCE

Since the Industrial Revolution, social life in the West has been split into two distinct parts: On the one hand, the public community; and on the other, private life centering on the nuclear family (Kovel, 1981; Michie, 1987; Shorter, 1977; Zaretsky, 1986). This division of society and its ideology have had a profound impact on the lives of men and women.

The public world, the dominant sphere, is the world of men and paid work. Here feelings of neediness and dependency are not to be expressed; the human need for nurturance is repressed. Other sorts of feelings, however, such as competition, the urge to mastery, and the impulse to power, are acceptable. These feelings are congruent with the production of profit, which is the bottom line in the public sphere of industrial capitalism and in advanced consumer culture. Behavior in the public sphere is meant to be systematized, regulated, civil, and formal. Paid work (a "real" job), formal law, the state are all defined by abstract and rationalized norms in rigid opposition to what is considered feminine, nurturing, and belonging to the realm of natural human dependency and interdependency so paramount in the private sphere (DiSalvo, 1983; Lichtman, 1982; Luepnitz, 1988; Poster, 1978).

Private life, on the other hand, centers on the institution and the symbol of the nuclear family. The private sphere of life is the foundation for notions of women, childhood, and home. It is the world of emotional need and growth, of private pain and joy, inner hopes and disappointments. It is the world of feelings, both pleasant and unpleasant, that privileges subjective experience. Here women are the workers, and the work begins with that humbling human truth: Everyone begins life absolutely dependent, usually on women. Women's work is an emotional labor. It is concerned with relationship.

In this division of labor, women have generally developed their abilities in the labor of nurturance. But this development has been constrained and marked by social exploitation of the work of caring, largely taken for granted even as it is idealized. The work of personal care and emotional nurturance is considered subordinate to the "real jobs" of the public realm. Much of it goes unpaid (such as mothering) and is banished from public life, while the rest (such as homemaking, nursing, teaching) is poorly paid and denigrated. Scorning the labor of nurturance is rationalized because it is considered to be unskilled women's work.

There are many unfortunate consequences of this historical division of labor between public and private spheres, men and women's work that ultimately play an important role in the creation of the current epidemic of eating problems. As the private sphere of life emerged around the time of the industrial revolution, it supported the development of the family and, with that institution, a new culture instilling hope for the possibility of personal satisfaction and identity. These concepts were anathema in the worldview of those living in the Middle Ages, prior to the development of this split (DiSalvo, 1983; Zaretsky, 1986). The notions of individuality and subjectivity were truly new historical entities and actors. As private life enhanced possibilities for subjectivity, so too did it encourage the desire for personal, individual fulfillment and happiness. But even as the private sphere opened up this new frontier for the recognition of personal life, needs, and wishes, this very frontier was fundamentally constrained by the relationship between public and private life, as it was, of course, by the realities of social class, racial domination, and ethnic oppression. In other words something was stimulated that inherently would be frustrated. This theme returned and intensified with the development of consumer capitalism and it became the cornerstone of culturally created attitudes toward women's appetites for food, emotional care, power, sex, and initiative.

As public life dominates in the hierarchy over private life, so its concerns, institutions, and power structures mark and impinge on individual experience in the private sphere of life. Thus, for example, although public life is a proclaimed democracy, there is, in reality, unequal opportunity. Instead, the imperatives of social class, gender, and racial inequities quite seriously limit the potential of most individuals not only to be fully part of public life but also to have the kind of self-esteem that is so basic to the growth of a healthy sense of subjectivity. Thus, although the very existence of the sphere of private life promises happiness, racial, class, and gender restrictions make most people deeply unhappy. More generally, the very fact of using people instrumentally and mechanically, so graphically depicted in Chaplin's *Modern Times* and basic to capitalism's relations of production, is personally injurious to people's sense of self. Another contemporary example of this inevitable contradiction between promise and reality is the massive layoff of workers, often in mid-life, after years of service and with few prospects for future employment. These examples remind us that people are very personally and privately hurt by their experiences in their public community. Although social institutions can be split—public and private, personal and instrumental—human beings do not so easily split themselves. People have needs for attachment, security, and community wherever they go, in their nuclear families as well as in their larger human community. Public life, dominated by the institution of private property and profit, cannot adequately accommodate human needs for a safe, caring community enabling individuals to recognize each other's humanity.

To the extent that public life is organized so much according to the principle of instrumentality, it denies responsibility for those human needs that do not fit its rationalized framework. Instead, those needs are relegated to the private sphere. But private life, without the backing of the public realm, also fails. Families without child care, day care, health care, or adequate financial support—all of which are further affected by class and race—are profoundly restricted in meeting the personal needs of their members. Moreover, private life is all too frequently anything but the safe haven it is advertised to be. For women and children it can be the site of major physical, sexual, and emotional abuse, a place of tyranny against them. Subordinate to public life and hidden, it is a world beyond public scrutiny, where men and parents are not held accountable.

One reason why private life can house so much private abuse is that because public life is more or less absolved from responsibility for an ethic of care, frustration is relegated to private life, where it is ultimately considered women's responsibility to repair emotional damage. Caught by the ideology of a world split between public and private, men and women alike are seduced by the myth that private life, the family, and especially women can meet *all* personal needs and that the family itself requires no community nurturance; that people require nothing that cannot be provided by mothers and wives at home. Consequently, the very most personal or emotional of needs, such as those for recognition and social connectedness, disavowed as they are in public, must be channeled into the family and toward women (Chodorow & Contratto, 1989; Kovel, 1981, 1984; Luepnitz, 1988). Unmet and unrecognized individual needs and wants swarm like wasps from their nests in public life to family life and alight especially on women, who are held responsible for the satisfaction of inner desires, for the calming of personal fear, and, in general, for connectedness to others. How impossible and overwhelming these expectations are. No family, alienated from a full, nurturing public life, no woman, lacking the power to match her responsibility, can meet the need stimulated by and created for private emotional lives. In this way women come to signify not only care and dependency but also more generally free-floating desire and disappointment.

Thus, the public/private split creates, structures, and supports a reservoir of frustrated desire that in part erupts in violence: battering, rape, and sexual abuse. In addition, this tantalizing reservoir fuels the development of mass consumer industry, so that it can deeply engage people's imagination, participation, and ultimately, in important ways, subjugation.

THE FEMALE PROBLEMATIC OF THE OBJECTIFICATION OF WOMEN

One of the most difficult and demanding aspects of women's hidden labor, deriving from this split between public and private life, is the internalized discipline of styling themselves into desirable objects not only for men and romance but also, for many, for work and social opportunities. This is not to say that women have no subjectivity and are only objects for men. Instead, women have a marked and constrained subjectivity, part of which includes their wish not only to attract men but also to please and assuage their own internal critic who carries social standards for character and beauty (Bordo, 1993). Despite the patriarchal ideology that women "naturally" come to be wives and mothers, the reality is that women discipline themselves carefully so that they may fulfill their gender roles. That women earn 65% of what men earn is not an empty statistic. The feminization of poverty shows that women on their own do not fare as well as do women who are attached to men, at least socially and financially (Fraad, 1990). Therefore today, as has been the case for centuries, women must sculpt themselves into marketable objects to enhance their objective and subjective sense of security (Barsky, 1990; Berger, 1972; Bordo, 1993; Fraad, 1990).

To this end, a central requirement of women's social position is that they develop a critical, self-observing sense about themselves. Seeing themselves reflected, the passive object of another's view, defined by their bodies, their looks, and their demeanor, women achieve their role by endlessly disciplining themselves and their appetites. There is an art to being female that teaches women how to suffer in order to create a visual appearance, often called the "look," that changes yearly, how to spend innumerable hours, thousands of dollars every year (Wolf, 1991), and incalculable angst to "improve" their appearance, present their body, and enhance their attractiveness to men and to meet female internalized critical standards. All this is basic to what it means to be a woman. Having internalized this functional misogyny, women, simply out of self-preservation, have had to become hypercritical. Frantz Fanon might call female consciousness a psychology of the oppressed, in which a woman inevitably joins with her "colonizer" (Fanon, 1968). The French social critic Michel Foucault and his feminist interpreters call this process "normalizing," inscribing in time and space and on the body—and, therefore, internalizing the forms and "discourse of domination" (Barsky, 1988, 1990; Bordo, 1993). Just as it was feminists who have theorized women's social position, so it has been feminist psychoanalytic theorists who theorize about how women's place in this gendered division of labor shapes female and male psychology.

WOMEN'S PSYCHOLOGY

Although it is true that today men nurture more then they traditionally have, the work of nurturance still primarily belongs to the private sphere where women are the predominant workers. In this care-giving capacity, women symbolically continue to represent early life—the vulnerable, the dependent, the uncontrollable, frightening, and powerful part of human experience. It is in this world that little girls become women (Dinnerstein, 1963; Eichenbaum & Orbach, 1983a; Westkott, 1986).

Mothers and daughters identify with each other (Chodorow, 1978). Girls, being "like" mother, are better able to maintain throughout their lives a sense of emotional continuity with the mother, with early experience, and with the value of relational continuity itself. On the other hand, in order to become men, boys need to break contact with their early nurturers, their mothers, and, therefore, with their experience of primary care and dependency itself (Chodorow, 1978). Alienated in this way from their first and most personal relationship, men are ever more dependent on women, making it natural for them to hold women responsible for knowing and meeting many of their emotional, especially dependency, needs.

Through identification, projection, and introjection, boys and girls come to different ways of knowing and being in the world (Belenky, Clinchy, Goldberger, & Tarule, 1986; Gilligan, 1983). For girls it is often not only connection to others that is primary but also a special kind of heightened sensitivity to the needs and feelings of others *before the needs of self* (Stone Center, 1991; Westkott, 1986). Thus Luise Eichenbaum and Susie Orbach argue that although women need to be given care and to take initiative, they learn to repress these parts of self in the interest of becoming "midwives to the needs of others" (Eichenbaum & Orbach, 1983a). This gender role is trained into and through the body.

In her book, *Hunger Strike* (1986), Susie Orbach argues that women are actually trained to feel body *insecurity* in regard to their own desire and initiative and to be fearful and mistrustful of their internal signals such as hunger, satiation, and impulses for physical activities. According to Orbach, the mother, also raised as a daughter in this culture, must raise an "appropriate" daughter if the daughter (and therefore by identification, the mother) is to succeed. Therefore the mother's holding, feeding, and handling provide her little girl with contradictory messages: those that encourage and those that discourage female hunger and bodily expression. The world is not nearly so welcoming to female appetites of any kind—for food, love, sex, knowledge, or physical mastery—as it is to male appetites (Orbach, 1986).

Food, hunger, and bodily appetite are an original form of and major symbol of the problematic of desire, need, and vulnerability. Women, in learning to be primarily nurturers of others and to be fearful of their own dependency needs, fragilities, and power and initiative, understandably come to experience and express their fear in relation to eating, hunger, and bodily need. The historical split between public and private, which denigrates dependency and puts women in charge of meeting needs rather than entitling them to be receivers of emotional care and privilege, is thus symbolically translated by women into suspicion and repression of their own hungers.

Women are set up very early for self-hatred at worst, and insecurity and lack of confidence at best. Because they feel obliged to repress their own appetite, need, and desire, they inevitably come to feel humiliated by the eruption of these feelings within themselves. But because to be human is to experience appetite, need, and desire, a basic sense of shame and humiliation, frustrated desire, and smoldering rage is built into the female condition and into women's everyday experience.

Benjamin (1988) argues that desire, by which she refers to women's sense of subjectivity, can be supported or forestalled by relationship to the father. The father, for Benjamin, represents the figure of the outside unlike the mother of dependency, unlike the mother of regulation, a figure who represents entitlement to and fulfillment of subjectively determined desire. In this position, if he allows and mirrors his daughter's attempt to identify with him as subject, the father enhances and permits female subjectivity. If the father accepts and reflects his daughter's identificatory love, he can help to create female desire. Unfortunately, Benjamin concludes, because of gender pressures, fathers all too often eschew their daughters' identificatory love, undermining their daughters' subjectivity.

Thus, feminist psychoanalytic thinking about the culture's impact on the mother and father—and, subsequently, on the daughter—describes a female psychology that leaves women hungering for something that can take away their psychic pain and allow them to feel more powerful and whole. Consumer culture, to which this chapter now turns, offers tantalizing and imperious solutions. One of the ways women make repair for the subjectivity stolen from them is to identify with those for whom they are objects. Thus, women learn to take pleasure in and feel powerful when they strive to achieve perfect object status. Consumer culture, the second contributing factor to the current epidemic of eating problems, shows them the way.

Women's Environment: Consumer Culture

Mass consumer industry requires mass consumption and, therefore, ever-expanding markets. Thus, to grow (and grow it must or be taken over by the competition), an industry has to stimulate in people needs for new products. The historian Stuart Ewen has documented that industry leaders, in order to protect sales, quite self-consciously fashioned themselves into what Ewen calls, "the captains of consciousness" (Ewen, 1976). American industrialists, embarking on mass production of consumer products in the 1910s and 1920s, reasoned that to sell their new consumer products they would have to alter the sentiments, the politics, the felt needs, the consciousness, the family life, and indeed the very inner life of the American public (Brumberg, 1989; Ewen & Ewen, 1979; Schwartz, 1986). They understood that before mass production Americans were, on the whole, hard-working and hard-saving. It was not a culture of consumption (Ewen, 1976). Moreover, in the same period, as mass industry developed, industrialists were also concerned that many Americans were being radicalized. Women were fighting for the vote and against the war. Workers were organizing and striking, and many were looking to

Bolshevism for guidance and inspiration. Intellectuals and artists were espousing new and radical ideas about art and politics (Tax, 1982, 1990).

To get Americans to focus on buying, on needing, and even on coveting consumer products meant that they would have to be persuaded or "sold a bill of goods." To this end, the captains of industry hired the new advertising industry to "educate" Americans (Ewen, 1976). Advertisers, rising to the task, dubbed this process "civilizing the masses" to consume. They argued that Americans, especially immigrants, should and could learn to *buy* "democracy," thereby protecting profits and weakening any radical and critical threats to the social order. Advertising defined democracy, synonymous with consumer capitalism itself, as the good fortune of being able to buy the objects of the new consumer production. The captains of industry were clear: People would have to feel the need for different things, things they had never needed before. Therefore, people had to be made to feel inadequate in new ways. Advertisements taught the fear and hatred of body odor, cautioned about the need to monitor weight, and prevent dry skin and stained teeth. Through subliminal suggestion families (especially immigrant) learned that only with the latest consumer products would they be able to raise their children as "real" Americans (Ewen & Ewen, 1979). In essence, this process required no less than the transformation of the basic social, political, and interpersonal relationships in which people came to understand themselves and in which they came to feel their own needs.

Hiring experts in human behavior and psychology, the advertising industry undertook to learn how people function psychologically, and to use that knowledge to create and stimulate needs that could become attached to the products, ideology, and authority of the corporate giants. There followed a breakdown of traditional authority patterns. For example, in the old family, social relations of dependency and authority were signified by titles— "mother," "father," and "children." Advertising, in effect, created a new family through the projection of images. The new members were called "mom, dad, and the kids," each with their own personal relationship to the product and, less obviously, to the corporation for which it stood.

"Mom, dad, and the kids" was a tactic of advertising to break traditional relationships and constraints and to offer a new version of nurturance and authority promising social mobility, independence, and open-mindedness to the consumer. In two ways, advertising intentionally aimed its message with great precision at women. First, women were targeted in their role as nurturers, wives, and mothers. Advertisements suggested that the mother, the protector of all, should do much of her loving and protecting by means of buying. Advertisements incited terror in mothers that, without the proper product, they would spread germs and create complexes in their children. "Indeed family safety and survival were at stake for the mother who had become the buyer and dispenser of goods" (Ewen, 1976). Although today advertisements emphasize less a clean house and more a perfect and ageless, totally controlled beauty, a smart housewife must still know her calories, her vitamins, and the importance of appearances for success. Advertising, in its "civilizing mission," carefully trained women in the transmission of consumer culture—a job that has withstood the test of time.

Second, advertising promoted in women eternal vigilance about their body and looks as the key to personal happiness, security, and personal control in rapidly changing social contexts. Advertisements taught that instead of achieving self-respect and a good character, in the old Calvinist tradition of good works, it could be purchased through good looks. As the historian Joan Brumberg writes: "If beauty could be purchased, then consumption was a form of self-improvement rather than self-indulgence. If beauty could be earned, then a righteous woman could achieve it through her good works; careful attention to complexion, hair, and clothing as well as healthful exercise and more important, restrained eating" (Brumberg, 1989). Today, says Brumberg, all this is still true: women's looks are still deemed to offer a glimpse into the "state of her soul."

On their part, and for their own reasons, women welcomed and joined advertising culture and its messages. Advertising challenged many of the more obviously brutal and harsh aspects of patriarchal authority. It pictured women making decisions and being important in the home and also engaging in activities beyond home and hearth. Women had staged a successful fight for the vote and expressed their desire for control over reproduction and sexuality. Working-class women were organizing and struggling in new trade unions, and they too became acquainted with and took up some of the ideals of feminism. The "new woman" was a very real and exciting historical achievement, not merely advertising's creation. From her own genuine desire, she wanted shorter skirts, brassieres instead of corsets, and inexpensive ready-to-wear clothes instead of hours of sewing. She wanted to move, to think, to be out in the world—to make her mark. And the fashion industry helped in a very real way. The industry's response to the felt needs of women was not simply a corporate manipulation: Women also took much from it.[*]

But what is relevant to women's eating problems is a more hidden aspect of the new consumer culture. The 1920s was the era when the public first learned that Sunmaid raisins would give the energy of youth and Palmolive soap would keep skin young. Raisins, soap, lotions, style, all became the vehicles of safety, personal security, and sensuality. The products stood for youth, beauty, and control. But youth and beauty really are fleeting; disappointment is inevitable; complete personal control is illusory. When the

---

[*]Men and women alike welcomed products that made life easier. They welcomed the chance to choose, to express themselves, to enrich, and make their lives more pleasant and less bleak. For an interesting literary depiction of these phenomena, see Tax (1982, 1990).

products failed to change these existential truths, women often blamed themselves, just as do children when disappointed by parents. Indeed, an insidious authority, hidden in the new images, had replaced that of the patriarch and conservative politician. It came in sheep's clothing. It came in calorie counting. It came in fat-phobic images and in shrunken bodies. Its main job was the "authoritative" and "scientific" creation of insecurity for the purposes of profit and social control. It ignited the self-hatred of women in this generation into an epidemic of eating problems and other forms of real self-mutilation such as those found in the increasingly popular kinds of cosmetic surgery.

The "beauty myth" has a particularly strong hold over Americans, whose history began with endless expansion, killing the old order as they pioneered the new. Americans have continually remade and mobilized themselves, first in the expansion westward and then in attempts at upward class mobility. Today, the body is the new frontier and market, especially women's bodies, required to be hard, thin, and tight, the site of tummy tucks, face lifts, intestinal staplings, breast implants, breast reductions, nose jobs, and, of course, diets.

Previously women's bodies had been corseted, raped, intruded on in hundreds of ways; now the invasion has been exponentially multiplied and hidden behind the happy, giving face of the corporation. For it was not simply the size of the female body that was changed. Mass industry went for the very fiber of fantasy life. Targeting both the most primitive of people's needs and their more adult aspirations toward freedom and armed with the psychological weapons provided by advertising, mass culture has aimed at nothing less than the institutionalization, the rationalization of fantasy life around sales that focus predominantly on female slimness and beauty. Thanks in part to the true needs and desires of women and in part to the power of suggestion by advertising and industry, women and mass industry became partners.

The Shared Ideal and Master: Thinness

The partnership between women's bodies and advertising has produced in women and in the culture as a whole a rigid ideal of thinness and hardness. This is the last of the three major factors contributing to the epidemic of a fat-phobic, obsessive pursuit of thinness among women and men, especially among women. The ideal of extreme slenderness gets its significance first from its power to symbolize a rich and varied array of powerful personal and cultural symbols. It means different things at different times, to different people, to different parts of individual people, and in the culture at large. Thinness is taken up for reasons that are highly overdetermined.

Breaking patriarchal constraints in the 1920s, the 1960s, and the 1970s has signified to women freedom from cumbersome reproductive roles. Many women sought to leave the isolation, the roundness associated with the home; to this end being sleek, lithe, and active seemed very attractive, appropriate to a business woman, a working woman, a woman with a modicum of independence. In these periods of radical thinking, thinness was also associated with the ability of the working and middle classes to break the bind of class stratification. The thin body itself could be the tool and site of upward mobility and class transcendence. In mass culture, buying products and being thin were important ways to move up and especially to leave an immigrant, old world consciousness behind: Consumerism seemed to be a movement toward equalization upward, "a democratization of surfaces" (Brumberg, 1989; Ewen, 1988; Orbach, 1986).

Yet, as industry absorbed these democratic aspirations, the radical aspects of the symbol of thinness were turned on their heads. Thinness, exploited by advertising, became a bogeyman, a judge, an accuser, an impossible standard, a drain on women's emancipatory goals. The advertised image of thinness, closely associated with beauty and "health," has become central to the notion of a "good woman" who is "trying her best" to look right, live right, and be right. Although today advertised thinness on the surface promises that women can "have it all"—work, family, and freedom—its most powerful, secret message is to remind them of their subordinate status as women, still judged on the basis of their bodies. They must take up less space, fit into prescribed molds of standardized beauty, restrain their desires by disciplining their hungry bodies. No one wants a fat woman, someone out of "control." In these ways the ideal of thinness plays its role in efforts to negate feminist resistance through the absorption and degradation of its symbols.

But thinness has also evolved as a solution to a more general social dilemma, the need in consumer-oriented culture to believe in infinite possibilities for both self-expression and, paradoxically, for self-control. The very rigid split between public and private life discussed earlier laid the foundations for this social conceit; the further development of consumer culture exaggerates it.

There exists in consumer culture a tremendous contradiction between what is demanded of people in their role as consumers and what is demanded of them as producers (Bordo, 1993; Brumberg, 1989; Ehrenreich, 1989; Kovel, 1981; Schwartz, 1986):

> On the one hand, as "producer-selves," we must be capable of sublimating, playing, repressing desires for immediate gratification: we must cultivate the work ethic. On the other hand, as "consumer-selves" we serve the system through a boundless capacity to capitulate to desire and indulge in impulse; we must become creatures who hunger for constant and immediate satisfaction. The regulation of desire thus becomes an ongoing problem, as we find our-

selves continually besieged by temptation, while socially condemned for overindulgence. . . . Food and diet are central arenas for the expression of these contradictions. . . . Conditioned to lose control at the very sight of desirable products, we can only master our desires through rigid defenses against them. The slender body codes the tantalizing ideal of a well-managed self in which all is "in order" despite the contradictions of consumer culture. (Crawford quoted in Bordo, 1990b, pp. 96–97)

The ongoing, never-enough drive for thinness thus represents an attempt to solve the contradiction in what has been called the body politic. Food and body are the first sites of, and become symbols for, desire, gratified or frustrated, the ancient place of deprivation or satisfaction. Intensified by the split between public and private life and later by the development of mass consumer culture, the female body also has become a powerful signifier of desire, possibility, hunger, need, and vulnerability, something potentially voracious or frighteningly vulnerable and powerless.

As individuals and the culture at large all call on restrictions in eating and body size as a metaphor of control, eating and body image themselves become polluted and confused. Eating and living in the body—things that might seem to be responsive to an internal knowable rhythm—cease to be so or do not develop. Women, buffeted by cultural forces, learn to distrust and be ignorant of hunger and satiation and to lack an accurate body image. Instead, women's relationship to eating and the body is overprescribed and overdetermined by a culture that constantly intrudes with ever-changing advice. In this way eating and body image, already so confusing within female psychology, easily become metaphors and ways to express myriad insecurities, including those about how to eat. Food and body have become areas of intense desperation.*

---

*Although a good deal about the symbolic meaning of thinness is now understood, the way it has become institutionalized should also be mentioned. Particularly, since the 1910s and 1920s, the insurance industry, the profession of home economics, and the clothing industry, all systematized the ideal of thinness and the fear of fat in their efforts toward standardization (Brumberg, 1989; Schwartz, 1986). Thus thinness came to have a bureaucratic life of its own, an organizational base with an inner tendency to maintain the status quo and its powerful adherents.

The insurance industry developed its now famous standard height and weight tables. These experts taught that body size could no longer be left to natural processes, and promoted the sale of new tools of body measurement and regulation. The scale and the diet became very profitable business ventures. Housewives and mothers were trained in scientific nutrition. Thinness and health became a moral imperative for women; fat, especially women's, was associated with disease, dirt, and smells.

As for the clothing industry, we have seen the progressive side of women's desire for ready-to-wear fashions and less restrictive clothing. However, standardization of clothing sizes also had an oppressive effect on women. It may be hard nowadays to appreciate the power of standardization because we have never known anything else. But the strange notion that people should fit into clothes replaced the idea, perfectly good until then, that clothes were made to fit the person. Standardization in the clothing industry foreclosed forever the celebration of variety of the female body. Only small sizes were in fashion, only slender bodies could feel safe, that is, if feeling safe is possible at all.

In today's world women are not only promised that they can and should "have it all" but also admonished that they can and should "have it all *together*." Today's woman is "superwoman." At home she should be soft, subordinate, and concerned with the care of her family. At work she must be hard, competitive, competent, rational, and instrumental (Fraad, 1990). It is no wonder that very often women feel confused and inadequate to compete in the public world of men. Contemporary feminist psychologists argue that one determinant of the ideal of thinness is that the "superwoman" wants to make her body hard, like a man's, precisely because she really doesn't know how to be in a man's world (Chernin, 1981; Wooley, 1991). She wants to make her body like a man's body because her woman's body is not respected.

Being extremely thin is an attempt to be beyond reproach, beyond contempt. It helps to bridge all the contradictory roles: A thin woman complies with the requirements of femininity and therefore eases her confusion; but simultaneously she may be expressing, in its extreme form of anorexia, her secret rejection of the humiliating aspects of the female role. Moreover, as women are asked to enter a man's world, they are asked to leave the world of connection and affiliation that characterizes the home. They are asked to leave a role in which they express continuity with the mother and enter the world of men. They are asked to disavow their concern with relationship and take on a greater commitment to the abstract instrumental goals of the public sphere. Under these conditions women often feel a confusing loss and sometimes, unconsciously, a fear of betraying their mothers (Chernin, 1985).

The psychologist Catherine Steiner-Adair has done a useful and pertinent study that clearly shows that to swallow this culture, literally and uncritically, makes women sick (Steiner-Adair, 1990). She has shown that girls who are uncritical, who buy the superwoman myth, and who expect everything of themselves, are those at the highest risk for eating problems. On the other hand, girls who are critical of the conflictual and unrealistic social expectations and standards for women today are far less likely to have eating problems.

Although the ideal of thinness is particularly oppressive to women, we see that it is increasingly affecting men as well, thereby becoming even more powerful in the social order. Thinness is for everyone a solution to fear and hope, to the contradiction between freedom from restraint and freedom from need. Thinness is about illusion in a culture that sells both real and illusory choice, in a system that holds out both real possibilities and outright illusions of possibilities.

Thinness is a perfect solution because it represents meeting needs by shrinking and hiding them. It stands for "having" by means of containment and deprivation. It gives the illusion of having control when one feels out of control. Thinness symbolizes the containment of inner vulnerability. And vulnerability itself is represented by the female body. Thus, it is no wonder that this culture moves to shrink its shared social limits and vulnerabilities by shrinking the signifier of need, women. As a society and as individuals, we return to food and body to express ourselves because they contain primal memory and meaning. They are at the origin of ancient and formative joys and hurts.

Thus far this chapter has surveyed the three main factors in contemporary eating problems: women, the consumer culture, and thinness, the ideal promoted in that environment. What has yet to be understood is why and how women "buy the lie," taking up the culture's painful, if not deadly, mandate.

The Internalization of Culture: How Women Buy the Lie

What is quite certain is that clients with eating problems *do* buy the lie. In their deepest unconscious, they have profound relationships with key symbols and categories, artifacts and prescriptions of consumer culture. We refer here to those notions and symbols that relate only to the female body and appropriate appetite. These symbols are hegemonically sold, reinforced, and upheld by advertising. They make their way into popular culture—music, film, television, and novels. In these media there is, however small, some room for varied images of women. The advertised image of women, on the other hand, presents a monolithic view of women, and it does so mostly through visual means. It is to this monolithic pictorial symbol of the "right" female that the following theory applies. Words and notions like: fat and thin; hips, cheeks, thighs, and breasts; pizza, ice cream, Twinkies, Snickers, chocolate, Haagen Dazs; the diet and the scale; size 6, 12, or 22; flab and muscle; old and young—these are all categories inviting intense psychological investment. Women speak of the exact moment that they were a size 6, when they "lost it," and when they became a size 12. Each pound on the scale, each doughnut and chocolate live on as markers of profound inner experience. Together, these many images and personal memories of size, shape, and food, as they compare to the advertised ideal, constitute a metaphoric map of personal and social history.

OBJECT-RELATIONS THEORY AND IMAGES OF WOMEN IN CONSUMER CULTURE

How exactly do these images derived from social organization mark individual subjectivity? Is it the "air we breathe," ubiquitous and unanalyzable? Are women no more than objects of the cultural assault? Or, as subjects, do they reach out to their culture in a particular way? Where is female agency in the face of this demanding and destructive part of culture? Sociological theories tend to see people as objects of their cultures. Object-relationally oriented psychoanalytic theories by contrast, underestimate or do not account for the role of culture in shaping emotional life (Craig, 1990). The notion of agency—in this case female agency within a hegemonic symbol system—is important in correcting these two biases and bridging the gaps in understanding how individuals internalize their culture. But agency does not have to be understood as conscious purpose. It can belong to the unconscious as well.

Behavioral theorists concentrate on the transmission of culture through learned behavior and conscious attitudes. Clinically, they emphasize the need for cognitive and behavioral work. They propose educating women about the dangers of dieting, for example, or the false hope that bulimia can control weight. This kind of cognitive and behavioral intervention is very important, but emphasizing rational, conscious choice underestimates the power of culture over the unconscious part of self.

Feminist object-relational and intersubjective theorists have been most useful in exploring the role of the unconscious in the internalization of cultural prescriptions. These theorists have suggested that culture is unconsciously passed along in and through the family (Benjamin, 1988; Chodorow, ther-daughter relationships, limited and formed by patriarchal culture, mold women and leave them in jeopardy, susceptible and needy in the presence of an exploitative consumer society (Orbach, 1986).

Feminist object-relational and intersubjective thinkers have made seminal contributions in turning attention away from an exclusive focus on oedipal patterning and toward the effects of society on the mother/child dyad. Their work refuses to marginalize women's contribution to psychological growth or to view her outside of her social context.

For example, Eichenbaum and Orbach argue that women's position as nurturers of others makes them fear and repress their own needs for dependency and individual initiative. Caught by this social role, women unconsciously teach their daughters to restrain their own needs for care and mastery. In *Hunger Strike*, Orbach extends this notion by arguing that since women transmit culture by virtue of their social position as nurturers, this painful and restrictive relationship to their own bodies and bodily wishes is passed on to their daughters. Insofar as these theories (like those of Dinnerstein [1963], Chodorow [1978], and Benjamin [1988]), boldly bring culture into the analysis of maternal influence, they represent important steps forward. Stopping the analysis here, however, still implies that mothers are too much responsible for the pathologies and vulnerabilities of men and women. Though admittedly their responsibility is mitigated by the social requirements of their role, further theorizing is necessary to understand the ways culture, especially the monolithic values of consumer culture, shapes individual conscious and unconscious life.*

CULTURE AND PERSONAL AGENCY: THE ROLE OF SYMBOLIZATION

Consumer culture is what sociologists call a "mass culture," a culture in which appearances really matter. An individual is required to accept or reject so much that is available not by gaining deep knowledge of a person or thing but by what that person or thing advertises itself to be, by its appearance. No one can open all "the packages" as it were; one must really choose based on the wrapping. Moreover, these "packages" of consumer culture are forced into consciousness. Neither mothers nor families are major pedagogues in our day; TV and other media are the major actors in consumer culture; they outsparkle the teachers and babysitters.

How do individuals internalize the notions and values of mass culture within varied family contexts as well as directly, from society, without family mediation? The question is not how people learn to behave, how they are consciously socialized but, rather, how the cultural life of advanced mass consumer society becomes part of, and an important actor in, the unconscious worlds of inner representation and object relationships. Bringing in the culture need not be occasion to forget the role of fantasy in psychology in favor of input from external reality or environment. People's "real," objective, external relationships need to be brought into psychoanalytic thinking.

---

*One way to reduce mother blaming is to explore the role of the father, a father also situated in and limited by patriarchal culture. Benjamin's *Bonds of Love* (1988) is one such effort. Exploring the impact of culturally situated family systems is yet another important route toward redressing the overstating of women's responsibility (Goldner, 1991; Luepnitz, 1988). Chodorow and Contratto (1989), Benjamin (1993), and Bassin (1992, 1993) are other feminist authors concerned with seeing mother as she is and not only as a reflection of the child's fantasy.

We need theory about how consumer culture and its dominant symbols directly relate to unconscious life, how they are taken in as parental, often maternal, introjects and compensatory objects versus how they may facilitate development in a constructive way. In my opinion, without this kind of study, it is inevitable that theories about the pathogenic role of mother, father, and family, even when they represent a giant move forward in that they are socially situated, must end up overstating the argument. Take the case of Orbach's *Hunger Strike* for example, so central to the thinking in this book.

In this work Orbach makes the first extended and deep analysis of the relationship of women's eating problems to the commodification and objectification of the female body in consumer culture. Her analysis of the mother-daughter relationship as transmitter of culture is too narrow to contain all she puts forward about women's bodies in contemporary culture. However, it is not as Elizabeth Young-Bruehl (1993) argues, that Orbach sees "mother as synonymous with culture." But rather there is a need to theorize psychoanalytically about how the symbols of commodification and objectification of the female body and appetite are internalized by women *directly* from their culture. Without this additional theorizing, the mother is naturally overresponsible for transmitting consumer culture. Feminists need to develop this kind of theory now, and then to explore how mother, father, family system, and cultural symbols all have an independent, but interactive, role in "reality" and in fantasy life.

However, this does not mean that intrapsychic maneuvers or fantasy life are unimportant. Instead, the more clearly the affects of "the real" are understood, the easier it is to hypothesize about the ways external reality and internal fantasy interact and affect each other.

According to Fairbairn (1952) the individual is not merely passively acted on by her culture but is a person with agency who engages with the world around her. People are unconsciously driven to attach to their world, their dominant culture—whether in compliance, defiance, or both—in ways similar, though not exactly the same as those by which they naturally attach to their mothers and to their nuclear families. This is implied by the phrases "culture home," "culture family," or "culture mother or father." The concept of a "culture mother" (Laura Kogel coined this term in 1991, personal communication) or "culture parent" is new in psychoanalysis and may be controversial. It is therefore important not only to compare in detail how people attach to cultural and familial parents but also first to analyze why such a concept has not appeared hitherto in psychoanalytic thinking.

As Stephan Mitchell (1988) argues, the analytic constructs of beast and baby are better seen as metaphors for lifelong needs and issues. Similarly the psychoanalytic concept of "mother" is best viewed as a metaphor for aspects of environmental provision required throughout life and provided, for better or worse, in a sociocultural context. The mother is not only the first and actual mother but also, insofar as the culture is seen as a facilitating environment, can be called a "culture-mother." The culture-mother is a designation for the kind of relationship that does or does not facilitate growth, a sense of liveliness, including a rich psychic fantasy life. Some kind of holding and care, possibility for recognition and mutuality, mastery and negotiation are needed throughout life in the public sphere and in the relationship of the individual to the culture at large.

Psychoanalytic narratives about the mother-child dyad are useful not only as theories about the actual first dyad but also as metaphor for lifelong needs that people have in relation to their adult environment, in this case including culture. Mitchell (1988) has criticized psychoanalysis for what he calls the "developmental tilt," that is, the psychoanalytic tendency to privilege early experience at the expense of understanding the lifelong struggles all people have. Such issues include tensions between merger and autonomy, finding one's authentic voice versus compliance, developing a healthy sense of grandiosity while recognizing others and external reality (Mitchell, 1988). In these struggles as well as in many other human projects, people are personally and unconsciously affected by life in the public culture at large. It is our argument that this public culture is another facilitating environment for intrapsychic life and for people to feel interpersonally connected.

The culture, however, is obviously not a person; so how does it provide or fail in the provision of such relational possibilities? One way is through the creation of institutional opportunities of various sorts such as education, job security, civil and human rights. Another way, discussed by Winnicott, is through the role of major social symbols in the cultural field.

Our starting point for exploring the psychological mechanisms people use to attach to their cultural environment is Winnicott's work on the use and power of symbolization as applied to the monolithic symbols visually presenting women's bodies and appropriate eating behavior. According to Winnicott (1971c), the baby comes to use transitional objects symbolically in order to negotiate the tensions, needs, fears, and impulses that inevitably occur in relationship to self and others (Ogden, 1990). The baby's relationships to objective reality and inner experience are thus mediated by the psychic experience of and ability to use symbolization. As the child becomes older and relates more and more to the world outside infancy and even outside the home, the capacity to symbolize becomes greater and greater, and psychological fate becomes increasingly tied up with cultural symbols and how they are used. As in any relationship, a central concern is the balance between objective, external reality, and subjective, individual will. (Benjamin, 1988; Flax, 1990; Ogden, 1990; Phillips, 1988; Winnicott, 1984).

At the beginning, the baby develops the capacity to symbolize as a creative response to regulate affect and gratify desire and impulses. Inevitably, the mother cannot—and should not—meet her baby's needs perfectly; also the baby wants to be more effective in regulating herself and her environment. In Winnicott's example, when baby uses her teddy bear or blanket to imagine controlling her mother's comings and goings or closeness or distance and her own sense of security or danger, she is using a transitional object to calm and soothe herself. She is using the arena of play and illusion provided by the process of symbolization. In reaching for the symbol—the blanket—and using it, seeing, touching, and feeling the not-me external reality, the child has the potential to bridge the space between inner and outer realities for herself. Only she can bring herself, her subjectivity, and agency into contact with the external, the outside, the non-me reality in a way in which the self survives and grows rather than being impinged upon and dominated. In Winnicott's language, as the baby reaches for the blanket, she is making her way from absolute dependence to interdependence.

Winnicott argued that it is by means of a paradox inherent in the use of the symbol that the baby's disappointments and longings contribute to the growth of desire and the possibility of fulfillment rather than the schizoid withdrawal subsequent to too much disappointment. This paradox was that the object-symbol—the blanket for example—seemed to baby to be its own creation. From one perspective, mother put it there. From another perspective the baby's subjectivity and desire make it useful, and therefore the baby created it. The object is a transitional object if the baby's illusion that she created it is unchallenged, if the mother never asks, "Did I give this to you or did you create it?" In this way, by playing, the child's healthful illusion, the place from which desire flows, is supported. Then, once the object is established, it can be useful. The actual and desired combine in a truly supportive environment. Now, through the transitional object, self and other are connected. But also through the transitional object, self and other are separate, allowing the baby to grow into her own person and feel real, not merely a reflection or product of the other.

Thus through this paradox, the symbolic use of transitional objects, a "potential space" has been created in which one learns to reconcile inner imaginative experience and external circumstances. Self and other, difference and sameness coexist in the potential space; they engage in playful negotiation, supportive of a healthful sense of individual desire and illustrative of healthful grandiosity even as the reality of the other, an external and different reality is also affirmed. Self and other both exist, joined and separated.

This capacity is the basis for individual potential to creatively transform that which exists intrapsychically and some of what is outside, in the environment. In this sense the individual, "the subject is not only signified but can also disrupt or transform the pre-given chain" (Flax, 1990, p. 119). Moreover, this capacity to play and the process of symbolization associated with it eventually expand into creative living and the whole cultural life of man. In other words, the transitional object is just a beginning step in the development of the lifelong potential of transitional experiencing, the use of many different kinds of transitional phenomena (Winnicott, 1984). For children, adolescents, and adults the symbol, as part of the whole cultural field, has the potential to be an instrument and site of mediation and dialogue between subjective agency and external social reality. How the symbol is used, something that varies over time and as its relationship to fantasy life changes, is one important basis for creative living or failures of creativity, in which case either culture or fantasy would dominate the potential space (Ogden, 1990).

WOMEN'S INTEGRATION OF CULTURAL SYMBOLS

This chapter focuses on the relationship between visual symbols of female body and appetite in consumer culture and an individual woman's subjective use of those symbols. Can a woman give life to her new dress, her old jeans? How do lipstick and liposuction affect her sense of herself and her relationship with others?

In Winnicott's theory the cultural symbol can become a channel for relationship, a way to transcend traumatizing separations and live on in reality—the world external to and separate from self. But it is also a construct around which people interact. This aspect of the symbol is less frequently discussed, yet it draws self and other together through introjection and projection (Finlay, 1989). Thus, it is a channel for both intrapsychic and interpersonal relationships. The symbols of external life relate to the inner object world, especially in their role as mirror of the self. The mirror is a preliminary stage of the use of symbol (Finlay, 1989, p. 64). In understanding the relationship between individual and symbol it becomes important to know the extent to which the symbol acts as the Winnicottian mirror, holding and containing the self, and the extent to which it acts more like the Lacanian mirror, decentering the self or creating it from outside (Flax, 1990). This is a question, however, that cannot be answered at the level of generalization; it is best analyzed in the specific interaction of person and symbol. What is clear, however, is that the object-seeking subject will be molded and shaped by its object. Thus, it is essential to understand the nature and character of the symbols with which she interacts. For longing is formed by self "but also by the object it seeks expression through" (Williamson, 1991). The symbol, like any other object with which the individual relates, carries its own charge and influences the potential space between self and other.

So what of the case of contemporary advertised pictorial images of women? And how do Western women use these images of themselves? One must question Winnicott's assumptions about transitional objects. Winnicottian symbols are benign; they are the unquestioned gifts of the mother and of the realm of private life that she represents. The blanket and the teddy bear are objects that are meant to bring a message of care. Even with regard to adult life, Winnicott speaks of the transitional realm as quite benign, a region characterized by adults using and enjoying music and painting (Winnicott, 1984). With this example from the fine arts Winnicott implies that people use—or fail to use—only the benign objects of their environment, only those symbols which leave room for individual experience and authenticity. Even though Winnicott knew a world that was at war, his conceptualization of the culture of the transitional realm does not reflect this context and history. In the same way, his wonderfully sympathetic study of the "ordinary good mother" minimized the role of the mother's sociocultural context and resources. Perhaps this is because Winnicott assumed the ideology of the public/private split, where motherhood is protected from the cold, cruel public world. Perhaps the private sphere, mother and home, seemed very far to him from the harsh world of profit and war.

Although on the one hand, Winnicott gave psychoanalysis the gift of theorizing a narrative that finally paid tribute to women's work, to the role of female nurturance, on the other hand, even with the concept of "good enough," his work idealizes this ordinary, devoted good mother, if only by not seeing her within her sociocultural and politicoeconomic confines. As if she had no limitations, this mother carries a most impossible responsibility. Winnicott's work, in this sense, was profoundly a product of the public/private split. He expresses such hope, such longing, such desire, and so much of this is directed at the mother. It is she who can make it possible for her child to feel real and authentic, or dead and cut-off. In this same idealized way, Winnicott saw people using objects and symbols creatively; but he did not analyze the nature of those symbols or how different culturally given symbols and objects might impact on the possible outcomes of the use of transitional phenomena throughout the life span.

The symbols in consumer culture, however, are far from benign or even neutral. The TV acts as babysitter; Barbie changes her inner life by changing her clothes; young girls are offered diets and exercise regimes even before they reach latency age; and the images of women, and increasingly of men, are uniform and impossible to achieve. How do these images, all major objects in the transitional realm, mirror? Do they serve to contain and honor the one who looks at her reflection in their glow? Or do they impose on and dominate the potential space between the subject and her external reality, the world represented by the symbol?

Before responding to these questions it is important to emphasize that these symbols, these images of contemporary consumer culture, are impossible to ignore. Just as the child must attach to its family, so must the individual in postmodern mass consumer society find some way to attach to her (or his) larger culture home. This attachment may vary in its character depending on individual personality and history; it may be hostile, rebellious, conformist, compliant, or otherwise; but everybody must somehow reckon with the objective nature of the symbols of consumer culture. They inevitably exert a powerful influence over the transitional realm used by people, especially women, in postmodern mass culture. Because these symbols are designed precisely to penetrate private life and fantasy, they are in active pursuit of their subjects. This is what I mean by saying that while individuals are object-seeking (Fairbairn, 1986), the symbols of consumer culture are subject-seeking.

Although people attempt to use symbols to connect and differentiate, to soothe, encourage, validate, express aggressive fantasies, reach for mastery, and otherwise guide themselves, the symbols of consumer culture are created precisely to manipulate people's needs and desires. In consumer culture, images of women are deliberately, subliminally, and opportunistically forced on the inner environment by visual, aural, and symbolic means. As such, it is not surprising that they do in fact affect kinesthetic and emotional experience of and image of self. The job of these carefully constructed symbols is to exploit human need, in this case female, for relationship with the world—what psychoanalysis might call the surround, the social home.

The advertised symbol deliberately attempts to manipulate psychology in order to boost sales and profits and to ensure social control. When consumer culture, for example, bombards people with images of female buttocks in tight jeans, it suggests that the female in the image is in great demand, someone with whom men want to appear, whom women want to emulate, someone who is intensely secure, sexy, and confident. It is as if the jeans were enormously perceptive, generous, and nurturant to the viewer of this image. The power of the jeans is not only magical in terms of the state of mind they promise to deliver but also insofar as they "know" a woman, recognize her in her innermost needs and fears, and are willing to offer themselves to her for her greater happiness. The sale of the jeans is based on a psychological exchange for which the advertised image has laid the foundation. The symbol is in a parental role to the subject, using that role for the advantage of the symbol makers.

Looking at this psychological exchange from another perspective, the symbol is a wolf in sheep's clothing. It insinuates that the viewer is, or at least should feel, inadequate about her looks and about whether she is appealing. Good looks, in this culture, are the equivalent of good works in Calvinist terminology (Brumberg, 1989). Thus, suggesting an inadequate appearance is tantamount to suggesting badness as a child—and overall failure as a woman.

Once this suggestion is taken inside, the implication that help is available from these jeans supports and intensifies preexisting insecurity about self. It is now impossible for the woman to discern, far less challenge, the part played by the jeans in the insecurity-making exchange. It appears to have begun with the woman actively looking at the advertisement. Even the received wisdom of consumer culture states that advertising meets consumer need and consumer-initiated demand for product education. Thus, it appears that consumers are in need and that the images of the products can both authoritatively comprehend that need and nurturantly meet it. Authority and nurturance, the two chief parental roles (Poster, 1978), are enacted by the culture parent through the relationship of consumer to image.

In this depiction the culture parent exploits and plays out the role of a narcissistic, engulfing mother or father. Some students of popular culture may disagree (Bassin, 1992). They might argue that people take in meaning in multiple ways and that there is no essential way, any one way, to understand the impact of popular culture on men and women. Sarafina Bathrick (1991), examining the impact of TV on women in the 1950s, argues that the question of the impact of popular culture on women can only be analyzed in historically specific ways. How, for example, does the historical legacy of the split between public and private life as it impacts on women in consumer culture, fare among African-American women? How does this gendered history affect women in different social classes? How does it differentially affect ethnic groups? And how do lesbian women fare? Each group requires and merits its own historically specific investigation.

In general, however, an analysis of the intersection of racial with sexist oppression shows that there are contradictory forces at work (Bordo, 1993;

hooks, 1990, 1992). On the one hand, consumer culture is, by nature, homogenizing. The ideal is young, thin, hard, and white. Even the increasing numbers of African-American models are idealized only insofar as they can resemble the white ideal. Susan Bordo (1993) gives the excellent example of the sale to African-American women of products they can buy to make their hair caucasian "hair that moves when you move your head" (p. 255). Insofar as African-American hair, skin, and body types are not like those of the idealized caucasian, women of color are doubly oppressed. Bordo argues further that the objective legacy of slavery intensifies the subjectively felt objectification and commodification of the black female body. Toni Morrison's *The Bluest Eye* (1972) depicts the profound harm done by the homogeneous white ideal to the growing African-American girl. It is, by now, common knowledge (e.g., Bordo, 1993, p. 262) that little girls of African-American descent more often prefer white dolls to black ones when they are given the choice.

On the other hand, as bell hooks points out in her essay "The Oppositional Gaze" (1992), sometimes the very marginalization of Black women from the dominant cultural ideal, as well as their oppression within patriarchal, racist institutions, can give them more power and intention to resist the normalizing influence of the hegemonic ideal for women. Sometimes, hooks argues, especially in relation to film, a Black woman can more easily than a white woman, stand apart from the ideal and see it with a critical, oppositional gaze. There is probably less room for resistance in relation to visual, advertising-based images of the ideal woman. However, to the extent that African-American women, or any group of women for that matter, can stand apart, "see apart," and feel solidarity within a community that is outside the dominant culture, their burden of oppression is relieved.

Returning to the question of general resistance to the cultural ideals for women, our argument is that, although contemporary movies or even television may leave potential for individual resistance, current advertised images of women do not. Instead, although there are pockets of resistance, especially those born of racial, ethnic, and class divisions as well as those deriving from the strength of the feminist movement and from individual differences, nevertheless, to one extent or another all women have to reckon with the noxious relationship to advertised images of women described here. Very few women leave this relationship unscathed. Inner negotiations with the impact of these images directly mark almost everyone's life.

Women must negotiate the impact of the ideals for female appetite and body on them. The majority of women in the increasingly poor and multicultural population of the United States struggle with what has been called by Becky Wangsgaard Thompson (1992), among others, "a simultaneity of oppression." Women frequently respond to exploitation by class, oppression by race, ethnicity and sexual preference, and all the associated traumas of poverty or discrimination through eating and body hatred. In therapy with working-class women, women of color, and lesbians, the therapist should be thinking about the interplay of these types of oppression with gender requirements.

THE RESONANCE OF DEEP PSYCHIC STRUCTURE AND SOCIAL STRUCTURE

These kinds of inner negotiations are evident to the interested and skilled clinician and have profound implications for clinical practice. If given a hearing, women clients will speak about their intense relationships to food and their bodies, and the imaginary landscape of which they speak will smack of images such as those Fairbairn uses to describe inner fantasy life. Women articulate again and again images of seduction followed by rejection, of exciting hopes—a diet, a surgery, an outfit, a new way of thinking—and of dashed dreams and self-recrimination—"I'll never get it together, I'm fatter than ever, I cannot stand myself, I don't understand why I can't just stop, why don't I exercise." These images cycle and repeat in ways that try client and therapist alike. The fantastic tenacity derives from resonances among three sources: (1) the contradictory messages of consumer culture; (2) their fit with deep psychological structures in the self; and (3) the gendered division of labor that assigns to women the impossible task of representing all objects of desire and being the nurturers to satisfy others.

First, the symbols of consumer culture themselves seduce and then reject. In essence, by their very nature, these symbols' dynamics are analogous with Fairbairn's libidinal and antilibidinal objects and ego structures. On the one hand the symbols and images tantalize. Revlon lipstick, for example, like tight jeans, promises that if bought and used, the consumer will feel as pretty, poised, and appealing as (by implication) does the model in the ad. On the other hand, the implicit message is rejecting and treacherous: If the consumer fails to buy and use this lipstick, she will *not* feel pretty, poised, or appealing. The advertising would never talk about Revlon's sales. On the surface it seems as if the lipstick—like a sensitive, protective parent—cares enough to know what is wrong and can fix it; as if this is all for the good of the child. However, if the child fails to heed the advice, she will pay the penalty.

Second, the dynamic use made of these central images and symbols of consumer culture also resonate with already existing internal intrapsychic organization, that Thomas Ogden (1990), following Noam Chomsky (1968) in the area of linguistics, calls "deep psychological structure." Ogden proposes that Kleinian concepts, like language, are best understood as almost biologically wired, predetermined avenues built into the human psyche to be used for internal mental representation (Ogden, 1990). Amending

(1952), Isaacs (1952) posits a deep, psychological structure in which individuals adapt to frustrations from their environments by internalizing them. First, inner representations of the frustrating external objects called tantalizing and rejecting objects, develop. Second, pieces of the central ego Fairbairn called libidinal and antilibidinal ego structures break off. Relationships between these object and ego structures then drain energy from the central ego, keeping the person in isolated schizoid experience. This endopsychic structure is a perfect mirror and match for the most important symbols of consumer culture. The Revlon lipstick is sold precisely by tantalizing or seducing on the one hand, and by implicitly threatening rejection, on the other.*

In other words, internal psychic structure and the message of advertising media are profoundly homologous. The fit is seamless. The advertised message piggybacks on "deep psychological structure." These two sources interlock and explain a good deal about the pervasive, tenacious grip of eating problems on women today.

Third, this seemingly inbred tendency both to blame and imagine oneself as utterly powerful, but failed, is in women's case not only homologous with the advertised image but also joined and intensified further by structural imperatives derived from the split between public and private life that gives women the same message. The historical split between work and home, men and women, and emotional life and the world of work, all engender an experience of stimulated but frustrated desire. As described, the public/private split sets up tremendous expectations for private life and emotional fulfillment for which the gendered division of labor makes women responsible (Kovel, 1981).

The gendered division of labor and the hegemonic, dominating symbols of consumer culture both scapegoat women, as if women were the culprits, the seducers holding out the possibility of the fulfillment of infinite desire. The female body thus becomes an object of impossible desire in the social landscape as well as in psychological life because of the power it holds for all human beings, who, as infants, first depend on a woman's body for life. As if

---

*A Kleinian perspective of this process would argue that the symbols of our culture tease us back into the paranoid schizoid splits of good and bad. Women come to know and to think about their selves in these images, good and bad. Good self and bad self are easily transformed into good body/bad body or good eater/bad eater dichotomies. From this paranoid-schizoid position women judge themselves and seek relief from the "bad self" experience in the false and addictive euphoria of the culturally defined good self, one that has the perfect eating, body, and exercise habits. From a sociological perspective, a student of Foucault's critical social theory might postulate that women's lived experiences with themselves discipline them further toward internalizing a self-improvement regime, as women in consumer society learn to discipline their use of time, money, body, and psychic energy to make themselves equal to the ideal demanded of them. However, because by its very nature this ideal is not really achievable, the discipline of everyday life never ends. Women have internalized their jailor, they live in the Foucauldian prison called the panopticon (Barsky, 1988, 1990; Foucault, 1979), where they are under the constant surveillance of the critical, rejecting, demanding, distrusting guard.

human beings, who, as infants, first depend on a woman's body for life. As if in a hall of distorted mirrors, a fun house, everywhere contemporary Western women look, they see themselves enlarged or shrunk but always distorted. The message that they have infinite power to fulfill the desire of self and others as sexual objects and as nurturers and that much of that power rests in the perfection of their bodies resonates everywhere around them. From the social world and from their inner experience women come to feel that the chasm between possibility and failure can be closed by perfecting their bodies and containing their appetites. If they take in less, they will get more.

As powerful, controlling, and overdetermined as all of this is, it is essentially a secret, unverbalized part of personal and social unconscious life. It is all-powerful but unknown that the three sources—consumer culture, deep psychological structures, and the gendered division of labor—validate one another as their message resonates back and forth, creating the epidemic of eating problems we have today. These deafening resonances are behind every chronic dieter, every "normal" eater who feels inadequate and ashamed of her body and her eating, behind the thousands of elective cosmetic surgeries, and the thousands of women who die annually of eating disorders. No matter what the individual situation—early food allergies, a rejecting parent, a history of sexual abuse, cruel peer group pressures—all women are set up by these overarching forces to be ready to binge, starve, and hate their bodies. Clinicians need to understand again and again how women's experience of eating and of their body image relates to the theme of seduction turned sour, hope stimulated then frustrated and how it is created, supported, and overdetermined in three spheres: (1) the public/private split and its ideology; (2) the culture of consumerism; and (3) individual intrapsychic adaptation to frustration, what is referred to here as deep psychological structures.

In asking how the individual so deeply takes in her culture we have thus far argued the following: (1) Individuals actively seek out and engage with the symbols of their culture home as transitional phenomena throughout their lives. (2) The culture is a psychological matrix and environment. (3) The symbols offered to women by consumer culture are not benign. Instead, they are both inherently tantalizing and rejecting, resonating perfectly with Fairbairn's notions of endopsychic structure and experience.

Now let us look at how this works in the dramatic example of the diet.

CHAPTER 2

The Diet: Personal Experience, Social Condition, and Industrial Empire

SUSAN GUTWILL

A T ANY GIVEN moment 85% of American women are on diets. (Hirschmann & Munter, 1988; Orbach, 1986). They diet several times each year. Between the diets, they live in the prison of what we call a "diet mentality": begrudging and fearful of every bite of food eaten. Women diet for many reasons: to be thin, to be acceptable, to meet the culture's standards for the female body. Sometimes they diet as an expression of their perfectionism, sometimes to express hatred of their hungry selves. Dieting, however, is not only a behavior of individuals but also big business and a cherished social ideal. The goal of this chapter is to examine the interface, so central to the work of therapy, between these dieters, the diet business, and the zealous overevaluation of slenderness and dieting.

The Personal Diet Experience

The internal diet tape is familiar. It usually goes something like this:

> I feel so rotten, depressed, disgusting, anxious. I don't know *what* is wrong with me. I wish I hadn't had that fight with my mother (girlfriend, husband, lover). Other people could manage all I have to do today. But *I* dread walking in the door and starting to prepare dinner again. God, I feel awful. . . . I feel so fat. Why did I eat last night? I make myself sick with my eating. Yesterday, shopping for clothes I couldn't stand the way I looked. Every magazine I open makes me feel uglier and fatter. I hate the way I feel, and I *know* it's very un- healthy. What kind of person am I that I do this to myself? Am I some kind of weak-willed imbecile? I *know* what that ice cream does to my body—not to

mention my emotional state. Why do I do this? I can't bear to look at this waist or these legs. But I don't even need to look; I can feel it all shaking. I am disgusting! I have got to look better, to get it together. I refuse to go to that party (wedding, reunion) looking like this.

That *new* diet promised you could lose ten pounds in two weeks. It was so nice when I was 10 (50, 100) pounds thinner. Remember life really *was* different then. I could be so perfect, so sexy, so confident—if only I could lose that weight. I never even appreciated how thin I really was. This time I would really appreciate it, and I would stay there.

If I could just lose the weight, all the rest will follow. I can't stand myself for another minute. I am going to spend the money and join the diet program. After all, if I am not worth that much to myself, who else will care about me? Really, what else is more important? It's the bottom line. I am going to call and join tomorrow.

I feel better already. I made the decision.

The decision to act feels momentarily empowering, but the needs unmet will not be silenced. They are expressed in a binge—usually the next thing that happens—"just one" before the deprivation begins.

This obsessional mental tape plays and replays even though the dieting process is obviously a dismal failure. More than 95% of women dieters end up gaining more weight than they lost (*Consumer Reports*, 1993a; Hirschmann & Munter, 1988). Each woman knows this about her own personal experience with dieting. As a group, women collectively know this. Yet, somehow this real knowledge, based on their own individual and combined experience, is repressed and remains unconscious. It is as if women wear blinders to shut out half the truth about diets. On the one hand, women know how to lose weight—and they do so. In any room filled with chronic dieters, you will find them all knowledgeable about calories and nutrition. Dieters are not short on information on "proper eating." They know everything possible about all kinds of diets, from the liquid protein to the "sensible," moderate, balanced diets. Most women have been on numerous and varied diets and lost weight on all of them. This is the part they remember. The second half of the experience—gaining back more than they lost—is routinely forgotten.

Psychologically this phenomenon is an example of rationalization, denial, or, in its most extreme form, of dissociation. The majority of dieters need to split off the truth about the weight gain, the "failure" part of the cycle, in order to cling to the other side: I dieted and lost, and I can do it again.

It is not only desperate female dieters who blind themselves to the realities of diet failures. The culture at large, especially the "experts," similarly refuse to make use of their personal experience and of the results of scientific studies on dieting. For example, doctors see that the diets they prescribe do not work over time and lead, instead, to long-term weight gain. Nevertheless, they prescribe the diets as compulsively as dieters diet. In addition, there is a reliable body of knowledge in the fields of social psychology, clinical psychology, sociology, and medicine that conclusively shows that diets do not accomplish anything but create eating problems. Studies show that dieting causes desperate and frightened eaters. As a result of dieting, adherents binge and learn to ignore their physical cues of hunger and satiation. Instead, like starving prisoners of war, they eat to make up for the feelings of deprivation (Bennett & Gurin, 1982; Hirschmann & Munter, 1988; Polivy & Herman, 1983). From the psychoanalytic and developmental perspective, this makes sense. Anyone threatened with the withdrawal of food—that earliest medium of relationship, life, and soothing—is bound to rebel somewhere in the deepest unconscious self. Food is basic to security.

Why do the blinders exist in the face of all the evidence of failure and of all the pain that dieting causes? Why does the obsession with dieting overcome individual and scientific wisdom and experience? First of all, dieting is obviously a panic response to the violent and unrelenting obsession with thinness in our culture. This social obsession both newly creates and attaches itself to already existing individual anxiety and shame and feelings of inadequacy. The fantasy of the diet momentarily relieves this anxiety and the longing for its relief. "After the diet," the fantasy goes, "I will be better, different, redeemed." Like the gambler, the dieter feels that if she can just do this, the future will be better. It will not be marked by this ugly present, this ugly body, this shameful self. Thus, one reason why the evidence about the dangers of dieting is ignored is because diets do promise relief from shame and anxiety.

But the addictive power of the diet does not lie only in its value as a relief fantasy. The actual experience of dieting creates addicts. As one engages in the diet, the need to diet is re-created and enforced. Look closely at what happens to the dieter in the objective experience of a diet.

The Dynamics of Dieting

The experience of chronic dieting can begin with many things: disgust, desire for relief, and for some, self-hate. Whatever the reason, on the surface, it is felt to be about body size, but in reality it is about the inadequacy one feels in relationship with oneself and others. So, for example, an attack of self-hatred can be triggered by a fight with someone, being hurt by a friend, failing a test, being afraid of rejection, being tired of taking care of everyone else, or being angry. Whatever it is, the original motivation, thanks to the fat-phobic and diet-addicted culture, is instantly and unconsciously translated into the language of fat, food, and one's body. Once the bad feelings have been thus transformed into culturally acceptable and understandable ones, they are alleviated by the promise to deprive oneself of food. Salvation through deprivation. The dieter is born. However, eventually, inevitably, both the actual and promised deprivation of food result in a rebellious binge. Whether the binge is an "illegal" grape, a meal, or five pizzas, everyone eventually breaks out of the diet. The diet creates the binge, not vice versa. A dieter eats according to rules that disregard her internal signals of hunger and satiation, and because of this she loses touch with those reliable signals. Alienated from her internal signals and feeling the need to make up for deprivation, she creates the factual experience of herself as an out-of-control binger. More and more, she feels the need for a diet and a diet surveillance group. The diet has polluted the natural human eating environment. The original and the resulting feelings of personal failure do not remain limited to one's role as eater. They are transformed into a conviction of being quite generally unreliable, untrustworthy, and insatiable. In this sense, chronic dieting undermines a person's sense of self. When there is a lack of security and safety in something as profound and basic, as omnipresent and unavoidable as the ability to feed oneself, one experiences a more general starvation and confusion: an inhibition of one's basic sense of trust in oneself.

The Psychodynamics of Dieting

Psychodynamically, dieting is best understood from the perspective of Ronald Fairbairn's (1986) reading of object relations theory discussed in the preceding chapter. Dieting and the diet mentality become socially created modes used by individuals to gain a sense of control over the frustrations and disappointments of their lives. The libidinal objects and egos are the tantalizers.

"Go on—try the diet. If . . . if only . . . I were good enough, giving enough, sexy, pleasing, or thin enough. . . . If only I could stay on this diet, I could be acceptable and lovable." In this inner dialogue the diet represents the exciting, tantalizing object promising thinness as the route to happiness. The libidinal ego holds the hope that one day all this will be attainable. The relationship between rejecting object and antilibidinal ego suggests the opposite, however: "But the truth is that I am *not* good enough; I am selfish, fat, stupid for wanting and needing, ugly, and weak. I deserve all I get. It's my own fault." Here is the inevitable rejection. Fairbairn calls this the moral defense: original environmental failure is blamed on the self here, the self using the culturally suggested form of the diet (Fairbairn, 1986). In this way women stay connected to the original, unconsciously known bad experience, either in its false good or false bad form, by feeling personally responsible for its occurrence. Here the diet represents the split—the hope and the need, as well as the smashing rejection.

Because dieting inevitably breeds failure and, therefore self-hatred, it also inevitably expresses and encourages ties to unsatisfying internal object relations, characterized by intense cycles of the stimulation of desire and then its brutal frustration. Diets actually strengthen the hostile aspect of the ego, corroding what Fairbairn calls the "healthy central ego," that part of the self that stands apart from total seduction or total self-blame. The weaker the healthy central ego, the less available for living and relating, the stronger the antilibidinal and libidinal ego. With the diet the individual repeats, continuously reenacts, and projects this internal object configuration on the external world. In this way, through the chronic, compulsive repeat, the individual maintains a knowable, familiar, predictable, if painful, drama.

The power chronic dieting has over the hearts and minds of women derives partly from (1) these powerful psychodynamics and the way they are intensified by their perfect fit with (2) the actual effects of dieting, and (3) the place of dieting in the cultural discourses and political economy of consumer society.

The Diet Empire

Dieting is big business, a business that thrives on failure. At least 65 million Americans diet annually (*Consumer Reports*, 1993a, 1993b; *Newsweek*, 1989; *U.S. News & World Report*, 1990). Many of these dieters do it on their own, without purchasing a diet plan, but many others buy membership in one of three types of diet organizations: (1) liquid diets, such as Optifast; (2) fat farms or other live-in places, such as Pritikin; or (3) the local diet franchises, such as Weight Watchers, Nutrisystem, Diet Center, and Jenny Craig. All together, the diet industry is currently estimated to be worth $33 billion a year. Even though anti-diet consciousness is increasing, the industry's profits are up from $29 billion in 1988 and are expected to exceed $50 billion by 1995 (*Consumer Reports*, 1993a; *Newsweek*, 1989; *U.S. News & World Report*, 1990).

The painful reality that most people gain back more than they lose is covered up by the advertising industry, which profits enormously: $285 million for TV, newspaper, and magazine advertisements in 1987 alone (*U.S. News & World Report*, 1990). Given the reality of dieting, advertising is almost always misleading, if not downright false. Only recently, however, has Congress opened hearings on the diet industry, investigating the health risks, false advertising, and profiteering that, according to Representative Ron Wyden, are "the bedrock of the nation's weight-loss industry" (O'Neill, 1990).

Moreover, the dieting industry spawns and supports related industries, such as technical and popular media, exercise, food, and beverage. All of these are very profitable—and expanding at phenomenal rates—and strengthen the general culture of slimming. The 1980s provide a clear example of these trends, which are continuing into the 1990s (*Consumer Reports*,

1993a, 1993b). By 1984, there were 300 diet books in print in the United States, and between 1980 and 1984 there was an average of 1.25 dieting articles per issue in *Ladies Home Journal, Good Housekeeping,* and *Harper's Bazaar;* 66 articles on dieting appeared in 22 contemporary magazines in January of 1980 alone.

The culture around exercising and the profiteering connected to it also contribute to fat phobia and the general cultural obsession with thinness. The growth of exercise gyms is indicated by the fact that in 1947 all the gyms across the country were making a total of $50 million a year, whereas by 1959 Vic Tanny alone was making $21 million from his health clubs, Slenderella was taking in $25 to 35 million, and Stauffer system $40 million (Schwartz, 1986, p. 246).

The sale of diet foods, which expanded at an annual rate of 10% between 1960 and 1980, continues to rise. The diet soft drink market is growing at a 20% annual rate. Diet food and diet beverage sales in 1984 were advancing at triple the pace of other foods and drinks with a market of $65 billion projected for 1995 (Schwartz, 1986).

As a result of the development of the diet industry and its obsessional promotion of slimness, more and more people agonize over whether or not they would be defined as "fat." Women, of course, suffer the most, but men also have an increasingly critical view of themselves. A comparison of various surveys shows that in 1950, 21% of men and 44% of women believed that they were overweight; by 1973, it was 38% of men and 55% of women (Schwartz, 1986). By 1980, 70% of college-aged women felt themselves to be overweight. Dieting and fat have become such a national obsession that when Congress threatened to prohibit the production of saccharine in 1977 because it appeared to be a carcinogen, "the Calorie Control Council, a consortium of industrial users of artificial sweeteners and weight-watching groups, lobbied in Washington against the ban. Some 100,000 irate letters reached Congress—more, it was claimed, than ever arrived in any comparable period during the Vietnam War." Congress dutifully put a moratorium on the ban (Schwartz, 1986, pp. 265–266). In the light of such facts, one must question whether health is a serious factor in diet prescription. A 1990 study found that 78% of women see themselves as overweight (more than three times that which the charts would call overweight) (Jacoby, 1990). Although it is hard for many to believe, the majority of these women, according to these studies (and this concurs with our clinical experience) feared wearing bathing suits, often refused social engagements, avoided sex, were significantly apprehensive of being rejected, shunned bright colors and shorts, and were reluctant to get involved in athletic activities—all because they felt fat (Jacoby, 1990). This level of self-imposed inhibition of activity is affecting younger and younger girls.

Dieting and the Medical Culture

Today's generalized prescription to diet allegedly comes out of a concern for health and fitness. The association between thinness and health on the one hand, and fatness and disease on the other, has a long history. It is partially substantiated by statistics on longevity compiled by life insurance companies. The industry originally wanted to find correlates of longevity to be used as predictors. Their original charts and tables have been criticized on the grounds that they represent actuarial analyses of mortality and morbidity done on an unrepresentative sample of the general population, namely, those who sought life insurance and were deemed eligible (Polivy & Herman, 1983). The studies do not look at the whole population, nor do they control for age, sex, or height differences.

More reliable information comes from a new area of medicine that has studied the connection between fat and heart disease and between fat, high blood pressure, and diabetes. It seems that the risk of heart disease is not based on fat alone but, rather, on fat in connection with other risk factors such as hypertension, diabetes, and cigarette smoking. In *Breaking the Diet Habit,* Polivy and Herman (1983) argue that what is dangerous to health is not simply being overweight, because not all overweight people are in fact overeaters, but overeating itself, coupled with rapidly changing weight. These risk factors aggravate heart disease, diabetes, and hypertension. Current hypotheses linking fat and weight with heart disease and diabetes (or any other health problems) are not invalid or unimportant. However, such information alone used as a motivating force in a person's recovery from an eating problem rarely works. Instead, most eating-problemed patients use this information to strengthen the antilibidinal self-hater instead of promoting the role of the central ego. For example, women tell themselves: "See you really are out of control, stupid, and hopeless." Guilt and shame make rational and nurturing decisions about their health impossible.

An unspoken health risk for overweight people is actually the stigma against them: Because of the phobia against fat in our society, overweight people do not get proper medical attention. All too frequently, they feel too embarrassed to go the doctor, and doctors, on their part, dismiss the ailments of the overweight person as the simple products of their being fat. In this way fat people are routinely discriminated against by the medical profession.

Moreover, for many fat may be almost impossible to be rid of, for there is evidence that the body has a "set point" or a "natural weight" (Bennett & Gurin, 1982; Polivy & Herman, 1983). This is the weight, genetically set and differing widely from person to person, that is natural for each individual and that one's body attempts to maintain. Many studies have shown that people tend to stay very near their set point. If they try to lose or gain a significant amount of weight from that set point their bodies will rebel, requiring ever more drastic measures. This helps to explain why chronic dieting fails. Because the body attempts to return to its set point, one's metabolism actually adapts to chronic dieting by economizing, by maintaining its set point with fewer calories. Thus, a dieter must eat ever fewer calories in order to even maintain, let alone reduce, her weight. Hence, the strange phenomenon that some very large people can eat very little and still have difficulty losing weight. Apart from a genetic predisposition to fat, people can drive their set points so low that very minimal eating supports a large weight.

In addition, because dieting leads to the loss of knowledge of physical hunger and satiation, dieters are left without internal signals. This causes them, as a rule, to eat more than normal eaters. In other words, as studies show, chronic dieters do eat differently from nondieters. (Bennett & Gurin, 1982; Polivy & Herman, 1983). Fat or thin, dieters are less sensitive to true hunger and lose control of their eating easily. Diets inevitably create binges. Diets lead to yo-yoing up and down the scale. This fluctuation in weight, and the over- and undereating causing it, is the unacknowledged culprit contributing to ill health. Thus, the hazards of being overweight tend to be exaggerated, whereas the hazards of the yo-yo syndrome are ignored. The denial of personal pain, especially women's pain, is manifest in this denial of the damage caused by dieting. Doctors, so uncritical in their thinking on this issue and so frequently obsessed with thinness themselves, readily prescribe the same diets over and over again to women whom they see do not benefit from them. When one doctor we know was asked why he compulsively prescribed what he knew would inevitably fail, he stated that this was how he was trained and he found it impossible to imagine not prescribing the diet even though he had no hope it would help. In many ways, doctors prescribing diets to overweight women are very much like those who prescribe Valium to a battered woman rather than confronting the socially sanctioned violence of which she is victim (Stark, Flitcraft, & Frazier, 1979).

Chronic dieting, paradoxically, strips women of the capacity for making self-determined, healthful choices about food and their nutrition. Dieting is not about good health. It is about ill health. Dieting is a disorder in itself.

Food and the Food Industry in the Culture of Dieting

To appreciate the contribution of the food industry to the dangers of dieting, first consider the early, fundamental meaning of food. Food represents relationship: hope for it, experience in it, fear of it. In this way relationship to food parallels deep needs and fears about both attachment—the ability to connect, to make contact—and individuation, the need to be recognized in one's uniqueness. The food industry is empowered by this early, primal, and continuing significance of food. Moreover, it is also important to remember that food is central to the mothering role. Women and food are inseparable. As Orbach puts it:

> A mother's presence is always implicit in food. It is almost as if food in its many and varied forms, becomes a representation of the mother. From the child's point of view, the essence of its mother is distilled through food. The mother's personality comes to fruition in the meals she prepares. Food is a statement of her love, her power and her giving in the family. Food personifies the mother and she is rejected or accepted through it. In this way food, divorced from its biological meaning, takes on a prism of reified projections. (Orbach, 1986)

Food is the product of women's labor. Most of the time, the labor is hidden. Advertisements show immaculate kitchens with mothers offering beautifully prepared food. At the same time that women learn they should offer food to others, as if it were not much trouble at all, they learn they should deprive themselves. All these contradictions are embedded in food (Orbach, 1986). Food is a medium of communication to self, others, and the larger culture. It represents the emotional as well as the physical act of eating. Eating, for an infant is a transformative experience; it alters psychosomatic states of being. Even for adults, eating is an expressive act, emotionally charged with whatever meaning belongs to current experiences and with memories of early and lifelong relationships. Eating and food connote not only the personal relationship of feeding but also the way people are fed by their culture, their society. The culture of food takes over where mother began, extending the feeding relationship into the larger cultural environment.

In this context it is important to understand the implications of three major changes characterizing today's food industry (Brumberg, 1989; Schwartz, 1986). First, the food industry has changed to respond to the radical critique made of it by the alternative life-style and natural food movements of the 1960s and 1970s. In its effort to absorb and tap the market of the "small is beautiful" vegetarian food movement, the food industry has practically made a fetish out of the word *natural*. The meaning of "natural" has been subverted by being coupled with "diet" food. Diet food, also called "lite" food, accounts for a major proportion of the food industry's growth. These two influences make contemporary food appear to be practically magical. You can stay thin and young, fit and pretty, healthy and happy. If you make the right choices, you will be in charge of your destiny, you can defy nature, and obtain youth and eternal good health.

Second, the variety of food available has greatly increased. Today one can buy all sorts of ethnic foods (even in the form of fast food), ice creams, frozen dinners, pasta sauces, and so on. Gourmandizing has made food an item for conspicuous consumption and given it the power to prove one's social status and tastefulness.

Third, the changes in the food industry mean that this new, huge choice of food is now available—to those who can afford it—at practically any time and any place. Traditional mealtimes and mealplaces have been undermined, and grazing is the new form of "au courant" eating. The market has desocialized old meal patterns, creating what Joan Brumberg calls a new "promiscuous eating" pattern, leaving individuals without a comfortable and reliable pattern for knowing how to eat.

Although some critics might blame "promiscuous" food offerings for eating disorders, a wide range of choice of foods, of places and of times to eat is not in itself dangerous or bad. Therefore, we disagree with the term *promiscuous*. It is only in the absence of reliable internal signals about when, how much, and what to eat that eating in this culture becomes such a painful and confusing event.

The implications of these three major changes in the food industry are in line with the general trend in mass consumer culture that was described. The culture of food, like consumer culture in general, leads to the combination of an intense stimulation of and simultaneous frustration of desire, recalling a central contradiction of the split between the public and the private. The food industry calls for hedonism, but the diet industry requires intense self-discipline. The striking contradiction between these two required stances underlies addictive disorders of all kinds but is particularly powerful in creating a generation of women with food problems and of people very confused about their relationship to their own bodies. Food is seen as both incredibly desirable and terribly dangerous.

For women, this contradiction is even greater than it is for men (Bordo, 1993). Women, as Orbach states, are taught to starve themselves amidst plenty:

> Consider for the moment the following shocking fact: a woman comes to know that the food she prepares for others as an act of love and an expression of her caring, is somehow dangerous to the woman herself. Every day women read in any newspaper or magazine of how they must restrain their desire for this very same food. Throughout history women have occupied this dual role of feeding others while needing to deny themselves. Women must hold back their desires for the cakes they bake for others and satisfy themselves with a brine-canned tuna salad with dietetic trimmings. Diet, deprive, deny is the message women receive. . . .
>
> Food for literally millions of women . . . is a combat zone, a source of incredible tension, the object of the most fevered desire, the engenderer of tremendous fear, and the recipient of a medley of projections centering round notions of good and bad. (Orbach, 1986)

Fed by the social world people drink from the breast of their culture. This "feed" is characterized by the social arrangements of that culture. Today, the cultural "feed" for women is what psychoanalysts might call a "false feed": one that gratifies but doesn't necessarily satisfy. It is offered in contradiction: Eat, but don't eat. The culture feeds women while it starves them. The joining of overabundance with deprivation of food confuses and starves the heart. The fact that all of this confusion focuses on food—that original object of love, that original holding environment—has profound significance. The culture not only provides a metaphoric "feed," but it is also an adult holding environment. Thus, the contradictory, enticing, and rejecting messages attached to food easily make food into tantalizing and rejecting objects. Food, as a status item, makes promises that cannot be met. Diets, sitting in judgment, condemn and make other false promises. Food appears to offer everything; abstinence appears to offer everything; war is peace. In this most important area of living, people are met with a combination of real abundance and false seduction. To quote Hillel Schwartz:

> As the honey-coated words drift over each platter, each invisible offering, day after day, month after month, the language excites an infinite longing, and we are not likely to be satisfied when the actual dinner is served. . . . Dieting in the midst of plenty . . . is the other half of longing. Dieting cannot subdue longing; it can only suppress it. The culture of slimming draws its enormous power from that longing and from two fears spawned by that longing: a fear of abundance and a fear of never being satisfied. (Schwartz, 1986, pp. 306–307)

The example of the diet offers an excellent and rich example of the way symbols and prescriptions of consumer culture piggyback on already existing psychic structure as it develops in early life. The notion of "deep psychological structure" reread through Fairbairn's theory would posit a psychic structure characterized by response patterns that are seductive/tantalizing and rejecting/frustrating. These patterns attach to parts of the ego so that people tend to compulsively repeat experiences and have feelings in which they are alternately seduced and then inevitably cruelly rejected. These experiences, of "the empty core," are increasingly attractive once this structure has taken firm hold and dominates central ego activity (Seinfeld, 1991). Here is a psychological structure that is the partner of consumer culture. The culture champions dieting. Diets are sold as seducers, tantalizing with false, magical possibilities. In reality, however, they create compulsory overeating that profoundly betrays and frustrates libidinal needs, wishes, and yearnings. Thus, actual experience with the practice of dieting and the advertised culture of dieting both support and strengthen the schizoid object relationships of early psychic structure. This is the seamless fit. An alternative to these maddening contradictions is elaborated in the rest of this book.

Although a woman cannot step outside of her culture, she can find a more comfortable place for herself within it. She can and must make a knowledge-able and nurturing relationship to her own body with its signals, desires, and limitations. She can and must come to notice and acknowledge the culture's impact on her and grieve the pain it causes her.

CHAPTER 3

Tracing Development: The Feeding Experience and the Body

Carol Bloom and Laura Kogel

The Meaning and Function of Food in Early Development

We need to eat to live. This fact makes food a very powerful force and symbol in life. Along with care, warmth, containment, and appropriate stimulation, food is a central aspect of the holding environment that facilitates a baby's growth and development. Hunger, being fed, and satiation are everyone's earliest and most basic experiences of desires, needs, soothing, and satisfaction and occur within the first intimate relationships. Moreover, how the relationships to food, eating, and the body develop affect the individual's feelings about what she wants, her experience of need, excitement, energy, creativity, the reliability and consistency of others, the ability of others to enjoy her excitement, her capacity to be satisfied, soothed, and so on. For this reason food and the feeding experience always resonate within each person for they touch powerful, evocative, sensate memories that reflect and shape connection to self, to others, and to the larger world.

It is useful to think about food and the feeding relationship as having its own line of development. The feeding infant moves from a nondifferentiated state of dependency of being to increasing autonomy and interdependence. Several important signposts and critical steps appear along this journey, and it is useful to keep these in mind as clients discuss their struggles with food. No specific one-to-one causality exists between how one was physically fed and how one feeds oneself now, but clients' current difficulties with food usually harken back to difficulties in how they were physically and emotionally fed. Thus, food has a metaphorical dimension as it contains and expresses developmental and relational issues.

For the infant, food is not usually differentiated from the mother. The infant takes in milk, and through endless repetitions of hunger and satiation, need and response, she begins to develop an awareness of inside and outside, self and other. Milk does not just appear when needed: There is another person who provides the milk, and therefore more than milk is being ingested. The mother's and, more and more now, the father's feeling toward the infant, toward food and feeding, their own experience of being mothered and of being fed, and in general their internal and external unconscious and conscious reality are all part of what is being digested by the infant. When the feed is relaxed, the infant takes in the good nourishment along with the good feeling of being held, cared for, nurtured, and supported (physically and emotionally). Here physical care and emotional care are joined at the root. These good feeds, continuously repeated, take hold and form a "home base" inside, a place of comfort and safety from which to grow. With the caretaker's attunement to hunger and satiation, the infant gradually comes to feel that the environment is trustworthy and reliable and that food is an appropriate response to hunger. This begins the psychological process that will eventually enable a person to become self-soothing. "If my parent(s) fed me on demand, I know that I am worthy of care and therefore will care for myself" (Kogel & Munter, 1986, p. 9). The development of self-regard is inseparable from the early feeding experience.

Hunger is one of the first intense, urgent, repetitive, internal experiences. If hunger is quickly followed by satisfaction, the infant learns that hunger is manageable. Over time with proper care bodily sensations become organized, knowable, alive, personal, and even pleasurable. Hunger itself comes into existence, that is, it is increasingly registered as a distinct internal need state. In fact, hunger is one of the most basic and discrete avenues by which need is learned about altogether. *Through the repetitive experience of hunger and satisfaction through food, a model about needs is being established.* If the infant has a need, it can be understood and met; pleasure then accrues to both parts of the experience, the need itself and the response. In the beginning the baby depends on others both to understand and discriminate what the need is and to provide the response.

This process is a delicate one. Freud (1961) and Winnicott (1971b) postulate that at the moment of the meeting of hunger with the breast or bottle, the infant feels that *she* has created exactly what she needs. This is developmentally appropriate omnipotence. It means that the child is not aware of the mother's separateness, that is the mother's subjectivity, when the child cannot psychically manage that fact. Omnipotence allows her to develop an internal sense of control, creativity, and ultimately symbol formation. As food, the mental image of nourishment, the symbol of satisfaction, slowly becomes associated with the actual provider, the infant comes to understand emotionally that she has needs and that she depends on this person to provide for her needs. If the feeder is reliable, then she comes to this realization gradually. The lessening of omnipotence is compensated for by the joys of bonding with the nurturing other and the increased power to affect another and thereby to contribute to getting one's needs met. In this way, need, hunger, desire, wanting (as in wanting apple juice, not milk), and one's power to command within a reliable dependent relationship all become associated with pleasure and a robust sense of entitlement, the building blocks of a secure sense of self.

When the environment is unreliable or inconsistent, the infant then needs to hold on to her own omnipotence to survive. Omnipotence must now be used defensively to deny the inadequacy of the environment, to deny one's dependency on the caretaker, and to defend against overwhelming feelings of helplessness, powerlessness, and chaos. Critical to grasping the meaning of clients who are obsessed, for example, with chocolate, chips, pasta, or bread (either reaching for or restricting), is to understand that they are continuously generating the fantasy that magically they can create or re-create the solution, the symbol of satisfaction to their internal conflict or need. But as with the unfortunate infant, the magical creation is a defense. When real needs for relying on another for relatedness and for help with discriminating and meeting other needs go unmet, distress is exacerbated, requiring the fantasy to be re-created and the cycle to begin again.

When there is poor attunement and the infant either continuously gets fed when she is not hungry or remains hungry for too long, she does not establish hunger as the signal for when to eat. Hunger then becomes a frightening and disorganizing experience. Hunger for adult clients is often just that, frightening or disorganizing and is either denied as a bodily experience, as in anorexia, or avoided by compulsive eating. For the infant, the experience is one of a lack of trust that the environment can provide and meet her needs. Food given when one is not hungry or in response to other needs will be experienced as an impingement and will be essentially a "false feed." When distress is countered with candy instead of holding or soothing words, the child learns that food is a substitute for closeness and comfort. This is demonstrated by clients who in turning toward or away from food are trying to get something for themselves, some momentary gratification, while simultaneously denying what they truly need. Then the child is left with a situation where other needs (for example, holding, stimulation, calming of anxiety or distress) become less easily discerned as discrete needs that require something other than food. This early denial can start the child on a path of a more basic confusion that prevents discrimination of one need from the next, leaving her susceptible to and dependent on others' interpretation of her inner experience. Becoming alienated from hunger also begins the severing of one's connection to one's body and its most basic function- ing. This early confusion plus later chronic dieting accounts for the dramatic fact that 100% of clients with eating problems do not use, and have rarely ever used, hunger or satiation as a guide for when and how much to eat.

Thus, precisely because food is at the heart of the early relationship, what is here being called normal eating is not a given. In other words using food pleasurably and straightforwardly to satisfy physical hunger is a develop- mental achievement. Because eating is an act that is never far removed from this earliest caretaking, there is always a pathway that makes even the adult vulnerable to regression in the way she feeds and cares for herself to cope with psychic distress.

All babies are initially fed. With the development of motor coordination, all babies begin to feed themselves. As the infant and caretaker continue sorting out the me/not me experience, food similarly is being sorted out from the provider. The introduction of solids and weaning, which varies so widely from culture to culture and from decade to decade, are major devel- opmental processes for the feeding couple. They mark not only further levels of separation* but also of having to find new ways to remain connected. Food is now moving from being solely under the auspices of the caretaker to being quite literally in the baby's hands. Issues of control, differentiation, au- tonomy, and identification of one's own needs come into the fore. The actu- ality of baby in the high chair (not in the caretaker's arms) with food put be- fore her to be handled, chosen, rejected, spit out, thrown is a beginning piece of the work of separation and differentiation. Although the foundation for the registering and the meeting of needs is laid in earliest infancy, the ability for the child herself to make the *conscious* connections between hunger, food, and satiation comes roughly 2 years later. This is a slow process. First, the in- fant can signal only through making sucking movements or crying. Then, later on she may be able to reach for food. Other times, she can only whine. To translate the physical sensation or discomfort of hunger into a verbal re- quest for food requires physical and cognitive maturation.

For example, a toddler, coloring, starts to get irritable and cranky. The caretaker helps to interpret this particular kind of distress, which she knows is probably physiological hunger, by offering food. Slowly, the child learns to say "I'm hungry"; she learns that hunger and food are her own domain. They are becoming more connected to herself than to her mother. Her taste buds are hers alone. As she separates food from her mother or father, the next issue is the selection of food, which is a step in the building of one's

---

*Throughout the book, *separation* is used to describe the psychological process in which the individual develops a greater sense of her or his own boundaries and selfhood through the continuous relating and interdependency with others. This idea first put forth by feminists (Chodorow, 1978; Eichenbaum & Orbach, 1983a; Stone Center, 1991) was a challenge to a model of separation based on the male experience of individualism.

own identity. For example, Gina is a child who likes strawberries, not peaches. When the baby's choices and actions are understood and respected, then the baby is allowed to become a person who likes peas but not apple-sauce. Food thrown down and, when older left on the plate, is understood as signaling that she has had enough. These moments witness selfhood being proclaimed and then affirmed. The baby is on her way to becoming a whole person with needs, wishes, rights, and boundaries.

Even when food has become differentiated from the feeder, resolving the primary developmental task of food and feeding, food continues to be, at every age and stage, a vehicle that expresses more general personal develop-mental issues. Nicky at age 4 will only eat his orange if it is cut the way his father does it. Aaron at 5 refuses to eat vegetables. Jesse at 8 suddenly would only eat peanut butter and jelly sandwiches like his friend Sammy. Louise at 9 wants to change the seating arrangements. And, at age 12, Sarah must al-ways phone Kate about their favorite teenage TV soap opera before eating supper. In each of these situations the child is using food and the feeding sit-uation to work through normal developmental issues (e.g., parent identifica-tion, rebellion, independence, peer identification). If these are recognized for what they truly are—expressions of autonomy or control or a need for con-nection—then the food phase passes. If the eating behavior itself gets fo-cused on as the issue, then a power struggle is sure to ensue, imbuing food with greater and more magical power.

Parents bring their own issues to the feeding situation. Although their at-titudes and feelings about authority, control, need, autonomy, closeness, and the desire to provide obviously affect the total relationship and formation of the child's young developing self, they also shape the feeding situation and attitudes toward food itself (Hirschmann & Zaphiropoulos, 1993).

The ethnic cultural heritage of the parents is the larger tapestry on which the individual family weaves its design. This design is created by all the members of the household, but often it is the primary job of one member, traditionally the mother, to do all the stitching. She not only cooks for the family but also plans all the meals, does the shopping, budgets the food bills, and now worries about the family's cholesterol consumption. Feeding is one of the ways in which parents nourish and care for their young. But for the mother it may be a primary way in which she expresses love, carves out her identity, and exercises power and control. It is often grounds on which she feels accepted or rejected, ushering in a multitude of conscious or uncon-scious interpersonal interactions.

Anna Freud (1965) and Mara Selvina Palazzoli (1986) talk about how the mother rightly knows she is being rejected when the child rejects the food. The question then is whether the rejection is stage related or signals that the whole relationship is disturbed. However, they do not discuss the possibility that the rejection may not be rejection of the mother but, rather, statements of physiological and psychological autonomy. Some people prefer string-beans to broccoli. For example, the mother has spent the last hour making chicken, rice, and broccoli, setting the table, washing the pots. When Alice and Jake refuse to eat most of the meal, she feels downcast, all her efforts gone to waste. She feels irritated; her husband sides with the kids. The whole scene quickly escalates into a battleground. This is an example of the way in which food takes on meaning and becomes enmeshed in the family dynamics. In this case the father did not know how to empathize with his wife so that her need for recognition and appreciation would have been responded to while supporting the children in being able politely to refuse food not desired.

There are particular pressures for mothers and daughters in any family constellation that make food more problematic in that dyad. Through the mother's identification and/or sometimes merger with her daughter, she projects on to her daughter her own anxieties and fears about her body and body size. She may try to control the quantities and kinds of food her daughter eats. It is the rare client who can remember having been allowed dessert freely without a struggle. The mother is anxious about her daughter's appetite, for the daughter's appetite may represent the mother's own appetites, needs, and passions that she has so arduously learned to keep under control. At earlier and earlier ages, concerned about their own and their daughter's weight, mothers are imposing a dieting mentality on their daughters, thus interfering with the daughter's ability to discern and interpret her own hunger. This leaves the daughter alienated from relying on her own internal processes for when and how to feed herself.

Even mothers who are consciously struggling not to be critical of their children, but who continue to speak in a belittling way about their own body and eating, are transmitting a constricted image of female acceptability to their children. Through identification with the parent, the child then becomes concerned with her own weight and eating practices.

Although the mother-child and particularly the mother-daughter relationship have their specific dynamics, there are also common scenarios of both parents foisting rules, such as cleaning one's plate regardless of satiation, eating food that feels unbearable, doling out quantities against the child's protest or need, eating according to rigid time schedules, and demanding compliance regardless of individual need or desire. In particularly dramatic ways food behavior can become not only the medium for intrapsychic and dyadic struggles but also an expression of family pathology. For example, clients have revealed an array of these kind of scenarios in which, as children, they were force-fed hated foods until they vomited, they were force-fed while they were sleeping, or they were made to go hungry for long periods; food, especially the "bad" foods were greatly restricted, locks were put on cabinets, such extreme tension gripped the dinner table that they ate voraciously, did not eat at all, cannot recall one bite of food that was pleasurable, parents hovered over every mouthful, or their families' sole connection to each other was through food and mealtimes. Dieting parents have visited their pent-up rage and deprivation on their children in various ways or have forced them to partake in their bizarre eating practices. Sadistic parents have made use of food in rituals of abuse.

Food and feeding can and ought to be a pleasurable, sensual, satisfying, nurturing, and nourishing event. But given that food, caretaking, and the caretaker are inextricably interwoven from the beginning, when there are problems and difficulties in the parent-child relationship, there will be problems and difficulties in the experience of being fed, in how one comes to feed oneself, and in the meaning of food itself. From the feeder's side, giving or denying food can be used for control, punishment, bribery, favoritism, reward, and connection instead of emotionally attuned relating. From the perspective of the one being fed, taking or refusing food can be used to express acceptance, rejection, protest, identification, identity, compliance, pleasure.

At different times food can take on different meanings, but in general and over time what food always holds is the quality of the primary caretakers, for better or for worse. In becoming an independent person, the adult reproduces both sides of the relationship, for she is now both the feeder and the one being fed.

As the life story of the woman with an eating problem unfolds in the office, practitioners must invite her to talk about the sometimes subtle but always powerful dimension of her life that relates to food and feeding. This itself will be a rich and revelatory journey as it speaks of important past and present relationships, developmental issues, actual food and feeding practices in the family, and the symbolic way she is currently using food to make meaning in her life. In talking about food and feeding, clients may take the therapist quite directly and quickly to the essence of their emotional experience. Even their difficulties talking about it tell a story. Talking about food helps to illuminate what might have remained hidden and unavailable, thereby laying the groundwork that allows practitioner and client jointly to begin knowing the heart of the issues to be worked on in the years to come.

Body Experience, Development, and Image

INFANCY

Living in one's body, like learning to interpret hunger accurately, is something that cannot be taken for granted as it too is a developmental achievement. This process that Winnicott (1972) so aptly calls "indwelling" and "personalization," also called body/self integration, is a long, slow one that can only happen in the context of a relationship with a caretaker whose loving hands and emotional involvement support the child to become a person. The child must feel accepted, valued, and loved for her own unique shape and temperament in order for development to occur. To quote Winnicott:

> Healthy feelings of personalization (the existence of a satisfactory working arrangement between body and mind) have their origins in and are based upon positive parental attitudes toward the child's body. When these are not present, the child's resultant attitude toward his own body will be critically impaired or otherwise compromised; that is he will have a weak basis for the formation of a valid and acceptable sense of self in his own body. (Winnicott, 1972, p. 1)

In the beginning, the baby's body and psyche are not fully separated out from that of the mother. New evidence from the research of Daniel Stern (1985) suggests that there are alternating states of separation and merger from the very beginning. It takes a couple of months before the baby can consistently hold the knowledge that those two hands that can move, sometimes curled under the blanket and sometimes waving wildly, are her two very own hands. The baby goes in and out of unintegrated states, moving toward fuller integration of body parts and body functions. Over the next year a mental representation of the body coheres as the child's sense of its own somatic shape and boundaries develops. The skin and the mouth are important first boundaries, establishing both contact and connection as well as separation. This sense of one's physicality, one's insides as a mass of physical sensations that later become organized, and one's body as first permeable then bounded, first unintegrated, and then integrated forms the core of the psyche. As Freud (1961) said, at first the ego is a body ego.

To shed light on an aspect of how this sorting out of me/not me takes place, Winnicott made an important contribution in his 1971a article, "The Mirror-role of Mother and Family in Childhood Development." He states that for the baby the precursor of the mirror is the mother's face. He points to the use of the mother's face and how she looks and what she reflects back while she is looking at her baby as the way in which the baby comes to know herself. The baby needs to find herself in her mother's face to feel recognized. If the mother (parent) does not reflect back the baby's state but can only reflect back her own, then the baby remains lost to herself and has trouble personalizing her own being. If the baby's looking results primarily in seeing a critical face, a hateful face, an empty face, or a depressed face, essentially an unaccepting experience of who the baby is, part or whole, the outcome is troublesome. The parent's face cannot be used as a mirror for baby's self-discovery. Without a mirror, it is difficult, if not impossible, to feel seen and recognized by the other, which is how a person comes to experience her or his own subjectivity. This leaves one always struggling to be seen by the other, to know from the other that one exists, to gain confirmation "I am."

When the baby is forced to be oriented in an age-inappropriate way to concerns about her mother's or father's state or to nonacceptance, there begins a hypervigilant attitude to the external world, leaving the baby more or less depleted without the richness that builds up from relatedness. This can be the beginning of false self or body development where true authentic relating is sacrificed to the needs of the other.

Being seen authentically is important to the immediate discussion because "being seen" carries both a psychological and physical meaning. In the beginning of life, if one's body is not seen and accepted, then one's self is not seen. Likewise, if the self is not seen and accepted, then neither is the body. Normal development assumes this psychosomatic unity. But this unity can be disrupted in infancy or at any later point in development. The adult woman who converts feelings into bodily states that have little to do with the psychic event, and vice versa, bodily states or thoughts about one's body into feelings that are unrelated to the bodily event is a manifestation of this disruption. For example, when one feels loss, the sadness is felt throughout one's body. But when the body is experienced as too large or too ugly as a response to the loss, the body then is functioning as a defense against an affective state.

As Winnicott points out in "On the Basis for Self in the Body" (1989), even a child that has a physical deformity can feel normal and whole if loved and accepted from the start for her own sake and shape. In fact, that is the only way she can later accept and integrate her deformity into her mental image of herself. To understand early psychic/somatic development more fully it is essential to understand the importance of gender for both baby and caretaker. Gender identity is shaped by culture, and gender profoundly affects in very different ways the journey boys and girls take regarding psyche-soma formation and the development of a social identity.

A major component of a daughter's body image is developed through identification with her mother. Body image as defined here includes three meanings: mental representation of one's body, perceptions of body size and shape, and comfort or dissatisfaction about one's body. As women mother, their experience of themselves and of their mothers as women is brought forward into their relationships with their daughters. Accumulated experience with gender thus has a powerful impact on how the mother "sees" her daughter and, subsequently, on how the daughter comes to "see" herself.

Sadly, for women, truly being seen and recognized, which is such a critical piece of healthy development, is too often only skin deep. Both historically and currently, women are meant to appear, to reflect, to be mirrors for others, to be the containers for others' desires (parent's, men's, children's), to support the passions and fulfillment of men. Women are valued insofar as they service another: either attending to others' needs or being their object of beauty. Women's very ability to see, self and other, is born in this context.

How and what women see is cultural. Just as experience is mediated by language, a cultural exchange, so too is vision a cultural artifact. Because women are not seen, they learn not to see themselves as they truly or potentially are; thus, they cannot act in the world on their own behalf but, rather, come to see themselves as what Berger calls an "object of vision: a sight" (Berger, 1972, p. 47).

CHILDHOOD

In this culture, little girls, like little boys, go through a narcissistic/exhibitionistic phase in early development in which they flaunt their bodies and make use of their physical abilities; this is a central part of gender consolidation. Rather than being seen as a phase to pass through in order to accept and integrate a piece of their sexual identity, a little girl's mandate to appear (rather than to act or be) and to focus on her appearance is confirmed as intrinsic to her being and equal to being an adequate female.

In the classical psychoanalytic literature, the explanation as to why boys are more active physically and girls more concerned with adornment is made along phallic lines. The little boy makes use of his penis in phallic play—guns, swords, running—but the little girl having no penis compensates by attending to her body in general—hair play, dressing up, makeup, and so on. We see this explanation as insufficient in that these activities are being shaped by a powerful vision of male and female identity from the very beginning. Research now reveals that babies in the first couple of months of life have more capacity to discriminate experiences than was previously thought (Stern, 1985). They can distinguish their parents' voices and smells. So too, early on little girls can, in some ways, perceive, become initiated into, and identify not just with the mother but also with the "female culture mother."

Historically, little girls have not been encouraged to explore either the possibilities the world holds in general or the more personal world of their own bodies. In these ways the culture ordains a narrow, and ultimately perverse, emphasis on appearance. When little girls fulfill these cultural expectations, they get locked into these constraints by the adult world: "Oh, how pretty/thin you are." No other complement is given with such generosity of spirit to the little girl. Dare she not comply by not focusing on making herself pretty or by being larger than acceptable, she often finds herself rebuked and rejected, which undermines her tenuous sense of self.

At the same time, the little girl is also contending with powerful prohibitions against displaying her body. Examples of these kinds of prohibitions are seen in clients' memories of being told: Cross your legs, don't be so wild, stop showing off, cover up. These warnings reflect cultural/parental anxieties and fears about women's power, place, and burgeoning sexuality.

These warnings also speak to the real ongoing threat of violence toward the female body.

Women thus contend with appearance as essence and yet must balance their exhibitionistic wishes with the concomitant prohibitions against them. Women continually work to transform their appearance through remaking their bodies—redoing their hair, nails, bellies, thighs, and so on to make an acceptable presentation. On the other hand, women feel compelled to hide or obliterate their bodies. Underneath both, however, lies the deepest hunger, which is to be seen for one's whole self, to have one's needs, desires, and sexuality accepted, to be understood in one's entirety for the complex being one is.

The last few decades have brought increased tensions to girls as their bodies develop. Infancy and childhood are no longer a safe haven from the pressures, anxieties, and demands of a more mature sexual identity. The worry and concern about one's body, which used to belong to the period of puberty when girls bodies are actually physically transforming and an interest in a more mature sexuality is awakening, are now being foisted on younger and younger children.

The notion that thin equals acceptability equals adequate female equals sexually desirable has opened the way for both mothers and fathers to be overly concerned at inappropriate ages with the size and shape of their daughters' bodies. Parents who have been raised under the specter of Twiggy often have their own eating and body image problems. Mothers consciously and unconsciously project/inject their anxieties, their fear, and hatred of their female bodies on to their daughters. Toward this end little girls are weaned earlier (Belotti, 1975), put on skim milk, and given less food more anxiously. Several clients report that they were clinically starved in infancy as a result of their parents' fears.

Chubbiness is no longer seen as cute baby fat or as a symbol of a well-cared-for child or as necessary prepubescent body fat. Rather, it is seen as parental and child failure. Young girls are made to feel increasingly insecure and anxious about their bodies and appetites by little comments about second portions, be careful, don't gain, and so on. Many longingly watch their fathers and brothers eat substantial portions, while they are put on diets, dragged to diet doctors, given diet pills, and sent to diet camps. One client reports walking into her friend's house, seeing the friend's 3-year-old alone in front of the television, exercising to Jane Fonda. The mother walks by and says, "Oh, what a beautiful body you have. Feel the burn, honey."

Little girls are exposed to the current exercise craze not with pleasure, enjoyment, body dexterity, strength, or prowess in mind but, rather, in search of the "perfect" body. Whether all of these concerns are those of the well-meaning parent who wants her daughter to fit in or are used by the more disturbed parent as the tools of hatred, envy, sadism, or pathological narcissism, the result, on a continuum, is still corrosive to the ego and interferes with positive self/body image development. Little girls increasingly do not feel good about their bodies or in their bodies. These intrusions promote the growing confusion a little girl has between body shape and size and self-worth, as well as about who really possesses this body and who and what is this body really for. When one poses the question to adult clients: "Who does your body belong to?," many readily respond, "my mother" or "my father." Body/self integrity has not been achieved; the process of "indwelling" has gone awry.

PUBERTY

Puberty is an explosive and dynamic time in a young girl's life, a time when she faces psychological challenges and when her body takes on new shape and power. The developmental demands of puberty require further steps in separation and differentiation, often restimulating earlier patterns and conflicts in the individual and among family members. This is a challenging time for every family. Often, there is a question about whether the family is healthy and secure enough to let their daughter have a life apart from them and among peers and whether she has enough internal resources, enough of a sense of self to both want to and be able to take this step.

In attempting to find her own unique place in the world, the adolescent girl is in a passionate struggle to be both similar and different from her mother. The mother's role, once again, is quite important in being able to accept the young daughter's needs for both closeness and differentiation. The identification (can I wear your sweater?) can feel good, warm, and close. The differentiation can be, yet doesn't have to be, at times aggressive and rejecting ("I hate you!, you never understand me, I never want to be like you or look like you!"). If the mother is comfortable with her own body and her sexuality, she can be helpful in educating her daughter. She can be a model for self-acceptance, contain her daughter's fears, and help to create an environment where both mother and daughter can each experience excitement and pleasure in the daughter's more mature state and the mother's new position. This accepting and respectful involvement contributes to the consolidation of a daughter's positive body image and arm her with better defenses against cultural obsessiveness regarding the female form. What is strikingly apparent in clinical experience is that mothers or parents who were able to advocate for their daughter's unique body size and shape fare better psychologically than those who could not differentiate from the cultural norms and exerted pressure on their daughters to conform. This clinical experience confirms Steiner-Adair's study (1986) that shows that girls who can differentiate from current cultural expectations to be a "super woman" are less likely to develop an eating problem.

Given that most families are reared by women, the fact that the mother and daughter share the same gender makes differentiation more problematic. Frequently, the boundaries between mother and daughter are blurred or merged; the mother can fear rejection, and some mothers fear abandonment and even disintegration. The mother can find herself struggling with anxiety about her own body and aging as well as with competitive and envious feelings toward her daughter's youth or freedom from responsibilities. The mother's own difficulties and unresolved conflicts in puberty can come back in full force. All these issues in the context of her second-class place in society often make it difficult for the mother to help her daughter to face this journey with confidence and security.

In families where there is a father, his role in this differentiation process is important to the daughter if he is available as another identificatory figure. If the mother and daughter are overly enmeshed, father can offer relief as the figure of separation (because he is other), especially if he can help his daughter not only to differentiate from her mother but also to recognize her subjectivity, as Benjamin (1988) argues, is so critically necessary. Given the fact that the father is a male, he is the first important man in her life and her introduction to what she can expect and hope for from men. His acceptance and respect of not only his daughter's autonomy but also her budding sexuality can contribute to her self-esteem and her positive self and body image.

But fathers too have unconscious fears about women's bodies and power, their own sexual desires and dependency needs. As their daughters mature, these fears can be aroused and, unfortunately, can become sexualized. Over and over again women clients report how their fathers were not helpful during this time, many experiencing abrupt disruptions in their relationships with their fathers at this age. Some fathers were abandoning, literally and metaphorically pushing daughters off their laps. Overnight, it would feel as if their fathers changed or withdrew, even as their need to "sit on his lap" still persisted. Some were inappropriately emotionally involved, and others sexually and physically transgressed their daughters' boundaries.

Coming to terms with sexuality is so difficult for adolescents because it is intertwined with separation and attachment dilemmas and struggles. It is also difficult because the powerful physical and sexual changes are complicated both intrapsychically and in the world. The development of hips, breasts, and secondary sexual characteristics with the onset of menstruation requires a change in both the body and psychic schemata. When a girl already feels insecure in relation to her body, these physical changes can elicit fear, confusion, and terror of being out of control, or they are seen as proof that she is already out of control. This fear can be expressed in a blurring of body states with psychic states, as seen in clients with eating problems.

The cultural mandate for girls to "appear" and the equation right body = self-worth combine to make it likely she will use her body as a way to negotiate the world and gain acceptability. Gilligan and Brown and the Harvard Project discuss the impact of culture on girls as they are heard less, are seen less, and called upon less. Girls react by "losing their voice" and becoming dissociated from that which they formerly knew about relationship and ways to be in the world (Gilligan & Brown, 1992).

Therefore, more than ever, the girl's body becomes the tool or currency by which she tries to attain power and feelings of importance as well as gain status in her peer community. Not only the right body but also the right hair, the right clothes, and the right look (hip, punk, gay, tough, straight, preppie, etc.) become increasingly important in expressing a more mature female identity as she begins to take her place in a particular social milieu. If she is allowed and able to separate and differentiate, this peer world becomes an attempt to create a secondary holding environment where (in this culture) she practices becoming an adult. Now she can attain new levels of emotional growth, interpersonal relatedness, and sexual maturity. But this peer group is insufficient as the new holding environment is shaped and held by the larger culture and feeds off its symbols, its modes of being, and its vision of what is possible.

As Kim Chernin points out in *The Obsession* (1981), in Western culture there are no rites of passage to welcome young girls into womanhood. Dieting and looking right fill this vacuum, allowing girls to bond together, to attend to each other's plights, to share secrets about the mysteries of their bodies, and to care for one another in their daily struggles to grow up female. These are the nurturing, positive interpersonal attributes the young girl gains and brings to adulthood—to the men, women, and, later, children who may enter her life. But the rituals and symbols themselves speak of restriction and constriction; they enjoin young women to seek definition and esteem through external criteria. Women bond and try to find strength and community not as much from the positive and powerful symbols of a matriarchy but, rather, from patriarchal consumer culture that fosters women bonding through the mutual dissatisfaction and even self-hatred of their bodies and selves.

Certainly for women with eating problems and, to some degree, for all women, the critical work of separation, differentiation, and integrating sexuality are displaced on to a struggle to manage one's appetite for food and to transform one's body. The body increasingly becomes not a place to live in but, rather, an object not only for others but also to oneself. The young girl is a long way from the infant seeing her mother see her. She now gazes directly into the mirror herself. Her expanded experience of the world and her expanded critical, emotional, and cognitive faculties (greatly increased during prepuberty) are now fully employed to evaluate herself. Sadly, under patriarchy, the mirror usually reflects back a critical, harsh, judgmental picture that is often made of bits and pieces, a fragmented version rather than an integrated whole.

Thus, it is common, if not universal in America, for women to diet during their adolescence. For some this is a short-lived attempt to fit in, "be a good girl" and maybe to try and take off some of the weight gain that accompanies hormonal changes. For others, the dieting and concern with body image remain for years, perhaps forever, without therapeutic intervention, a silenced dialogue woven into daily life, a silenced way to deal with anxiety and feelings of inadequacy. For still others, the obsession with food or food intake, the dieting and bizarre eating behaviors and the urgency to transform one's body no longer accompany life but rather become life.

There are women who do not develop an eating problem in adolescence. For some, it takes further or later developmental stages involving both separation and more complex attachments to precipitate an eating problem, the most common being leaving home for college, work, or living together or marriage, bearing children, or the loss of a loved one. It is common for women who have been raped or battered or who are working through memories of childhood incest to respond to those traumas by attempting to control their bodies and food as a way to take charge over the intense powerlessness they felt from being victimized. In fact, the concurrence of eating problems and sexual abuse is extensive enough that the latter part of the book is devoted to this phenomenon.

ADULTHOOD

Given the cultural and psychological impingements and interferences in a woman's developing sense of body/self integrity, it is a great struggle and challenge for any woman to live vitally in her gendered body. What is the female body and what meanings does it hold as the young girl moves from puberty to adulthood? Feminist theorists, clinicians, and social theorists have understood the power and import of the female body. They have read the female body as the medium of culture, the arena for social control, the emblem of consumer culture, and the site of both courageous protest and excruciating compliance (Jaggar & Bordo, 1989; Orbach, 1978, 1986; Szekely, 1988). As Bordo says, "our bodies are trained, shaped and impressed with the stamp of prevailing social forms of selfhood, desire, masculinity, femininity" (Jaggar & Bordo, 1989, p. 14). Women's complicated relationship to their social position and consequent gender requirements are inscribed on the body and enacted through daily social practices such as dieting, makeup, involvement with fashion and beauty, or exercise.

Although there are uniform cultural ideals and images of and for women in each historical era, each woman makes her own unique relationship to these symbols. Both the common and idiosyncratic forms of relationship to these symbols, as mediated by the family and self, structure multiple layers of meaning about the body for each individual woman. The substantive issues of development that are the challenge of being human are read by women as the surface presentation of self by the overseeing of the minute details of the body "look." Although this preoccupation and this wish for transformation and mastery drain all women, it actually erodes emotional life and satisfactory living for the woman with an eating problem.

Having to house psychic life, the body becomes overly burdened. To the extent that the body speaks for the self, it is subject, albeit narrowly defined. However, the body is rendered object and "thinglike" when daily practices are about control of desire and need, rather than possessing and living comfortably in the body. The greater the body/self disintegration, the riper the body is to serve as the arena and container for the displacement of emotional life and social relations. For the women with eating problems authentic relating, real care, and negotiating need and desire are moved to the body. The body thus imbued with relational needs becomes the stand-in for real people and, for some, the primary and compelling relationship in their lives. Some of the expressive and defensive uses of the body that need to be deconstructed in treatment are the following: the body as internal object relationship (exciting, rejecting); the body as false body; the body as sexual object; the body as undeveloped expression of needs and feelings (i.e., a vehicle for separation, independence, autonomy, power, differentiation); the body as hated self; the body as container of memory; and the body as manic defense. These psychic maneuvers are not exclusive of one another or fixed. Often, contradictory and competing forces and relationships can reside in the same person.

Clinically speaking, if one is to understand the meanings of the body, one must enter the patient's discourse about the body, which primarily gets distilled to talk about fat and thin (Orbach, 1978). The omnipresent images of fat and thin, the pursuit of thinness, and the hatred of fat are the primary ways in which women organize and experience their bodies. They are the umbrella constructs forming the language used by women about their bodies. They are the magnets that attract all other meanings and psychic maneuvers used in relation to the body.

The cultural splitting of fat and thin and the consequent internalization of these rigid images mask and express a profound misogyny: a woman's nonentitlement to live in her own body. Fat and thin talk is ultimately regressive: It oversimplifies and bifurcates the world into black and white, good and bad images; it impedes the development of more complicated thought processes, linguistic expression, and symbolization. The fat/thin obsession means one is outer directed, seeking approval from others and using one's body to endlessly improve oneself. This body preoccupation thus depletes her energy for real societal interaction and impact.

In addition to the search for thinness, as women enter the work world, the traditional province of men, a new categorical imperative has come to the fore. The hard, toned, fit, thin body is preferred over the rounded, soft, fleshy body. This new dichotomy represents the split between the masculine values of autonomy, competition, rationality, and mastery over needs and the denigrated female world of caretaking, nurturance, emotionality, and relationship.

Although thinness does represent success, power in the marketplace, the power of will over need, it encodes another equally significant emotional polarity as well. Lack of power, vulnerability, inhibition of desire and appetite, fear of sexuality (flesh) can be heard if listening carefully to the undertones of the discourse. On a representational level fat is seen as weakness, lack of control, powerlessness, but also it embodies an opposing configuration of meaning. Substance, strength, power, and the wish to take one's place and space in the world constitute a deep and unshakable inner experience, which women reveal when given permission to contact the whole of their experience. These polarities of fat and thin, good and bad, strong and weak, successful and incompetent, sexual and asexual, independent and dependent, and masculine and feminine need to become more fluid, less hierarchical and value-laden. These attributes need to be named and freed from fat and thin body states. The ego will then be able to integrate and use them. With self states integrated into the ego (self), the body can become a body, a place to live in.

CHAPTER 4

Symbolic Meanings of Food and Body

CAROL BLOOM AND LAURA KOGEL

Consuming great quantities of food or eating no food at all without
    regard for physiological hunger
Chewing food but not daring to swallow
Waking up with thoughts of not eating
Poring over diet books
Eating lunch with colleagues and slipping into bathrooms to throw up
Pouring Comet over leftovers
Taking laxatives and Dexa-trims as magic potions
Obsessive thinking and overinvolvement with the body
Attacking one's body curves by exercising for 6 hours

All these are prominent metaphors in the symbolic language of
women with eating problems. They must be treated as metaphors
for a persistent, gnawing, emotional hunger that will not subside
no matter what food or exercise strategy is employed. The seemingly gar-
bled code of their images, actions, and thoughts must be deciphered.

Although each woman and each treatment are unique, it may be generally stated that a woman with eating problems cannot fully rely on herself or
others. She has withdrawn into the inner world of unsatisfying relationships,
which, bad as they may be, substitute for people and provide a holding environment, which the circumstances of her past or present failed to provide.

This reality was poignantly expressed by a client who said: "Food is my
lifeline. It's the thing I hold on to that prevents me from sinking into a terrible black emptiness. My mouth is the gate between the inside me and the

outside world; and food and my constant thoughts about it are the draw-bridge—what brings them together and keeps me alive."

The range in severity of these symptoms is very great indeed. There are women for whom the symptom substitutes for life itself. The focus of every single day is activity (mental and physical) in the service of eating or not eating, running, sneaking, bingeing. For these women, the defenses and symptoms act as a safeguard against greater anxiety, disintegration, and fear of exposing their neediness to themselves and to others, thereby leaving them less open to rejection and abandonment.

The majority of women, however, are not totally "taken over" by their symptoms and obsessions, yet, they are involved with a riveting preoccupation, an encapsulated piece of "madness" that moves from background to foreground, depending on triggers in their inner and/or outer life. For these women, the symptom is not a defense against disintegration, but, rather, it serves to modulate anxiety, need states, and esteem.

Without a direct or with only a partial connection to her needs (here defined broadly to include bodily, narcissistic, sexual needs along with needs for power, autonomy, comfort, soothing, recognition, connection, etc.), a woman uses food to represent them, to control them, or to thoroughly disavow having them altogether. Because of her fear of being seen as needy, she tries, for example through dieting, to ensure that no one—including herself—will see her needs. This part of her feels too young, too selfish, too irrational, too threatening, or too vulnerable. So, this needy little girl part is split off, leaving the woman without access to a substantial part of her being.

Her eating problem gives her a way to explain her agony about what feels so dreadfully wrong in her life, which she cannot (or does not think she can) tolerate more directly. To say "I have an eating problem" is a less agonizing, more familiar, a predictable and self-contained "disaster" than to face the pain, humiliation, and rage of acknowledging "I have been neglected." Moreover, she feels that she can have better control over this experience and outcome (eat less, eat more) than over her feelings of internal neediness, terror, and chaos, or in her relationships. Her symptoms are the means by which she psychically survives and copes. Thus, she falls apart in a controlled and private way, having little trust that the environment can care for her any better. But over and over again these techniques fail her. Devoid of real people and real relating, they cannot meet real needs, and so she must keep repeating them addictively in what is called here an "action symptom."

Emotional experiences (pleasurable as well as painful) are discharged as action, so as to symbolize good or inadequate caretaking. She thus is able to bridge psyche and soma. In extreme cases, those who are severely anorexic never close this gap. This group bears closer resemblance to those people who suffer from psychosomatic symptoms, as Joyce McDougall (1989) describes. Overwhelming anxiety is expressed only through the body because the trauma occurs so early that there are no word or symbolic representations.

Many women with eating problems are less extreme in their reaction. These women do not split their minds and bodies to such a degree that all their wishes and fears are expressed through the body. Their experience is still quite fractured. They are using food as a mental construct, a symbol of care. They use this symbol to contact and speak about the psychic part of their distress, and they use "food/body" actions or thoughts to communicate the nature of their difficulty. Their symptoms are thus a bridge to their inner lives. The woman with an eating problem has only her symptom as a way to signal her distress, her protest about her world, past and present, inner and outer.

Although some factors and dynamics are common to all eating problems, there are identifiable differences between compulsive eating, anorexia, and bulimia. These three categories can be viewed from the perspective of the relational matrix: the relationship to the real caretakers, the internalized caretakers (the internal objects) with the attending affective states, as well as the relationship to self needs (recognition, comfort, agency, connection, power, sexual fulfillment, etc.). Food is a substance that satisfies self need, but food is also the medium for relational transactions from birth. The need for food can come to represent all need.

Although these syndromes can be seen as separate entities, there are many women who shift back and forth, making use of the different behaviors as needed to express different and shifting psychic states. The anorexic woman can become bulimic; the bulimic woman can suddenly become anorexic; a year later she is a compulsive eater; and so forth.

The Compulsive Eater

The majority of women with eating problems are compulsive eaters who eat for emotional reasons without regard for physiological hunger. There are all kinds of compulsive eating behaviors. There are those who eat compulsively when with others, those who eat compulsively primarily when in isolation, others who eat all the time, those who eat when hungry during the day but compulsively in the evening (most compulsive eaters have trouble in the evening when the structure of the day is no longer there to hold them), and others who cannot make it through the night without a 2:00 A.M. feed. Some eat sweets, others starch, and there are those for whom sheer quantity is the essential. For some, preoccupation with food may substitute for having a life. Others have a life with meaningful work, relationships, and sex, yet many experiences still need to be punctuated with a dish of ice cream. For example, Julie had just had a short, inconsequential interaction with her supervisor. When the coffee cart came around, she found herself taking and gulping down two donuts, although she usually got just coffee. Her supervisor's tone had bothered her, and she felt she was foolish to be bothered at all.

Debbie, in a different example, had a nice evening with her lover. They made love; her body felt satisfied, but there was some small gnawing experience inside that she was not able to really define or to grab hold of, but she knew a piece of cake would touch the level of the emotional gnawing. She said she was hungry, though she was not physically hungry, and got up and ate cake. She was then able to go to sleep, but not without first castigating herself for having had the cake.

These two women both reacted to an emotional moment by means of an action symptom—in these cases, eating—in order to respond to their feelings in the only way they knew how. For some compulsive eaters, chewing or sucking the food may be the most important component of the action symptom; for others, the taste, the sense of fullness, the ongoing obsessional thinking (providing in its own way a loyal companion), or the activity itself—getting up, going to the fridge, looking around, making crackers and cheese, remaking them over and over again. In this way the whole experience structures time for many compulsive eaters, filling in the gaps and providing the only way they know to be with themselves.

The schema of understanding the compulsive eater's use of food as a symbolic representation of the internalized object and of self needs provides insight and a basis for a treatment approach. Compulsive eaters lack an internal soothing presence to tolerate anxiety; they turn to food, as symbolic of the good mother, to find comfort and connection in order to allay anxiety. Beyond this generality compulsive eating cannot be located diagnostically because it can be found in every diagnostic category, every family constellation, and every characterological profile (unlike the case with bulimic and anorexic women). With each individual client, diagnostic concerns play a part in the psychic issues being eaten about—fears of fragmentation for one person, loss for another, narcissistic injury in another, and in others conflict. Myriad thoughts, affective states, a glance in the mirror, conflicts, an interaction that went well or did not go well, forbidden feelings, and undeciphered needs can send someone toward food.

Although food symbolizes a time when the merger of mother with baby was a soothing experience, in actuality food is a concrete separate substance under one's own control. Food is accessible, available, legal, and relatively cheap (Thompson, 1992). Nothing can replace food. Lovers, spouses, friends, work, sports, sex may help or temporarily stave off a feed or a binge, but the compulsive eater ultimately always returns to food to solace her for the types of distress, internal and external, she cannot psychically metabolize. The food is there just for her. It makes no counter demands, requires nothing of her; it has no needs of its own. In this way food can be viewed as a transitional object (Winnicott, 1971b), albeit a failed one, or as a self object (Kohut, 1971).

Like any transitional object, food offers itself as the solution from birth on to all a woman's needs. In later life food is used in the transitional space to rebel and protest against her deprivation of both food and a fuller emotional life. Her binges announce that her needs and desires refuse to be silenced. Even though she may not be aware of what she is symbolically swallowing, and no matter how mismatched her responses are, she affirms that she has a right to her experience, a right to eat, a right to her needs, and a right to exist more fully.

But whatever relief she derived from taking in a piece of caretaking, that very relief is soon derided and rejected by other parts of her psyche (the anti-libidinal ego or rejecting object) and the culture's internalized saboteur. These resistances to care make it impossible for her actually to structuralize the transitional object's functions into the ego. Self-rebuke weakens her attempts at expansion and self nurturing. For as soon as she asserts her rights and needs, she then yells at herself. "I shouldn't have eaten the cake!" "If I had only lasted on that diet!" She is upset that the food/caretaker fails her and is angry with herself for needing to return home for support. She is angry that she now has not only had the cake but that the need or bad feeling still persists. She is angry that she needed anything. This self-rebuke about eating also hides her self-condemnation about whatever—the injury or conflict or loss or terror—sent her to the food. She tries to listen to her "yelling voice," her "trashing voice," and manages to suppress her needs for a while and does not eat the cake. But then she is angry about not eating it, and her needs arise again. She eats. She yells, unable to appreciate her appropriate protest and anger. This is a cycle that continuously repeats itself. For some compulsive eaters, the "yelling" or "trashing" voice represents and strengthens the tie to the rejecting or traumatizing object, thus corroding the central ego. Cultural symbols and signifiers continually reinforce this internal criticism. In this way the transitional space is neither fully transitional nor benign. It cannot facilitate the growth of the ego.

The Anorexic Woman

The anorexic woman dramatizes the mandate that women should "appear" but not "be." In her struggles for recognition through her symptomatology, the anorexic woman is trying to give shape and substance to her inner emptiness, believing (for good reason) that love, connection, and food only mean danger. Her libidinal energy is turned inward, her passionate ties are to her internal demons.

Her anorexia is both the logical extension and the exaggeration of some of the perverse demands of femininity on women. By constricting herself, she stretches and pushes her limits and boundaries. She plays with the borders of her psyche and her body. She takes the cautionary message to watch and watch out for her needs, desires, and appetites to the extreme: She tries systematically to exterminate them.

When we look in horror at her emaciated body might we not be looking, horrified, into the soul of a patriarchal and misogynist culture? She is the living embodiment of what this kind of culture can do to women. She ferociously takes up the cultural vision for acceptable femininity and paradoxically turns it into its antithesis: She cannot and will not participate in adult female life and sexuality, no matter what her age. Her anorexia is not a refusal to grow up but a protest and rebellion against the life that is offered her as a woman (Orbach, 1986).

The denial of needs and food and the wish to transform oneself are most strikingly manifested in the anorexic woman. For her there are no benign transitional objects. Food represents the rejecting or traumatizing object internalized as the inadequate, intrusive, or poisonous, controlling, and overly enmeshed caregiver. As Orbach (1986) points out, the cause of anorexia is the preservation and protection of the unemerged self. Because of environmental failure this self is not only unable to develop but also feels so much under attack or submerged that it needs to split itself off and remain in hiding. Elaborate defenses and barriers are constructed to protect this hidden self from any further exposure, rejection, abandonment, or annihilation. The anorexic woman feels that the smaller she is, the less room she leaves inside to be attacked internally. Invasions, control, or enmeshment by the caregiver leave the anorexic with overwhelming feelings of worthlessness and impotence, which also need to be defended against. To protect herself, she takes control by refusing to eat, by perfecting her body, and by the obsessional thinking and activities that organize her psychic life. She thus keeps at bay her extreme vulnerability, her feelings of powerlessness, terror, and anxiety. Control over herself becomes the goal of her life.

A battle takes place within her. When the internal self component moves toward the object component, it faces merger/annihilation/total control by the object. In fleeing this state, the self component faces abandonment and aloneness. The anorexic woman moves internally from one state to the other, and, projecting these states (originally experienced in the external world) back into the world, she relives them interpersonally. The obsessing and the quest for perfection attempt to negotiate these two terrifying places.

Food as the object is dangerous. Her body as container of frightening needs, feelings, demands, and wishes is also to be rejected and controlled. But she is not to be daunted. With no other tools at hand, she uses the very same ones (food and the body) to create a more acceptable being; indeed, she aspires to be a "perfect" being. She hones, tones, sculpts, and carves a body that is invincible. Fat, a culturally horrifying female attribute, will exist for her no more: Her life needs to be beyond reproach. Her body is to make no demands for food, sex, comfort, and so on; it must require nothing, literally. Having no needs and feelings, which she has deemed impermissible, she is thus guiltless.

Her anorexia provides the solution to these intensely bad feelings and impossible goals. She attains a semblance of power as she triumphs over her needs and desires. Because she was not allowed to differentiate, her needs for recognition and to feel special become an intense motivation for her anorexic stance. "I am anorexic" is a self-affirmation of uniqueness; it provides an identity. Her ferocious exercising and denial of her need for food and sleep are unique ways for her to feel momentarily successful, accomplished at something. Her skinny (but never skinny enough) body is both the longed-for prize (in that it is linked to a fantasy of finally being loved) and the symbol of achievement and mastery. Her true self in hiding, she omnipotently creates a fiercely independent, stubborn, dauntless false self to function in the world.

The anorexic's antilibidinal ego is in a winning position. But because it forbids her from experiencing any satisfaction, she can never feel good enough. She must therefore continually push on to get even skinnier. What she does not know yet is that her body will never get skinny enough to change her internal reality or her perception of a world that feels so unwelcoming to her. Without therapeutic intervention, her striving for self-esteem, through victory over her appetite, becomes a constant struggle, one that can eventually lead to her death.

The Bulimic Woman

The bulimic woman is caught in a dramatic, alternating cycle of bingeing and purging (through laxatives and/or vomiting and/or overexercising) and often starving between the two. She shares, on a continuum, many concerns and characteristics with her compulsive eating and anorexic "sisters." Women, of varied ages, sexual orientation, class, ethnic and racial background, respond to a whole array of psychological distress, traumatic experiences, and deprivation by bulimic behavior. By controlling what goes in and out of the body, women attempt to master what feels uncontrollable and even unnameable. They transpose their distress or trauma to a struggle around their own bodies, unconsciously hoping to heal the injuries of neglect, narcissistic exploitation, poverty, homophobia, racism, and so on.

Currently more and more young women are becoming bulimic. This phenomenon requires a sociocultural analysis as well as an understanding of the individual's personal history. Bulimia can be understood as a response to the terrific stress and demands of being the "new" woman who is entering the professional workforce or in college preparing to do so. These young women are attempting to navigate a rapidly shifting social world and find a role for themselves with a genderized internal psychology that does not adequately prepare them for this task.

In many young bulimic women we see gendered life in its raw form. Traits and values traditionally assumed to be masculine and associated with the work world—independence, competence, distance, rationality, and lack of emotion—are crystallized as one part of the self. Feminine traits associated with home and hearth—nurturing, interdependence, relating, emotion, nonlinear thinking—constitute another crystallized form of self. These crystal selves remain rather separate; they do not mesh into one larger structure. They represent different ego states with different ways of being in the world, different values, aspirations, fantasies, and interactional patterns. The bulimic woman struggles with each set of traits. She moves back and forth between them trying to find her right place. Because each move represents a sacrifice of part of herself, no move is quite right. The bulimic woman experiences these ego states as antithetical to each other, and the contradictions feel overwhelming and insurmountable.

These two worlds are, in reality, sometimes antithetical to each other. When Melinda's boss screamed at her, she said that the "natural" thing for her to do was to cry. Instead she stood there "like a man" and faked being as in control as she could (probably the smart thing to do in her case). It is the impossibility of reconciling these two different worlds that women are literally throwing up. Women's bodies become the place both to contain and to eliminate the contradictions. It is the therapy room and the therapeutic relationship that become the place to acknowledge and understand the contradictions, to come to terms with the fantasy of being perfect in each world, to bridge the polarized gender splits and to learn to manage the external world as well as possible given its real limitations.

Encountering these contradictions leads us to speculate about what life would be like if there were a shift in role expectations, a feminization of the workplace, equalization of child-rearing arrangements, less rigid conceptions of masculinity and femininity, elimination of pressure for women to be better on the job than men, and changes in mandates to look the right way. Without at least some of these changes, women will continue to turn to such dramatic means as purging, sacrificing inner security for outer success.

In addition to a social analysis, there is a common familial pattern described by many bulimic women, not only some of the younger women just discussed but other women as well. These women describe their experience in their families as one in which there was no psychological room for them as a full person. They were not to take up space, ask for anything, or make demands. They were the good girl. Normal feelings of anger, assertion, or rebellion were sent underground. Very commonly, someone else in the family had a serious physical or emotional problem that consumed the available space and attention. The bulimic's role in the family became that of caretaker. Her needs appeared to be unimportant, but her caretaking role was essential in enabling the family to function. Since she could not develop herself based on recognition of her full emerging self experience, she used her role as caretaker to define herself. She secured a place in the family by being whatever they needed her to be: smart, understanding, perfect, sexy, sexual, successful, or not too successful. In these ways she gratified her parents' emotional needs. This familial pattern that perpetuates the "good girl" syndrome contributes to the difficulty in the larger world of integrating the relational world of women and the individualistic world of men.

But in clinical experience, we often find that inside this well-functioning, contained, competent "good girl" is a fuming "wild" child desperately clamoring for recognition. Like her anorexic sister, she introjects the spoken and unspoken parental and cultural demands and expectations. She pushes and drives herself to become the best (false) self she can be. This drive functions to defend against her inner emptiness, neediness, anger, and feelings of abandonment and powerlessness.

The bulimic symptomatology is a perfect mirror of the bulimic woman's basic struggle. Even in her suffering she cannot be visible or take up space. People do not know she has this secret. Her normal weight or overweight belies her problem. No one sees those pills she is taking by the handful. No one knows why she disappears after work presentations or dinner. No one is privy to her despair, her chaos, and her shame. Because her symptom allows her privacy—a condition uniquely hers—and the bathroom becomes "a room of one's own," she can go unnoticed and therefore receives less help. This "illness" is the perfect metaphor for a society in which one's desires are kindled in the small family unit, yet are treated as disruptive and illegitimate, and therefore must be hidden in the family as well as in the culture.

On the intrapsychic level, her needs, conflicts, fears, pain, desires, and feelings (rage, lust, envy, love, hate, etc.) are all deeply split-off and displaced onto food. Because, she believes, the food may never be there again, just as it is never okay to eat or feel, and because she might be truly hungry, she voraciously, greedily, and secretly gobbles it up. If food is not permissible and if food is not truly for her, then the only way she can eat is to sneak, steal, or binge it. (This is also true for the compulsive eater.) It is not uncommon for bulimic women to steal food and other things, because the act of buying something requires a conscious acknowledgment of desire and need.

Every day—sometimes 10 times a day—she battles to keep these difficult feelings and circumstances at bay. Sometimes she feels successful; she separates from her inner turmoil and despair and can therefore stay away from food. But she is unable to tolerate the accumulated stress of deprivation and denial of emotional life and food itself. Her needs burst forth expressed in her desperate desire for food. As with the compulsive eater, her move toward food may be an attempt to resurrect a good mothering experience, but more often the food is the exciting object that inflames desire, seducing with the promise of nurture and succor that it cannot truly provide.

Once inside her, food pierces the defenses she has erected against her urgent needs and the bad object, causing a state of panic (Bloom, 1987). She now feels invaded and overtaken by all the feelings and conflicts from which she has worked so hard to distance herself. She experiences internal boundary loss: She is in a merged state with an intrusive, overbearing, or annihilating object. Quickly she turns her terror and chaos into ferocious self hate. She is defeated, out of control, fat, grotesque, and filled with profound shame about her responses. The food inside and her fear of fat symbolize the fear of being stuck in this intolerable state forever.

But purging offers her a solution. She can take action; she can do something about her agony and panic and the dreaded fat. Through severe dieting, vomiting, laxative abuse, or all three, she reestablishes her boundaries by unmerging and getting rid of the traumatizing object. She thereby regains her equilibrium. Although she is temporarily relieved by the hope that maybe finally she has just flushed away what feels so dreadful, it is only a matter of time before these feelings reassert themselves and the cycle begins anew.

Some women experience a more chronic state of boundary or self loss and resort to bingeing (an intensification of the state of boundary loss) as a means to get to the purge, which creates the boundaries once again. Women have described this by reporting that when they throw up and for a while thereafter, they know they exist and that they feel alive.

The bulimic woman is symbolically repeating that what she has gotten, and continues to get, is not just insufficient—it is toxic. Again, depending on the extent of damage of sense of self and the corrosive effect of her symptoms and her actual situation, she will be more or less overtaken by her bulimia, therefore becoming more isolated and withdrawn. Bingeing and purging are the only ways she knows to deal with her loneliness and despair.

CHAPTER 5

Beginning the Eating and Body Work: Stance and Tools

CAROL BLOOM, LAURA KOGEL, AND LELA ZAPHIROPOULOS

THE TREATMENT model described in chapters 5, 6, and 7 is predicated on a psychoanalytic relational framework, in which the dyad of therapist and client is the medium for working through the client's problems. The journey is complicated, challenging, and idiosyncratic; and it is always shaped by both the therapist's and the client's subjectivities.

In treating eating problems the therapist must always bear in mind that the client's food and body behavior actually constitute (among other things) reenactments of object relations and of relationships to consumer culture. This treatment sets the stage for weaving together the threads of food, body, hunger, gender, internal object relations, interpersonal engagement, and ego functioning. It does so in terms of a model of attuned eating and of living in one's body and in consumer culture.

Traditional psychoanalytic thought holds that symptomatic behavior reflects underlying deficits and conflicts and, thus, cannot abate without resolving the conflicts and repairing the deficits. The literature abounds with cautionary tales of analyses being derailed by focusing on the symptom. Unfortunately, however, we have found that many people finish good analytic treatments with their eating problem intact precisely because no direct work was done on the symptom or on the interactional communication embedded specifically within the symptom. Some clients feel that their lives have been much improved by treatment, but they still suffer enormously, though often in silent shame, over their troubled relationship with food and their bodies. We believe it is essential to address the symptom from an analytic and psychoeducational, behavioral, and cognitive perspective.

Upon beginning treatment, clients differ in how conscious they are of their symptoms and in their relationships to them. Some enter treatment focused on their symptom, either because that is what they are seeking help for or because they are so "captured" by their symptom that they cannot talk about anything else. For some, the symptom organizes inner chaos; for others, it also gives them identity. Others do not talk about their symptom; they may not see their eating as a primary problem, or it seems inconceivable to them that anyone could help. Some clients experience too much shame about their eating and/or body size to reveal these concerns at first. Disclosure of the symptom may also be affected by whether the therapist is male or female, has a feminist critique and sensibility, and is known as an eating problem specialist; sometimes a therapist's expertise in this area eases the client's shame of disclosure.

A woman who starts treatment talking about her food obsession may be revealing her deepest intimate needs and her psychic organization. From the start she may need the therapist to focus with her on the symptom. However, another woman, although she reveals her symptom, may be best helped by first focusing on the rest of her life more generally before direct work on the symptom can be useful or tolerated. This is a clinical judgment that the therapist determines through careful listening. For example, although one very large woman may need to talk about the shame she carries with/in her weight, another may finally need to be seen and engaged without any attention to her fat. At some point in the treatment, however, the eating and body problem and ongoing practices must be disclosed and eventually made central to the analysis. It is useful for the therapist to become familiar with a person's weight history and her family of origin's attitudes toward food, to eating, and to her developing body. Exploring this terrain provides entrée to core dynamics. In addition, the therapist needs to put forth an alternative model of attuned eating and the possibility of living comfortably in the body. Not only must the symptom be analyzed but also a solution must be made available.

Stance and Detailed Inquiry

A stance of compassion, curiosity, empathy, and attention to boundaries is especially necessary when working with people with eating problems. The therapist must demonstrate an open, questioning attitude that neither judges nor pathologizes the client. In the face of the patient's great shame or trivialization of the problem, the therapist must create a safe place in which the problem can be articulated, dignified, and eventually worked through. The very process of detailed inquiry about eating behavior and the feelings that trigger and accompany it dignifies the symptom by making it worthy of serious psychological investigation. Therapists need to communicate tolerance for the symptom itself, for the intensity of feelings, as well as for the symbolic content of the symptom. They can do so by inviting the actual lived experience to be part of the therapeutic dialogue.

The therapy must also emphasize curiosity about all aspects of the symptom. Explication born of empathy and curiosity provides access into the patient's chronic isolated experiences. The following exchange between patient and therapist illustrates simple ways to make inquiry and show empathy for typical statements by patients about their bodies.

P: I lay awake for hours last night after the party thinking how different I would have felt if I'd lost the 10 pounds.

T: Can you tell me more about what it's like to have those 10 extra pounds?

P: My thighs are grotesque!

T: What about them feels so unbearable, and why your thighs? *or* I can imagine that if you're in the world all the time feeling grotesque, it must be painful! *or* Do others think your thighs are grotesque, or do you just think that yourself?

The examination of these eating incidents and moments of body distortion is part of the basic foundation of any woman's therapeutic journey. These discrete moments, reported over and over again, can seem as if they are all the same, just so many repetitions of an obsessive, compulsive coverup of underlying depression or anxiety. Even the repetitive, ritualistic tone in which many are presented can lead the therapist to believe that once she has heard one, she has heard them all (Gutwill, 1992). The therapist then may believe there is no need to pursue the details of any incident further. In fact, psychoanalytic training teaches that to "gratify" the client by letting her obsess endlessly about what she ate or how fat she feels is countertherapeutic. And this can be so, but only insofar as the real purpose is to get past the obsession to that which it defends against and represents. The therapist must listen carefully to the content, eventually moving beyond the obsession into the meaning. Therapeutic success entails working precisely with that obsession (which may sometimes include deemphasizing it) and understanding how the obsession itself is defensive and adaptive.

The monotonous or hysterical presentations of these incidents belie the profound and varied meanings they contain. The challenge to the analyst is to add to the reservoir of ever-widening meaning. The analyst will necessarily have certain hypotheses about the significance of each particular eating or body distortion experience. She must, however, simultaneously maintain an ability to enter each moment with fresh curiosity—as Bion might say, "without memory or desire" (Bion, 1967). Each time she creates the attitude of curiosity, she is likely to obtain new information and to have a new opportunity in the therapeutic relationship.

Through detailed inquiry the therapist joins the client in her concerns, core experiences, and dissociated aspects of self. Therapeutic questioning paves the way for the client to entertain the idea that another way of thinking and being exists. In this way the therapist differentiates herself from the general cultural assumptions. "Is it possible that your obsession with candy has to do with the prohibitions in your family that you maintain now in your adult life?" Or, "Do you think that getting less in your family has to do with being female given how you and your sisters were treated compared to your brother?" Moreover, these questions call for mental elaboration, which creates psychic space for feeling and thinking, not doing. The creation of psychic space in which the patient can experience her feelings and reflect on them is critical for the client to be able to master her action symptom. The conviction that the client's problem is not just the 10 pounds allows the therapist to hold forth the hope of relief and eventual internal integration in the face of the patient's overwhelming sense of inadequacy and failure. Finally, these exploratory questions exist in the context of relationship; and it is this relationship that brings about change in the client.

The therapist has to hold the tension between the patient's desire to fit in with her culture, to be an acceptable woman, to have the "right" body, with the danger of being captured and taken over by oppressive aspects of the culture. The patient's symptom encodes the desires for an expanded view of herself by which to take a fuller place in the world. The therapist must also create an anchor within herself to withstand the power of the intense desire to transform their bodies that patients bring to treatment. The patient exerts tremendous interactional pressure to enlist the therapist in helping her to lose weight. The therapist must reject this induction because she cannot know the meaning of these wishes until they are analyzed. This is a highly vulnerable area for transference/countertransference enactments, given the therapist's potential for blind spots about or identification with the cultural mandates regarding body size (see chapters 8 and 9). ("Of course my patient should lose weight. She is 50 pounds overweight.") Relinquishing or at least monitoring her ambition to change the client's body size allows the therapist to use countertransference as a tool to understand her patient's unconscious life rather than as the truth about what needs to be done about her body. The therapist can feel concern about weight, but to be invested in weight loss as a goal is to be aligned with the cultural and internal saboteur. When there is a change in body size the therapist will need to clarify whether it is due to a constructive outgrowth of or defense against the therapeutic work; this understanding will then guide the therapeutic action.

Establishing a framework about weight helps the therapist to manage medical situations that might accompany working with patients who suffer from eating problems. The therapist needs to become clear about the limits of what she can handle if she is in private practice. The person who is 75 pounds, 5'4", stable, and functioning may be an acceptable candidate for treatment for one therapist but not for another. The same is true of the person who is 100 pounds overweight with a heart condition. The therapist must know her own bottom line and realistically appraise each situation. It is advisable to make a contract with anorexic patients about an agreed-upon weight below which they will not go, because otherwise the medical and psychological risks make outpatient treatment untenable. It is the patient's responsibility to maintain her weight above that negotiated figure. This is a critical treatment strategy in which the anorexic patient takes charge of her own body and recovery. It also allows the therapist to function with a safety necessary to do therapeutic work. Patients can be required to agree to hospitalization as a therapeutic alternative if they cannot maintain their weight. The other requirement to secure the frame is for the high risk person, large or small, to be under ongoing medical care.

Four Treatment Tools

Beyond the basics of a general psychodynamic treatment, there are four additional tools that are essential for working with eating problems: (1) psychoeducational work; (2) exploration of the adaptive functions of all aspects of the symptom; (3) identification of internal and/or external triggers; and (4) encountering the internal object and working through the tenacity of the symptom.

When the therapist includes cognitive, behavioral, and psychoeducational work she must then assess and track the reactions of the patient to direct teaching and suggestions (and the accompanying dynamic formulations). This process requires closely monitoring the transference and countertransference.

Psychoeducational Work

Although many clients come to treatment with detailed information about caloric content and different diets, clients must learn certain essential and basic facts about their bodies, food, and eating. In some cases therapists can include this information when treatment begins, but other clients may not be ready to hear the information for years. Because cultural and familial misinformation, perhaps even disinformation, is so pervasive, it is important to discover what the client believes are the facts about eating and her body. Then, the therapist should begin gently to expose the contradictions, inefficiencies, and harm inherent in holding on to these kinds of fallacious thinking and entrenched fantasies as well as propose an alternative model of feeding oneself in an attuned way.

For example, medical concerns about purging, starving, laxative abuse, and chronic dieting with yo-yo weight gains and losses must be thoroughly discussed. Over time these practices are harmful to the body and can result in any of the following:

Electrolyte imbalance
Damage to teeth and esophagus
Broken blood vessels
Loss of normal peristaltic and sphincter functioning
Protein deficiency
Changes in skin tone and color
Hair loss
Changes in body temperature
Fatigue
Erosion of the lining of the heart, which can lead to heart attack
Slowing of metabolic functioning (need less and less food to maintain weight)
Impairment of cognitive functioning

Clients need to be reminded of or learn the effects of chronic dieting as well:

Diets create binges, inflame appetite. They are the prisons of deprivation that create the jail break of bingeing (Orbach, 1978).
Yo-yo dieting changes metabolism and alters set point. Studies have shown that forcing people to either gain or lose a lot of weight disregarding their set point (natural body weight) has proven difficult (*Consumer Reports*, 1993a).
Diets tamper with hunger as a reliable signal and lead to loss of and confusion about interoceptive sensations.

Clients also want and need information about weight that challenges obsession with hyperthinness:

800–900 calories was the starvation diet used in concentration camps in World War II (Wolf, 1991). If you are already thin, you may need more food, not less, to lose weight.
You can be too thin. Underweight adversely affects menstruation, menopause, pregnancy for mother and child, and stunts bone development and normal growth.
Being overweight does not necessarily mean being in ill health.

Most clients desperately want help with relating to and managing medical professionals. The following may help to empower clients:

Clients with eating problems are often treated in a biased and unfair way, with either disregard or alarm. Often, their weight is blamed for all medical problems.

Encourage clients to realize they are entitled to respectful medical relationships where they can expose all physical concerns and experience mutual communication.

Advocate for patients' rights so that they can obtain all the information they need. Help them to feel entitled to get a second opinion, to come prepared with their questions in writing and a notebook to write down the answers, to get clarification throughout the consultation, to think critically about glib explanations that make weight the sole reason for their problem, and to feel free not to know their weight (i.e., to turn one's back to the scale if knowing the weight causes distress).

Research the medical community for those who have expertise and a philosophy with regard to eating problems that is compatible with the therapy.

Many doctors do not understand the psychology of an eating problem and treat it as a diet, nutrition, or weight problem, which results in further problems iatrogenically created. Avoid treatments in which other health professionals routinely take total charge of the patient's food and eating and, therefore, organize a treatment plan without consulting with the therapist.

Anti-Diet Approach

Although knowing these facts is useful, psychoeducational work primarily centers on teaching the anti-deprivation, "true" body method of feeding oneself. This includes teaching the recognition of physiological hunger in order to know when to feed oneself and legalizing all foods to demystify them. Clients should learn to distinguish which food will match a particular hunger experience and to recognize and use satiation as the signal to stop. Understanding the psychological meaning of each of these is woven into the treatment (see chapter 6). Understanding the meanings of fat and thin states in working toward body size acceptance and body/self integrity is also part of the psychoeducational work (see chapter 7). To this end the therapy can integrate, when appropriate, guided fantasy work, body image work, food logs, journals, and recommended readings into a psychoanalytic framework. Again, the therapist must track the meaning of these suggestions to the client as well as the meaning of the client's reactions. For example, one client felt cared for and understood when the therapist suggested keeping a food log. She felt ready to face what she actually took in. Another client felt that same suggestion to be undermining and even punitive, a reaction the therapist ascertained only through a close reading of derivative material.

EXPLORATION OF THE ADAPTIVE FUNCTIONS OF THE SYMPTOM

The symptoms of eating problems are major defenses erected by the client to keep herself from experiencing and examining certain feelings, thoughts, conflicts, identifications, needs, fantasies, and material situations. At the same time, the symptom expresses these same feelings, identifications, and so forth. This expansive view of the symptom is why it must be accepted and welcomed into the therapy room. The symptom can be a "pan defense" (Kogel & Munter, 1986): a response to all thoughts and feelings, a noisy distraction from knowing anything but the manifest content of the symptom. On the other hand, the purpose of the symptom can be to defend against certain very specific feelings (e.g., anger) or to push away or obscure a particular aspect of self or experience. The psychological function or purpose of the symptom, that is, its relation to the ego and to internal objects, can change throughout life and the course of treatment. As the symptom is deconstructed, all the defenses and self/object configurations will emerge for analysis.

To comprehend the purpose of a symptom or an aspect of it, the therapist must first slow down the client's rapid presentation by asking for a fuller, frame-by-frame account of the eating moment or body hatred experience. This detailed accounting is absolutely essential. The client usually tells the story as if she were a train hurtling by at 120 mph with her full focus on the final destination: self-blame and self-recrimination. Self-blame, although a critical part of the cycle, and for some a primary one, often masks or hides major psychological issues that cannot be dealt with and integrated if continually bypassed by focusing only on the blame. It is important for the therapist to "slow the train." He or she needs to explore each car for its valuable contents and to wonder whether the scenery along the way can be experienced as part of a journey. In the elaboration of her client's story, the therapist seeks the psychological purpose that the symptomatic thought or action is serving. This quest is critical in working with any addiction if the goal is more than symptom removal.

For example, Reni, a 48-year-old client in treatment for the first time, found herself eating a whole box of doughnuts, although she was not at all hungry. This detail was part of a longer story that she was telling the therapist, who did not want to interrupt. But she made a mental note that it would be important at some point to bring Reni back to this moment, and to ask how reaching for the doughnuts attempted to solve some unconscious psychological difficulty. When the therapist tried to explore this eating experience, Reni could only discuss how angry she was at herself for eating the doughnuts. This is a common point in the work when it was crucial for the therapist to dissect the experience further. The therapist commented that the anger Reni expressed toward herself seemed to be subsequent to the eating, a response to it; and asked what Reni was experiencing at *the moment* she reached for and then ingested the food, that is, before she felt angry at herself. Reni thought for a while and then realized that she had been extremely anxious. She then understood that, for a split second, she had felt soothed by the food. She was surprised by what she had just said. The therapist elaborated, "So this is a way you have to calm yourself, and this is important to know; perhaps in your own way or the only way you have, you were actually trying to take care of yourself, to soothe your anxiety." For the first time Reni appreciated her unconscious efforts on her own behalf; for Reni food functioned as the good external object which needed to be digested and made part of the self. For some clients, this understanding of the function of food as comfort achieved over time can be transformative. However, for others it is important to explore more fully what comfort itself means for them. Clients frequently tell their therapists that they feel they should not need to reach for comfort and this disclosure opens the door to work on the crucial issues of dependency, need, and mutuality. Many clients come to realize that they do not know how to soothe themselves, which leads to an understanding of the paucity in their early experience of attuned soothing.

Finding the adaptive function of the symptom breaks through self-hatred, validates vulnerability, particularly the vulnerability of having and expressing a need, and then affirms the need for self-care and agency. The therapist satisfies a critical developmental need on the part of the client: to be understood, mirrored, recognized, and affirmed by an important other. In this way, the therapist helps to establish entitlement to and ownership of self experience. The client thus expands her range of ego functions as she comes first to appreciate and then to internalize the positive adaptive functions of the defense. In other words, the client cannot structure the self-regulating function of the symptom into the ego until she has first acknowledged it. Over time the therapist replaces the functions of the food, and the client transfers her dependency on food into the therapeutic relationship where the feelings can be interpersonally processed, recognized, mourned, and satisfied.

Another example illustrating the adaptive function of the symptom is provided by the case of Joan, who often described her eating as anesthetizing and numbing rather than calming, as was Reni's experience. To Joan eating felt like taking drugs. Food was her chief defense against emotionally acknowledging extreme emotional neglect by her family of origin. In the transference, Joan used food to numb herself to the impact of the therapist.

Sometimes the adaptive function can reflect a momentary conflict or thought, but it can also express the raison d'être of the whole symptom. For example, an anorexic client named Joyce reported that starving was a way of providing psychic space for herself in a family that consistently annihilated her individuality. Refusing food was the one way that she could be in control and survive. By repeatedly acknowledging this adaptative function, the therapist began to make contact with Joyce. This provided a positive context in which the difficult work of dealing with internal persecutory anxiety could unfold.

Another patient, a 25-year-old bulimic woman named Marcia, after spending 3 days throwing up and staying home, could focus only on her guilt, self-revulsion, and fear of judgment. The therapist asked her to slow down and describe her experience in detail. Marcia eventually found words to describe how scared she was to go out of the house, to be in the world, to interact with others. Together Marcia and her therapist realized that the bingeing and purging took up all her time and provided an activity that felt safer than going out into the world. Marcia felt relieved that this dreadful, terrifying behavior could be understood and worked on.

IDENTIFICATION OF TRIGGERS

When Marcia and her therapist next explored how her latest episode came about, it emerged that a few days prior to the binge, Marcia had made a successful presentation at work, something she would not even have tried 3 months before. In the narration, she mentioned the experience quickly, almost in passing. The therapist "slowed the train down" and went back to inquire more about the presentation. It seems that Marcia was very anxious after the presentation, flooded with concerns about having been too visible and too powerful "for a girl." She feared the envy of coworkers. Marcia now began to wonder if these feelings could have sent her back to the house, feeling so scared that she became constricted in her repertoire, eager to make herself smaller. Recognition of this trigger—the success of the presentation—initiated a period of the therapy that focused on the meaning of visibility and power in Marcia's life. This work eventually enabled Marcia to understand her binge trigger, namely, the fear of being envied, which then itself needed further analysis.

In the session following Reni's exploration of the adaptive function of eating the box of doughnuts as an attempt to soothe herself, she reported a dream in which the central theme was abandonment. Feeling abandoned seemed strange since Reni appeared to feel understood by the therapist in the preceding session. Again, they went back to the eating event, the doughnuts, and looked at the "scenery." In discussing what had preceded the binge, Reni recalled that half-an-hour earlier, she had had a telephone conversation with her lover, Sonia, that was one of many recent contacts after which Reni had had a "funny" feeling. With the therapist's help, Reni was able to articulate the fear of abandonment during these contacts. Given her history, she understood why needing to soothe herself in any way possible would seem urgent. Reni and her therapist acknowledged that in the preceding session they had gotten to the "adaptive function" (the soothing) of the food but they had not gotten to what had set her off (the trigger). To Reni the failure to complete the discovery process had felt like an abandonment by her therapist that paralleled her experience with Sonia. In their discussion of this theme of abandonment, another aspect of Reni's eating and its accompanying dynamics came to light. If Reni did not have all of something she wanted, she would feel lost or abandoned; nothing less would do. She compulsively needed her lover's entire attention, and she reproduced this compulsion to have everything by eating the entire box of doughnuts at once.

Triggers thus can be conscious or unconscious conflictual thoughts, feelings, memories, behaviors, actions, interpersonal situations, material conditions, and internal object relationships. A trigger can be a look in the mirror, the smell of a certain food, a glance from someone, an "unacceptable" feeling, a developmental step. Triggers can be multidetermined, can change, and can be a function of the content or the process of the treatment.

Exploring the triggers helps to introduce the connection between the patient's psychic and interpersonal life, on the one hand, and the mechanics of her symptom on the other. When therapist and patient make this connection over and over again, they create more room for the patient's psychic life, and as her psychic life is validated, it becomes more knowable and manageable. Through the client's new insight and experience, her symptom, which previously felt out of control and bizarre, comes to be known, understandable, and controllable. Her need for the defense diminishes. The client's insight and growing knowledge of her own experience strengthen her sense of self and protect her against self-hate. She develops more compassion for herself. She discovers more options for managing the triggers, both behaviorally and emotionally, as she becomes curious where she would have been self-blaming.

With some clients it is important to explore every single trigger in order to help them establish the existence of their emotional life. For others, who eat (as a pan defense) in response to every emotional stimulus, it is difficult to distinguish individual triggers and this technique is thus less useful. It is then more fruitful to begin by gaining an understanding of the client's life and history. Making sense and order of her life, of how she came to be who she is, must come first. Exploring the triggers then will have meaning in this context. With yet others the converse is true: Some order must first be brought to the food and eating before meaningful life exploration can be undertaken. In this situation teaching the client how to eat according to hunger, choice, and satiation is the first step. After she begins to have experiences of eating with hunger, she can then make use of the times she does not do so by exploring the triggers. What was operating as a pan defense begins to function more as signal anxiety. It is not enough, however, for the client to recognize the triggers. The therapy must also explore the adaptive functions, so that, as mentioned, the client can internalize the self-regulating function of the action symptom into the ego.

ENCOUNTERING THE INTERNAL OBJECT AND WORKING THROUGH THE TENACITY OF THE SYMPTOM

To view psychic life and structure in terms of object relations theory and specifically the tie to internalized unsatisfying, rejecting, or traumatizing objects gives a theoretical hold to patients' struggles and suffering. Negative aspects of parental care and cultural impingements are taken inside, stifling patients' development and ability to form satisfying relationships without therapeutic mediation. The grip of and devotion to thoughts, feelings, ideas, behaviors, and relationships that seem so painful and undermining to what another part of the self wants and needs can be a baffling and arduous challenge to therapist and patient alike. The chronic and entrenched involvement with internal objects, which undergoes yet another psychological transformation through displacement to food and body symptoms, accounts for both the complexity and long-term nature of the work. The therapist must be prepared to work with what seems like the same material over and over again. It is through this repetition that new meanings and relational shifts emerge.

The client's use of food, body, or exercise always contains a paradox. At the very same time her symptoms defend against her feelings, they metaphorically express those feelings. As such, while her use of eating and body action symptoms work to resist the transference, they simultaneously reveal the transference. Just as the client defends against feelings, she is also reenacting her internal object relations. The therapist must understand that she is cast in the part of the abandoning or omnipotent parent from whom the client must withdraw. Through slow complex work the therapist must prove herself to be more reliable than the former caretakers and the food, even if the only way she can demonstrate her reliability is by reliably understanding this dynamic. Then the client can correspondingly slowly relinquish the intensity of her attachment because a better caretaking experience is being internalized and new ways of relating and coping can be explored.

For example, patients may stuff themselves or throw up before each session with the metacommunication of "I don't need you," or "I'm going to stock up or empty myself of need or hope, so if you fail me, it won't hurt so much." Others may binge or purge after the session to eject the care, bury the conflictual aspects of receiving and connection, and protest and rebel against the all powerful controlling authority.

Women with eating problems erect formidable defenses against care, dependency, and intimacy. They frequently block their dependence on others and reinvest it in food, body image distortion, or exercise regimes, all of which substitute for reliable interpersonal relationships. It is inevitable that the client's dependency needs and her own strong prohibitions against them will emerge in the therapy relationship. She may have ambivalent feelings about the contact and care she receives from the therapist; although this care and contact is ultimately curative, it can also be very painful. Repeating earlier intimate relationships clients often express fear that they want too much or that they may devour the therapist. They also fear being devoured by their own needs, disappearing in a merger with the therapist, or being exploited or imposed on by the therapist.

It is a tremendous risk for the client to experience and tolerate feelings not only of need and dependency but also assertion and autonomy without knowing that the therapist will treat her differently from the ways she has been treated in the past. Responses of care, understanding, empathy, insight, pleasure, play, and mirroring from the therapist not only release memory, pain, deprivation, moments of joy, hope, and desire but also rage. Clients frequently fear that the rage that has been stuffed down by the food will be unleashed to destroy the therapist, themselves, or both. Or they fear drowning in pain, with no relief, reliving their early history when they suffered alone. Will the consequences be different if they let themselves feel it all over again? Should the therapist, rather than safe food, be taken in to that place of terrible pain and if so how?

A typical initial response of women clients to an authentic relationship with their therapist is to feel they are selfish and undeserving—fearing that their "having" is indulgent and will deprive others of what they need. They fear reprisal and abandonment, as their growing sense of entitlement to much more than food threatens their false self organization. The "good" and the "having" feel too strange, different, separate, or unfeminine. How will a woman know how to relate and connect to others if she is okay and not bonding through deprivation or self-denial, as she has learned to do all her life?

In the experience of being better cared for by herself and the therapist, the client retrieves from repression or dissociation the anguish of how poorly she was cared for, what she lost or never had, or what was done to her. Her recognition of pain that she could barely experience at the time helps her to mourn what was done or unmet, and frees her to detach these losses from food and body obsessions. She begins to feel that needs can be met, that unsatisfied needs are not bad, and that she is not bad for having them.

But, then clients often retreat from these new ways of being and from care and continue or return to bingeing or starving. They try to hold on to their safe and familiar ways of coping, to restrain their desires and appetites as well as their fear and guilt for wanting and having more. They are reasserting their loyalty to internal objects. As the client establishes a more positive relationship to the therapist she threatens this internal tie, which was all she had. This loosening of the tie creates tremendous anxiety as well as feelings of betrayal and guilt. The client constantly makes and breaks the separation from the internal object, often manifesting these phases in weight gains and losses, and the return of aspects of the symptom. These experiences must be tolerated, explored, survived, and worked through.

Because food and the body are symbolic of an object relationship, learning to feed oneself well and to accept one's body is to free oneself of, or at least lessen, the impact of negative parental and cultural introjects. As clients take charge of recognizing and satisfying their food needs, they learn a paradigm for real self-care. This enables them to assume greater control in all areas of their lives; it empowers them and fosters and solidifies their ego growth and self-esteem.

Work with the internal object must also be taken up in its cultural form. Working with the cultural bad object does not necessarily mean politicizing people or being an ideologue or dogmatic, but it does mean cultivating an awareness of the harmful effects of internalizing the cultural ideal female image. The omnipotent "helpful" torturer, in whose hands no one can feel right, is often hidden in concepts such as fitness, health, and "balanced" meals. The following example illustrates working with this internal cultural introject. Annie, a 47-year-old woman, reported feeling she suffered with feeding herself all her life. She had begun trying to eat in a self-attuned way, but recently she had been "going out of control" and gaining weight. She proposed going to a Weight Watchers group. The subsequent discussion clarified that only in the last year Annie had placed food at center stage, and it was just 6 months since she tried to eat when hungry. In fact, she was becoming more and more able to wait for hunger. Moreover, her weight gain totaled only 5 to 6 pounds. The therapist acknowledged the positive steps that Annie had already taken, calming the more dramatic and judgmental presentation.

A: But I'm not losing weight! So, on the one hand I think I should just accept myself, and I do love eating mayonnaise in my tuna. But, on the other hand, I think there are too many calories in the mayonnaise, and I should be in a structured program like Weight Watchers.

T: When you eat your tuna with mayonnaise, part of you says it's OK, but another part of you says you shouldn't really have the mayonnaise. So in a way with every bite you are taking the pleasure away because there is always a Weight Watchers waiting for you around the corner.

A: Yeah, I have this tape in my head, which I cannot get rid of, that says

"I'm bad" over and over again. I don't know what to do; I love tuna and mayonnaise but just don't think I should have it.

T: I'd like to know more about the voice that says you're bad. Is it the same voice that says you should go to Weight Watchers?

A: Yes, it says I'm bad, I can't be in control, I'm no good, I should go to Weight Watchers and be under their control and not eat mayo. It's the same voice from my family, my history, and it's been there forever.

T: So Weight Watchers and the tape are one and the same. Weight Watchers represents a punitive, depriving voice inside you, which is scared to trust you?

A: [very passionately] But I don't want to give into that tape, I really want mayonnaise with my tuna, I really want to listen to myself. I want things to come from myself. I want to accept myself, I want to be myself!

T: This part of you is full of want and desire; and I notice how passionately you express this desire to claim yourself.

A: I want to want, and I read *Fat Is a Feminist Issue,* but I don't want to keep gaining weight.

T: It sounds as if you have a major battle going on inside yourself, which tuna with mayonnaise completely expresses. On one side are your desires, your wants, your passions, *Fat Is a Feminist Issue,* acceptance of yourself, and a wish to differentiate yourself from what you know to be mad; and on the other side is the part of you that feels you are bad, which is aligned with the punitive aspects of your parents, distrust of yourself, Weight Watchers, the diet industry, and the cultural pressures to look a certain way. This battle is something to be quite upset and conflicted about. Every time you eat the mayo in your tuna, this war inside yourself breaks out. When you eat what you want, you take on your family and the culture; and perhaps you feel disloyal as well as rebellious, because a piece of you feels that they are right, and who wants to risk this even if they aren't right?

A: That's exactly how I feel. I feel these two camps, and I really want this side (she points to the accepting, authentic side) to win.

T: But you're secretly worried that the other side may be right.

A: That's it! What if I can't do it? What if this way I'll gain weight?

T: You mean what if you really are bad and can't trust yourself? It's hard to hold on to your adult female voice when everyone around you feels you can't make a choice and you feel so undermined.

A: Especially when I've been told I'm wrong my whole life. I must not feel good about myself because they are right.

T: So our work for now, rather than focusing on which side you should choose, should be to appreciate the depth and pain of the conflict inside yourself. Let's understand both sides better and better.

Including a cultural critique provides a more profound understanding of the world outside and inside and allows for more highly developed and varied sets of responses. People can get angry, develop a sense of humor, work out their own compromises more consciously, take actions politically, change the nature of friendships and love relationships, and create less oppressive subcultures, thereby living a more authentic and vital life.

CHAPTER 6

Learning to Feed Oneself: A Psychodynamic Model

CAROL BLOOM, LAURA KOGEL, AND
LELA ZAPHIROPOULOS

BURIED BENEATH the symptomatology of all eating problems are the dynamics of compulsive eating: a lack of entitlement about eating, prohibitions against knowing and using internal physiological signals, and an absence of internal structure that is self-soothing. Even in cases of anorexia or bulimia, once the defenses are analyzed, the same restless foraging, seemingly out-of-control behavior, and obsessive thought processes come to light as in compulsive eating. Thus, all clients with eating problems must be taught about hunger, satiety, and food choice. Although teaching how to eat in an attuned way is in part didactic, it is also best understood as a psychoanalytic task, in that working through the conflicts and defenses just discussed in chapter 5 is necessary for each step in the process of reclaiming an integrated body self. Within an analytic relationship, working on the symptom is what we call doing the food and body work. The components of this combined didactic-psychoanalytic work are elaborated in this chapter.

Working with the Diet Mentality as Psychic Organizer

Therapists must work with the reality that most patients with eating problems are dieting when they enter treatment. In fact, on the conscious level many are seeking better ways to restrain themselves. Chronic dieting serves different functions, from helping to organize food intake to helping to organize inner and outer life. The diet functions as a manic defense, a "high" of resoluteness and control against the depressive aspects of life that are out of one's control. Dieting is a cultural prescription for appearance and self-care and an aspect of female bonding and identity. Dieting as psychic organizer is a defense against anxiety or even disintegration. For the chronic restrainer the diet is a tie to the unsatisfying or traumatizing internal object. Therefore, letting go of the diet, a piece of familiar, familial security, signifies profound internal change.

Clients may say, "Who am I?" "Who will I be if I do not diet?" "Can I do this radical, almost antifemale act of eating what I want?" "Can I really have, and am I really entitled to this bountifulness?" "Do I really deserve this kind of self-acceptance?" "I don't trust my insides." "I know what food is nutritious, but I can't be trusted to eat it." "I deserve to be screamed at and punished for my reactions." "I have to keep myself under control lest I be wild, too much, voracious, bad, and huge." Over the course of treatment the goal is for the diet to move from being ego syntonic to dystonic. This change requires that the therapist be aware of the deleterious effects of dieting as well as its uses in psychic organization.

The degree of entrenchment of dieting in psychic structure is a good diagnostic indicator of both psychic distress and the psychic availability needed to feed oneself in an attuned way. A continuum exists from those who can easily give up the diet to those who cannot for many years, and some who may never give it up, even as it leads them to the point of death.

Some women can change fairly quickly when exposed to a feminist critique and anti-diet information, whether these new ideas come from a book, a therapist, a self-help group, or a friend. These new ideas can help them to break decisively the diet-binge cycle. As these women discover and feed their hunger, they are able to calm down relatively easily about eating and their body images.

For example, Jane was a bright, young feminist who did not understand why her weight fluctuated. She reasoned that her dieting and overeating would balance each other. During a 6-week workshop focused on eating and body image problems, however, she had a powerful revelation. She was thrilled to hear that precisely by refraining from dieting she could stabilize her body size, and she gave up her diet immediately, feeling she actually could not bear to diet one more day. Her ability to eat when hungry easily fell into place. However, choosing foods that specifically met what her body needed and wanted occurred more gradually. During the workshop it became evident that Jane had many good friends, was glad to be in college, and was managing separation from home fairly well. She simply needed help in acquiring a new vision of herself as an eater, which actually complemented and affirmed her basic vital stance in life. Didactic information about an anti-deprivation approach was the primary tool needed to open the way for Jane to become comfortable with food and body. Her first discovery in this direction was to experience stomach hunger, and then she was helped to try eating every time she felt hungry. Since she was hypoglycemic, the group leader suggested that she carry food with her at all times, particularly sources of protein that her body needed. In this way Jane could protect herself from having to wait too long to feed herself and thereby risk other uncomfortable physical reactions. Not only was her body hunger relieved, but on a psychological level Jane proved to herself that she could trust herself to provide solid, reliable care that accommodated her own particular needs. Jane also recognized that the mandate to eat less and keep herself small was part of the oppression of women. This understanding helped to liberate her from her own struggle to limit her food intake to less than what she actually needed.

For Jane and others, the ideas of not dieting and of broadening the scope of the food choices are deeply relieving, exciting, and affirming. Jane is an example of someone who psychologically welcomes the idea of freedom, self-attunement, nurturance, and acceptance and who is interested in pursuing the therapeutic work needed to accomplish this end.

Lisa presented a similar but somewhat more complicated psychic situation. Lisa was an energetic, 26-year-old graduate student who came to treatment with a variety of concerns: conflicts around both professional and sexual identity, an underlying low-level depression, and chronic internal loneliness. Her eating was uneven, with bags of cookies attending the depression, followed by a day here and there without food, in hopes of compensating for the cookies. At other times she ate and enjoyed hearty meals, though often without regard for hunger and satiation. Her weight fluctuated by 20 pounds, and she was preoccupied with food and her extra weight.

Lisa entered an ongoing theme-centered group on eating with an anti-diet perspective. She enjoyed and digested the ideas of the new approach as much as she enjoyed food itself. In the consultation, one of her first questions had been, "How do you know when to eat?" The idea of eating when hungry was exhilarating, and the idea that hunger should be met with food felt profoundly satisfying. Although it took years to work through the psychological issues that caused her compulsive eating, Lisa immediately began the process of attuned feeding. Both the therapist and the new idea provided the good care and holding for which she had been searching. The group was crucial in alleviating Lisa's isolation and shame. The consciousness raising function of the group enabled Lisa and the others to see that many of their choices and behaviors were dictated by deeply internalized cultural norms and expectations.

Supported by other women, Lisa felt empowered to try new ways of eating that were consistent with her needs and desires. For example, she loved eating a particular chocolate danish with a big glass of milk every time she was hungry. She was shocked to find that on the fourth day of this regimen, she desperately wanted a salad and she began to listen more closely to the demands and rhythms of her own body. Her confusion, shame, and anxiety faded, and she learned to have fun exploring the experience of eating.

Jane and Lisa both found that an alternative approach was all they needed to stop dieting and begin responding to internal signals. In a group treatment modality, both felt sufficiently supported to forge a new relationship to hunger, satiation, food, and body. Jane needed no further treatment, and Lisa went into long-term individual treatment to work through the issues embedded in her symptom. A theme-centered eating group is a useful model to introduce clients to this new approach. The psychoeducational work in the context of group members' support and shared experience is a good beginning to work on food, eating, and body issues. This holding environment provides a powerful challenge to negative cultural introjects.

Unlike Jane and Lisa, however, many other people cannot give up dieting without great effort and a thorough analysis. Depending on internal and external issues, they usually oscillate between dieting and relying on their bodily signals of hunger and satiation. Under stress they look to the diet for safety, security, continuity, and reliability for care. But the diet is a problematic caretaker. For the security provided by a diet is the security of an object that admonishes, "Restraint! Restrict! Don't want too much! Don't be spontaneous! Do it my way!" In such a situation, it takes a long time for the client to accept the therapeutic relationship's offer of an alternative kind of security, one that provides limits, structure, and reliability, without the continually depriving, punitive, and manic aspects that accompany the diet's care.

For example, Joanna exhibited a cycle of dieting and overeating. Every so often, she would come in saying, "I know I never want to diet again. I want to eat when I'm hungry, but I first just need to lose 20 pounds, get a little jump start, feel a little more confident, feel better about my body." A few weeks later she would say, "I've been on my own for 5 days trying to eat with my hunger, but I can't put my fork down. Look at me! I'm a mess. I'll never get a job in my field [public relations]. Skill is one thing, but 'looks' is really where it's at." In discussion Joanna revealed that at this period, as she interviewed for jobs, she was feeling great anxiety.

T: I see you are very distressed about how out of control you seem to be. But I'm wondering if you could say more about what you have been facing since we last met.

J: I went for that interview. They used computers I'm not familiar with; but I can do my job without computers. The worst thing was that everyone seemed so young and so skinny there.

T: Are you worried about learning a new system?

J: I'm sure I can, and the man said they'd train me, but I get so anxious when I have to learn with people watching. I know you'll think this is crazy, but I'm sitting there the whole time thinking if I were 20 pounds thinner, this wouldn't be an issue.

T: It sounds as if you were very anxious about your competence for that job, and then you tried to soothe and protect yourself with the idea of transforming your body. Do you know why this is such an inviting idea?

J: [Laughs] I just thought how my parents' favorite refrain was 'If you look the part, you'll get it,' whatever that meant. They never knew how to help me with the substance. They said I could do anything I wanted, but they really didn't guide me or give me helpful ideas. [Joanna started to weep.] I really love my work; I feel so alive when I'm being productive and smart. I want to feel solid. [She laughs.] Maybe I eat when I'm not hungry so I can try to be "more."

T: That's an interesting idea. Maybe eating more is about being more; maybe that really is the way you try to give yourself a feeling of solidity. Trying to change your body becomes a way to address your fears and desires about being competent and respected, and even attractive and desirable as a woman.

Joanna felt deeply inadequate; she felt that she was not "doing it right," and that she was not proficient in the latest technology. She relied on her looks, which she felt she was losing because her nondieting was supposedly causing so much weight gain. Dieting was a way to bind her anxiety. She hoped that a cultural prescription for how to "do it right" in the food and body arena would translate into feeling better about her whole self. Dieting reenacted the basic dynamics in her early family life, where her parents praised her for her looks and cheered her on to do anything she wanted while instructing her to do everything their way. The weeks of dieting would always collapse when she could not bear the restraint, both of food and the guidance she felt was lacking. Over time, she came to see why food and body became the arena in which to play out her struggles, while the therapist consistently worked to understand the adaptive function of the symptoms, both the diet and the compulsive eating.

In Joanna's field, as is true in others such as acting and dance, physical appearance is highly regarded. Although it is important to validate this fact, it is also critical to make clients understand the psychic cost of this reality; and in Joanna's case to tease out the overestimation of appearance because of family dynamics and values. The question must become, how does one take a stand of integrity? That is, how does one not lose oneself in the process of fitting in to one's larger world?

The next example along the continuum of those who can and cannot relinquish diets is Rachel, a 19-year-old college student. (Rachel will be discussed several times in chapters 6 and 7.) She exemplifies the use of the diet as a major psychic defense against dissociated parts of self. Rachel felt very fat, although she was thin. Her eating was quite chaotic: Not only had she been dieting since she was 13, but she also seriously abused laxatives. Unlike Lisa who first asked for guidelines about when to eat, Rachel anxiously blurted out her first question, "How should I diet? Should I go back to Weight Watchers?" Later in that initial session she described early incidents of sexual abuse and revealed that both parents were bright and creative, but unpredictable alcoholics. Perhaps, suggested the therapist, the work to be done together would be to understand the relationship between eating and family history. But, in addition, Rachel needed to know about an alternative to dieting, which consisted of getting to know herself, emotionally and phys-iologically, including her own body's signals for hunger and fullness. Part of this alternative approach was to help her eventually to become comfortable with food and her body and to understand what dieting has meant to her. This integration could be done at her own pace and as the therapist got to know her. It was not until months later that Rachel referred to these ideas; initially, the therapist thought the idea of an alternative approach had no meaning for Rachel. Although Rachel could, in fact, feel hunger and at times could feed herself in response to it, she could not do so reliably each time she was hungry. She still felt that losing weight was what was most important. She tried to join Weight Watchers, but because she was not even 5 pounds overweight, they refused her. So she dieted on her own. The therapist ac-cepted this, proposing that they still try to learn what the dieting meant. To Rachel, even starving felt more acceptable than being at her current weight.

With the therapist's help, Rachel discovered that her current weight was related to dissociated parts of herself: the frightened, out-of-control Rachel, insecure in her parents' chaotic home. Her image of an even thinner self rep-resented both an image of her younger self when she was popular, accept-able, and in control and an idealized image of her home characterized only by her parents' creativity.

In all of the work with Rachel thus far discussed, our model of attuned eating and body acceptance gave the therapist a route to weave together dif-ferent strands of Rachel's life: (1) inquiry about food and body; (2) inquiry about her life, past and present; (3) the relationship between food and body and her life; and (4) her reactions to being in treatment. It became clear that Rachel could not attend to the eating problem so long as her body repre-sented the troubled, out-of-control part of her emotional self. Dieting and laxative abuse were attempts to gain control over a body that had naturally gained weight in the passage from adolescence to young adulthood. Rachel's weight gain was also associated with her own burgeoning sexuality, about which she was quite conflicted, and which, like her early history, she wished she could erase.

After discussing all this, Rachel suddenly took a step back: Although she presented a more controlled, organized self, the laxative abuse escalated to crisis proportions. The therapist used this as an opportunity to interpret

Rachel's great anxiety about beginning treatment and the advisability of her coming more than once a week, which would provide more security for her worries, fears, and conflicts. Rachel was relieved. The therapist also suggested that Rachel communicate her reactions to the therapist's interpretations, in order to let the therapist know what she was feeling within the therapy relationship. Rachel was very happy to do so, and was, indeed, quite forthcoming. Thus, a more authentic dialogue ensued.

In attempting to bridge the gap between Rachel's bulimia and her emotional life, the therapist made three kinds of interventions: (1) discovering the adaptive functions, that is, establishing the psychological need for the symptom as a whole and its different aspects; (2) identifying the triggers; (3) cognitively educating, by saying for example, "Eating so little doesn't necessarily mean you will lose weight" or "Laxative abuse will affect your sphincter functioning." Meanwhile, the therapist was doing the crucial work of reconstructing the context of the symptom. She interwove what she was learning about Rachel's past and present life with the knowledge gained about the function of the dieting and laxative abuse. Rachel soon understood that her "food disorder" was not about food but was instead about providing comfort for all that had been indigestible to her. Her new understanding and her positive connection to her therapist enabled her to discontinue daily laxative use. With her bulimia no longer operating as a "pan defense," the treatment proceeded by tracking the specific triggers of the binge-purge events through discussing food and its meanings and working to understand her distorted body image.

The therapist explained that although Rachel had over time completely stopped her abuse of laxatives, her compulsive eating, restricting herself and obsessing about her weight would take much longer to work through. Indeed, Rachel remained tormented for a long time by her constant desire to eat and her bulimic mentality, which insisted that any food ingested turned bad, which for her meant turned to fat instantaneously.

On the dieting continuum Josie's restrictive eating represented her tie to the traumatizing object that dominated her internal world. Josie was a 40-year-old woman, a "restricting bulimic," who stated that she was not on a diet. Nevertheless, her eating pattern was marked by great control and rigidity in terms of when, where, and what to eat. Only a few restaurants were deemed ok, and only a few people could eat with her. Any disruption of these ritualistic patterns threatened her "control" and with it her sense of inner equilibrium. Her rigidity was counterbalanced by periods of chaotic, terrifying bingeing and purging that would go on for hours, leaving her devastated, debilitated, and exhausted.

Josie's psychological need for this rigidity to keep her psychically intact was so profound that it could not be directly addressed until the fifth year of treatment. This was a case in which working with the diet and diet mentality consisted of not challenging her eating behavior until a more secure bond was established within the therapy relationship. Slowly, Josie revealed enough that the therapist could interpret the restrictive behavior as a defense against overwhelming dependency needs with a concomitant terror of abandonment resulting from physical abuse in childhood. In the third year of treatment, Josie alternated between taking the therapist in and spitting her out, longing for connection and defending against it by devaluing the therapist; concurrently, there was an intense exacerbation of her bulimia. The therapist both bore witness to and survived these attacks, which she understood as the internal object asserting itself in response to the possibilities of a different kind of relational experience. Only after demonstrating the therapist's strength and connection to Josie could the therapist interpret to her the relationship between her restriction with food and her emotional states.

When the Diet Emerges Well into the Treatment

It is very common for patients to contemplate or actually resume dieting during the course of treatment. The return to the diet or diet mentality can be the harbinger of painful undisclosed material. Returning to the diet later in treatment is often a communication to the therapist about emerging transference/countertransference issues. The use of the diet for an array of psychological and interpersonal maneuvers needs to be analyzed eventually and not acted out.

For example, Jackie, a 29-year-old administrative assistant who had been in treatment for 6 months, started a session by announcing that she had joined Weight Watchers. This announcement followed a period of more attuned eating. When asked what was entailed in her decision, she said that she had visited her family over the weekend, and her mother and father had become very anxious when they heard she had stopped going to Weight Watchers. She also informed them that she was in a therapy that was not encouraging her to diet. Throughout the weekend her mother and father constantly questioned her choices and her judgment and expressed concern about her future. On the train home Jackie began obsessing about her body. The next morning she woke up with the resolve to rejoin Weight Watchers. The plan to diet served to keep her tied to her parents in a familiar way that would ensure their acceptance of her. Because this incident occurred early in the treatment, Jackie and the therapist had not yet carved out an internal space in which Jackie could differentiate from her parents. But this latest resolve to diet did provide such an opportunity.

Melanie, 32 years old, decided to fast after a particularly poignant session in which she was overwhelmed by realizing that her therapist was neither disappointed in her nor hated her for bingeing and purging, thus disconfirming Melanie's transference expectation that the therapist would be repelled by her bulimic behavior. Here Melanie's wish to fast was a way to defend against the hope of finally being understood and accepted. Hope for such a relationship was dangerous because it entailed confronting the idea that the relationship could be lost and threatened her tie to internal objects. Instead, she chose the diet, that familiar depriver and rejector: It felt safer, more predictable, and more under her control than did a person. By understanding this process the therapist proved steadfast in containing Melanie's rejection and hopelessness. As Melanie's trust in the therapist grew, so did her ability to trust herself. The diets decreased in frequency, and guided by bodily cues she began to eat more reliably.

In a similar vein, Dorothy dieted for the first year of treatment, all the while absorbing and savoring the ideas of a different way of relating to food, eating, and her body. When she was certain the therapist would neither betray nor exploit her, having tested her often, she was ready to let go of the structure and buffer against others which the diet represented. A human relationship became more substantive and interesting than a diet. (As Guntrip [1971] states, "a person is better than a pill.")

Sarah had several weeks of eating exactly what she wanted, following her hunger cues and without bingeing or purging, and was working steadily on critical issues in her treatment. She then resumed bingeing and throwing up and started a stringent diet motivated by intense self-hate. When she and the therapist wondered about such a dramatic return to her symptom at this time in her treatment, Sarah reported a dream. In analyzing the dream, which was about shifting terrain, Sarah was able to put into words that she was terrified about losing her problem, her bulimia, because it gave her a sense of uniqueness and place. She slowly revealed that she was most worried about how to be special to the therapist, and this revelation was the start of her working with her transferential feelings.

For some clients, such as Jane and Lisa, dieting is relinquished early on. For others, such as Rachel, Joanna, and Melanie, the diet is too entrenched as an internal object relationship and thus will continue as a salient issue in the treatment. However, once the client no longer *continually* enacts or thinks about dieting as a solution, it is then possible to recognize such enactments or thoughts as signals of psychic distress or relational communication. By analyzing the psychological communication, the client can metabolize the material rather than act it out or act it in.

Attuned Eating: Hunger

To feed oneself in an attuned way, it is necessary to discover physical hunger. Learning to discriminate and to label internal bodily sensations is critical; it establishes a basis for the integration and regulation of the body-self. Hunger is the only reliable personal guide to feeding oneself with integrity. As stated, the patient learns to recognize hunger in an interpersonal relationship. The therapy relationship provides a current opportunity for hunger to come into psychological and physical existence. Hunger establishes that the self has an inside and an outside; it provides a basis for differentiating discrete internal need states. Hunger thus establishes autonomy as well as differentiation of self and other. To feed oneself other than when hungry is to leave oneself vulnerable to external definition and alienated from inner experience.

Clients with eating problems do not rely on hunger as a guide. In getting to know themselves as eaters by asking themselves if they are hungry, their psychic terrain begins to shift. The question itself presupposes a self with a body that speaks, that can be heard and known. For many patients it takes years of intensive work to reach this point. As patients notice that they are rarely eating out of biological hunger, the therapist must engage their curiosity about the expressive functions of their eating. What seemed like disordered and out-of-control eating can now be organized as psychological phenomena available for analysis.

The process of helping clients to discover their hunger begins by the therapist asking about the history, memories, associations, and fears of clients' bodily experience of hunger, about the responses of others toward their hunger, and about what and how they were taught regarding hunger. Was there ever a time when they ate naturally out of hunger (at camp, grandma's, when alone)? Likewise, clients need to learn how they negate hunger by keeping themselves constantly full, by suppressing their hunger signals, or by misinterpreting or interfering with their signals. For example, some clients find it difficult to differentiate physical hunger from anxiety, excitement, or physical exhaustion. There are those who know hunger only from their experience of dieting in which either they are not eating quite enough or food consumption is based on an external time table. For them hunger is associated with discomfort and deprivation on the one hand or a virtuous feeling of triumph on the other.

For some clients hunger can be terrifying and disorganizing. When unmet hunger is an intense experience, it can feel like a persecutory attack from within or like a depriving assault from the external world. If people experience needs and feelings as assaults and humiliations, then their hunger will be similarly experienced. Furthermore, because hunger and food represent internal object relationships, they generate issues that are felt in the transference. The therapist should note that the transference is not only to her but also to food and body as they are representative of relationship. So long as patients do not feel entitled to feed themselves, hunger remains a terrifying prospect. When hunger, however, is met with food, when need is met by the good object, hunger becomes less terrifying, more manageable, and eventually pleasurable.

Two contrasting examples follow. Doris and Beth are both at least 100 pounds overweight and came to treatment to work on their weight. Within the first year of treatment, Doris was able to imagine hunger and even experience it, albeit infrequently. Although it made her anxious, she understood the concept and engaged in treatment that interwove the meaning of hunger and food with the experiences of her life. By the fourth year of treatment she was developing consistency in her experience of hunger and an ability to feed herself with assurance, as she worked through her guilt about her early desires for more independence, which had threatened her mother. To Doris, hunger unconsciously meant autonomy, and becoming comfortable with hunger thus required mourning her mother's death when Doris was 9 years old. Simultaneously, she was able to acknowledge dependency needs which had been repressed since her mother's death.

Beth is in her eighth year of treatment with the therapist who treated Doris. Beth still cannot feel hunger. Even when she has no food all day long, she does not experience hunger, only a headache indicating the bypassing of hunger. Throughout her life, her body has been dissociated: She has never had a consistent internal body image. Having a body, like having feelings, represents vulnerability: Her family's mode of relating tolerated no vulnerability. The father was always right and always righteous; the mother concurred. Highly legalistic verbal discourse defined interpersonal transactions and had the effect of denying the children any subjectivity. Beth, like her parents, was often intellectually brilliant; but she completely lacked a sense of subjectivity and viewed others as part objects as well. The legalistic mode of discourse encoded a harshness that tolerated no imperfection, no need, no ambivalence, no acting out. Growing up in such an environment meant that feelings and needs had no place except when presented in a rational way, as in a legal brief. Helplessness, the predominant feeling generated by this atmosphere, had to be split off entirely.

At the age of 35 Beth's first task (which took years) was to differentiate enough from her parents to begin the process of finding her own subjective reactions. She then began to find a fuller range of feelings. For example, as her numbness slowly dissipated, she learned to distinguish sadness from disappointment. Perhaps once she becomes comfortable with feelings and integrates them into an internal self schema, true self experiences will permit true body experiences, and she will begin to develop an internal body schema as well. Until this happens, hunger, because it represents her most desperate vulnerability and her feelings of helplessness, will remain too terrifying a reality to experience. In normal early development, true body experience builds true self experience and is interwoven with it. But Beth lacks a self that can help her to negotiate what it means to have and experience a body, because her own has existed hitherto in such a dissociated state. The possibility exists, of course, that some trauma to the body might be discovered; but at this time the psychological trauma alone is devastating enough to seriously damage body/self integrity.

When clients cannot experience hunger, but are ready to learn, they can be helped in this process. In the security of the therapy relationship, clients can imagine, in fantasy, what hunger might feel like. The therapist can ask them in what part of their body they might feel their hunger. People report experiencing hunger in different places along the digestive tract, usually in the area of the stomach. At times, people report headaches or dizziness, which usually means they have let themselves get too hungry before eating. If hunger is experienced in areas other than the stomach or in unusual places, the possibilities of depersonalization, dissociative phenomena, sexual abuse, or psychosis must be considered.

As they imagine experiencing hunger, what feelings and associations emerge? Does hunger begin as a mild sensation that gathers strength and leads to eating; and does this feel comfortable emotionally? Or is hunger an acute pain to be ignored or feared? Or is it experienced as a boiling cauldron of needs that can never be satisfied because, after all, hunger is the signifier of all need? Clients need to learn the physical sensations that precede acute pain so that they can eat more promptly, breaking the identification of hunger with pain and deprivation. It is most important that the therapy constantly work on the client's defenses against experiencing needs.

For those people who in fantasy can organize an internal experience that is not too anxiety ridden, the therapist can suggest that they choose one day during the week when they wait for their hunger, emphasizing that as soon as they experience hunger, they must feed themselves. Knowing that hunger can and should be met with food constructs and reinforces the experience of hunger: that hunger is knowable and that it can be satisfied by food, and only by food. Psychodynamically, the client discovers by means of this technique that she can both validate and meet her own needs. She begins to become her own good parent. Her new ability to nourish herself loosens the tie to an internalized depriving or intrusive object. By recognizing and satisfying hunger two, three, or four times a day, she forcefully reorganizes her psychological structure and reinforces her sense of self with needs that can be met.

Another client, Penny, a 40-year-old woman with a compulsive eating problem, always had difficulty eating when physically hungry. By constantly "grazing" she rarely let herself feel hunger. Hunger was associated with dieting, a most painful and depriving experience that she had endured on and off from the age of 8 years old. As she became capable of feeling hunger and of letting herself have food in her house, the therapist suggested that on a day when she did not have major obligations, Penny stop herself from beginning the day with grazing but instead wait to eat until she first experienced physical hunger.

Having followed the suggestion "to the letter," Penny reported in her next session that she was surprised by the outcome. Initially, she had had no problem just waiting, trying to focus now and then on her body and what it was feeling. But after an hour and a half, she felt flooded with loneliness and a terrifying physical sense of emptiness which gave rise to an intense longing for contact with someone, anyone. In exploring these feelings, Penny remembered similar ones from her childhood and sadly expressed how lonely she felt now. Until Penny could better examine, understand, and nonjudgmentally integrate her affect and experience, hunger would remain problematic; but her new awareness was the first step toward change, toward a more attuned way of being with herself.

Penny's desire to please the therapist, as evidenced by her complying with the therapist's suggestion "to the letter," was explored in the transference. Penny and the therapist reached a deeper understanding of the pressure Penny placed on herself when she was with others. She always had to be the pleasing "good" girl, so as to never experience their displeasure or her own anger. This put pressure on her interpersonal interactions and thus led her to avoid social activity, which reinforced her loneliness and isolation.

REACHING FOR FOOD WHEN NOT HUNGRY

Once hunger and attuned eating are introduced as guiding principles, clients will continue to report a variety of incidents of eating when not hungry. These usually occur at moments when they cannot bear mounting anxiety, and they take action to relieve the tension. Eating is thus a frenetic effort by the client to quell her anxiety, in order to distract, suppress, numb, or soothe herself, so as not to experience deeper, less manageable feelings, needs, or aspects of self. Particularly in the beginning of a treatment in which an eating problem is the primary presenting symptom, tracking the adaptive functions and triggers is critical in offering help, establishing a relationship, decoding the symptom language, and creating a mutual language. This is the foundation for building a historical and emotional narrative.

Rachel, the 19-year-old college student previously mentioned, began a session talking about how she knew whether or not it would be a good or bad day based on whether or not she woke up with a craving for food without physical hunger. The therapist asked Rachel to tell her more about the craving itself.

R: Well, it's a craving to take the world into my mouth, to eat something solid so I can feel solid. [Silence] But then, I feel terrible that I've eaten.

I feel guilty. It's a horrible feeling, and I have to take laxatives to get rid of it.

[The therapist decided to explore the adaptive function of the craving, understanding that to experience feelings or express need and desire were taboo for Rachel.]

T: We can get to the guilt and the need to rid yourself of what's bad in a while, but can we start at the beginning with the craving so that we can understand that better?

R: Well, the more I think about it, when I think about putting food in myself, for a moment I get calm. That makes me think about an incident this week.

[Rachel recalled bumping into an old boyfriend. After a short visit, the joy of seeing him turned into sadness. She then found herself eating pizza. Since she had already had ice cream that day, it was clear to Rachel that she would have to use laxatives. After recounting this, Rachel realized that she had stopped thinking about her ex-boyfriend after she ate the pizza; her entire focus had switched to food, eating, and her body.]

R: Oh, my God, maybe this bulimia isn't about food!

T: Previously, we've understood that your eating helps you feel solid and substantial and calms you. Now you're adding that it helps you get rid of uncomfortable feelings.

R: So the craving is about getting rid of those feelings? And then I take the laxatives to punish myself for the craving, and I can punish myself to all different degrees depending on how many laxatives I take.

[During the session Rachel continued to be astounded that the pizza had obliterated her whole emotional experience with her ex-boyfriend.]

R: [Beginning to cry.] I'm just realizing that I have been torturing myself for 3 years, and I really believed it was all completely about the food, and now I see it's not about the food at all.

Rachel now understood that "craving" had nothing to do with physiological hunger but was an intense, out-of-control feeling that could overcome her at any moment during the day, often hundreds of times a day. This helped her to realize that her problem was neither the food nor even her craving but being afraid of her feelings about people and herself. It was a shocking, but liberating, realization. Because she now understood the "craving" and thus had more real control, she no longer needed to punish herself for her uncontrollable food urges. After this session she took laxatives only twice more. These occasions were processed in session, and shortly thereafter she ceased using them. Now that she let hunger be the internal guide for feeding herself, Rachel began noticing those moments when she reached for food without being hungry. She thereby strengthened her observing ego and expanded it to incorporate dissociated painful experience. The struggle with the "craving" feeling remained torturous. She just no longer punished herself for it by taking laxatives.

Food

In the course of treatment clients should learn how to give food its rightful place as a source of nurturance, succor, and care as well as learning about how they use food as a "bad" caretaker.

FOOD AS OBJECT RELATIONSHIP

Just as reaching for food is rich in psychological meanings, the exploration of the food itself, why it is chosen, and the way in which it is eaten reveal early and ongoing internal object relationships. Food represents caretaking in the client's earliest familial arena and in her peer and cultural milieu. How these relationships have been internalized in their primitive, fantasized, and real forms will determine how the client uses food: whether she devours it, spits it out, rejects, avoids, swallows, chews, or enjoys it.

For example, Penny, who was discussed in relation to hunger, was living a very isolated life. She gradually began to make contacts with another woman; this was a very new experience for her. In describing a date with this new friend, she named the foods they each ate. Penny had just recently begun to eat with physical hunger after years of chronic restraint. A few days after this date she found herself eating more than usual and not in response to hunger. She was perplexed by her own behavior. After pursuing this incident in many ways without getting anywhere, the therapist asked what she had been eating, and the answer was rice pudding, a food Penny did not usually care for. The therapist could finally make sense of this particular eating episode. She reminded Penny that rice pudding was precisely the food her friend had been eating the night they had gone out together. Penny's jaw dropped with astonishment. Then she realized that this was not an isolated experience. She remembered many eating experiences in which specific foods had substituted for contact with particular people. Penny saw how she used food to express both her desire for connection and her terror about the perils of connection. Here food, and a very specific one at that, was the object of a need, a need that had gone unmet from an early age. The rice pudding also represented the good object, in this case, her friend. To accept her need of the rice pudding and to feel the rice pudding as "good" once inside her was part of Penny's process of transforming her compensatory object relations. Again, the discovered meaning liberated from the eating inci-

dents must be worked and reworked until the client can internalize its function. Toward this end the food must be honored and the client's need to take
something in for herself must also be respected during what may be a long
time when meaning and affect are still embedded in the food. The therapist
and patient may have to sit together through periods in which they work on
the meaning of compulsive eating and food choices without the work trans-
lating into better eating experiences.

Sheila requested a consultation to evaluate her current treatment, which
focused on her eating problem. She found she had been able to eat noncom-
pulsively until she began to explore her relationship with her mother. The
salient fact of her family history was that she had been put on diets by her
mother at a very early age and had had a compulsive eating problem ever
since. When she and her therapist began talking about her mother, she began
to binge again. Now three years later, she was finally eating "sensibly"
again, balancing her meals, allowing the occasional sweet, but fearing that
the next binge was around the corner. The consultant heard the word "sensibly" and understood it was fraught with meaning, leading her to comment
on how (overly) sensible and reasonable Sheila seemed to be about her food
and eating. In response Sheila eventually elaborated how she felt she was
balancing the conflictual infantile needs of each of her parents. The consultant validated her worry, stating that she seemed to be reenacting her relationship with her parents in her "sensible" manner of eating and that this
could lead to rebellion, namely, the binge she sensed was around the corner.
Perhaps Sheila needed to learn to eat from internal, subjective desire rather
than from being "sensible." The consultant also reframed the binge, suggesting that Sheila use it as a signal that, on an emotional level, "something was
up," something that could then be explored and resolved. Here, unlike the
case of Penny and the rice pudding, what looked like new-found control was
actually a recapitulation of ongoing unsatisfactory object relations.

Dana is a teenager who restricted her eating so severely that she had to be
hospitalized. She is the daughter of an anorexic mother, who was narcissistically preoccupied with her own inner demons, and of a workaholic father.
Her three brothers received markedly different treatment than she did: They
got more food, desserts, more attention, and more support in striving for autonomy. Dana's terror and refusal of food reflected an identification with her
mother, a competition with her, and a wish to be noticed by her and to
please her father. She also tried to control her rage at the deprivation and the
inequities she endured by displacing her suffering on to the food and then
rejecting this toxic substance. As Dana learned to tolerate her rage and desires and grieve the realities of her life, she came to understand that the food
itself magically contained her traumas, which was why she had to reject it so
profoundly. During an arduous and lengthy therapy, as Dana's emotional
life became more available to her, she came to view food as less treacherous

and eventually to see it as comforting. This ushered in a period of compulsive eating and weight gain. Dana and the therapist used an anti-deprivation approach to demystify and legalize foods and to work with the urgent longings for relatedness that the food now represented. The therapist came to be the good object, an adult who could stay focused on Dana, unlike her self-absorbed parents.

In the foregoing examples, as food comes to serve a more pleasurable, bountiful, and nutritive function, the client can experience emotional life more freely.

SPLITTING FOOD, BODY, AND SELF STATES

It is important for clients to understand how their constructs about good and bad foods become linked to good and bad conceptions of the self. How is it that eating cottage cheese makes someone feel thin, good, virtuous, and desirable and that eating chocolate can make someone feel instantly fat, out of control, bad, ugly, stupid, and alone.

In this culture foods are imbued with magical properties of goodness and badness that transcend basic nutritional value and appropriate psychological function. Foods function as magical potions and transformational objects, able to repair, destroy, enhance, or undermine life. Food, characterized as good or bad, links up with internal self states that represent split self experiences such as good-bad, active-passive, strong-weak, virtuous-immoral, or desirable-undesirable.

These self states and ideas about fatness and thinness join and influence one another. Because fat and thin states are also split into rigid categories, the food, the self state, and the body size all become transforms of one another. A person can feel bad, choose the foods that are deemed bad, feel fat and ugly, and then stay in the house because she is the hated, bad one. Or she can start the day with cottage cheese and feel momentarily good and entitled to a good day ahead.

Another person feels good, until a disturbing thought or feeling occurs that she does not know how to acknowledge, metabolize, or understand; so she eats one cookie (or a bag of cookies) to calm or distract herself, and now she has a way to explain feeling bad: "I ate a cookie. I'm disgusting, worthless; I can't keep myself in control. I really deserved to be yelled at by my boss." Eating a cookie simultaneously acknowledges the problem and denies it. It confirms that something is wrong, while substituting a false cause for the real one. This is a closed, fragile, brittle, unstable, and self-perpetuating system whereby emotions exist only insofar as they are associated to food or body states.

How might one work with this phenomenon? To stay with the example of the cookie, the therapist can ask or point out that this cookie holds tremendous power as it allows the client to explain complex feelings and interactions. "How did this cookie get so powerful?" This question implies that there is more to the eating event that needs to be identified and explored. Or the therapist might ask any of the following: "What does it mean to you that your boss yelled at you, that he's a man, he's your father's age, that it was in public? Did you feel enraged but dared not express it, and therefore needed a way to muffle and shut yourself up?" This addresses the adaptive function of eating the cookie, to stuff down the rage. The therapist could also wonder with the client whether there was anything about the cookie that needs to be understood. Why was it so exciting, so riveting? Did she see a cookie on a coworker's plate at lunch? Or was it a cookie from childhood that she dared not then have but that she finally got to eat thanks to this upsetting situation with her boss? Or was this some generalized restlessness, some familiar feeling of anxiety, a gnawing, unnamed wanting that the cookie helped to soothe? In this case, the therapist might point out the positive aspect—the adaptive function—of giving herself something, of letting herself have something in an otherwise depriving inner world. And now or later the therapist might ask, "How can a cookie be so very bad—and you so despicable for eating it? This may not be something you had wanted to do, but why such self-recrimination?" In addition, the therapist could begin to wonder whether there was something in the transference to herself that the client enacted with the boss.

In this example many psychological tasks and issues are being addressed. At the same time a particular stance toward food and a model of eating is being conveyed: The therapist invites the client to be curious about her behaviors, inner life, and interpersonal interactions; together they label and question the splitting; they identify and interpret the symbolic and adaptive functions of reaching for the food; they challenge rigid ideas about food and eating; they ascribe psychological meaning to the food itself as well as to reaching for it and eating it; and they elaborate transference and countertransference. After this analysis, the patient might be able to take a more compassionate stance toward her own impulses and feelings. As in any other analytic endeavor, this kind of exploration—or perhaps only a piece of it—must occur over and over again. Given that food is so intertwined with psychological phenomena and given the patient's attachment to thinking that the symptom is the only problem, this reworking—teasing out food from life, body dissatisfaction from self-worth, putting everything in its place—is the work of treatment for a very long time.

FOOD CHOICE

How can people feed themselves what they enjoy, and what will be satisfying both physiologically and psychologically if they have never had that option or have had little experience in knowing their tastes and preferences and are constantly bombarded by advertising ploys and health claims about what is good and not good to eat? For the most part, women with eating problems have spent a lifetime abdicating control of what they eat and being discouraged from discovering what their preferences or dislikes are. They are unaware that different foods can give them many possible sensations, that their moods or bodily states prefer various foods at different times. Food groups are seen as good or bad, fattening or not, high- or low-calorie; women often have almost no clue beyond these highly charged notions about how to nourish their hungry bodies in a sensually satisfying way.

When asked, "If you could eat anything you want, what would that be?" patients can feel overwhelmed, confused, perplexed, and at a loss regarding this most basic self-knowledge. They feel fearful as they imagine consuming great quantities of all the "bad" foods they have been so ferociously battling. To be allowed to have can feel painfully conflictual when having has always been associated with danger, selfishness, and greed.

Food choices, embedded in an ethnic, historical, and cultural milieu, are further complicated by the rapidly changing, contradictory but ubiquitous messages about what to eat. Establishing a personal relationship to food preferences requires effort and attention to sorting out advertising influences, medical claims, and one's own habituated regimens. This lengthy process is challenging and confusing, but through critical thinking, satisfaction when eating, and learning to live with ambiguity, it is possible to come to a peaceful resolution.

Some women have a better sense of what they prefer or have had periods of noncompulsive eating. But these experiences are transitory because these women do not believe that they can eat what they enjoy over a lifetime without losing control. They will need much encouragement from the therapist. By trial and error they must prove that this is a deeply satisfying way to eat and that food eaten when one is hungry does not harm one's body. Provided there are no medical conditions requiring special care, the more precisely a person is aware of what she wants and what her body physically requires, the more efficiently she can satisfy herself, thereby fostering psyche-soma integration. For example, if she eats three bites of chocolate cake that hit the spot with company, she may avoid starting a 3-hour binge the minute her company leaves.

For patients who have no experience with taking charge of their food, and therefore no clue as to what to feed themselves, there are many ways in which the therapist can help them to discover their preferences and choices. She can encourage them to look through cookbooks, walk through food shops or survey menus, imagining what foods might taste and feel like once inside their bodies. She can use focusing techniques and guided fantasies or imagery in the safety of the therapy relationship to stimulate new ideas and sensations in the client. One such guided fantasy is:

Imagine you start to feel hungry. This makes sense: you have not eaten for a few hours. The only thing to do now is to take care of yourself by feeding yourself. Now, try to imagine what might really hit the spot. Is it salty, crunchy, creamy? Is it a lot of little tastes of many things or a meat and potatoes meal? Is it the delicious smelling soup your grandmother cooked, the breads you have not eaten in years, the pie you would not even consider making for yourself, or the one that is a car ride away? When you find something that appeals, imagine letting yourself have it. Make it or buy it. Now imagine eating it—what does it taste like, feel like inside your mouth, going down? Once inside, how does it feel? If it is not right, put that food on the list of possibilities, and try something else. You never again have to eat something you do not enjoy or want, and your choices will always be changing.

Another fantasy exercise is the banquet table:

Close your eyes. Now imagine a huge banquet table in front of you. On the table are all your favorite foods in great quantities. Let yourself really see and smell all the luscious foods that you enjoy. You can add foods or change them. Now put your name on the table and say, "This is my banquet table; and anytime I'm hungry I shall go to my banquet table and choose the food that will satisfy me." Remind yourself that there is an endless supply, ready for you. Food can always be replaced or new foods added. Now imagine that when you locate the food you want, you also figure out a sure way to actually get it. What does it feel like to know that for the rest of your life you will have your table available to you as your guide for feeding yourself?

These fantasies become the basis for taking the next step with greater awareness and confidence, which is actually to eat the truly desired foods when hungry. When the client plays with and enjoys this process, she turns what has been anguishing, painful, or denied into an opportunity to discover needs, desires, and preferences that she can satisfy with regularity, pleasure, comfort, and increasing confidence. As she becomes attuned to hunger and food, attentive and responsive to her own body, she opens up the whole area of body need and awareness of her subjective experience. Learning to eat with hunger can help her to address other physiological states of need and to take advantage of opportunities to satisfy them.

Therapists should remind their patients that when they are hungry they should be doing nothing but feeding themselves with food that will nourish and satisfy them. From now on they are in charge. No one knows better than they do what their bodies need. Gradually, this will become second nature and less conflictual, difficult, and time-consuming. They may find that sweets they previously craved are really "memory" foods that no longer satisfy them (Milky Ways eaten at age 5), or that they are having food jags and only want pasta for weeks. They may discover an interest in gourmet cooking and making dinner parties, thus replacing compulsive eating by enjoying eating food with others. Or they may discover that their food choices have been overdetermined, either by their family repertoire or what's easy and available, like fast foods or packaged goods.

There are some women who move quickly away from the deprivation and dieting stance once they permit themselves to eat whatever they want. Their chaotic relationship to food abates, and compulsive eating, starving, and bingeing diminish. More typically, it takes clients a long time, with many steps forward and back and much "doing" and "undoing," to discern their tastes and choices and to figure out what they need or want at any moment. Because choosing food is ultimately about self-definition, autonomy, entitlement, and differentiation from familial and cultural pressures, this new sense of agency, becoming one's own good caretaker, reflects changes in the relationships to internalized parental and cultural strictures. Becoming one's own good caregiver, although exciting, can be a long and rocky road.

LEGALIZING FOOD

Once a client has a vision in which food is nurturing and nourishing instead of forbidden, threatening, dangerous, or bad, eventually she will create a psychic environment in which she can regulate herself. If she releases food, all food, from the enemy camp, truly allows it in her life and feels entitled to it, then she no longer has to binge or sneak, and food will no longer intrude on her thoughts in response to deprivation.

Because food unconsciously can substitute for real relationships, it is important to make a satisfying and peaceful relationship with food itself, so that food is no longer experienced as abandoning, rejecting, or tantalizing. As the client works out a better relationship to food, she also rearranges her internal object relations. Women talk to themselves about food all day long. The therapist must carefully consider and work with the manifest content of these ideas, as well as the underlying conflicts and patterns which they express. The manifest content of thought about food is in itself very important and can perpetuate disordered eating and corrode ego functioning. At an unconscious level these food thoughts often contain conflicting inchoate ideas and experiences that must also be illuminated. For example, some people tell themselves that they are eating all the time, that they are disgusting and out of control, but they are not conscious of a more entrenched belief that they are never supposed to eat for any reason. So although on the manifest level someone is saying she eats all the time (which she might be doing), psychically she is ejecting her experience of the food with every bite, and therefore can never have an integrated experience of a good feed.

Obsessional thinking binds anxiety for some and defends against disintegration for others. Although this kind of thinking concerns withdrawal from others, it is also a way to stay connected to real people and to internal compensatory objects. The therapist must hold the tension of the dual function of the obsession, the simultaneous withdrawal and attempt at connection, and help the client to become conscious of the moment when she begins to retreat. When the client accepts the idea that this tortured, repetitive thinking provides a "loyal companion," she has achieved a fundamental shift in perspective, which lessens self-flagellation and engages her curiosity about her responses and what triggers them.

The therapist's task is to help clients to say both "yes" and "no" to food. This does not mean, as many clients fear, that when saying "yes" they have to eat it immediately, or all the time, or 10 times more than they need, or only fats and sugars. It means that all food goes on the list of what is permissible to eat when hungry. This kind of psychic environment supports freedom, choice, abundance, passion, and dignity—certainly a radical change for women used to messages about restraining appetite. This new attitude toward food becomes the client's model for relationships to her own needs, to other people, and to occupying space in the world. If the cheesecake or the broccoli or the bread looks delicious in the shop, the question is not, "May I?" or "Should I have it?" but, rather, "Am I hungry?" "Do I want it?" "Will it hit the spot?" "Is this what my body can use now?" If the client is not hungry, then the question becomes, "What feelings, conflicts, or interpersonal situations are causing me to want to eat?"

The timing and the quantity of foods brought into the home are two important variables in the process of legalizing food. Clients are often afraid to have "the forbidden foods" in their homes and the therapist may find it necessary to suggest introducing foods one at a time. If sweets as a category are "forbidden," then the client's first step in legalization should be to eat one sweet, the one she really wants at the time, and to keep it available. Quantity plays an important and different role for each of the three sisters with eating problems. For the compulsive eater, and for some bulimics who are ready to deal with their compulsive eating problem, 1 gallon of ice cream may not be enough. They may need to have 5 gallons in their freezers to reassure themselves that the ice cream will be there and that they are entitled to have it. The therapist should ask the client to imagine how much ice cream she would need to feel neither deprived nor overwhelmed. This provides a useful guide for how much to purchase the next time she goes shopping. It is also important to remind the client to replace the ice cream before the supply gets too low. In this way she will let herself know that she is committed to abundance, not deprivation, that there is a new caregiver at work, allowing a shift in her internal object-world. Although some clients may be ready to discuss these ideas at the beginning of treatment, clients who severely restrict their food intake may take years before they can entertain them.

This process meets much resistance, largely because of people's terror of being out of control when faced with abundance. The chronic deprivation of actual food and of the psychological experience of being denied food as a soothing symbol perpetuates both fear of food and out-of-control behavior around food. Spending money on food can function as another resistance. Although the therapist needs to be sensitive to the realities of her client's economic life, people who are compulsive eaters from all economic classes, even the poorest, spend money on surplus food. If a client is going to buy food, at least she should buy the food she likes. The client's fears of having, bringing in, and replenishing food need to be analyzed repeatedly.

HEALTH CONCERNS

Of course, eating too much salt, fat, or carrots, for example, entails negative consequences. Certain diseases are linked to particular dietary patterns. For example, if a client is recently diagnosed diabetic, the therapist can ask her what it means to continue eating so much sugar. The therapist can explore the meaning of putting something potentially harmful into one's body. Many people give their medical conditions short shrift when the psychological need to eat is more powerful than the facts about nutrition. In these cases the dangerous foods must be demystified. Legalizing food is an essential part of this process, so that the client who eats foods that are specifically unhealthy for her does so with curiosity about her choice instead of self-recrimination. In this way she can begin to understand the function of her eating. She may need to go through a period of eating ice cream and candy bars despite medical restrictions, allowing herself to eat with dignity, tasting slowly rather than gulping down, putting food in a bowl rather than eating surreptitiously from the box, or focusing on taking food in rather than on watching TV. Eventually the foods will become less dangerous psychologically so that the real dangers can be dealt with medically. In addition, the therapeutic relationship must provide the kind of connection and recognition that helps the client experience her body as worthy of care. Then she can begin to make different kinds of food choices, in harmony with the real needs of her body as it actually is, neither denigrated nor idealized. The restrictions and limitations due to medical considerations constitute deprivation, both literally and symbolically. The therapy must explore, mourn, and work them through until the client reaches a stance that is directed inward rather than outward.

The whole process of listening to internal signals of hunger and food preferences does eventually enable people to better care for themselves on a medical level. Body signals previously ignored can now be heard. Patients respond to inner body requests for legumes, vegetables, garlic, orange juice, or meat for many reasons, such as using nutrition to medicate the flu, digestive problems, iron depletion, and so on. Patients also report diagnosing more serious conditions such as thyroid problems or diverticulitis sooner than they would previously have done, precisely because they had developed a new attuned relationship to their bodies.

Yet these are confusing times regarding diet and health. It is difficult to sort out the facts from the quasi facts, myths, and incorrect ideas. For example, what is the role of fat and cholesterol in relation to our health? Fats pose a threat to our coronary functioning (Framingham study) and possibly contribute to the development of certain cancers. The recent transformation in nutrition from meat, potatoes, bread, and butter to pasta and salad or vegetables may save countless lives as people's arteries get less clogged with animal fat. It may also be important to direct concern to the pesticides, dyes, hormones, antibiotics, preservatives, and now radiation that are overused in most food products.

From a different perspective, is all the concern about health and fitness causing anxiety and health related problems as well as binge behavior with food? As Professor Barsky of Harvard Medical School argues, Americans "don't live exuberantly but apprehensively, as if our bodies are dormant adversaries programmed for betrayal at any moment" (Barsky, 1988, as quoted in *Time*, July 25, 1988). According to Barsky, polls show that those people who say they are satisfied with their health dropped from 61% in the 1970s to 55% in the 1980s.

The therapist helps the patient juggle these diverse and often conflicting realities, giving each its due. Sometimes the therapist's stance is to help the client live with the different tensions. Other times, the therapist explores why one set of beliefs is adhered to over another. For example, is the client worried about her fat intake in a particular period because she is uncomfortable learning to pleasure herself with food (love, work, sex)? Or is she now comfortable enough with pleasure that she will not feel deprived if she limits her cheese intake in order to lower her rather high cholesterol level? What is most useful to the therapist is to have the internal flexibility (as well as some knowledge) to sort out with the patient what the priorities are for that particular patient in that particular moment of the treatment. For many people with an eating problem, their concern with health functions as a cover both for their preoccupation with thinness and for calorie counting—that is, maintaining a diet mentality. The therapist eventually must work with this defense in order to move out of an inner depriving and threatening world.

BREAKING INTO THE BINGE

Simply by permitting herself to eat and choose from the full range of foods, a client often manages to abate her bingeing. Nonetheless, binges do not entirely disappear; and so clients need strategies to help them to interrupt and understand their binges. At the moment of bingeing, the client should ask herself compassionately one of the following important two questions: "Why am I eating this if I'm not hungry?" or, if that does not help, "Am I eating what I truly want to eat?" If ice cream is what she really wants, then eating cookies only makes the binge and its psychic repercussions worse. The point is that the client should attempt to make the right choice for that moment, one that satisfies her and helps her to define herself in a positive light. These questions to herself help interrupt her state of panic and her robotic action and allow her to think about what she wants, and therefore, to organize herself internally. To this end the therapist can never ask these questions too often. The therapist, by stressing compassion toward a binge, is essential to the process of the patient creating an internal soothing presence. The idea that even if she is bingeing, she ought to eat what she truly wants helps the client to challenge the part of herself that is rejecting and critical of her feelings in general and specifically of her entitlement to eat.

Some therapists think, as do some patients, that to focus thus on one's food and bodily states is to replace one obsession with another. This assumption is not true. The process just described promotes feeding, having, allowing, choosing, and enjoying rather than controlling, counting calories, and feeling disgust and hatred. As the process becomes more and more integrated and familiar, it requires less and less psychic energy. In the beginning of the process, however, when the client is still learning that a caregiver that is better than her action symptom is now available, what is most important is for her to determine precisely what food she desires at each outbreak of the symptom. Eventually, if she is hungry but not sure exactly what she wants, yet has something she basically likes, she will not feel bereft, undone, abandoned, and hopeless as she might in the beginning of this treatment process.

FOOD AS A METAPHOR FOR LIFE

The method and examples given so far are based on clients who experience difficulties in their relationships to food. The therapy helps the client to understand that her painful food, body image, or eating experiences represent unresolved issues in her psychic structure and emotional life.

In other words, in the cases hitherto discussed, the techniques of treatment are designed to decode the metaphor whereby food stands for life. Sometimes a statement about the client's life experience, which she could not absorb if made directly, will be taken in if expressed in terms of food, eating, and body image. For example, Jeanne, an anorexic woman, told her therapist that she could not let herself eat. The therapist asked, "What might you want to eat?" Jeanne replied that she wanted to be able to eat a piece of toast with jam. As this was early in treatment and Jeanne was at a starvation weight, the therapist took this opportunity to ascertain what the reality of food intake was. Jeanne informed her that she could indeed eat a piece of toast, but not with jam. The therapist queried, "You eat part of a piece of toast?" She replied, "No, I eat a whole piece; that's no longer a problem; but to eat it with jam, now that's really too difficult." The therapist queried further, "Because to eat with the jam would mean . . . ?" Jeanne replied, "I'm deserving. I'm good enough to be a regular person who could have that much." Several sessions later, Jeanne came in upset about an incident with a family member. The discussion centered on feelings of abandonment, deprivation, and indirectly on the core feeling of unentitlement. At some point the therapist said, "Like not being able to have the toast with jam." Jeanne nodded yes, slowly and sadly, and a deep moment of shared silence followed.

What happened in this seemingly simple interaction? The parallel between an experience with food and feeding and an interpersonal interaction was clearly established. What Jeanne symbolized and enacted in the feeding situation was exactly the same as in the life situation. The fact that Jeanne understands this parallel furthers her working-through process and serves to establish a powerful interpersonal connection between herself and the therapist. Jeanne felt deeply understood in that moment; and the silence was pregnant with both her sadness and the bonding she experienced in that moment between the one being understood and the one who understands. On the one hand, they decoded the language of eating problems (in this case, adding jam to a piece of toast equals entitlement); on the other hand—and this is the point of the example—they used that language to express mutual understanding.

Nancy, a talented, intelligent, and extremely beautiful woman, came to therapy lost in her internal object world that alternately abandoned and seduced her. Without the shared experience and language of food, and, in her case, a feminist intellectual sophistication, there would have been little way to establish connection and hope. Her feminism challenged the emotional basis of her life, that her only value lay in her appearance. Her beauty only made her more insecure, because on the one hand, she felt not quite beautiful enough, and on the other, she felt unappreciated for who she was as a whole person. Although she resented this construction of femininity, she could not free herself from it. But she did take the initiative of coming to a feminist therapist with an anti-diet approach. Nancy and her therapist waded together through Nancy's feelings of envy and fear of being envied. She used her tantrums, rage, and intense self-hatred like a machete to defend against vulnerability and dependency needs. Meanwhile, the therapeutic relationship and endeavor slowly affected one area of her life: her eating. The therapist had not only to withstand Nancy's storms of rage, but—what was even more important—the therapist had to be comfortable with the issues of food, need, and greed. After direct work with Nancy on these issues through the metaphor and reality of cookies, Nancy eventually was able to eat two or three cookies without devouring a whole bag at a time—a miracle for this embattled woman. In doing so, she had mastered a piece of existence that had always been as impossible to conquer as everything else still was. At first, the cookies had represented desperate need, experienced as greed and accompanied by feelings of shame and humiliation. After mediation by the therapeutic relationship, they came to represent a more autonomous, intact piece of self. Nancy continued to grow comfortable around food. She had found a way not to banish need but to integrate it. Her relationship to food and eating had become a more integrated, less conflictual, more autonomous sphere of ego functioning; no longer did it represent intense psychological and cultural splits, such as dependence-independence, selfishness-selflessness, good-bad, or fat-thin. As work continued in other areas, there were long periods during which the therapist could not reach her, could not break through the internal deadlock created by her tie to internal persecutors. Only when the therapist drew the parallel between a current crisis and the former one with the cookies, which now represented a piece of unfettered self and hope, did an internal shift take place so that at least some mutual processing of the impasse could take place.

Satiation

Satiation signals the completion of a feeding experience. It is a physical, emotional, and subjective sense of comfort, satisfaction, and well-being, of a need appropriately met. Satiation is self-care at its most refined; it requires the ability to discern and appropriately label bodily communications, and ultimately concerns trusting and accepting them. Hunger and satiation are the guides to natural body weight.

Some clients have never internalized satiation as a discrete and knowable experience. This occurs when the client has been overfed or underfed or has had no experience of linking bodily sensations with behavior such as putting a fork down. Furthermore, years of chronic dieting, purging, or fasting may have damaged and distorted her perception of internal cues of satiation as well as hunger. A dieter identifies satiation with having consumed the kind and quantity of food dictated by a particular diet. How can a total stranger know that four ounces of chicken, one slice of bread or its allowed substitute, and a fruit, but not a banana, is the right quantity and choice of food to provide a personal and comfortable sense of satisfaction? This prescription presumes a universal appetite and body size. The culture dictates that people achieve and maintain a particular body size. People ignore the cues of satiation, fearing that having enough food would lead to weight gain. In the course of treatment it is not uncommon for a patient to be able to wait for hunger, to choose from the full range of foods, but then to have difficulty stopping at a point of comfort.

To acknowledge satiety is to own a profound piece of self experience. Women's psychological rearing does not encourage them to recognize or meet their own internal needs. Satiety is yet another internal experience from which women are alienated. Like hunger and food, it easily evokes psychological issues because it represents object ties and self formation, including awareness of interoceptive experience. Satiety can encode separation, differentiation, autonomy, entitlement, limits, and boundaries. When food represents one's earliest attachments, the difficulties in those relationships (and their ramifications in later life) shape one's relationship to satiety as well as food and hunger. To say, "I've had enough for now, and I'll find you again, food, the next time I'm hungry," requires a good-enough internal object experience. When many patients with eating problems put down the fork, they say "good-bye" and experience intolerable loss, grief, or abandonment. On the other hand, there are patients who are in a constant state of pseudo-separation and who bypass satiation and needs entirely.

Four years into treatment, Ruby, an anorexic, took some risks by eating more food than what she had previously allowed herself. After a week of eating more, Ruby noticed she was having more fights with her husband and was being provocative with her therapist. She linked her anger, her wish to overturn the table and kick the therapist, with her increased eating. The therapist asked Ruby to describe the feelings of eating beyond the point at which she had previously stopped. Ruby described with glee the wonderful feeling in her body when she had eaten more than her usual amount. The therapist asked what it would mean if she ate and felt satiated. Ruby replied that if her needs were met, she would have no right to want anything from anybody ever again. If she actually let herself have the food and feel satisfied, then she would no longer be in a state of need. For Ruby, being in a state of need felt safer and more comfortable. In her need she felt connected to the possibility of care, that someone would come and respond to her needs. This configuration of feelings represents Ruby's internal tie to a tantalizing object, one that promises care and connection, but never fulfills the promise. Her psychic situation replicated her relationship to her mother who was cold and terrified of intimacy but a compelling and glamorous force in the larger community and business world. From the outside her anorexia appeared to be about the assertion of independence, but internally, her state of semi-starvation constituted a plea for her dependency needs to be met. She would only express these needs by her avoidance of satiation. By never feeling full, she kept herself continually needy, because that was the only way to keep herself attached to important people in her life.

As the treatment progressed and Ruby's dependency needs were attended to, it became clear that a continual state of dependency also functioned as a defense against her desire to differentiate. Because women function in society as the carriers of connection and attachment, their freedom to differentiate is often problematic. A genuine experience of satiation implies the uniqueness of one's body-self, because no one else can decide, "I've had enough. I feel satisfied."

Very often when asked what stopping with satiation would mean, clients respond by noticing how stuffing themselves is an attempt to circumvent loneliness, as one client tearfully said:

> L: It's never enough food not to be alone. If I stop eating I'll be abandoned. At least if I have food I won't starve as well.
>
> T: So stuffing yourself seems to address how lonely and alone you felt for so much of your life in the past, and sometimes even now?
>
> L: Yes. I cling to it for dear life. Every time I leave people, as you know, I have to have food until I get calm again.
>
> T: Separating from food feels the same as separating from all human connection. Eating promises that you won't have to feel fear, grief, or aloneness; but they really exist.
>
> L: How will I survive if I feel my grief? I'll be so scared, and I won't know what to do.
>
> T: It will feel less overwhelming and terrifying than it always has if we work on it together and you allow yourself to feel these feelings with me.

Besides separation and attachment issues, entitlement issues are often encoded in satiation. Satiation is a feeling of "fullness," that reflects feeling entitled: to have needs met, to live a full life, to sustain healthy feelings about one's own greed, desire, and lust, and to have a comfortable body sense, neither too hungry nor too full. Both in the culture and in family life, women are told to eat like a "lady" or a "bird," which compromises having a robust appetite and feelings of comfortable satiety. When the therapist and client explore and analyze the vicissitudes of the client's sense of entitlement, her emotional deprivation—sometimes physical, too—will surface as a significant theme in relation to both food and other aspects of the psyche. For the client to develop a sense of when she is satiated, she must distinguish emotional neediness from the demands of her body.

By definition satiation is a limit and a boundary. Limits and boundaries provide safety, a sense of well-being, and wholeness. They establish essential boundaries between inside and outside, fantasy and reality, self and other. By the same token they can feel injurious to one's narcissism and omnipotence. When parents excessively impinged and intruded on the client as a child, limits no longer represent safety; instead, they are experienced as oppressive, depriving, or self-annihilating. Satiation then is experienced as one more unbearable external imposition. Eating beyond satiety or never reaching it are ways to rebel, express opposition, or try to assert one's autonomy.

When a client's boundaries have been trespassed, she alternates between rebellion and compliance and experiences satiation as overwhelming, terrifying inner chaos. Under the stress of physical or emotional neglect, her internal limits and boundaries disappear or feel foreign to her; and her notion of
satiation is compromised by boundless eating or rigidly imposed limits, to
compensate for what was and remains missing.

When cultural rearing practices put pressure on women to be thin, they
are forced to deny or distort hunger and thus to tamper with satiety. The
widespread concept of "superwoman" reinforces their confusion about limits and boundaries by implying that there are none: women must do everything, have everything, and be everything.

EXTRA ANALYTIC TECHNIQUES

When clients are already eating with physiological hunger some of the time,
demonstrating some ability to eat foods of their choosing, they are ready to
start working on satiation. The therapist may find some of the following
techniques helpful. A client cannot experience satiation unless she eats in response to hunger cues. A client who stays constantly full can never know satiation based on internal physical cues. One who waits for extreme hunger to
start eating will find it difficult to know when to stop. So will a client who is
not completely sure that more food will be there the next time she is hungry.
These are the guiding principles to teach clients, so that they can stop eating
when they are satiated.

There is no physiological signal for stopping except for the eventual re-
placement of the feeling of hunger by a sense of fullness. And her feeling of
satiety will not be truly comfortable unless she ate foods that she desired and
chose herself. In this case desire joins physiological need, and she experiences complete satisfaction. With only physical satiation, that is if she eats
carrots when what she craves is ice cream, she can be physically sated, but
psychologically still hungry.

The client must first learn to recognize when she is satiated. The therapist
may have to discuss at length with her the sensations of fullness, both physically and psychically. Some clients report that occasionally they find a moment or a "click" when they recognize that they have had enough to eat. For
others both the concept and experience of satiation are completely baffling
and anxiety provoking.

As the therapy explores the function of not stopping when satiated, complex issues in the patient's internal object world will be revealed. For example, Lois's therapist suggested that she recall in her imagination the last time
she ate and then asked, "What were you feeling, thinking? Can you imagine
that you are no longer physically hungry and that you feel satisfied? Look
down and notice that there is still food on your plate; and now imagine say-

ing 'good-bye' to the food, 'no more for now.' How does that feel?" Lois placed her hands across her chest and described a sensation as if something were being torn off her body, "maybe my skin, as if everything then would be exposed and hanging out." This allowed them to explore Lois's extreme fear of exposure and inhibitions about being known.

The therapist can suggest that, after eating what seems like a satisfying amount, a client wait 20 minutes to see if she is still hungry. Another suggestion is that when the client stops eating at the moment she feels full, she should remind herself that more food is available. This step is particularly relevant if the client formulates her desire to continue eating in terms such as, "But it tastes so good." With this reminder, the client may escape the internal experience of deprivation, despite physical satiation.

The therapist can help clients to ask what they really want or what they are feeling when they are satiated but still want to eat. If they feel full, then it is not literally food that they need but, rather, what the food symbolizes. Can they tolerate sitting with whatever feelings or wishes might surface?

The client may not fear feelings or wishes connected to food but, rather, the change in body size that she anticipates if she learns to stop eating when full. Can she tolerate a change in body size? What does that mean to her? This questioning introduces the work of understanding the meanings of body size (see chapter 7).

The goal is to make satiety a reliable internal signal. Thus, satiation, rather than being determined by outside stimuli such as the size of the plate, the end of lunch hour, the second half of a sandwich, the whole croissant, becomes an inner experience. Clients learn to know themselves from the inside on both the bodily and psychic level.

This non-diet approach does not aim at perfection. It is to be expected that from time to time a client will eat beyond satiety, eat when not hungry, or select food based not on internal need or desire. However, if any of these difficulties persists regularly, it indicates psychic distress.

Trashing: Working with the Internal Saboteur

The term *trashing* denotes the activity of the berating, yelling, negative inner voice. Its corrosive effect on the sense of self is pernicious. In classical terms, trashing is the evidence of a "harsh superego." In object relations terms it is the work of the "internal saboteur," an internal attacker that is structurally embedded in the psyche by identification with the rejecting and depriving aspects of the caregiver. This saboteur viciously attacks the needs and weakness of the suffering, unsatisfied libidinal ego or the needs of the buried true self. In interpersonal terms trashing is experiencing oneself over and over again as the "bad me"; external disapproval heightens anxiety, becomes internalized, and diminishes one's sense of self. Because the culture makes eating and body size moral issues, self attacking thoughts are like punishments for sins one has committed: the sins of when, what, and how much one has eaten and/or about a body size that does not conform to cultural norms or the latest aesthetic.

Trashing is central to all eating problems. It is the internal voice of self-hate, the harsh judge, the cruel critic, and as one client put it, "my upwardly mobile gestapo commander." It completely dominates any compassion clients might have for themselves. Trashing is central to perpetuating a vicious circle: Dieting leads to bingeing, so bingeing leads to trashing, and trashing leads to more bingeing or dieting. Trashing can be loud and blatant—"I'm such a fat pig, slob, wild, and out of control" or subtle, a slight internal disruption manifest when the client compares herself to others and feels diminished or uncomfortable. How pervasive and entrenched this self-hater is depends on the extent to which early psychic deprivation has fused with continued neglect. Early deprivation and privations lead to unmet and unbearable dependency needs often well hidden.

Therefore, feeling dependency needs as an adult evokes vulnerable childhood feeling states. She may have been rebuked, denied, forcibly controlled, abandoned, or exploited by her caretakers, and she reenacts this treatment because it is the only way in which she knows to treat herself and because she believes that the "best" way to avoid fear or vulnerability is to deprecate them as "weakness" and to organize a self-hating, falsely independent stance toward these dependency needs. Without this pseudo-independence the client desperately fears falling apart, crying forever, not functioning, or feeling too weak and young to carry on without help. She may tell herself, for instance, "I'm just a big baby; stop this indulgent, greedy behavior and grow up." "Good, I deserve to be fat; look how disgusting I am." When the client allows help she recognizes her own dependency needs and thereby directly challenges the internal saboteur. Clearly strivings of all kinds, for autonomy, sexuality, creativity, and so on, can be met with the same internal attack if the familial and cultural messages prohibited them.

Psychodynamically this internal judge, jury, and executioner can serve a number of purposes. First, trashing punishes the client both for the pain that drove her to the cookies and for the attempted solution, eating the cookies. The original pain is numbed; she now focuses on food, eating, and how bad she has been. The "solution" to the new problem: further food deprivation.

Second, trashing also controls the client's unacceptable feelings by blaming and yelling at herself for eating or for her choice of food: "It was fattening." The client magnifies and lingers in this area of life that she can control.

Third, trashing manifests and maintains the client's attachment to unsatisfying internal objects and object relations, thereby inhibiting or preventing her form developing her own voice and sense of self. The client's first step toward changing is often to become aware of how pervasive her internal saboteur is. To help clients to make this step, therapists can ask them to reflect on the last 24 hours or to look over the coming week and to notice how often they criticize themselves for either their behavior or their very existence. Trashing is usually so automatic and ego syntonic that often a client is not consciously aware of its pervasive influence.

After the client has become more conscious of this way of talking to herself, the therapist might ask her if she notices any connection between trashing and her behavior. Does trashing lead, in the moment, to eating or if she is already eating, to more eating? Does it make her stop eating? What happens after some time? In the case of a compulsive eater, trashing often leads to further eating; and the therapist may find it useful to explore with the client her internal state prior to eating, continually exposing the trashing which so often precipitates episodes of compulsive eating, which may not be obvious to her.

The therapist might then consider with the client the possibility of talking to herself in a kindlier, more concerned way. If she can shift to a more empathic voice, this will give her a respite, perhaps for a few minutes, from the harsh, abusive jeering. Then it is important to explore this experience of changing the voice. Or, if she cannot find a more empathic voice, then what or whose voice gets in the way of doing so?

The kind voice is generally not a familiar one. Fostered by the therapist's compassionate stance and tone, the client gradually develops a voice of understanding. The therapist's voice may be the only kind voice the client has ever heard in relation to her food, eating, and body size. She can shift from interpreting the trashing as a statement of fact to interpreting it as a signal that something is troubling her externally or internally and use it as a cryptic clue to what that something may be. It is this shift that can open the door for the client to begin to reconsider what she was taught about food, hunger, eating, and her body. She no longer has to direct a critical eye solely at her self, her body, and her behavior, but can now turn it outward to her material situation and how it may be contributing to her dilemma. This kind of subjectivity and individuation may be problematic because it goes against the internalized cultural mandates for femininity.

Grappling with the internalized rejecting object's strength and tenacity, is the work of treatment. With those clients whose internal object is particularly vicious, punitive, and dominating, something positive must be found and acknowledged in that brutal object, if only its strength. If not, it will fight back even harder, asserting its right to survival. Only when its positive aspect is acknowledged can it relinquish its tenacity. Then the client can integrate this positive aspect into the rest of her self.

CHAPTER 7

Working Toward
Body/Self Integration

CAROL BLOOM, LAURA KOGEL, AND
LELA ZAPHIROPOULOS

WOMEN'S COMPLICATED relationship to their social position and consequent gendered psychology is inscribed on the body and enacted through daily social practices. Because women primarily organize their perceptions and experience of their bodies through body size and image, an essential component of treatment is the work of deconstructing fat and thin, the dichotomy clients utilize. This deconstruction promotes a more integrated and realistic sense of body-self.

The meanings ascribed to fat and thin, to particular body parts, to body image, to body wellness, and to the body as a whole are slowly and painstakingly revealed through this deconstruction and analysis. Furthermore, the therapist must help the client to reintegrate those fantasies, parts of self, lived experience, aspirations, personality attributes, affective states, and needs that have been dissociated and deposited into fat and thin body image states and other bodily experiences. For example, when needs such as mastery and dependency are experienced as too conflictual, clients defend against them by transforming them into the wish for the illusory "right" body and leave the actual body hated. Together, the therapist and client must understand this defensive wish for transformation, the hatred of the body, and the etiology and meaning of the original need. This wish for transformation fosters a split in body/self integrity. Although the splitting divides psyche from soma, the person's preoccupation with and hatred of the body simultaneously maintains a connection, albeit a painful and distorted one, between body and self.

The endless pursuit of thinness, which provides the illusion of salvation, redemption, love, and acceptance, is a manic defense against intolerable feelings of deprivation, despair, and depression. Utilizing this manic defense, splitting, and displacement, the psyche sets about transforming the body as a means to gain control of unbearable affects and unsatisfying internal object experiences and as compensation for unsatisfactory real ones (Orbach, 1986; Palazzoli, 1986; Sugarman & Kurash, 1982).

A client named Carla told the following incident in one of her sessions, which exemplifies the process of splitting in the wish for bodily transformation: She is sitting with Ray at a restaurant. She finds Ray handsome and interesting but has decided not to sleep with him and has planned to tell him this tactfully. She feels good about this decision; it reflects her newfound ability to know what she does and does not want. Her real interest in this man is their shared passion for the visual. She loves their conversations about art and architecture and has decided that is all she wants because he would not be a good partner for her. At the table Ray talks about other women, and his eyes subtly roam the room. In this kind of interaction Carla is unable to grab hold of the emotionally elusive experience, elusive precisely because it is so familiar and familial. Her father had affairs outside his marriage, although this was an "unthought known" (Bollas, 1987) prior to treatment. As she and Ray continue to talk she begins to have bad feelings about her body. She feels her body is too old, not quite slim enough, not perfect. In addition, she explains that whenever she has these kinds of bad feelings she always links them to concrete plans to eat "right" and to exercise. "It's not what am I going to do, rather it's I am going to do X and Y. I am going to gain control." Transformation on the interpersonal level may feel impossible, but she can remake her body. Only by the end of their session did she get to the core of the experience. "Being the 'good' girl in the face of some jerk getting to do just what he wants always makes me feel bad about myself, and I transfer that to my body."

Therapists must listen to the body on the metaphorical, representational level as well as the literal, physical level. Listening on these levels is important but difficult because the conversion from emotional self states to body (size) states and body states into self states is instantaneous and usually unconscious. For example, one client reported feeling upset about an interaction with a friend and felt fat all day. As she processed the interaction and felt she understood better what had transpired between her and her friend, she commented with surprise that she also felt thinner. Someone else reported eating cottage cheese and then in a flash felt thinner. Later she ate one cookie and just as quickly felt fat. In feeling fat she immediately felt bad, disgusting, and worthless; her internal saboteur had taken over. In all these examples body states, self states, and food all become instantaneous transforms of each other that result from cultural and psychological splitting and displacement. The therapist works to interpret these transforms by illustrating how the same issues are manifested in each.

Clients talk about their bodies as if what they are saying or perceiving is fact, whereas it is a subjective experience based on a distorted view of themselves. "My large hips are disgusting." "You can't go to the beach if your cellulite is like mine." "My belly is huge." These convictions are presented as the only truth, and misery and deprivation are presented as the only possible responses. This "truth" always contains and conceals intense self-hate, which itself is a defense against such overwhelming feelings as confusion, vulnerability, or despair.

The therapist uses detailed inquiry partly to indicate that embedded in a patient's talk about fat and thin is a broader, richer terrain to mine. For example, Joanna continuously talked about being overweight as if the therapist, she, and, of course, the rest of the world felt equally judgmental, hateful, and repelled by her "fat" (her subjective assessment). She always linked her "fat" self to being inadequate and out of control, and she envisioned her "thin" self as totally competent. The therapist responded, "I understand you assume that I too am repulsed by your 'fat.' But, for right now, let's first try to look at how your 'fat' got to be so terrible in your mind." Her responses helped to explain how these categories became so entrenched. She was born to upwardly mobile immigrant parents to whom thin meant success in class terms. Moreover, she was a chubby adolescent, often teased by her peers, who wanted but received no help from her family concerning her weight and her painful interpersonal experiences. Furthermore, she worked in a profession that demanded a certain look and body size. All of these pressures required still further exploration in order to unravel the bigger picture: a more complicated, larger truth that included her past, her identifications, her dreams and aspirations, her familial, professional, and social worlds.

The therapist, aware of how much a person's emotional life can be displaced to the body, listens to non-body material to hear possible metaphors, connections, and explanations with previously reported body experience. Amanda, who was constantly preoccupied with control of her food and her body, came one day to a session deeply upset about an interaction with her grandmother that had involved herself, her parents, and her siblings. At the last family gathering, Amanda's grandmother had behaved in an exceptionally controlling way. Amanda was understandably upset about how the family interaction had been shaken by her grandmother's pernicious control. The therapist connected this theme of familial control with Amanda's intense control of her food and body. Although her body and eating problem were central to her psychological life, Amanda had not been focusing on them for awhile.

When the therapist made the link between Amanda's hating her grandmother's oppressive control and how tightly Amanda controlled her own eating and body, several processes were set in motion. The patient felt

deeply heard and understood, and she felt that her eating problem was dignified and taken seriously. Both feelings aid in solidifying the relationship to
the therapist. This kind of empathic intervention also tackles the patient's
problem with splitting because the link is made between psyche and soma.
When these connections are made repeatedly, the patient can then give dimension to her bodily experience by taking it out of its narrow confines as an
isolated, shameful, and concrete problem. Although the body is a tangible
entity—and at times this is the important aspect to address—the patient is
beginning to learn that the body is also psychically elaborated.

More typically, the patient discusses her body but does not connect it to
other internal or external situations. It is helpful then for the therapist to
wonder aloud about how the patient's feeling states affect the experience
and perception of her body. Rachel provides an example. She repeatedly de-
spaired over her being "fat" (she wasn't), explaining, when questioned
about her history, that her bulimia began 3 years earlier when she gained 7
pounds and was revolted by this "fat." The therapist remembered that 3
years ago was exactly when the patient learned about a suicide in her family.
The therapist suggested that perhaps this concurrence wasn't just by coinci-
dence; "Would it make sense to you that you suddenly had acquired or been
'filled up' with traumatic knowledge that you wished to get rid of, and
maybe that's what the 7 pounds in part are about?" Her body had indeed
"filled out" more at that time as she moved from an adolescent to a more
womanly body, which accompanied a move from a certain kind of inno-
cence to, in this case, knowledge of a traumatic adult reality. Flowing from
this dynamic the therapist continually worked with Rachel on the possibility
that when she feels fat or sees herself as fat, her most painful felt experience,
she is probably experiencing pain about something else; something possibly
even connected to her body. But she is attaching the pain to body size, as if
her more mature body were the problem. Although it is a means for her to
have her pain, this painful experience of "fat" (the more mature body) denies the real pains of her life. This attempt at solution, of using displacement
to manage her pain, this cultural defense, simultaneously robs her of that
very pain and of a voice with which to express it. Furthermore, her bulimia
had created dire consequences for her actual body. For many patients such
as Rachel body size becomes identified with particular periods in their lives
that must be untangled in order to curtail the phobic or fetishized responses
to the body.

The therapist holds the connection between the body hate and the idea
that these feelings have meaning other than hate of the body. This endeavor
is difficult because the body hatred is so intense and incessant, but it is not
impossible because body hatred always contains a narrative. Weaving the
narrative of body hatred in its current defensive uses with its historical evo-

lution eventually diminishes its singular power, and it becomes part of a larger pattern. It can then be used as signal anxiety in the same way that a binge can be used as a helpful indicator of psychic difficulty, once it is no longer the sole way of eating.

Image versus Lived Experience of Fat and Thin States

Almost all women could make a strikingly similar list of the emotional meanings of "fat" and "thin." Not surprisingly, these meanings correlate to the cultural images projected from the diet, fashion, beauty industries. Often, fat represents feeling: out of control, gross, unlovable, repulsive, greedy, self-indulgent, dirty, worthless, imprisoned, incompetent, stupid, unemployable, offensive, asexual, damaged, unhealthy, unentitled. Conversely, thin represents feeling: competent, sexual, attractive, clean, desirable, in control, in charge, powerful, healthy, successful, accomplished, guiltless, transcendent, virtuous, free.

"Fat" and "thin" are not superficial categories about the body. They are used to describe personality traits for some and for others to define the very essence of who they are. However, these traits and this essence should not be assumed by the therapist. They must be made explicit between therapist and client so that the therapist learns what are the precise issues or states of being with which the client is struggling.

P: I want to be thin.

T: How come?

P: So I can date.

T: You can't date unless you are thinner?

P: No! Men always choose the thinnest woman. If you bring a man into a bar and ask him to choose, he will choose the thinnest woman there. I am sure of this.

T: So, for you very thin equals sexual attractiveness?

P: Of course!

T: How are you so sure that the man will always choose the thinnest woman?

P: It's funny you ask that because I was thinking the other day about Rob, who is drop-dead gorgeous, and how he chose to go out with Phyllis who is 20 pounds heavier than Janis, whom I thought for sure he would pick.

T: Some men actually like flesh, and Phyllis may have more in common with him.

P: Flesh, ugh! That's revolting!

T: Tell me about flesh. Why is it so revolting?

[The patient then had an association to her nephew who is the same age that she was when she was sexually molested.]

The therapist did not assume anything about the client's desire to be thin and invited her to describe her experience. When hearing more about her association to being thin, the therapist was able to raise questions about the patient's (stereotyped) formulation. This questioning allowed the patient to notice the complexity of the world around her and then to articulate this perception, making it more real and thus expanding her consciousness. The therapist takes the opportunity to probe further what turns out to be the "real" problem, the client's revulsion to flesh; this understandably creates a turning point.

Although the therapist first works at surface-level articulation of what thin or fat means, she must go beyond the manifest presentation. When the therapist explores further and hears about the actual lived experience of being fat and thin, both therapist and client discover complicated and contradictory images and feelings. Thus, fat, when seen without the hate and stigma, often represents several concepts: keeping a boundary, strength, substance, power, sexuality, protection, rightful anger, protest, rebellion, and safety. Treatment includes distinguishing—unlodging the lived experience from deeply held attitudes regarding the cultural ideal of fat and thin.

Betty discovered over time that her fat provided a feeling of much-needed protection. She felt less vulnerable when she walked in the street. She began to appreciate that the fat was serving as a defense (adaptive function) against fears of sexual revictimization. Her therapist asked, "Unless you could find another way to protect yourself, why would you want to get rid of your fat?" For the first time Betty was able to feel compassion for the way in which she responded to her own psychological distress. Understanding the adaptive function of the fat alleviates some of the self-hate and additionally challenges dichotomous thinking, feeling, and being (splitting).

Partly because women are never encouraged critically to explore their actual experience of being thin, they find it difficult to believe that being thin has not met their expectations. But when they review their histories in depth, many discover that when they were thin they felt vulnerable, weak, easily penetrated, trivialized, infantilized, objectified, hyper, ungrounded, frail, sick, incompetent, externally defined, emptied of desire, unentitled to need, or insecure. Lucy illustrates this point. When she was questioned about the times in her life when she was thinner, from ages 19 to 24, she recalled feeling vulnerable. She didn't feel she could take herself seriously. She felt small; neither her words nor what she had to contribute seemed "weighty" enough. She felt overwhelmed by sexual advances and did not feel entitled to her own sexual needs or to her say in these situations. This life experience, as associated with body size, remained a shaping force in her inability to maintain a stable weight. The acknowledgment of her own life experience and its relation to body size marked the commencement of deeper work around her intense wish to be thin.

Object Relations and Self States

Body and body image can be used to externalize and dramatize internal object relationships. In viewing both as object relationship the therapist has a progressive way to look at seemingly intractable and destructive behavior with the client. The hated "fat" can unconsciously represent the hated self; in Fairbairn's (1952) schema, the internal saboteur (anti-libidinal ego) is living in "the fat." The hated "fat" can represent the rejecting object, that is, the representation of the neglectful, hurtful aspects of the caretaker, or the tantalizing object, or an identification with the real caretaker. "Thin," too, functions in several different ways in the unconscious. It can represent merging with the tantalizing, exciting object and then function as a manic defense; the ascendence of the internal saboteur in its mastery over need and desire, as exemplified in anorexia; a defense against merger; or an escape from an intrusive or annihilating object. The following illustrates a few of these categories in which the client's relationship with her body functions as an object relationship.

FAT AS THE GOOD CARETAKER

After many efforts at trying to discover the meaning of Doris's large body size, the therapist suggested to her that they use guided fantasy. With Doris's permission the therapist asked her to imagine that her fat had a voice and to let her fat speak. At first Doris began to experience bodily sensations that were new to her and difficult to articulate. As the therapist encouraged her to free-associate, she conveyed through the voice of the "fat" that the fat felt like a warm pressure, a covering, like a coat providing protection, safety, perhaps even a home for Doris. Emerging from the guided fantasy, Doris associated to the loss of protection she experienced, at age 10, when her mother died. Her fat was the physical representation of her mother's loving care. Her father, well-meaning but emotionally depleted from the loss of his wife, was only able to care for Doris economically. Doris took over many of the household responsibilities, including the care of her younger brother. She did not have the time to focus on herself, nor did she know how to work through the loss of her mother. In burying her mother, she had buried her hurts, anger, resentments, wishes for separation, and dependency.

Over time she came to understand that her fat unconsciously represented her conflicted relationship with her mother. This understanding allowed her to acknowledge her need for mothering and to separate these feelings from the "fat." For the first time she expressed her desire to come to treatment twice weekly. She realized that although her fat preserved her mother, it had also been used to keep out others, including the therapist. As Doris mourned the loss of her mother, dependency needs were named and came alive in the transference. In experiencing these needs Doris felt anxious; yet, she also found pleasure in her new closeness with the therapist. The mourning, the feeling of being emotionally held, and the beginnings of allowing pleasure all permitted Doris to begin internally differentiating herself from her mother. The fruits of this process were manifested in her increased ability to eat when hungry and to make food choices in response to her own desires as opposed to those associated only with her mother. Her steps toward the autonomy that had threatened her mother could now be taken and these too were gingerly tested in the transference. Life was growing more lively. She was thrilled. Enjoying pleasure became the next theme of the treatment requiring further shifts in self organization. Anxiety continued to decrease over the years of treatment. She developed a more differentiated sense of self, took great pleasure in her growing autonomy, and she felt more genuinely connected to others.

Through her body Doris had found an unconscious, secret way to hold on to her mother. With the exposure of the secret, she began owning and integrating her feelings and no longer had to use her body or eating as the only way to manage, honor, and defend against the complexity of her relationship to her mother.

Considering the construction and constriction of female development (Eichenbaum & Orbach, 1983a), it is not uncommon that dependency needs and the defenses against them emerge in food, eating, and body/self integrity. Needs for both dependency and autonomy coexist in a complex way, and what is required is to work with them simultaneously.

FAT AS THE INTERNAL REJECTING AND TRAUMATIZING OBJECT

Julia's mother was neglectful, narcissistic, harsh, and critical to both her children, but particularly to Julia, the eldest girl. In this behavior Julia's mother repeated her own experience from her family of origin. Julia's body was the target of relentless criticism and denigration as far back as Julia could remember. Diets began by the age of 7. She was to eat less and have less while the rest of the family ate more and had more. Her mother constantly scrutinized her attire and would comment without mercy on her hair style, clothing, height, weight, and so on. By the second year of treatment, Julia came to feel that her fat represented her mother. Her fat felt like an unbearable weight, oppressive, more than she could handle. She declared that she felt she was carrying around her mother in her fat and that she could not get rid of her. Through her relation to her fat, she kept her mother always present, ready, and able to make her life miserable. To some extent this insight helped to create a context in which to do further work, but it did not diminish her hatred of her fat, that is, her tie to the internalized rejecting object. These insights, however, were a part of Julia's defensive structure, because they served to keep her emotions split off, deposited into her fat. This defense had to be worked with gently so as not to repeat the critical aspect of her mother and further wound Julia narcissistically. The same careful processing held true of her anger, which also functioned as a defense.

For years most sessions began with the same opening phrase, "I need to lose weight, and I know how to do so, I have to exercise, but I don't do it." Most of the time, the therapist's attempts to work with this repetitive opening proved fruitless, at least so far as Julia's body image was concerned. However, Julia did begin to develop more regard for herself, for her capacities and abilities in other areas of her life. And over time the therapist came to realize that the rejecting and traumatizing object was not only in the fat but was also the author of these opening phrases as they couched intense self-hatred. In the countertransference the therapist felt that her power was being annihilated. Understanding this helped better to comprehend just how annihilated Julia had felt. The experience of annihilation was carefully, gently, and at times humorously processed in the transference/countertransferrence. The annihilating effects of the real mother, lived through in the therapy relationship, finally loosened the grip of the internal, "bad" mother. Julia could not possibly let go of the weight (her goal) until she mourned the illusion of an idealized mother with whom she identified her "thin" self. Although she lost weight, only 25 pounds over an 8-year period, which was much less than what she had hoped for, she became more accepting of her size and was pleased with new ways of dressing. Although her appearance changed only moderately, she greatly appreciated that her quality of life had dramatically improved. She began to feel that her size no longer determined her self-worth. She was still a large woman, she said, but so much happier. She felt more accepting of her husband and her children because she was no longer such an angry person. In this last stage of her treatment she is working on the tantalizing nature of her relationship to her father. She is still grieving the mother she never had, is accepting that her real mother will never give her what she wants, and she is freeing herself from feeling that she caused the harshness and neglect of the environment in which she grew up.

Despite many years of treatment, Harriet, a social worker in her fifties, had struggled as far back as she could remember with body hatred. Looking in the mirror, going to the beach, monthly bloating at the time of her period were times of great anxiety when she attacked herself viciously. Having resolved many issues during the course of former treatments, which enabled a greater sense of freedom and enhanced self-esteem, there remained this self-denigration about her body size. In her transferential experience she and her current therapist linked her occasional times of fear of her therapist with early experiences with her father when he rejected her and was verbally abusive. Through the use of the "moral defense" (Fairbairn, 1952), she blamed herself rather than her father for her bad feelings. She reenacted this with her therapist. She was unable to speculate about what went on between them and processed complicated interactions as due to her "neurosis," never to anything that the therapist did or said.

Harriet recognized that, in fact, her father was not able to give very much emotionally to his children because of his own early years of deprivation. Harriet's father projected his own self-hatred onto her. This was painful and hard for her to truly comprehend. She put the unbearable experience of feeling hated by her father into her fat in order to get relief: Instead of the painful acknowledgment of her father's hatred, Harriet would say she hated her body. Once this defense was understood, Harriet confronted the devastating legacy of her childhood and lived through periods of excruciating pain and sadness. Her conflicts about aging, fueled by cultural ageism, paralleled and converged with this hatred from her father. Her conflicts about aging were a comment on both the loss of years lived unfulfilled as well as real concerns about growing old in a youth-obsessed culture.

THIN AS A BARRIER TO THE REJECTING, ANNIHILATING OBJECT

Many women, some of whom are anorexics or bulimics who restrict, describe getting thinner as a way to control or keep out the annihilating intrusive object both in its real and internal fantasized forms. These patients say that when they get smaller and smaller there is literally less and less room for that other to exist within. It is as if their internal traumatizing object takes up so much psychic space that on a fantasy level they feel as if they are actually being taken over and controlled by someone inside their body. Because care from others has been experienced as self-serving and exploitative, they counter by suspending dependency and bodily needs to be certain no further violations will occur. The body becomes the site for the struggle to exist on one's own terms, even if that existence is minimal. The primitive defenses of splitting, denial, externalization, and projection must be repeatedly confronted and analyzed in the context of an especially personal and nonintrusive therapeutic relationship.

Orbach (1994) extends theoretically the discussion of the body as object relation. She uses Winnicott's notion of true and false self to argue that just as the false self in the context of unsatisfactory early object relationships comes into existence to protect the true self from insult, injury, and abandonment, so too a "false body" sense and reality develop to protect an un-emerged "true body." The false body, like the false self, is compliant and malleable, the container of societal and parental projections. It allows the true body to stay on hold waiting for a better environment in which to grow. This caretaker "false" body will only dissolve in importance when a new and different kind of relationship of care and nurture is present. This raises the question whether it is valuable to postulate a "true body" given all the social impingements and mandates about the body and body ideal in any culture. While the following does not do justice to such a philosophical question, eating when hungry, stopping when full, and listening to all internal bodily cues are at least guides to establishing the possibility of a "true body" self rooted in both physiology and psychology.

BODY SIZE AS CONTAINER OF MEMORY

Body size can hold specific memories from a particular period in a person's life. The work with Faith exemplifies how a therapist made use of this concept. Faith had successfully worked on a history of compulsive eating in adolescence in an anti-deprivation, psychoanalytically oriented treatment in her twenties. At age 35 she reentered treatment to work on a particular issue at the beginning of her fifth month of pregnancy. Her body had reached the size it had been during her teenage years. As she described it, her body felt familiarly painful, burdensome, confusing: "Is this me? Is it not me? What's happening to me? My body feels out of control." Faith saw her body as "too much, too big again, fat," even though she knew she was not eating compulsively. In addition, she was generally more anxious, somewhat depressed, and struggling with self-esteem issues, none of which had caused distress for years. As she free-associated she heard herself saying that her pregnant body was now at the same size her body had been during her adolescence, a difficult time of life. Disturbing memories came back as a result of being at this body size. She and her therapist acknowledged that although these issues had been talked about and previously worked through, her experience of her pregnant body was recapitulating the earlier experience. Between the fourth and sixth month of pregnancy when a woman's body is larger from pregnancy, she could appear to be gaining weight because of the pregnancy or just getting larger. The therapist reassured Faith that she was not out of control as she had been when younger. The therapist validated pregnancy as a time of surrender, which is not the same as being out of control. Faith was excited and pleased to be pregnant and quickly sorted through the historical determinants of her body image problem. Once her body no longer symbolized adolescence, she was freed up in her mental elaboration to accept her body as the container for a new life.

Margo, a 22-year-old secretarial student, entered a group to work on her compulsive eating problem and her intense hatred of her body, particularly her thighs. She began her time in each group session with her negative preoccupation about her thighs. Through calm and careful exploration on the part of the group therapist about her focus on thighs, the meaning of weight in this area, and the history of this preoccupation, it emerged that there had been an early experience of vaginal sexual abuse. The critical need for heavy thighs was adaptive in protecting her violated self and body. The hatred of such a specific body part represented the trauma of her early abusive experience and her fear of losing the fat triggered a terrible, horrifying vulnerability. Margo's preoccupation was emblematic of a hypervigilance following the abuse (see chapters 10 and 11).

Memories can be stored in a variety of bodily sensations and states. It is common among women clients more generally to report with monthly regularity feeling "miserable, bloated, fat, out of control" about their bodies just before menstruation. After repeatedly hearing monthly reports, asking a woman where she is in her cycle helps to make the connection between bodily sensations and the biological event. Other women know they are about to menstruate, but they still feel simply "fat." Over time Cathy understood that the reason her premenstrual bloated feeling did not just have to do with water retention was that her father teased her when she got her period, leaving her humiliated and feeling ugly. The therapist may find it useful to explore memories regarding the onset of menarche and how the family responded to it. Was it discussed, welcomed, denied, ignored, or met with anxiety? These are important discussions around femininity, sexuality, and the integration of bodily processes. Fertility and menopausal concerns and issues may also need attention, specifically in relation to self- and body-image.

THE BODY AS CONTAINER OF NEEDS AND AFFECTS

Women defend against their own needs and feelings in numerous ways. When needs are presented in an overwhelming, hysterical, chaotic, and urgent manner, they are often defenses against direct expression of an underlying true self need because one feels unentitled, fears exposure, rejection, and abandonment. Another primary defense is to distance, disavow, or displace feelings and needs on to the body. The following experience with a patient demonstrates how emotional needs for connection and recognition as well as intolerable affects were converted into an attempt at body transformation.

During the third year of a twice-a-week treatment, Annie came into her session and proudly announced, "Yesterday I started a 5-day fast. I'm going to clean out all the toxins in my body and get my health back on the right track." Sensing that there was a lot going on that Annie was not fully aware of, the therapist asked her to say more about why her decision to fast seemed to make her so happy. Annie revealed that she beamed a constant message to herself when fasting: "I'm going to feel successful and really like myself. I'm going to get strong, healthy, and lose weight."

The therapist pointed out that while this message lasted, it certainly must have felt like a tremendous relief from the more usual judgmental, attacking messages that made her feel weak and bad about herself. At first Annie looked quizzical, then got teary, and agreed with the therapist's formulation. The therapist asked her to stay with the feeling of the tears. Annie said, "I'm so sick of feeling bad." The therapist silently thought about why she might currently need this manic state; why would she need this protective state of instantaneous but false good feelings that a fast can elicit? The therapist had seen a more vital Annie lately and thus asked her what had happened since the last session. She responded, "Not much" and quickly glossed over that she was going to spend the weekend with an old boyfriend, J, who recently reappeared on the scene. The therapist asked her about J and about the choice to go away with him for the weekend. Annie said that they were just friends now, but then went on to reminisce about their former intimate relationship, which had been a disaster. He was a very critical, judgmental, dogmatic, and sexist person who imposed his values and views on her. He had strong opinions on how she and others should be thinking and living, which included correct ways to eat and the correct body size to be. He was preoccupied with his own health, what he ate, and his belief that no one could be "too thin." Annie spent much energy in their relationship trying to gain his approval and acceptance and complained that she was confused about what she thought and wanted for herself. During that time, sneaking food was a common nightly occurrence. As might be expected, this relationship mirrored experiences with her parents, particularly her father, who had also been quite judgmental and domineering.

In their relationship J was sexually attentive, and Annie loved the way he touched her body; here she felt accepted and appreciated, which possibly made up for everything else. Currently having no other relationship and feeling quite lonely, Annie was tempted to be with J. She was lured by the hope that maybe things would go better this time. With a growing sense of awareness and upset, Annie said, "It sounds like I'm settling for crumbs again" and wept for a long time.

When Annie finished crying, the therapist interpreted her desire to fast as a wish to wipe out part of herself, to make a "clean slate" of all that was potentially conflictual within the relationship. She linked her fasting self with a state of not having needs—not even needing "crumbs." The fast was the vehicle to bind and gag the "bad" needs/self and to allow for the fantasized idealized "good" Annie to emerge. She feared that if she exposed who she truly was, a person with needs and vulnerabilities, she would be subjected to insult and rejection. Historically with J and others she was willing psychically to submerge and split off much of who she was in order to become more acceptable, to try and secure love.

The split between good self/bad self, good body/bad body, and food/no food was an attempt to protect her true self from threat, insult, and abandonment. By seeing what was problematic in the relationship as her problem, her shortcomings, and her neediness, she perceived that her needs, her body caused trouble. In this way she preserved the needed object and attempted to have control over deprivation and neglect. If she could only change enough to be that more likable self, then she could hold on to the hope of being valued and loved. The distortion in the relationship was experienced in her distorted perception of her self and body.

Much of Annie's preoccupation with good and bad foods and her revulsion and terror of fat were attempts to contain her felt sense of badness and her intolerable feelings that she would be exposed. She controlled her affective self states and painful identity issues by how and what she ate and through her body image. When she felt needy, messy, and chaotic, as well as conflicted and disappointed, she ate. The eating was, on the one hand, a rebellion against restraint and deprivation. On the other hand, it was her true self needs breaking out. But, fearing abandonment and rejection by meeting her needs this way, the initial comfort from the food quickly turned into a brutal internal attack. She now treated her own needs with the same neglect and harshness that she had experienced in her earliest relationships.

Like so many women, Annie feared and hated her "fat" because "fat" itself was unconsciously experienced as the container of her intolerable feelings. She felt trapped in her fat just as she had been trapped in the pain of living as a hated child. Even though she is not fat, she clung to the idea of being fat because fat is the mental construct symbolizing that change is difficult, if not impossible. In Annie's mind her "fat" exposed her bad feelings and her powerlessness, and it was these feelings deposited into her "fat" that were the real cause of her shame and humiliation. Once Annie and her therapist were able to identify all the feelings and needs that were expressed through her body, then Annie was able to make different kinds of choices. She stopped fasting, and she did not spend the weekend with J. Of course, these issues and psychic maneuvers were worked on for many years.

Women, raised to deny their own needs and feelings in deference to others and as a way to maintain attachments, often deny their bodily needs or delay meeting them. Hunger, thirst, need for elimination, sexual urges, body temperature, fatigue, aches, physical and emotional sensations of all kinds are bodily events that signify need. Therapists must pay attention to all these bodily needs and functions as well as working through the defenses employed to deny, delay, repress, or dissociate from these needs. It is not uncommon to discover that many women patients do not urinate when they have to, rest when they are tired, or take their sweater along on a chilly day, especially if this act would require exposing and asserting their need in an interpersonal situation. Listening to these symbolic communications about body-self is an entrée to otherwise inaccessible material and adds a richness to treatment.

THE BODY AS EXPRESSION OF DEVELOPMENTAL ISSUES

Eating disorders have been located in various different developmental stages: Wilson, the oral stage; Chasseguet-Smirgel, the anal stage; Wooley, Crisp, Strober, Palazolli, adolescent identity crisis; Sugarman and Kurash, practicing subphase; Sands, self-object experience; McDougall, preverbal. It is important not to limit an analysis to any one phase because clients present multiple and overlapping developmental issues and needs. Symptoms can abate or emerge as new developmental issues are confronted in treatment.

The developmental issues of autonomy and differentiation are illustrated in the anorexic behavior of a patient, Nell. Nell's family was somewhat paranoid and depressed. "Bad luck" was how her parents explained their misfortunes and their lower status. Everybody else had the "good things" from life, but they were deprived. People who "had" were to be feared, envied, and held in contempt. Professionals were denigrated as "smart alecks" and "too filled up with themselves." Nell's parents saw their economic and social status as unchangeable and out of their control. Although they projected all their hopes and fantasies of a different life on Nell, they also communicated another contradictory message to her. She was supposed to achieve, marry a doctor to redress the injustices of her parents' lives, but at the same time she was not to rise above them, a common working-class conundrum (Sennett & Cobb, 1973). Throughout Nell's life her parents experienced her striving for autonomy as abandonment and betrayal, or they were dismissive of this need. Nell grew used to hearing, "Who do you think you are, Miss Know-it-all?" Her parents' anxieties and fears controlled her and eventually interfered with her meeting developmentally appropriate challenges.

The family made connection, felt vitalized, and was able to "have" only through eating together and sharing their anguish about being overweight. Going out to eat on Saturday and Sunday and dieting on Monday was the way the family soothed, bolstered, denied, and made up for emotional deprivation. But for Nell the family dog was a very private and special source of comfort and she dates her depression as commencing when her pet died during her adolescence. At that time she tried to use food to replace the beloved animal and began eating compulsively to attend to her grief and growing anxiety. She soon gained weight that she maintained through college. Following graduation from college, she was back home, feeling lonely and lacking in direction. Despairing over her life, she began to exercise rigorously and put efforts into restraining her food intake to try and provide direction for herself and differentiate from the family. She entered treatment, first group and then individual, but seemed unaware that she was in the beginning stages of starvation.

Her anorexic behavior was an attempt to take control over how stuck she felt and to do something positive to differentiate from the family. Differentiation was so difficult because boundaries were seen as abandonment or exclusion. In Nell's family locked doors were forbidden, personal drawers opened, desires for privacy made fun of, and, if frightened, Nell could easily end up sleeping through the night in her parents' bed. In an effort to stay close enough not to be a threat, Nell said her body did not feel like her own. Her body boundaries often felt fuzzy and malleable depending on her thoughts and interactions. Her anorexia was a concrete manifestation of her profound need for self-definition. It also served as a defense against all the conflictual and painful feelings that belonged to her desires for differentiation and autonomy. Psychically she was unable to accomplish either because of her enmeshment with her family.

Carla exemplifies a woman trying to negotiate oedipal conflicts by preoccupation with her body. Over years in treatment, a picture of family life was drawn. Carla's family reflected the typical gender arrangements reminiscent of the 1950s. The mother was denigrated, her only power being over the children and household management. The father was hard-working, entrepreneurial, wielding power in the marketplace and at home. He showered his daughter with his time and attention but had little contact with his wife. This situation was overstimulating for Carla and shaped her fantasy life regarding love and romance. She reenacted her relationship with her father by seeking powerful men whom she desperately tried to please. They overwhelmed her and made her feel insufficient and inadequate, which also expressed her identification with her mother. These relationships inevitably were short term and ended in failure and despair. These failures exacerbated an already intense preoccupation with her appearance, particularly her clothing and stylish image, and led to an almost phobic response to going outside.

Although Carla's psychic energy focused on getting a man, her fears and avoidance of women stayed in the shadow. Interpretations around her fears of competing with her mother, although helpful, were not sufficient. In treatment a year later, she was able to let awareness of her father's extramarital affairs surface. The question for Carla was not only whether her body could be better than her mother's, but, more important, whether she could compete with "the other woman." Although she charmed her father, she was not woman enough to keep him home. Painful affect accompanied this insight. Her next libidinal focus was on her deeper attachment to her female therapist. As she worked on dependency issues in relationship to her therapist, she began to feel closer to her mother. However, both patient and therapist noted that with the closeness to women she did not allow herself any contact with men. After this phase, she began reporting dreams of seeing her therapist and her medical doctor cooperating in her care. As a result of having worked on oedipal rivalry she came to believe she could be close to a man and a woman at the same time. As she became secure in this way, she started to experience her intense involvement with clothing as oppressive and enslaving; this represented a developmental achievement. She was in the process of relinquishing a narcissistic defense, allowing more authentic involvement with herself and the world. Although she cared about how she looked, the compulsive preoccupation with clothing was replaced by feeling more alive inside and more secure about what she wanted.

SEXUAL OBJECTIFICATION AND SEXUAL SUBJECTIVITY

Throughout history the sexual objectification of women and of the female form has denied women full selfhood because they are rendered objects, not subjects. To be a subject who is also an object, in the sense of being desirable to and for the other, is to feel an aspect of one's power and the potency and pleasure of one's sexuality. However, when being an object of desire is the primary or exclusive experience, it distorts and maims a woman's relationship to her own sexuality. She becomes alienated from her own desirous strivings. To desire, to want the other, to feel one's power in activity—grabbing, having, lusting, wanting—is the necessary accompaniment to a satisfying sexual experience. Sexual objectification bifurcates the wish to be wanted and desired from wanting and desiring. This contributes to a fantasy life that is shaped around polarities, with women assuming the first side of each common split: object-subject, female-male, passive-active, submission-domination, thin-fat. In all these splits, duality exists where fluidity ought to be (Harris, 1991a). Generally, men are more entitled and thus more able to integrate both their desire and their wish to be desired. Women, barred from a freer relationship to their needs, aggression, and agency, have difficulty in experiencing their own desire as well as achieving full sexual satisfaction when they do want and engage in sexual activity.

The women's movement of the 1960s and 1970s challenged the sexual double standard where men attained manhood through sexual activity and women were left to worry about their reputations. Women's self worth was predicated on self-restraint although they still had to be the object of others' sexual desires. Feminists questioned the centrality of appearance and fought against the injurious role of being a sex object. They looked at language, dress code, social behaviors, economic arrangements, cultural mores, and sexual practices such as the "myth of the vaginal orgasm," which reflected and buttressed the objectification and trivialization of women. Women were encouraged to liberate their desires and to be more sexually active by claiming their own sexual pleasure within the context of a relationship of equality. Sexual expression including sexual preference was an area in which women came to feel more entitled to explore and expand.

But the dominant culture has interpreted and co-opted the demand of the women's movement for sexual equality. Removed from women's control once again, female sexuality has been used as a commodity in mass culture and advertising. Thus, at younger and younger ages women are pressured to be sexual and appear sexy. The rise of eating problems not only reflects compliance with cultural norms, but it is also a rebellion and defense against sexual objectification and the contemporary mandate to be sexually active (Young-Bruehl, 1993). As Rachel's story makes clear, it is important to help to release young women from this new imperative in order to restore greater agency to them and away from their eating problems. It is also important to analyze the impact of sexual objectification on women's desire as the follow-ing stories of Erica, Eve, Susie, and Marge illustrate. Even while many young women with eating problems seek the perfect sexual body, they are uncon-sciously retreating from the world of dating and sex. Although these young women do actually achieve looking "sexy" and some can even allow them-selves the pleasure of the play, many reveal a very different sexual story. They are alienated from their desire, sex is foreign and frightening, authentic sexual experience is beyond their reach.

As previously described, Rachel's coming of age included confronting a suicide in her family, the alcoholism of both parents, and her own sexual molestation by a non–family member when she was very young. After learn-ing about all this she became bulimic. She entered college, took courses, made good friends, and was sought after by men, even as her bulimic behav-ior escalated. As a sophomore after serious physical side effects necessitated hospitalization, she entered treatment. When the most serious aspects of her bulimia abated, she began talking about her relationships with men. Men were drawn to Rachel, but she was never interested in the ones interested in her. When she did go out, she felt obligated to have sexual intercourse. She bravely admitted to her therapist that she did not like sex and did not under-stand what the fuss was about, yet she did not know what she could do about it. In those sessions she seemed to be searching for something that would free her from what she perceived as sexual obligation without any idea of what that might be. She was visibly relieved when her therapist gave her permission to handle the dating process differently. She did not have to be sexually active until she was ready. She could kiss because she enjoyed that and could remain at that level of intimacy until she desired more. Over time they would come to understand the impact of Rachel's experiences that resided in her body and affected her sexual responsiveness.

Erica is an example of a woman whose self-objectification interferes with her own desire. Erica felt an intense hatred for her larger body, which could fluctuate 20 to 30 pounds above what she considered her ideal weight. Clothing, attractiveness, and presentation to the world were important values in her family of origin as both parents were involved with the clothing industry.

Erica spent, as she described, a lifetime trying to broaden the values so dominant both in her family and in the larger culture in the 1950s. She became a beatnik interested in poetry and literature, and began developing a more radical critique of society. Coming out as a lesbian at nineteen was a joyful and relieving experience personally, though it posed arduous challenges in terms of dealing with her family and the larger world. She became a lawyer, had friends, community, and eventually a committed relationship that was loving and satisfying on all levels.

Although she sought treatment for various characterological issues, her agony over her "extra" twenty pounds was for a long time kept private and trivialized by her. She could not acknowledge that it was important enough to affect her self worth. She remained unaware of the meaning of her fat or that the compulsive eating and weight gains were preceded by depression and anxiety. She only knew that she felt desexualized. She could not and would not experience herself as a sexual being during these periods of weight gain. When she could not view herself as conforming to the cultural ideal, as an object of desire, she lost her own desire as a subject. This loss of desire occurred despite her critique of patriarchy, the devotion, desire, and lust of her partner regardless of her size, and her expanded view of femininity in every realm but this one regarding a body ideal.

In treatment she began understanding the connection between her lessened interest in sex and her weight, and the import of her critical eye. Erica appeared comfortable in taking difficult and courageous stands, and on the conscious level, she was reasonably secure with her life choices (career, sexual orientation, politics, etc.). However, there were historic issues and early identifications with critical, imperious, and abandoning parental images that remained unconscious and caused cyclical anxiety and depression. Her eating symptoms were now linked to these emotional states and understood as a withdrawal of energy from external relationships to preoccupation with her inner world in an attempt to bind and manage her threatening anxiety and depression. There was an unconscious displacement onto food and the body to address issues regarding authority, conformity, and difference.

Although Erica seemed comfortable in all her independent stands away from the traditions in the family and, in part, truly was so, she had psychically left no room for anxiety or grief at separating from all that she had known. Her eating provided a controlled, small arena in her life to contain and express her anxiety. Her desire to conform, to be like everyone else, and to be accepted found an outlet in an obsessive concern with having the right body and losing the twenty pounds. Her weight losses were her attempts to yank herself back on track and back in life. This was a problematic solution for Erica as dieting also represented her submission and surrender to external authority. In order to consolidate her positive choices, she needed to mourn the loss engendered when one is different.

Eve is an example of a woman whose obsessive focus on and objectification of her body both inhibited her sexual desire while giving her an entrée into the sexual realm. At 30 years old, she had suffered with bulimia since her late teens. Body size, appearance, clothing, and image were a major parental preoccupation and were thrust heavily on her as the only child. Her family's economic privilege afforded easy access to fat farms, spas, and surgical procedures. Eve was the ugly duckling turned swan (she had had surgery to correct a congenital deformity). But she was extremely insecure and vulnerable in her interactions, especially with men. Objectification of her beauty and her body became a significant relational tool that temporarily masked her insecurity.

Eve had begun to appreciate her beauty during the course of treatment; potential partners flocked about and she had a series of relationships that came to follow a predictable pattern. She was active in her desire to sexually please her partner. Her sexuality, however, was compromised in that she could not really experience her own physical pleasures or desires. When routinely she faked orgasms, the "ugly duckling" feelings about her body returned. Under the scrutiny of male eyes, her new acceptance of herself was overpowered by feeling fraudulent.

The therapy relationship provided Eve with a place to reveal the details of her negative body image and fabricated sexual responses, and her disclosure alleviated some of her anxiety and depression. This alleviation then allowed for a startling recognition of her extreme self-denial and objectification regarding her own pleasures, sexual and otherwise. Eve had learned to inhibit and deny her feelings, thoughts, and reactions, which were experienced as too overwhelming and too burdensome in her family. Her parents' self-absorption left her unseen and neglected; she became withdrawn and isolated, and her bulimia began as an attempt to manage her extreme loneliness and confusion. The slow process of learning that whatever came from within her, including her desire (for food or whatever), would not harm her or anyone else and, in fact, was an aspect of her strength and appeal, proved immensely liberating. She made a psychic move from being a desired object seeking pleasure through other's desires to being a desiring subject in her own right.

Another patient, Susie, is a 23-year-old woman who was bulimarexic for many years. She is beautiful, thin, and shapely, looks sexy, and dresses with style. Yet, she is never free of worry about her appearance, especially during sexual encounters. If she rolls to the side, will her "flab" be revealed? Will her partner see the real her and be repelled? These worries interfere with her idealized, distorted, and fetishized view of love as it exists in her fantasies. Her bulimarexia is a defense against her problematic relationship to her desire and sexuality.

Susie's sexual fantasy life contained a theme that is a fairly common one for heterosexual women. She, the woman, is so beautiful and desirable that the man cannot help but be consumed with desire for her, sweeping her off her feet, passionately enveloping her. Her knees get weak, she is breathless, her desire is ignited. Sex is uncomplicated, completely satisfying, and sanitized. Suzie has actually reproduced in reality the situation in her fantasy, but she cannot sustain the intimate or sexual contact for any length of time.

Currently she is in a relationship that she wants to make permanent, but she rarely wants to make love. She fears this reluctance reveals that Gene isn't the "right one." Gene does not always want to ravage her. He wants to feel wanted, too. Their relationship is complicated—his imperfections in conjunction with his availability do not measure up to her fantasy.

Exploration of her fantasy life reveals that dynamics are the opposite of what they appear to be. Rather than seeing the man as the powerful one who can go after what he wants, in Susie's eyes, her partner's desiring her in an unbridled and uncontrolled way means she is totally in control. He desires, she is the cause of that desire, and therefore she feels powerful and in charge. However, to feel her own powerful desire and her own sexuality was too revealing, too out of control, and made her feel vulnerable to the other person. During treatment Susie came to realize that her need to control her body so rigorously, to objectify and reify it, and her desire functioned as a defense against profound vulnerability.

For some women confusion may exist between feeling attractive and being sexually objectified, as Marge's story illustrates. Marge, 40 years old, had always been overweight. She never felt attractive, and because of her body size she was treated poorly, teased, and generally not chosen or made to feel special in the sexual arena. Very accomplished in her work, she was loathe to talk about her desire for recognition on the physical, sexual level. She felt ashamed about what she would call her "unfeminist stance," saying, "I can't believe I'm sitting here wanting to be a sexual object." During the course of treatment, she grieved the fact that she had never had the experience of being whistled at, lusted after. She wished she could be like her friends who had at least been whistled at; who, although hating these street experiences, had at least had the chance to reject them. She wanted to have that experience herself, and this remained a secret wish. The therapist's gender empathic remarks about Marge's (and other women's) experiences allowed the revelation of this secret. It felt very shameful to reveal this wish to her therapist whom she saw as both competent and attractive. Her admiration and envy of her therapist made her "secret wish" only more humiliating to her.

Revealing her shame and envy ushered in a long, stormy period between Marge and her therapist. The experience of envy toward other women, which previously had been defended against, was now emerging with great intensity in the transference. Marge felt suspicious: She felt her therapist was gloating and victorious in the face of her envy. She thought all women secretly made comparisons and competed with each other to be the most admired. This thought was yet another admission, revealing that it was equally important to her that women admire her. "Don't tell me that women aren't sizing each other up all the time," Marge taunted, hiding her desperate plea to be noticed. When taken seriously, Marge's shameful wish to be whistled at powerfully shaped the treatment over the next few years.

Taking a stand against the objectification of women is complicated. When a person takes the courageous stand of accepting a large body size and gives up trying to get smaller, she is often faced with prejudicial treatment and attitudes. She may be vulnerable to loss of self-esteem and depression if she is not in a consistently supportive environment that challenges the cultural ideal. There are women who consciously create this environment for themselves and feel comfortable with their choice. In this case desire is linked to a different fantasy about female sexuality and female role options from those mainstream culture dictates.

As women age, they also differ from the youth-oriented mass culture ideal of desirability. The ageism of the culture means that many older women feel invisible and suffer a loss of self-esteem in response to being viewed as less desirable. Some older women, however, finally feel permission to get out of the sexual marketplace and struggle to find their rightful place in society with appearance now less of a priority. That desire is linked to youth-oriented fantasies has to be challenged, and alternative views offered of older women as sexually desired, desirable, and desiring.

THE SCALE AS REJECTING OBJECT

Each day the scale determines how thousands of women feel about themselves and how they will manage their food for the day. The scale is a most powerful instrument in today's society and many women have an intense relationship to it. "I lost a pound. I've been good. I'm OK. Today is going to be a good day"; "I didn't lose even one pound. What's wrong with me? I'd better skip lunch." Each day begins with this morning ritual (which may be repeated throughout the day) of weighing and evaluating one's weight and one's worth.

The use of the scale easily becomes addictive, even for people without an eating problem. For example, one teenager attentive to her appearance but not troubled with food or body issues, had thought her mother a little strange for not having a scale in their home. When visiting her grandparents who had one, she noticed how easy it was to get hooked on weighing herself. She said she now understood why her parents didn't have a scale. Life was much freer without it. For this reason either throwing away the scale or putting it out of sight is part of the recommendation of our approach.

Some women are only too relieved to put the scale in the back of their closets or to throw it out, but others cannot imagine life without their daily evaluator. It takes exploration to discover the meaning of the scale for each woman and how it is used to externalize different internal object situations.

Paula, an anorexic woman who wanted to eat more but could not, understood what a profound hold the scale had on her. She knew that to increase her food intake she would have to stop the morning ritual of weighing herself because even a half pound weight increase stopped her progress. In the beginning this change seemed impossible; it represented a level of separation that was too threatening. Paula was rigidly controlled and physically beaten as a child. Exploration revealed that the scale was "a way to pay homage to my parents," that is, to the power they had over her. When Paula was asked to give the scale a voice, its message was clear: "Don't deviate! Stay in your place! If you gain, you'll be sorry! You'll be anxious. You don't know what you're doing!"

Paula was creative in her attempts to alter what felt like the unalterable. She thought she should first change her morning regime; that is, continue to weigh herself but to vary the order. She also thought of doing something pleasant, such as listening to music, so as to begin to associate change with pleasure rather than disaster. Then one day she did not weigh herself, and the anxiety was not as overwhelming as anticipated, nor did there seem to be any retribution. Eventually, she was able to weigh herself every second or third day, which was a victory that she could appreciate. In this experience she was able to defend herself and her right to live freer of her internal assaults and external controls.

Rachel was terribly upset that she had gained 2 pounds. She was particularly upset because she had been eating so well (not compulsively) and had expected to lose or at least remain the same. The therapist commented on the discrepancy between Rachel's own feelings of satisfaction and those determined by the scale. Rachel responded that the scale was scary—and powerful. "Like anything or anybody you can think of?" queried the therapist. The scale reminded Rachel of her mother when her mother yelled at her. Her mother yelled rarely, and as Rachel adored her mother, these bad times felt as if her world were shattering. Internally, she felt devastated. Seeing the scale register 2 pounds higher felt the same as having her mother yell at her. This was an unexpected insight that allowed for a richer discussion of her relationship to her mother and then to her father. By not making concrete suggestions about the scale at this particular time, the therapist encouraged her client's own curiosity and observing ego about her idiosyncratic relationship to the scale.

Jane and Lisa who had given up the diet so readily and eagerly were as relieved to put an end to their using the scale. In their groups, a discussion of the scale and the suggestion that they did not have to use one were all they needed to end "the tyranny of the bad numbers." Jane felt freed; she joked that "a weight had been lifted from beneath her." Lisa felt similarly but was concerned about gaining weight and not even knowing it, especially because she knew she had difficulties in stopping eating when satiated. Getting rid of the scale, however, is not an exercise in denying reality. The therapist assured Lisa and the others in the group that there are other less obsessive ways to keep track of one's size. How clothes fit is one very helpful way. Difficulty buttoning one's waistband means weight gain and may be a signal that a client has been eating past physical hunger and satiety. Sometimes that realization simply means accepting one has gotten larger and the next clothing size is needed. Paying closer attention to hunger and satiety will provide a guide. Teaching clients how to use the mirror in an observational rather than judgmental manner is the other means to accurately perceive changes in body size. In addition, to put away the scale does not mean one can never weigh oneself. When the scale is no longer such a severe internal and external evaluator, weighing oneself occasionally can be nonproblematic and provide information.

THE MIRROR: THE TRANSFORMING OBJECT

The mirror, in addition to the scale, is what women use to harshly assess body size and body image. Without therapeutic intervention the mirror reflects a fragmented, imperfect, and inadequate image because the reflection is always judged against a cultural ideal. Learning to look, see, and be seen with minimal parental, peer, and societal injunctions is to learn to see from within. To see one's body self more objectively and descriptively a client must work through and accept one's limitations and boundaries, mourn the loss of the illusory body, and analyze the internalized negative familial contributions.

To look in the mirror without judgment or negative anticipation can be a useful suggestion at particular times in some treatments. Suggestions to view the total body, not just from the neck up, to see oneself nude or with covering, to look at oneself head on versus sideways or from the back, to focus on form, texture, and shape are useful in expanding ways of seeing. For those clients who avoid the mirror at all costs, it can be useful to suggest that the client, alone or with help, view herself for just a few seconds at a time so that she can identify what is so frightening or upsetting. For clients who are obsessively preoccupied with mirror gazing, it can be useful to learn to experience the body through other sensory modalities. Discussion of the visual and kinesthetic aspects of the experience can be helpful. (See Orbach 1978, 1982; and Hutchinson, 1985 for fuller discussion.)

When the Body Changes

Changes in body size may occur as the symbolic landscape of the psyche and psyche/soma shifts. Change in body size can be a productive outgrowth of or a defensive reaction to therapeutic work. The change can be either the result of an intentional, focused, articulated goal, or it can be an unconscious by-product of treatment. All responses eventually require acknowledgment and exploration.

To effect lasting psychological well-being about the body, two goals guide the treatment. One is body acceptance, a nonhating relationship to the body that includes a realistic perception of the body no matter what the size. The second is that eating becomes organized around internal cues that then determine body size.

For example, for the person whose bingeing is beginning to decrease or for the person who has been overly restrictive and is now eating when hungry, the analyst can utilize psychoeducational information to prepare the patient for change in body size. Psychoeducational preparation paves the way to explore fears, fantasies, and desires regarding weight change through the following kinds of questions: "If you continue not to bypass your hunger, that is, if you keep eating when you are hungry as you have been for the last couple of weeks, what would it mean to you to gain a pound?" "Since you feel ready to lose weight, what would it be like to spend this week imagining you weighed 4 pounds less?"

As people lose weight, they need to explore, analyze, integrate, and maintain the weight loss and the psychological impact before going on to lose more. This process is also true for those who need to gain weight. With a change in weight, patients can feel vulnerable, anxious; they can experience identity loss, gender loss, separation anxiety, or intense pressure to keep up the "good" work. These psychological stressors account for the fluctuations of weight gains and losses and the return of other symptomatic behavior. The therapist needs to encourage a gradual process that allows for internalization of a new body/self schema. What do those 5 pounds just lost or gained mean psychically? What fantasies and feelings emerge: rage? fear of being envied? competition? pleasure? a more autonomous sense of self? Can those feelings be tolerated? Do they represent terrible conflict? What is the physical experience of the new body size? What is it like to move with more or less weight? What parts of the body are most affected by the loss or gain, and what meanings do they hold? What are the interpersonal consequences to the weight change?

Fantasies, transference configurations, identifications, and memories may surface more prominently as the client's body is changing. The anorexic woman who is worried that her pain may be taken less seriously as she gains weight may continually test the therapy relationship to see if the therapist's respect for her is unwavering regardless of her body size. The woman who loses 10 pounds and starts bingeing because she is frightened of becoming sexually promiscuous needs to explore her sexual desires and fears. As she works through these psychological issues, she will need to make decisions about how she actually uses her body sexually, based on who she is and what her values are, not by body size and shape alone. Each time the body changes, the psychological issues embedded in the body will be continuously revealed and provide opportunity for deeper exploration and psychic change.

Interpersonal issues get revealed as patients report reactions to the changes in their bodies from those around them. They need to learn to negotiate and manage their own and others' responses. Because the body has been the focus of their attention and because this society grants permission for public remarks regarding women's bodies, other people's reactions exert great influence on patients. Weight loss or gain invites a new round of commentary, sometimes benign and well-intentioned but also intrusive and abusive, all of which affect patients. Patients need to find ways to establish boundaries that allow for safety, privacy, and different ways of connecting or responding without a return to weight loss or gain.

Change in body size through psychological work represents a change in the person's internal object world, providing greater control and autonomy. Thus, it is to be expected that patients will present themselves differently in the world, and important others will be impacted by this difference. This shift in self and in others' responses is true even if there is no weight change, but the person holds her body differently and, for example, stands straighter, begins wearing differently styled or colored clothing, and acts more confidently. If others have an investment in maintaining an old static interpersonal system, then pressures will be induced to undermine the patient's progress. Patients need encouragement to believe that healthy, loving relationships can tolerate their developing growth and vitality.

However, change in body size can be defensive, requiring vigilance on the part of the therapist. In those cases the therapist must not collude with the patient's manic feelings of success regarding the body change or abatement of eating symptoms. The cultural ideology that espouses weight loss (or gain for the anorexic) as the panacea for and victory over complicated life processes and challenges induces a cultural countertransference reaction that makes it all the more difficult to understand that a defense is being enacted.

The weight change can be a defensive communication about either conscious or unconscious material, including material about the therapist and the therapeutic relationship. The patient makes use of her body, once again taking action, because she is still unable to psychically process and verbalize her experience. Here the body must be read for its derivative meaning as one reads the dream for its latent content. Awareness that the patient is expressing something, particularly to the therapist, can be experienced in the countertransference as guilt, inadequacy, overconcern, and a zealous need to fix or do something, to take action. For example, a therapist felt personally uneasy each time she saw one client, Joan, who was coming to her sessions looking increasingly tired, drawn, with her clothes baggier than usual. It took many sessions to discover that Joan had felt injured, put down, and angry by a comment made by the therapist. Until the therapist deciphered the communication, Joan only knew she was feeling fat and had to lose weight quickly. Robin provides another example. She started bingeing, purging, and gaining weight after a long period of being asymptomatic. The return of her symptoms came at a time when she and the therapist were beginning to talk about another level of trust and intimacy in their relationship and because she recently revealed her private fantasies. The symptoms were the only way that Robin had to signal how frightened, confused, and ashamed she felt in the relationship and about her fantasies.

Some patients also turn to body transformation in order to cope with separation from the therapist and important others because of illness, vacations, and impending termination. The following example illustrates this usage. During the course of treatment Jackie and her therapist noticed a pattern of weight change. Jackie, having lived through early significant separations at different times from both of her parents, was loathe to admit under any circumstances her reactions to separations from significant others, always taking a pseudo-independent stance. As a matter of course her therapist took two vacations a year. Rather than discuss any feelings in regard to this, Jackie would consistently gain weight prior to her therapist's departure. It was not until this pattern was named that Jackie was able to put words to this bodily communication and to describe how emotionally disruptive these separations were for her. The weight gain was her visible but silent plea to the therapist to stay as well as the expression of a muted anger because she knew the therapist wouldn't stay. As communication was further elaborated, Jackie revealed her fear that her therapist would never return and that she would be left abandoned and alone with her fears and conflicts, not to mention a body and eating that felt out of control. Here the weight gain was not used in the service of ego growth, as it is when someone is learning to accept her actual body size or from eating when hungry, but rather as an unconscious communication to signal distress.

When the Body Does Not Change

For some, metabolism, chronic dieting, genetics, and aging prohibit weight loss or desired change in body size. Furthermore, some women cannot lose weight and perhaps should not for psychological stability.

For example, a person who eats with body hunger and satiety most likely would jeopardize both her psychological and physiological equilibrium if she persisted in attempts to lose the 10 pounds over which she agonizes. These attempts usually result in obsessive and anorexic-like thinking and behavior. Rather, she needs to examine her fantasy about the 10 pounds. The woman who has had intense psychological difficulty following previous weight losses, such as suicidal gestures, hospitalization, or decompensation, may for the present also need to integrate current body size while the work of establishing a more secure sense of self progresses. Some very large women make excellent use of treatment and do not change their body size. Through treatment they are able to accept and live full, rich lives comfortable in their size despite cultural taboos and discrimination.

When the body cannot, does not, or should not change, the work of treatment is to help patients to accept their body size by understanding, mourning, and relinquishing their relationship to a cultural ideal or whatever ideal they might hold. Accepting limits, differences, and one's ordinariness may be experienced as a narcissistic injury that for some women will be a major issue requiring analysis of all its developmental, adaptive, and defensive aspects. Issues of when to focus on food, when to focus on body, when either is being used as a defense or expression comprise the art of doing this eating and body image treatment.

CHAPTER 8

Transference and Countertransference Issues: The Impact of Social Pressures on Body Image and Consciousness

SUSAN GUTWILL

The first distortion of truth in "the Myth of the Analytic Situation" is that analysis is an interaction between a sick person and a healthy one. The truth is that it is an interaction between two personalities, in both of which the ego is under pressure from the id, the superego, and the external world. (Racker, 1968)

THIS QUOTE has captured the imagination of many contemporary psychoanalytic psychotherapists who are rethinking classical notions about transference, countertransference, and the relationship between the two. Transference, a key concept and tool of psychoanalysis, was originally understood by Freud as the patient's expectations of and feelings about the therapist deriving from repressed, unconscious, and unresolved experiences with and feelings toward parents and other significant caregivers from the patient's formative years. Countertransference, a response to the patient and to the patient's transference, was originally warned against by Freud, who understood these feelings of the therapist to be unresolved issues of the past that had a destructive impact on treatment. Today, especially influenced by the social constructionists (Gill, 1982; Gill & Hoffman, 1982; Hoffman, 1984, 1991), transference is seen as representative not only of unresolved historical issues but also as responses to the therapeutic relationship. This new thinking extends the contemporary theoretical paradigm that posits a two-person field where reality is seen as socially constructed. In the new paradigm, transference, rather than being understood as only genetic in origin, is now conceived as a "plausible" outgrowth of the "here and now" relationship in which the analyst acts more fully as a subject and is an actor in the analytic field (Gill & Hoffman, 1982).

Developing theories about countertransference and projective identification (Ogden, 1982) have both enriched one another in recent years and also established the way these two processes bring the analyst into the patient's unconscious experience. Far from something to be excised, countertransference experience has become the subject of detailed study in an attempt to help to classify what different countertransference experiences indicate about the patient, the therapist, and their relationship. Susan Wooley in a fine article exploring uses of countertransference with patients with eating problems defines the totalist view of countertransference as including

> all the therapist's responses to the patient, occurring at varying levels of awareness, to all of the patient's verbal and nonverbal communications. These include (1) what Winnicott (1949) called "objective countertransference," reactions with a basis in reality that would be shared by most people; (2) responses common to groups of people with some basis for a common outlook (e.g., gender, age, nationality); (3) "idiosyncratic transference" responses occasioned by one's unique developmental history; and, most important; (4) responses attributable, in Tansey and Burke's (1989) phrase, to "interactional pressure"—that is, to the patient's unconscious effort to direct the therapist into an experience of feeling as the patient does or feeling toward the patient as important people in the past have done. These include "concordant projective identification," in which the therapist temporarily shares the patient's experience (this is usually called "empathy"), and "complementary projective identification," reflecting the complementarity of the patient's internalized representations of important relationships. Complementary identifications can have two forms, one in which the patient plays his or her original historical role and another in which the roles are reversed. (Wooley, 1991, p. 255)

In other words, all the therapist's thoughts, reactions, feelings, roles, dreams, and her internal object world can be utilized as tools to understand a patient's unconscious life and experience. The shift in attitude toward countertransference from something that obscures to something that illuminates reflects a democratization and feminization of the therapeutic profession. And it is not surprising that in addition to Donald Winnicott, Heinrich Racker, and Harry S. Sullivan, female analysts such as Melanie Klein, Paula Heimann, Margaret Little, and Lydia Tower began understanding and working with preoedipal—and hence often nonverbal—material, asserting the value of using their own feelings to do so.

Thus, countertransference is now established as one of the psychoanalyst's most important tools. How to define it, how to make use of it, its relationship to transference, to the past and to the present, are part of current debate. Instead, it is now widely accepted that there is an interpersonal and intersubjective field created by two people who are continually influencing each other and that this field can be used as a major therapeutic tool.

The work of Edgar Levenson on the therapist's involvement (Levenson, 1983), of Donnell Stern on "the grip of the field" (1987, 1989), of Christopher Bollas on the "unthought known" (1987), of Darlene Ehrenberg's "psychoanalytic engagement" (1982, 1984), and of Stephen Mitchell on embeddedness and the relational matrix (1988) attest to the unconscious contribution of the two participants in creating a shared interactive reality that at times will enact and evoke different aspects of the relational world of each.

Not only are therapist and client interactive, but also they, together with the field of psychoanalytic theory itself, are all "embedded" in a larger world of hegemonic cultural symbolization and discourse about female body and appetite. This social holding environment affects the transference and countertransference issues that commonly arise in the work. Besides all the idiosyncratic transference and countertransference developments that arise in every individual treatment, working with clients with eating problems requires an ongoing critical examination of cultural notions about eating and the ideal body as they affect therapist and patient alike.

Another way to conceptualize this social "embeddedness" is to see patient and therapist as both being in a transference relationship to the same "culture home" or "culture parent." Although this social home is characterized by class, race, and ethnic hierarchies—and the therapist should be prepared to witness the impact of these influences—here, of course, the subject under investigation is the ideal image of women. It is especially important to repeat that we are referring only to the advertised image of the ideal female body and to the discourse about female body and appetite contained within it, not to the whole of popular culture. This part of the culture is hegemonic and monolithic and at this point in history not given to liberatory interpretations. The relationship to this symbol, as has been argued in chapter 1, becomes part of the unconscious object-relational world, affecting self and object representations and interpersonal relationships. Because this cultural symbolic impact is both socially and personally repressed, it is particularly important to elaborate it consciously. If the therapist does not bring this repressed material to consciousness, she may be quite unable to recognize, contain, and metabolize the experience the client has with the social discourse around female body and appetite.

This chapter is, therefore, devoted to describing the cultural impact on common transference and countertransference configurations, an impact that has not yet been thoroughly examined in the literature.

In this chapter the term *cultural countertransference* refers to the therapist's transference to the culture. And the attendant transference/countertransference configuration can be understood as a culturally affected configuration.

It is encouraging to note that the term cultural countertransference and related notions have been entering the literature from several independent sources, indicating a new generation of thinking in this area.* Susan Gutwill and Carol Bloom of the Women's Therapy Centre Institute (Spring 1992) and Catherine Steiner-Adair (1991) all have introduced this term in talks and papers about eating problems. In addition Mary Gail Frawley, on a panel about the treatment of sexual abuse (1993), refers to a similar phenomenon: countertransference to psychoanalytic theory and the psychoanalytic community itself. For Frawley such countertransference occurs in the relational matrix of the treatment setting but is stimulated by "psychoanalytic culture." The argument here is that transference to the cultural symbol of the ideal female body occurs and is contained within relational matrices as well as existing in the ties an individual makes to the symbols of her culture.

Analytic Resistance to Food and Body Material

One of the most unfortunate outcomes of the fact that psychoanalytic thinking is embedded in the larger culture is a tendency to minimize the analytic importance of the full range of eating and body image problems. As has been argued throughout this book, the underpinnings of compulsive eating and body image distortion problems are socially normative and, therefore, easily escape analytic attention. Anxiety about feeding oneself and living in the body are understood mainly in their extreme forms: anorexia and bulimia. Underlying assumptions about eating and body size thus may be hard to see in their fullest importance and insidiously difficult to question because of their general social acceptance. Even though these aspects may be repressed and unarticulated, both client and therapist experience transferences to these cultural practices and to the discourse about eating and body image. When cultural practices are normative, psychoanalytic theorists, practitioners, and clients more easily resist acknowledging the existence of transference and countertransference issues connected with those practices, both within the therapeutic dyad and in relationship to the culture, its institutional arrangements, and key symbols. In the case of eating and body image, such resistance reflects the patriarchal environment in which women's work is simultaneously invisible, denigrated, and falsely idealized. The ultimate female work—the manual and mental labor of feeding babies, the sick, needy, and elderly, spoonful by spoonful, meal by meal, day by day, year by year—is taken for granted, unpaid or barely paid. More generally, it is taken

---

*There is, of course, also a growing literature on the impact of gender on transference/countertransference phenomena. The reader is particularly referred to Susan Wooley's (1991) excellent article on gendered countertransference with patients suffering from eating disorders.

for granted not only in patriarchy but largely in psychoanalytic theory as well that women will attend to the requirements of both the concrete and the symbolic functions of digestion and excretion. The intrapsychic and inter-personal meaning of learning to feed oneself is so sparsely theorized that, in its absence, workers in the field of psychoanalysis can easily be left in the grip of obsessive cultural constructions around food, eating, and body. These constructions lead therapist and client alike to some level of despair, anger, confusion, and feeling overwhelmed in the face of wild, out-of-control eating and body image experience.

In a situation where the absence of critical theory leaves therapists unpro-tected from the prejudices around female (and increasingly male as well) ap-petite and body, it is no wonder that therapists' most basic transference/countertransference problem is perhaps simply to stay attentive to their clients' experiences around eating and body image in a clinically useful way. When patients are ready to and can be helped by focusing on the particulars of their eating and body experiences, it is essential for the therapist to be fully available for the dialogue.

Supervisees, for example, need constant help in comprehending the im-portance of, and in knowing how to ask about, again and again and again, the explicit details of eating, purging, dieting, or body image distortion expe-riences. In session after session, therapists must have faith in the importance of slowing down to observe the details of their clients' experiences with food and body. Questions such as the following, for example, do not wear out their usefulness:

"When did you begin to think about having that binge?"

"Why do think it was at 2:30 and not 6:30 that you began to feel so 'gross and fat?' What were you feeling at the time?"

"How do you feel about yourself when you are having that particular feeling? If there are no words, can you find the experience in your body?"

"Now, here in the room with me, could we imagine together why it is so hard for you to experience insecurity and neediness (or competition, inadequacy, envy, etc.)? How were you treated and how do you treat yourself when that feeling comes up in you?"

"Once you began eating, what was it like—the first bite, the second, and so on? What messages did you give yourself during the binge? What was it like after you ate?"

"What do you think you wished that food would do for you?"

"If you were trying to say something to me with your eating, what might it be?"

These questions could go on forever; essentially they aim to identify the experience and untangle it from its dissociated food or body image state in order to reconnect it to a fuller psychological and physical self-awareness.

The therapist's inability to sustain these kinds of experience-near questions is a countertransference difficulty that underlies the entire discussion in this chapter. The lack of a sustained ability on the part of the therapist to be curious stems from her lack of awareness that even though they may appear to all be the same because of their ritualized and obsessive form, eating problems can and do represent and express a large array of significant psychological difficulties arising at virtually every stage of development. Moreover, they emerge within almost any diagnostic category and can change over the course of a treatment. This is why it is so essential to pay attention to the enormous variety of moments of body distortion and eating problems. Eating problems are channels for the expression of multiple facets of self and change over the course of a lifetime.[*]

Common countertransference responses include an understanding of clients' repeated, monotonous eating incidents as defenses against "the real problems" or as the real problem that needs immediate and external controls. Feelings such as boredom, annoyance, guilt, fear, inadequacy, disgust, and despair are countertransference experiences that can inhibit therapists from sustaining their ability for this kind of detailed inquiry. Indeed, they are perfectly matched to the nearly universal transference expectation of the patient, namely, that her eating is a "stupid" pattern, something that she had better just "get control over" and stop indulging in, something that is just an infuriating annoyance, embarrassing, incomprehensible, worthy of no real careful analysis but only of profound shame as well as the self-hating badgering and berating that always accompany eating or body hatred. These expectations on the part of a patient are often a defense against consciously knowing that her eating and body image distortion may contain her core and most profound suffering and psychic struggles.

In the absence of a stance of compassionate, nuanced, and persistent detailed inquiry, two other transference/countertransference enactments typically occur: Either symptoms are more or less ignored, or else they become the center of treatment. In the latter case there is a somewhat desperate effort to control the symptoms rather than to "read" them in order to discern what they express for the client.

Missing the import of, and therefore trivializing, food and body image

---

[*]It is interesting to note that the monotonous, repetitive expressions represent the flattening and homogenizing of desire that is an ironic product of consumer culture. A similar phenomenon of discovering the importance of the details occurred in the field of sexual abuse. It took a wave of feminist exposure and theory to underscore the frequent necessity of being prepared to ask about details of the abuse—who, what, when, where, how, how long, how each aspect felt. Feelings are buried in details that are felt to be so shameful that they are dissociated and repressed.

concerns is a form of "cultural countertransference." There is a cultural pressure against subjecting eating and body concerns to careful and repeated examination because "the real" issue is thought to be, for example, relationship to mother, abandonment fears, sexual abuse, or envy of the therapist. Here the mass culture designates the eating and body image distortion as just so much female drivel, a product of vanity, although the psychoanalytic culture may see ongoing compulsive eating and body image distortion experiences as obsessive defenses against "real" treatment. There is some truth in these verdicts: Food and body obsessions both hide and give an opening to the deeper communication. The obsession simultaneously serves as a substitute for real relating and begs to be met with relationship.

Analyzing eating problems directly can be a particularly painful and challenging problem to a female therapist influenced by feminism and grappling with society's demands for her to conform to ideal images. A client with eating problems forces the therapist to bear witness to excruciating compliance (nothing matters so much as being thin) coupled with violent rebellion against the rigid regimens inherent in the eating problem. Supervisees and colleagues reveal how intolerable it can feel to see the brutality their women patients direct against themselves in the name of having the right body. It is easy to distance, to become annoyed or impatient with what appears to be a display of submission because it may resonate with a familiar but controlled internal state in which the therapist is capable of such self-flagellation.

At the WTCI we have consulted with a number of skilled and caring professionals who could not empathize or work with the level of body shame and guilt over eating seen in many such clients. Feminist-oriented therapists sometimes have particularly great difficulty containing patients' self-hatred. The level of punitive harshness that they direct at their body images and eating selves can be profoundly off-putting to those therapists who oppose the denigration of women and their bodies. The degree of sadism and masochism enforced, sustained, and enacted in the name of a cultural ideal can feel repulsive. Living in this culture is not comfortable; one may wish not to conform but be only partially able to defy that ideal. Whenever the therapist cannot maintain contact with his or her patient, it is generally a countertransference problem. In this case such a break in contact would be what Catherine Steiner-Adair calls a cultural countertransference error: The therapist loses contact because her patient is experiencing what Steiner-Adair calls "nonidealized" emotions. (Steiner-Adair, 1991) In this culture, women are encouraged to be victims to very sadistic internalized standards. Such standards and the feelings associated with them are indeed "nonidealized" in both feminist and traditional circles for different reasons. To feminist women, self-degradation in the face of materialistic standards of appearance and utter cruelty to women is anathema. To more traditional women, such sadism can be nonidealized because it is ugly, "not nice."

A contrasting cultural countertransference phenomenon noted by Catherine Steiner-Adair (1991) occurs when the client raises issues about the sociocultural context of her food and body problem that the therapist considers an avoidance of and defense against the work of therapy. Although reference to the culture can, and indeed sometimes does, operate as a defense, the client still can and should be helped to know the deep grief, shame, and confusion spawned by her relationship to cultural symbols and institutions.

In contrast to a therapist's proclivity to be overwhelmed by, defended against, ignorant, or denigrating of the importance of symptoms, the client's acting out with regard to eating and her body may be matched and reproduced by the therapist's exaggerated attempts to act, to mobilize, and to control the symptom—a concordant experience, to use Racker's term. For example, if the client ate too much, then she will wildly diet; if she dieted too much, she must wildly binge; if she feels bad, she assaults her body-self through denigrating her body image. There is intensely felt pressure to "change me now, fix me immediately, now, overnight, make it go away." Triggered by any number of feeling states and events, this mobilization to action responds to any kind of alarm.

So too with the therapist on whom the pressure to act is equally great. For not only is it the very nature of the symptom to act out in an attempt to control, it is also socially valued "to act," to "just do it," especially as regards eating and the medicalization of weight problems. The therapist in this situation, feeling the enormous pressure of the panicked client, may feel it incumbent on herself to act, to rescue, to solve. Moreover, when that therapist reaches to her cultural milieu for holding, she is met with yet another layer of hysteria: a call to arms, to Overeaters Anonymous (OA), to diet, to hospitalize, to get that woman's eating under control, to make her gain weight, make her lose weight, lock the bathrooms so she cannot purge. "She is killing herself," goes the social refrain; and it is the therapist's ethical duty to stop this suicidal self-destruction. This is obviously an interpersonal pressure in the form of projective identification, where the therapist is induced into action under the impact of an action symptom, a concordant countertransference. But it is also a social phenomenon; for the culture concurs with the action solution. Although the patient believes she cannot tolerate the feelings underlying her food and body action solution, the therapist's job is to remember that it is possible to do so—and is indeed the goal of treatment.

How does the therapist resist the pressure to enact this "mobilization to act" transference/countertransference configuration? One helpful thought is to remember that the manic quality of going on a diet, of getting "it" under control is the polar opposite of, and defense against, feelings of despair. Often therapists and clients simultaneously fear drowning in despair. Therapists, like clients, can feel immobilized, inadequate, and powerless in the face of entrenched and dangerous symptoms. And what the therapist must bear in mind is that rather than drowning in despair or leaping into emergency action, her job is to feel both sides, both temptations, both pulls, metabolize them, and give them back to the client so that she can work her way through the feelings and digest them, allowing them to take her deeper into the heart of her suffering.

Therapists are easily or subtly prey to the cultural mandates for the female body (and increasingly for men's bodies as well). This mandate is contradictory. On the one hand it is fat-phobic, obsessed with bodily control, in revolt against aging and its concomitant bodily changes, outraged at and contemptuous of the imperfect out-of-control body, and repulsed by immodest female appetites and hunger. Even the most critically minded therapists must do at least some amount of internal battle against this mandate, because it presents itself to everyone in the name of health as well as beauty. On the other hand, there is an implicit social mandate to "indulge," "enjoy," stop at McDonald's. Fast food, high-fat food, is omnipresent, intensely advertised, and frequently all that is available (e.g., on highways). This is a very frustrating and confusing combination of countervailing mandates that the therapist needs to manage.

It can be very frustrating in the countertransference for a therapist to sit in front of a 275-pound client, for whom she cares deeply, and hear that, once again, she has just eaten two pizzas and a box or two of Entenmann's cupcakes that were on sale and that her blood sugar is dangerously high. It can also be profoundly frightening and very easy to forget that every program in the world has already failed this client, probably increasing her weight 20 pounds per program. Likewise, if the therapist herself has concerns about eating and exercise, it can be confusing to sit in front of an attractive 30-year-old who eats carefully apportioned, low-fat, high-fiber, low-sugar veggies, works out faithfully five days a week, still has her period, and indeed "looks great," and reports that she "feels great." She really may be reporting accurately, but the theoretical environment of psychoanalysis does not consistently offer help in learning to distinguish a real choice about eating and body size from a defense against feeling shame or inadequacy. Was this client expressing terror through rigid compliance with a stringent diet program? Is she really sitting on a minefield, or is she truly providing self-care? And is it always the same? Is her experience on Monday the same as it is on Thursday or Sunday? The therapist's attitudes and resources in all these moments have a major effect on the transference/countertransference interaction.

UNDERSTANDING THE ROLE OF BODY IMAGE SHAME IN TREATMENT

Although the therapist's body has been theorized in preoedipal terms, in terms of the fear of annihilation through merger, in oedipal terms dealing

with competition, envy, and rivalry between women and in the female therapeutic dyad, women's relationships to each other's bodies as it is mediated
by the cultural ideal has yet to be understood. Women compare themselves
to the ideal and compare themselves to other women insofar as they, as well,
compare to the ideal. "Other women" certainly include one's therapist, one's
friend's therapist, and so on. These comparisons are meaningful, revelatory
material in therapy, and they play profound roles in common transference
and countertransference pressures and configurations. Therefore, psychoanalysis needs theory and language to comprehend the vicissitudes of body
image experience. When body image experience is ignored, trivialized, or
elicits unanalyzed disgust, there is an acting out (and acting in) instead of a
healing communication. In other words, the eating and body image distortion problem remains unchallenged as the solution to deep-seated conflict
chosen by the adaptive client.

For example, Sara, a therapist herself, had had several successful treatment experiences. But her persistent body image hatred never relented.
When she spoke about it in therapy, she would be temporarily relieved only
to find in disappointment and confusion that her pain returned and sometimes even intensified. Until she was in treatment in which she could effec-
tively and persistently mention and reflect her body image experience and to
connect it to many other subjects of analysis, Sara had never unearthed its
role in her life. Sara came to feel safe enough to acknowledge and track for
herself and her therapist the intensity of her body image self-hatred. She
began to take notice, and even to write about it. To her horror she realized
that she rarely walked down a street without comparisons stabbing at her.
One time she reported waiting in the car at the airport to pick up a dear
friend who was returning from a trip. She sat in the car staring into the
rearview mirror watching out for her friend's arrival. It was both poignant
and profoundly painful for her to become conscious of and to admit the significance of the fact that what she watched in the mirror was every other
woman's body. It was a truly compulsive internal rite; no woman passed by
without her judgment. Each woman was compared to herself and the cultural ideal. Sara's mind was crowded with hierarchies. Overtly they seemed
to be about the women in relationship to herself and to one another. The secret partner, however, was always the cultural ideal body image, the internalized symbol of consumer culture, the perfect woman busily taunting, tantalizing, and rejecting her.

When encouraged to explore her compulsive comparisons, Angie too discovered that the arms and legs of women she would notice were always seen
in comparison to the internalized images of the ideal arms and legs sold by
advertising. Thus, the subliminal relationships to cultural symbols mediated
actual and projected interpersonal relationships in the present.

In these cases, as in all others, the willingness of the therapist to sustain interest in a detailed inquiry of body image material enabled the profound and shameful relationship both women had to cultural images to emerge and to be contained and dignified. But frequently these compulsive comparisons are left unanalyzed, accepted as the background buzz always competing with the sounds of "real life." Such a failure of analysis is the outcome of the therapist's cultural countertransference in partnership with the client's transference expectation that devalues and minimizes the pain caused by these internalized relationships to symbols.

Seen more abstractly, women's body image distortions and comparisons will reflect their relationships to three interrelated phenomena: (1) The monolithic ideal in consumer culture of the fetishized, objectified female body. (2) The mythical image of female body as representative of the potentially all-nurturing, depriving, or engulfing mother (Dinnerstein, 1963). The female body, like the mother's, can represent every hope, wish, and dream, as well as every fear of destruction, deprivation, and rejection. (3) All the personal, idiosyncratic, and shared developmental issues of women's lives: conflicts about dependency, sexuality, desire, mastery, and recognition *as they are played out in their individual families, interpersonal, and class, race, and ethnic realities.* Body image difficulties exist on two levels, which live in paradoxical tension with each other (Ghent, 1992). On the one hand, body image shame is simply what it is—the burden of an unrelenting hatred of one's body, an albatross, a very painful experience that must be understood, acknowledged, and welcomed into the therapy room on its own terms. On the other hand, it is a metaphor for many intrapsychic and interpersonal issues, themselves both universal and gendered phenomena. The metaphoric meanings carried by body image experience come into treatment and are made explicit insofar as they are seen as contrasting background to the intrinsic body image shame as it exists in and of itself. A fat body is cruelly stigmatized in this culture. It is treated, seen, and felt as the object of disgust and fear. Many disabilities are so treated and seen; but fatness is also seen as reason to blame the fat person who ate his or her way into "freakishness." Because exclusion and inclusion issues are central to, if not the nightmare of, everyone's childhood, exclusion by virtue of fat goes to the heart of childhood experience. Objective exclusion on the basis of obesity can be a trauma so profoundly fragmenting to ego development that it is often at least partially dissociated. However, the severity of dissociated experience can be hidden by the socially normative complaints always present about how one feels having been rejected as a fat kid. It is as if the partial complaint can hide, rather than permit, an opening to the depth of the real complaint.

The subjective experience of fat, with or without the actuality of it, can also be truly traumatizing, as is evident in the case of anorexia. In all cases "fat" stigma enters psychic structure, perhaps has even organized it, exacerbating an internally split and self-annihilating experience.

When the therapist suffers in a similar manner as his or her client, it is no wonder that body shame experience is pathologized, denied, distanced, omitted, minimized, or treated with outright aggression in the treatment setting. The impact of body image shame is illustrated in the following four examples, in which each client has a somewhat different experience of body shame in and of itself and a very different experience of what it has symbolized for them. Moreover in two of the four cases, previous therapies had failed to explore this central aspect of the patient's experience.

Rebecca

At 400 pounds and 32 years old, Rebecca had almost died of sleep apnea, but her life was saved by a gastric bypass operation (stomach stapling). At the time she entered feminist psychoanalytic treatment, her biggest problem seemed obvious to her, namely, her eating and weight, although she was, in fact, comfortable at 250 pounds, her approximate weight at the start of this treatment. Rebecca was in a very loving marriage, and she had an excellent, responsible job as an accountant successfully managing a department of 100 people. These accomplishments seemed serendipitous to her. How could she, disgusting as she felt, have obtained this position in life? At best her success seemed like an accident, and she felt it was more likely a mistake.

She had been in therapy several times before this treatment and had learned that not all her pain was about her fat. She understood she had self-esteem problems and that there was more to her than her fat. She also understood that her family dynamics had been hurtful. Her father, a bitter survivor of the concentration camps, believed himself to be most entitled to pain within the family. An engineer reduced to factory worker by immigration and war trauma, he was enraged. His marriage was without happiness or peace, tumultuous, and full of paranoid accusations: He was sure Rebecca's mother was destroying his life. Rebecca was confidante to her mother, who felt victimized, angry, and pained. Rebecca was most easily designated the family caregiver because, more than either of her two sisters, she genuinely wanted to help her mother and her father and to ease tensions within the family. She became both emotionally sensitive and caring as well as physically competent to do household chores at a very young age. She cooked for everyone from age 8 or 9; she ran various small family businesses, and she listened to her mother's pain and her father's troubles.

Rebecca did not feel she was a typical child of a Holocaust survivor. In fact, she had been in a special therapy group for children of survivors and had felt she was not acceptable because she never fit with the leaders' expectations and predictions. Rebecca felt her life was characterized more by her fat than her experiences as the child of a Holocaust survivor. With the possible relationship between fat and the Holocaust in mind, the new therapist was able to provide Rebecca with a hearing for her experience as an obese child, teenager, and woman, and even to contain some of the pain too frightening for Rebecca to articulate. Rebecca was unlike many women in treatment who seem as if they can speak easily, even compulsively, about how fat they are, and who can complain in socially acceptable ways about their fat thighs or the vicissitudes of their weight loss schemes. Rebecca's stigma, based on her fat, caused her such total mortification that she found it difficult to talk about it, sometimes almost denying its centrality to her experience. She tended to think, in fact, that something was "wrong" with her for even thinking that her fat was as impactful and important as she experienced it to be. Maybe she was paranoid, she mused. Yet, if the fat did have as painful an impact as she felt, then she reasoned it must prove that she was truly "gross."

The therapist reported in supervision that she had very strong feelings when sitting with Rebecca. She felt deeply disturbed imagining how much weight Rebecca had carried and what it could have meant. She also reported feeling very moved and touched by Rebecca. Was it the weight? Was it Auschwitz in the wings? She reported in supervision that one day, walking down the street behind a very large woman, she felt herself flinch. She thought of Rebecca and felt frightened, as if those feelings about fat registered in the flinch or could harm her client. The supervisor simply suggested noting and storing this memory of the flinch. The supervisor felt that the key thing for the moment was to explore the feelings the therapist had about fat, about Rebecca's fat, and about being Rebecca's therapist. Not surprisingly it became clear that the therapist, quite naturally, had some negative feelings about fat: She, too, was a product of this culture. But having acknowledged and contained those feelings, she was then most disturbed by the fear that speaking to Rebecca about the fat would hurt her client. She was concerned that it would be a kind of reabuse, a reminder that would rub salt into the wound. She did not want Rebecca to be hurt—she had a deep sense of Rebecca's fragility, which existed alongside her great strength and many talents.

Having noted and held this in a nonjudgmental fashion the supervisor encouraged the therapist to move forward to explore Rebecca's experience with her fat. The supervisor hypothesized that the therapist's fear and hesitation and her sense of danger were countertransference responses of two kinds: one, an induced, concordant countertransference experience reflecting Rebecca's terror of knowing her history with fat; and the other, a reflection of the therapist's own memories and fears of being and feeling fat. If the supervisor had had an unanalyzed transference to cultural symbols, she might have either discouraged her supervisee from talking about and exploring the profundity of her patient's experience of being stigmatized by her fat, or she might have minimized it, rather than allowing for the therapist's strong feelings about fat in itself.

For her part, Rebecca needed the therapist's gentle encouragement to explore the details of her relationship to her fat and her history as a fat person. She was afraid of the material; and her unconscious transference expectation was that she would be blamed or ignored in her pain, reproducing early and intrapsychic experience. A therapist caught in a cultural countertransference might, however subtly, easily err in either direction and not be responsive to Rebecca's need to have the therapist's validation of her half articulated idea that her fat was as significant an experience in her life as she suspected it was. In addition, she needed to hear the therapist's suggestion that she could survive the act of telling about her experience of being fat.

She began slowly and over time finally found the words of truth in herself. She remembered the treatment by schoolmates: No one ever ate lunch with her. She had almost no friends. Because of fat phobia and anti-Semitism, she was isolated among her peers. To this day she is shocked when she is asked to lunch by anyone. The therapist ached, hearing about the painful scenes Rebecca described in the cafeteria sitting alone, accompanied only by her fat and the food that fueled it, as if she were on humiliating display. Perhaps the role of the fat became most clear to the therapist when Rebecca described her hospital stay for the stomach stapling surgery. Rebecca's humiliation in the hospital, a humiliation paradigmatic for her life, was profoundly traumatizing. She reported that the hospital gowns never fit her and that none was provided for her size body; that she could barely fit in the chairs or on the x-ray and operating tables; that the ridiculing comments of the aides pushing her body-self around were endless; and that, worst of all, she was profoundly humiliated by being taken to the hospital cellar to be weighed on the laundry scale, the only one that could accommodate her weight. She could barely say how ashamed and disgusting she felt. She was frozen in fear, terrified in the next session of what else she might remember and reexperience.

At this point the therapist reported in supervision that the image of Rebecca being weighed on the laundry scale was profoundly unsettling to her. She said it was as if something ripped inside her. Her associations in supervision were of the Jewish tradition of ripping one's clothes when someone close has died. Making room for these intense feelings and exploring them led both the supervisor and the therapist to feel Rebecca's truth at a very deep level. Rebecca's experience of stigma, the constant, unrelenting reminders that she was different, unworthy, disgusting, grotesque—like her hospital stay and even everyday experiences at school and in her childhood neighborhood—all were traumatizing. These traumatic experiences provided the organizing core to Rebecca's life and sense of herself. Because the trauma was so big and central, it seemed overwhelming; and Rebecca both repressed it and dissociated from it. She did not want to talk about it but could never overcome the painful belief that this fat undid any good in her life. All good felt fraudulent and illusory. In these ways Rebecca's center and core of shame make her like many people who feel apart and different from others in a variety of ways. But in the sense that all the world sees her fat, she can never even pass for being "okay." Moreover, in the sense that there is nearly universal social revulsion about fat, she is never spared from judgments by others, which directly confirms her experience with and beliefs about herself.

As discussed, it was inevitable that when the pain was explored in its fullness, the therapist should flinch and feel ripped in mourning; for a moment (a countertransference response), she came near to feeling the full brunt of Rebecca's pain. The therapist also realized that her own fat childhood, even though it was much less traumatizing than Rebecca's, hurt so much that she too could not quite remember or talk about it without somehow distancing herself from the most poignant moments. She knew that, like all children, especially those with any weight on them, she had been warned against becoming like Rebecca. These solemn warnings suggest that no one living in this world can be free of some internalized fat hatred. Like the experience of internalized race hatred or homophobia, the hatred of fat must be reckoned with, not hidden. The supervisor's ability to hold the therapist in her "flinch," her hatred of fat, gave the therapist the ability to do the same for Rebecca on the day she came in with the following story. She had spent the day driving around her 600-pound friend, Mark, a man entirely disabled by fat and utterly dependent on her. He was hopeless, increasingly agoraphobic and could not or would not do anything to help himself. Rebecca was furious with him; she was disgusted and found herself screaming inside herself, "Why don't you just *do* something about it, damn it?" Horrified at herself, Rebecca cried, "How could I even think this thought so painfully hurled at me daily?" The therapist had to help Rebecca to accept her inevitably sadistic disidentification as well as her legitimate complaints against Mark, who, like her father, was demanding, impossible, dependent, and irresponsible in dumping his pain all over her.

Because she had been victimized, she expected and feared its repetition. In the treatment setting, the therapist empathically felt this. In addition, she knew what it felt like to be stigmatized as well as to desperately want to disidentify with everyone or anything "fat." By knowing all this, she could stay close and witness Rebecca's terrifying and confusing feelings, understanding that Rebecca's telling the truth about her fat was not, in fact, reabusing her. She could understand but not stop at Rebecca's or her own worry about Rebecca's health. The sadism at the base of the ostracism and exclusion could be seen, felt, rather than hidden or repeated. Rebecca's fat and shame needed all the attention they demanded and all the respect they deserved.

Over time it became clear that Rebecca's body image was central to her experience and that this image was always in contrast to the ideal body image of her culture. Rebecca had always had two pairs of images in her mind. One pair contrasted an image of her fat, grotesque, and shameful self with that of a "normal" size person, and although the former image was the more obvious and painful to her, some comparison to the latter was always implied. The other pair of images concerned food: One was an image of all the candy she longed for—by the pounds—and another of the diet food she ought to be eating. If the therapist were to miss the way in which these images structured Rebecca's emotional life, it would be a countertransference problem. This would be the case regardless of the fact that, after relatively little time in treatment, Rebecca's compulsive eating had diminished significantly. She ate when hungry and stopped not far from satiation. Although she had bouts of compulsive eating, they became less violent, less gigantic, and less frequent. She did not, however, lose weight. Indeed, she put on some weight but was basically more stable that she had ever been in her life.

Rebecca's weight and eating had many origins, not the least of which was an attempt to provide a soothing parent to take care of herself. The fat led to, and eventually protected, her isolation: As a fat Jew she was neither welcome nor safe in her neighborhood. As her isolation increased, food became her only friend. Perhaps, also, her shameful fat created an image of a problem as big as Auschwitz. One might wonder if this fat expressed not only the depth of her pain in this family and the profound pain of the family relationships but also of the traumatic concentration camp history itself. But however and why it ever got there, once there the fat had a life of its own, in which cultural attitudes and symbols were significant players, both in her interpersonal life and in her inner object-relational landscape. Only when these were understood in their own terms would Rebecca really be able to see what her fat and eating represented and how they functioned for her psychologically.

Rebecca felt like a freak, mortified and condemned by her own hand, her own mouth, her own behavior. She needed to hear her experience of herself articulated. She needed to hear the actual word: freak. A therapist caught in cultural countertransference might maintain the social repression and be afraid to utter that very painful truth and to validate that, in her fat body, Rebecca was truly and objectively the target of people's worst fears, projections, and hatred. Rebecca needed the reality testing that such mirroring of her own buried knowledge articulated. Once articulated, she could see her experience and begin to grieve for it and also begin to trust other parts of her inner knowledge, including how lovely, loving, and competent she was. As with any survivor of trauma, Rebecca needs to own the truth of her past in order to move on from it. But the therapist was able to help her to this validation only insofar as she had a critical understanding of the powerful, destructive impact of the fat-phobic culture on Rebecca as well as on herself.

She had to be able to oppose harshness and blame with knowledgeable empathy.

Most people in the course of Rebecca's life, especially Rebecca herself, could maintain only carefully limited sympathy for her plight, because they saw it as her own fault, her own choice to have put food into her mouth. But a critical consciousness adds that: (1) she did so under extreme duress; and (2) once this adaptation of eating was established Rebecca became the product and the object of social forces far beyond her control, by which she was profoundly traumatized. Her deepest injuries were not only intrapsychic but also inflicted by others on her. She was put on infinite diets—her family's and her culture's solution—that caused her to binge; her metabolism was destroyed by dieting; the more isolated and outcast she was as a fat person, the more food was experienced as her only friend. In her object-relational fantasy life, Rebecca took these experiences in, merging them cruelly with her inner landscape. The full stigma and dynamics of Rebecca's trauma were not entirely acknowledged and remained shrouded in clouds of blame. Rebecca needed to be mirrored without the reserve born of this blame so that she could know the truth of her feeling like a freak. She needed to grieve for herself, for her life as someone tormented by her culture, by other people, by her internal relationships to cultural symbols and images and by the inevitable behavior—hating her body and fearing food—demanded by these relationships.

In the first place, with Rebecca as with everyone who suffers from body image shame, it must be recognized as a real experience, complete in and of itself. The burden of an unrelenting hatred of one's body is an experience that must be acknowledged and brought into the therapy room on its own terms. It is then possible to view the self-hatred and shame about the body as metaphors for aspects of self and relational experience (gendered as both of these are) that require translation from body image language into what the body image is expressing.

For Rebecca the experience of being ostracized as a freak stands on its own and is undeniably a major source of trauma. But however real this experience is, Rebecca's body shame also represents many other feelings and experiences for which she does not yet have words. Her hatred of her fat, for example, represents her sense of inadequacy as a child for not being able to heal her parents and to make up for the Holocaust and all the losses it caused. Her body shame expresses hatred of the needy self, the dependent, angry, hateful, resentful self of the child designated to be caregiver to her parents. It is the job of the therapist to feel and contain the affect Rebecca is still afraid of; and only by standing outside culture—through the achievement of critical consciousness—can such pain be seen and understood, allowing the therapist to feel Rebecca's experience rather than the cultural tale about her.

Colleen

The tension between seeing body shame in its own terms and as metaphor is different for Colleen from what it is for Rebecca. Colleen was not visibly fat, but her weight frequently fluctuated, and she was never at peace with food or her body image. Colleen's body shame was never addressed during 15 years of therapy before she came to a feminist analytic treatment that incorporated an anti-deprivation approach to eating. She needed to grieve for pain that had never been seen. She sobbed "I have always hated and attacked my body. I cried for my parents to help, at 17 I couldn't go out of the house for a year, I tried to tell my therapist. No one understood. They either told me that I looked normal or gave me information about another diet. No one saw I was seething, smoldering in self-hate. I have lived hating, fearing, and despising my body; and for 20 years I have not had a bite of food I didn't question and feel guilty about. I can't believe it—not a bite!" With the therapist's validation, Colleen could finally observe her own predicament with horror and empathy. In her previous treatment, Colleen and her therapist had been mired in a transference/countertransference configuration based on a culturally induced resistance to awareness of the impact of body image on the self. When these experiences could be honored in the new therapy, Colleen could permit herself to see how her self-hatred and shame were not only exhausting and painful to live with in and of themselves but also repositories for how much she hated and feared her father's daily alcoholic rages and her mother's ineffectual depressions. She realized the connection between her self-hatred and her childhood terror of watching her sister scapegoated for her fat. All this made Colleen insecure in the role of the "cute, thin, brilliant" child, destined to fulfill everyone's lost hopes. Helpless in the face of all this and still unable to articulate it, she deposited her pain in her body and hated it at whatever size it was.

For Colleen and Rebecca understanding the role of body image is crucial to successful treatment, but in very different ways. The cultural transference dictate about Colleen is that her pain is a metaphor, subjective, purely personal, "crazy," because she is basically a thin woman who has only a little eating problem and therefore need only take charge and avoid exaggerating it through gaining weight. Acquiescence in this transference to the culture had left Colleen and her previous therapist in a transference/countertransference configuration with two particularly unfortunate outcomes. First, Colleen's pain was minimized, leaving her abandoned again. Second, in the absence of a healing communication, the symptom was reinforced as if it were the solution. Colleen and her therapist colluded in seeing one diet or another, one exercise program or another, as the solution to Colleen's worry and upset, enacting the action solution described. Rebecca, on the other hand, is exactly what parents, husbands, and other "well-meaning" people tell a woman she will look like "if you keep eating like that." Rebecca, like many others, was indeed a socially designated, socially useful "freak," a warning to all. She was and is actively and repeatedly used as "the bad example." As such she, like many others like her, is the ongoing product of objective social injury and internalizes that abusive experience. But to fully acknowledge Rebecca's trauma requires a critical stance regarding cultural mores, so that it is possible to relate to her without the reserve born of the hatred of fat, a reserve that strengthens the internal saboteur—the cultural saboteur—within her. Rebecca cannot transcend her body image based on interpersonal stigmatizing trauma until she is understood in this history.

Claire

Although what Rebecca was too scared to talk about was screaming wordlessly in her sessions, Colleen, very normal looking, was sure she could not be understood in her body shame. Claire's story exemplifies a slightly different transference expectation that, if colluded with in the treatment, can also keep body shame out of the therapy room. Even though Claire was not severely obese, she was too embarrassed and humiliated to discuss her body image. Claire was in feminist psychoanalytic treatment two to three times a week for 10 years before she felt consistently able to discuss and pursue her body image shame in its real depth. One day, in quite a panic, she reported feeling as if she and her body were locked in a bad marriage. They could neither stop the hostility nor divorce each other. Part of her self was always degrading her body. "You are ugly, disgusting, no one would want you." She said it was bearable to talk about her body insofar as she had insomnia, drank too much, and was frustrated in her attempts to lose weight. But she could not bear to talk about the pure experience of hating her body. She remembered very clearly the session, several years prior, in which the therapist encouraged her to talk about her belly and what it meant to her. At that time she could not bear the intensity of humiliation she experienced by simply saying the word "belly" and thinking about what it meant to her. Then she went on to her thighs. Claire said her thighs now rub together. She is involved with, fascinated by, and married to just how disgusting it is, how it makes her walk a disabled waddle.

The therapist had a fantasy at that moment. As if in a film filled with special effects, she felt that she and her client were near a mountain surrounded by clouds of dangerous steam and vapors. The sky, the air, the sounds, an opening to a cave in the mountain were all profoundly ominous. She felt gripped by some reified, religious horror. This was a concordant countertransference experience in which she was identifying with the way Claire felt about her body and the "weight" it carried in her psyche. Letting this countertransference experience in, and with a critical awareness of the culture, her therapist came to believe that the image and Claire's feelings lived in the "cultural region of the devil": the large, soft, hungry, needy female body, evil and magic. She understood, and could help Claire to understand, that the "bad" body inspires and contains this level of horror—it is socially designated to do so.

Claire's experience of and hatred of her body image brings to mind Dinnerstein's (1963) image of the female body as an all-depriving mother, an experience that Claire had with her blank, emotionally absent mother, who hovered around her in body but not in spirit. With the therapist's help in revealing this "magic," Claire was able to observe the vapors of deification, demonization, mystery, and horror as evidence of the depth of her internal struggle. She was able, for a moment, to see all this from a somewhat separate place, outside the clouds that enveloped her. She could watch in wonder and with great sadness, the drama of the polluting clouds, socially designed and personally felt. The therapist's image let her know and feel her way into the intensity of her shame, which prohibited her from allowing the healing light of relationship to enter her private mountain cave of pain. This cave and her body hatred were symbols of her extreme emotional isolation.

Claire had given the message to her therapist that she did not want to look in detail at her body image: It was too sensitive and embarrassing. Claire's message was not trivialized or passed over in silence, as it might have been if the therapist accepted the repressive cultural countertransference. On the contrary, it was analyzed in such a way as to validate her experience that something was magically dangerous, carrying a power of some horrible "truth" with it. Only by seeing its "magic" could the magic be eliminated.

Ralph

Ralph grew up in the suburbs as a fat boy. After being beaten up on the school playground daily, he would go home and vent his aggression on his little brother. He was then repeatedly punished by his parents for his rages and violence. When he begged his parents not to send him to school and told them about the playground beatings, they emphasized their wish that he learn how to handle it because after all they said "this is all normal for a kid your age." His parents, both also very large, had each been stigmatized on the basis of their fat. A little boy growing up fat is stigmatized for his fat in terms specific to the masculine gender; he cannot be exempt from stigma any more than a fat little girl can. This experience of body image and all that became associated with it has never left Ralph regardless of how thin or successful he has become. Not only ostracized and humiliated but feeling invalidated by his parents, his experience needs much room within the therapy relationship.

But like Claire and Rebecca, Ralph offered only partial entrée into his experience. Even as he narrated it, he was angry but far away. A very fearful look would then come over his face. He became quiet, and seemed instantly young, and vulnerable. He did not want to talk any more or to feel or think. He stared as if struck, looking into the therapist's eyes with the look of one who has been hit. He seemed to say "stand back, danger, don't trespass, my heels are dug in." But he also stared at her as if to say "reach me, touch me, accept me, help me." He too was afraid to be known and held in his fullest experience. A therapist afraid of or insensitive to the impact of body image shame might leave Ralph abandoned again, instead of able to feel and interconnect his experiences in the world, in his family, and in his inner fantasy life.

CLIENT AND THERAPIST RESPOND TO EACH OTHER'S BODY SIZE AND IMAGE: TRANSFERENCE/COUNTERTRANSFERENCE CO-MOTION

A culturally critical psychoanalytic theory about body image can help therapists to acknowledge and investigate reactions such as the following that client and therapist may have to each other's bodies:

> How can *you* help me—you are too fat, thin, changeable, sloppy, gorgeous, perfect, ideal, and so on?
>
> How can I help her, she is so threatening because she makes me envious, she's gorgeous, perfect, and young; or she is disgusting, she is so fat and sloppy?
>
> I wish I could wear clothes like those, or I'd never be caught dead wearing clothes like those.
>
> She is so fat she would never understand how I could feel fat even though I am thinner than she is. I could never talk to her about it.
>
> Why is it that when I'm with a particular client I always feel dissociated from my body?

Although understanding and admitting thoughts like these can be hard, it is an important piece of the therapeutic work. Projections about each other's bodies that remain hidden and cannot therefore be translated and reassociated, provide fertile ground for unresolved projective identification. The likelihood of projective identification is particularly strong among female therapists because as members of this culture, they have a malleable (Orbach, 1986) and variable experience of their own bodies. They may feel too fat, too thin, pretty or ugly, old-looking, youthful, well-muscled, flabby, and out of control in their eating. Ripe for projections, a therapist may find it hard to distinguish when they come from the client, from herself, or from their common culture. On her part the client, too, can have all of these same kind of reactions. Clients' and therapists' varying experiences of their own and each other's bodies form what we will call in this chapter a transference and countertransference co-motion. Some examples follow.

The first is of Brenda, a therapist in supervision. Brenda reported that one female client, Terry, alternately perceived Brenda's body as just right, average chubby, round, and even fat. Terry's particular perception seemed to depend on her transference in a given session. One day Terry said she saw Brenda as round but not fat. After Brenda inquired how that felt, Terry said that "round" carried positive connotations for her. She said, "I feel comforted knowing you can tolerate some extra weight and still be okay in your body." At this point in Brenda's life she usually felt comfortable in her own body, and realistically she did in fact see herself as somewhat round but not fat. Thus Brenda's countertransference experience of being comfortably round could and did act as an emotional container and a model that held out hope for Terry to also imagine the possibility of being comfortable in her body.

By contrast, at a later point in the same treatment, Terry saw Brenda as quite thin, although Brenda's weight had not actually changed. This time, however, Brenda told her supervisor that she was disturbed to imagine herself being thought of as thin. In fact, she had found herself feeling fatter and fatter as the session went on. By virtue of these careful observations born of her capacity to tolerate an internal detailed inquiry, Brenda and her supervisor were able to surmise the following about the transference and countertransference "co-motion." At the point in treatment when Terry perceived Brenda as thin, several important developments coalesced. Brenda was not thinner. She was, however, developing her skill as a teacher in her field and struggling to maintain a professional self-image syntonic with her achievement. Her body image and her self-presentation may indeed have reflected her growing sense of mastery and confidence. It was quite possible that Terry read these changes as "thinner," more "in control," and self sufficient, and felt them as enviable. Terry, thus, probably translated her experience of these changes in Brenda into body size language. By sharing her transference experience, she triggered a countertransference experience in Brenda. Brenda was not comfortable with imagining herself as thinner. She associated being thinner with being a small and incompetent younger sister, an identity she knew well and was trying to shed. Brenda felt very frightened when someone envied her.

Another interesting twist in this transference/countertransference configuration is that Terry is an older sibling with many characteristics in common with Brenda's sister. One could hypothesize that a number of feelings of patient and therapist were being deposited in body image and body size perception. For example, Terry may have felt envious of Brenda's growth and "reduced" her body to rebalance the felt relationship. Brenda may be responding to her own sibling history, expressed in body image terms or to Terry's subtle message or both. But certainly recognizing these body size and image reactive experiences opens many avenues of exploration.

In relation to a male client, Tom, Brenda reported a very different countertransference experience with her body image. In this case Brenda felt uncharacteristically fat after Tom mentioned that he thought of her as "average" in size. This time, as she felt herself grow larger and larger in the session, she did not feel safer but, instead, in danger of being humiliated by this fantasized weight gain. Because of this body image experience Brenda hypothesized that Tom meant something quite critical in his description of average. When Brenda asked Tom how he felt about "average," he admitted feeling quite critical; average was not really up to snuff. It became clear to Brenda that this time her body-size-based countertransference was partly projective identification, but it also served to encapsulate her own feelings about not living up to her internalized cultural ideal, feelings triggered by her patient's contempt. Brenda further noticed that Tom had expressed his criticism just as the relationship was becoming closer, and she guessed that his contempt defended against his fear and conflict about being known very deeply by his therapist. Brenda stored this observation and hypothesis for a time when it might be helpful.

A last example of transference/countertransference co-motion is provided by Brenda's experience with Barbara, a severely obese woman in treatment for over 10 years with Brenda. Barbara felt far more satisfied in her life in many ways as a result of her treatment. Barbara had made friends, was no longer socially isolated, became capable on her job, and obtained recognition in her profession as a legal secretary. She set comfortable boundaries with her mother and father, each of whom had invaded her independence in different ways. She was able to begin very serious dating and had attained comfort with her bisexuality. In all these ways Barbara's world expanded. Her relationship to eating and her body image, however, were still areas of great suffering. She continued to binge and hate her fat. Brenda reported in supervision that from time to time she felt alternately thin and then fat when with Barbara. After some careful tracking and inquiry, it became clear that Brenda could not understand why with all these improvements, the eating and body hatred were not also significantly changing. She realized that although Barbara depended on her in profound ways, she was still not as safe or comfortable a companion as were food and body hatred. Thinking about what fat and thin felt like emotionally in this context, Brenda noticed that she was frustrated and worried. She wondered whether she was important to Barbara and failing her. In this context she came to believe that her strange body image alternations between fat and thin represented feelings she had in relationship to her client. When she felt particularly thin she noticed that she also felt somewhat contemptuous of Barbara; and when she felt fat, she felt panicky, ashamed, and confused about Barbara's progress. Monitoring these body size and image experiences anchored Brenda in facing her worry and frustration directly. Eventually she let go of her feelings of hyperresponsibility and felt more able to endure her patient's pace and symptoms, thus allowing Barbara to finally trust and herself to differentiate from her client's pace. Her patience grew as her self-blame and client blaming, encoded in body image experience, receded.

ISSUES OF DISCLOSURE, PLAUSIBILITY, MUTUALITY, AND ASYMMETRY IN BODY IMAGE CO-MOTION

Disclosing countertransference experience is a hotly debated issue in psychotherapy today. Just as it is no longer considered a technical error to experience countertransference, so it is no longer taboo to disclose such feelings. Breaking the taboo, as noted by Burke (1992), Wooley (1991), and others now allows therapists and theoreticians to consider when disclosures are helpful (e.g., when they provide new object experience that can be used by the client) and when they are harmful (as for example when they will only repeat an old object experience) (Burke, 1992). The issue of self-disclosure dovetails with contemporary writing about issues of "plausibility," "mutuality," and "asymmetry" (Aron, 1992b; Gill & Hoffman, 1982; Hoffman, 1984; Levenson, 1983). The following examples apply common experiences with body image transference and countertransference to this area of thought.

As her therapy progressed, Terry felt better about herself in general. However, she still did not trust that she could be comfortable in her own body if she were not always on guard against fat by constantly calling herself fat. In a sense, she was addicted to self-hatred as a way of coping with anxiety about her sense of personal adequacy. She was relieved by her wishful fantasy, reported earlier, that her therapist could feel comfortable in a body that was round. In discussing Terry's body hatred, Brenda reminded Terry of her fantasy that Brenda felt okay in a round body. Brenda suggested that although part of Terry felt committed to body hatred as a safety measure, another part longed for the self-acceptance Terry imagined Brenda to have. Brenda reasoned that Terry would be helped by analyzing the wish in the fantasy about Brenda, thus enabling Terry to take back the projection and own her longing to live free of such debilitating criticism.

Whether Brenda needs to disclose her own comfort at that time is another question. Perhaps such disclosure would hold out hope for Terry that she too could eventually live in peace with her body. Perhaps, on the other hand, it would set up a holier-than-thou, politically correct competition in which Terry felt guilty for her self-hatred. Or it might foreclose Terry's further fantasy elaboration about her therapist's experience of her body.

In relation to the question of disclosure, consider the incident in which

Terry saw her therapist as thin and Brenda, in her own personal discomfort, "rectified" this perception of herself that felt dangerous to her by immediately feeling fat. Brenda wondered if it would be useful to disclose to Terry that her fears about competency were sometimes expressed in fat and thin terms. For example, when Terry reported how fat she felt as she embarked on a new work assignment, the therapist could fully empathize with this conflict and fear expressed as a body size state. She thought about sharing a common struggle and tried to mentally enumerate some criteria upon which it would depend. Was treatment in a termination phase when Brenda might need to affirm some reality and the transference had been very much worked out? Alternatively, was it a time when Terry was in a rage at Brenda and needed no new input about Brenda's struggle with food and body image?

Brenda did feel clear about the value of eventually disclosing her experience of feeling fat with Tom. It was revealed in his treatment that when he got frightened of getting too close in love relationships, he typically began to feel critical of his girlfriend's size. In addition, it became clear that the women sometimes responded by feeling fat as well as wrong and unlovable and eventually distanced themselves from him. Tom did not connect his feelings about body size to his girlfriends' withdrawals and depressions. After observing and pondering her own countertransferential body image experience, Brenda had regained her equilibrium; she stopped feeling fat with Tom. Now she felt she could give Tom an important new experience by self-disclosing, so she decided to tell Tom about her own experience of feeling fat after Tom said he thought of her as average. She also told him that she believed his perception reflected his fear of the two of them becoming closer in the treatment. After the discussion Tom saw how his contempt, focused on body image, affected his girlfriends who were already wounded by this culture. He even hypothesized, probably correctly, why one of these women had actually gained quite a bit of weight at the time he began to feel critical of her: She internalized his criticism so deeply that she felt she ought to get thinner immediately, thereby creating an anxiety that led to frequent bingeing. The fact that the therapist could remain stable and endure his frightened and defensive assault was an important and reassuring new experience for him.

Therapists working with clients who have painful eating problems and body image distortions will often be asked about themselves. Clients frequently ask whether "you" have suffered with an eating problem and how "you" feel about and in "your" body. When investigated, this question often reveals a wonder about whether one can really feel better about food and one's body; the question can hold hope that such change is possible. But this is not always the meaning of the question. Sometimes a client really wants to say, "How can 'you' help me, 'fat' or 'thin' as 'you' are?" They may hope that you can do so but defend against such hope with contempt, disbelief, or disidentification. Each therapist will have to determine if and when disclosure will be useful to the client and either way be prepared to track her responses in the treatment. The growing literature in this area is helpful and stimulating in thinking about individual cases.

There is another set of questions frequently asked that are generally not useful to answer directly. When a client asks, for example, how much weight you lost, what you did or do weigh, how you eat, what you eat, whether your weight is absolutely stable, and exactly how free you are from eating and body image obsession, it is best not to provide a direct answer. The dangers of this type of disclosure are that the clients get lost in either identification or merger with the therapist; alternatively, they may attempt to differentiate by means of the manipulation of body size and eating habits. Moreover, the grip of the cultural "field" is so strong that once many clients hear a number on a scale or a typical set of eating habits, they easily may become stuck by the concrete and want to eat or weigh exactly that. Everyone wants to be 120 pounds and 5'7" and maybe 30 years old, but equally great is the pull toward being the same as the therapist—having that weight, that appetite, those food preferences, that exercise routine, and that length of treatment. Particular sensitivity to issues of merger and individuation is due a client suffering from eating and body image disturbance; there is already much too much pressure to conform to a uniform ideal.

In many cases, however, these general considerations must be balanced by honoring what is now called "plausibility" in clients' estimations of therapists' experiences, thoughts, and feelings. When for example, the therapist is not an ideal or average weight or when she has real weight gains and losses, this reality cannot be denied without compromising the relationship. Even so, the therapist must be careful not to overconcretize and to help the client explore the fullest fantasy and relational meanings of her observations about the therapist. In general there are dangers of being either too resistant and cut off from plausible inquiries or being too concrete and open about them.

This last example touches on all the major issues discussed: the possibility that client and therapists' perceptions of each other's bodies and that the cultural ideal of beauty will invade the therapy relationship and issues of asymmetry, mutuality, and disclosure.

A therapist called Ann told her supervisor that, in facilitating her therapy group for compulsive eating and body hatred, she frequently had very painful and embarrassing thoughts and feelings. As a thin woman, she said, she sometimes felt almost sadistic when sitting with the fat women in her group. She definitely felt superior and more virtuous than her clients. In having these feelings she felt complicit with the worst of contemporary social hierarchies: She was not being honest about her belief that she truly did have more power and prestige in this culture than did her fat clients. "We are not the same," she argued, "yet there is something about my treatment with these women and about this method that falsely implies we are."

Ann and her supervisor discussed these disturbing feelings and Ann's history, and their talk illuminated her experience in a number of ways. Above all, it was important to validate Ann's perception of social reality. Ann was not only very svelte, she was also an extraordinarily beautiful woman. People could be taken aback looking at her. The supervisor hypothesized that Ann had carried her beauty as both gift and burden in her life. For example, a colleague of the therapist's had remarked on meeting Ann that she was so striking that he felt embarrassed. The therapist also empathized with the sting Ann felt at having been toppled from the arduously gained position of being on a pedestal when, in her late teens, she had gone from being anorexic to the point of hospitalization to gaining over 100 pounds so that she looked quite heavy and was ostracized for being fat. They talked about Ann's beauty with all its complications. Ann knew and was honest about how her appearance was idealized, as well as the hatred, jealousy, and sadism that it aroused in those around her. To aggravate all this Ann had survived severe, sadistic, and systematic sexual abuse and knew all too intimately the experience of being helpless in a hierarchy. In these experiences her beauty had been both envied and abused, perpetrators had wanted to own her, to control the power she seemed to contain. She was aware that sometimes she could not help but identify with the aggressors and idealizers of her beauty. The superior/inferior schema about which Ann felt guilty, overtly based on beauty, encoded covert power systems that had touched her deeply in her experience of abuse and in the course of ordinary social life. Ann had been exposed to the worst in current social mores.

It was relieving and grounding for Ann to talk about all this in its fullest complexity, to analyze it, demystify it, and to be cared about in her upset and confusion. With this grounding Ann and her supervisor were able to recognize further that beauty was neither entirely personal nor just a social ideal. On the one hand, Ann's beauty was entirely her own, not simply a dividend of social standards. What was so striking about her was most of all an inner radiance and liveliness. Ann was a very attractive person, not for her appearance alone: She was powerful, deeply skilled, and committed to providing excellent care. Somewhere, somehow, her presence seemed to let people know that she truly was a survivor. On the other hand, Ann's svelte beauty and her clients' obesity did not exist in and of themselves, not even simply in relation to a cultural scale. The cultural ideal acts as a standard that passes critical judgment on anyone's body; no one escapes its sadistic and powerful scrutiny. This is what gives beauty so much of its power. The ideal is internalized, joins the internal saboteur, becoming an internalized "cultural saboteur" (term coined by L. Zaphiropoulos, 1994, personal communication), and inserts itself into the relationship between client and therapist. This process is hidden, however, so that the exchange between therapist and client seems to be purely personal, whereas, in fact, it is both personal and social, almost impersonal, and inherently objectified.

On the basis of this further discussion, the supervisor advised Ann to encourage her clients to reveal, at appropriate times in the course of their work, how they felt about Ann's body and appearance. In pursuing this analysis, Ann saw how it would be possible to help her clients to discover and name their experience with and relationship not only to her but also to the social standard and how that standard joined their individual emotional experiences. The following questions might be helpful to the clients. What do they feel about her and about themselves in relationship to her? Do they distinguish their relationships to her appearance from the social ideal? Or do they conflate them? How do their experiences of her and of themselves reflect both their individual histories and their shared social history? In the group setting, the supervisor advised, it would not be useful for Ann to disclose her own pain but, instead, to use her shared and related experience to guide her clients to knowing their inner truth, as it existed in their social reality.

CHAPTER 9

Transference and Countertransference Issues: The Diet Mentality versus Attuned Eating

SUSAN GUTWILL

A THIRD AREA around which transference/countertransference configurations typically coalesce and that does not yet have a place in the literature, relates to the impact on treatment of the therapist's stance toward feeding oneself. On the one hand, the culturally normative diet mentality stance—always the default position in very subtle forms—puts particular stresses on the transference and countertransference. On the other hand, a socially critical, antideprivational commitment to attuned feeding and body acceptance also has an impact on the transference and countertransference.

In almost every case the client with eating problems has had parents and many other loved ones who attempted to keep her or him on a diet. This history is kept alive by ongoing interpersonal and sociocultural relationships where the diet mentality reigns. Guilt about eating and wanting food, the inevitable product of the diet mentality, is always coupled with a rageful rebellion and with tremendous sadness at always feeling deprived. Clients live with their fantasy versions of the "diet generals" inside and act out their inner conflict again and again in particular eating incidents. The inner "diet general," the product of both fantasy and reality experience, is projected on to the food. For example, time after time, in a detailed inquiry, the clinician will hear something that indicates that her client began to eat the food then immediately attacked herself, feeling as if the food both admonished her and tempted her. She then rebels: "Goddamnit I'll eat as much as I want!" and eats way beyond even what she originally wanted.

This rebellion and rage are almost always enacted with food, but they frequently enter the transference to the therapist too. The transference may be loaded with rage at the deprivers, blamers, and manipulators that clients have felt the "diet generals" to be. The client may be so used to this prisoner-versus-jailor relationship that even the new therapist and her approach of responding to hunger can represent an impossible, rejecting, new diet standard. To the client, that is, waiting for hunger to eat and stopping with satiation may be experienced as a new diet. As such, it can activate the same old antilibidinal demanding, frustrating, critical, internal object relationships. In the attendant transference/countertransference configurations clients will often become enraged, seeing the therapist as an impossibly demanding taskmaster who has stripped her of her old diet defenses, leaving her bereft. Now, in order to achieve approval, she feels she must submit to the therapist's will, the therapist's "program," and live in the panic of having her old coping mechanisms stolen from her. A compliance-defiance cycle may materialize in the transference/countertransference experience.

For example, many clients come in feeling desperate, victimized, controlled, and so wildly threatened by gaining any weight that they feel they must go on a total 90-day fast or have a stomach stapling or jaw wiring. The countertransference provoked may be an attempt to prevent these extreme measures, but it may be seen by the client as the therapist controlling her, falling into the client's role expectation. If, however, the therapist takes no stance to protect but, rather, just explores the client's predicament, she can be experienced as the neglectful parent. As is most often true in treatment, there is no one right answer. The therapist makes individual decisions depending on the client's struggle and the stage of the treatment.

Alternatively clients may misconstrue an antideprivational commitment to eat with hunger and become attuned to the body as a license to eat anything and everything at any time. In this case the philosophy as well as the therapist can come to represent tantalizing internal objects that oppose necessary limits, as if "you can have it all, always." The implication here is that limits are hurtful, injurious, punitive, and critical. In the transference the client will both love and hate this mother who finally cares, but who is not effective, and therefore still fails her. "You *said* eat anything, and I'm trying, but. . . . " She must remain frustrated and in a struggle with her internal jailor.

The following represent examples of treatments in which the diet mentality (including body hatred) played a major and pathogenic part in the inner world of the client and had an impact on the transference/countertransference in complex and challenging ways. Each case required the therapist to dig out of or avoid stalemated transference and countertransference configurations dictated by the diet mentality in order to meet other important treatment objectives.

SARIT

Sarit came in one day expressing in a particularly dramatic way a characteristic experience she had in therapy. She felt she was gaining weight, was not being helped by her attempt to eat with hunger, and was thus being essentially set back by treatment. "I can't stand this any more, I have hit my limit. I have to do it differently. Maybe after I have lost some weight I can learn to eat and nurture myself, but not at this weight. I hate you. It's like you have stolen my liberty. If it weren't for you, I would do what I have done my whole life and just go on a diet. But because of you, I am in conflict; if I do diet, I lose your approval, and if I don't I hate myself. And what is worse, the truth is that I can't diet now even if I wanted to. [She had forgotten that she came to therapy in the first place, for being unable to diet anymore. But she could not lose the mentality either.] It's like you stole my only coping mechanism from me. I came here in good faith, and I am getting worse," she cried. "I feel like I have a solution. I almost asked the dentist to wire my jaw the other day. And I still might do it."

Sarit, whose mother had survived Auschwitz, had recently spoken about a horrible memory of having had her mouth taped shut as a child to prevent her from breathing through her mouth, something considered dangerous to a child. She had associated this mouth taping with another memory of having been tied into the bed clothes at some point when she was falling out of bed. Both these memories and other similarly dramatic incidents were connected to her experience of having felt like her mother's prisoner throughout her childhood—and still now, even though they had a long-distance relationship maintained through telephone contact.

On the day Sarit discussed the jaw wiring possibility, she felt toward her therapist as she did toward her mother. The therapist and her damn ideas, were making decisions for her. She felt like the therapist's victim, entirely disempowered. Her rage was cloaked in a whining tone, duplicating and exposing the powerlessness she felt with her mother. The therapist, however, was also being tested. Sarit was furious at her father for abandoning her to her mother's incompetence and wild rages. She felt her father didn't go to bat for her enough. He even left her with the mother after he himself had divorced her.

In the countertransference experiences, as will be true in each of the examples included here, the therapist must avoid the concordant experience, a position inculcated by the culture at large, that Sarit should "do something" now, diet now, and only then can she afford to think about her pain. This culturally syntonic position would contend that (1) Sarit hates herself now, partly because she has gained 10 pounds, and 10 pounds on a small person is serious; and (2) if she loses the weight she will have achieved something very real for herself and therefore be in a better position to deal with her many other conflicts. A variation on this concordant countertransference experience would be to so deeply identify and empathize with Sarit's upset about her fat that the therapist would support any measures whatsoever to help her out of her pain. The therapist would also have the advantage of appearing not to want to narcissistically control Sarit by imposing her philosophy as did Sarit's mother. In reality, however, the therapist would, in this situation, be in the position of the father, abandoning Sarit, not this time to a violating mother, but to a violating diet practice. In a less obvious way, however, the therapist would also be enacting the disowned, sadistic partner of Sarit's inner masochist: "Go ahead, have your jaw wired, do anything to get rid of that weight." The sadistic countertransference complement is always a danger: It is easy to perceive the client as only a masochistic, victimized, "hysterical" woman who cannot stop "whining" about how fat she is getting. It is important to avoid enacting this countertransference position, and it can be far more difficult than it may appear. For it is easy to accept Sarit's transference accusation as "plausible": that as a therapist one should not have a known position about feeding oneself, that one ought to be neutral, that to advocate against dieting would be simply for the therapist's narcissistic gratification. It is easy to forget that the therapist does not have so much power and that the client can, indeed, diet at any time she wishes. In fact, Sarit has dieted innumerable times, just as even in this treatment she has often been quite able to eat in a careful, nurturing, healthful way, attuned to physical hunger and satiation. It is essential not to accept this transference/countertransference trap. Sarit can do whatever she likes, regardless of what opinion the therapist has. Sarit needs to be helped to remember this so that she can begin to take back her projections and so that her internal conflicts can surface. Sarit's cruel, name-calling hatred of her fat hips and the needy self who eats both matches and reproduces the mother's criticism and the father's abandonment. Moreover, were she to have her jaw wired, she would be enacting this cruelty in images reminiscent of the violations that she believes her mother to have suffered in the concentration camps. Indeed, on some level this would relieve Sarit by expressing in physical pain the psychic pain to which she feels unentitled, because in her family system it was her mother who was seen as the one "really" hurt. The diet mentality—a victim-victimizer scheme, a compliance-defiance inner relationship—can easily seduce the therapist into related countertransference enactments.

The only way out of such a destructive entanglement requires first and foremost an understanding of the power of the diet mentality and its grip on Sarit. The therapist must have a critical view of hegemonic cultural messages; in other words, she must be somewhat free of an unacknowledged transference to the culture at large. Only from this position can the therapist help Sarit to observe with empathy and accuracy her fantasy world as well as her real cultural environment and relationships. Sarit needs to "recognize" herself and her predicament in order to leave the masochistic-sadistic enactments by which she is so pained and in which she is so stuck. She needs to become aware of how willing she is to violate herself in thought and deed and to connect this predisposition with the violations in her life. What happened to her mother and what happened with her mother resonate with the culture's constant critique of fat, all of which in turn then resonate with Sarit's psychological world, making life very hard. The therapist's awareness of the power of the diet mentality, as it activates and stimulates other painful areas of Sarit's life, gives her a perspective from which to observe the countertransference pulls.

CLAIRE

The conflict between the obsessive need to eat spawned by the diet mentality and the incessant admonishment not to eat gives rise to its own transference and countertransference experience. An example of this is shown by the case discussed earlier of Claire, who came to treatment one day with a complaining, frustrated tone quite like Sarit's. "I can't stand it any more. No matter what I do, I just can't ever do it. I've been here 10 years! And still I do well for a few days, and then I let go or something, I lose it, I end up bingeing, and then that day and the next wipe out whatever I achieved in the days prior. I can't take it. Ten years! Obviously I can't do this thing. It seems simple, so clear, eat when I am hungry, remember to be gentle and curious about overeating. I just forget everything. It just doesn't work. I am getting fatter and fatter." In this situation Claire feels inadequate and at fault and probably disappointed in the therapist who can help others but not her. It is very easy for the therapist in a concordant countertransference to feel blamed and then, in defense, to exhibit the complementary sadism to match her victimized client's. One of the best ways out of this trap, a form of detailed inquiry and specification used to extricate the client from the generalized, self-defeating language of why "it" isn't working, is to ask what happened the last time she tried to wait for hunger to eat. What particular incident does she have in mind? In this simple and profound way the transference/countertransference bind is avoided (to be understood and later used), and work can continue. The therapist did, however, note for future work, that she felt annoyed and, given Claire's presentation, was unable to fully empathize with her pain at that moment.

Claire said she was thinking about an occasion during the weekend when she was lonely and had no plans; characteristically, she felt somewhat humiliated by those facts. Trying to go on, she had determined to study and practice some music she was learning but felt quite overwhelmed by the task. She felt hopeless about mastering it. She then began to eat and have a few drinks. Although she immediately and repeatedly told herself to stop eating and stop drinking, she was unable to do so; and the more she told herself to stop, the more she indulged herself. Nonetheless, within a relatively short time, she felt able to tackle the music but was full of self-hatred for her food and liquor binge.

The therapist first asked what it felt like to hear the demand to stop the eating and drinking coming from inside herself. Claire immediately noticed that the more she admonished herself, the more she ate and drank. In doing so, she remembered countless similar incidents. It immediately became clear to her again how the diet mentality works; a realization that empowered and relieved her. Then the therapist asked how Claire felt about herself when she was insecure and overwhelmed upon looking at the music. Claire, considerably more centered, said she hated being so insecure and weak. The therapist then asked how she felt about her loneliness. "Ditto," said Claire. "This time," the therapist said, "it was easier for you to hate being a compulsive eater and too fat than it was to realize that you were hating a lonely overwhelmed Claire precisely for being lonely." They sat in a knowing and rich silence, having worked together long enough so that Claire was now capable of feeling sad for herself. Claire then asked, "Why is it that I use the fat?" To which the therapist replied, "It is a socially designated channel or repository for emotions such as insecurity that are personally hard and socially unpopular." Instead of enacting the cultural countertransference by considering Claire's question to be a retreat from self, a flight into the culture as a defense against self, the therapist explained and exposed the cultural contribution at a moment when Claire wanted to hear it and could make use of it. And again there was a full and important silence, after which Claire said she felt more dignified in her struggle, more respectful of herself, and more capable of trying again to eat with hunger.

Before the discussion of this episode ended, however, the therapist processed and made use of her feelings of annoyance and inability to feel compassion at the start of the session. She had understood that Claire was using her, as she used food and the diet mentality itself, to become involved in a characteristic compliance-defiance struggle, whose purpose was to cover her shame about feeling needy, vulnerable, and lonely. They discussed this interaction. As she had first presented her material, Claire had felt a little whiny and had experienced the therapist's listening as a somewhat cold response. Together they clarified that Claire's plaintiveness had expressed her expectation that the therapist would be impatient and disgusted with the bingeing and with Claire's failure. Claire was then able to observe how impatient and disgusted she herself had felt. Eventually they saw that Claire's self-contempt had been taken up momentarily by the therapist, thereby enacting, even though in a subtle form, relationships in

Claire's unconscious object world dominated by painful struggles between victim and victimizer, a form of contact that at least helped her to fill her sense of emptiness and isolation and hide her feelings of vulnerability and dependency.

In Claire's case, once again, the implications and dynamics of the diet mentality would have created a transference/countertransference configuration that were its enactment: a failing client coupled with an insatiable therapist who only demanded what could not be achieved; a client who feels like an unlovable failure and a therapist who, in defense against feeling like a failure and being blamed for it, instead feels annoyed with and defeated by this broken record of a client. If the therapist had been disgusted by Claire's eating, bingeing, or fat, if she could not see how the diet mentality itself created a double bind that always leads to bingeing, she could not so easily have penetrated the underlying work and psychodynamics and have achieved an effective intervention.

ERICA

The last example of diet mentality operating in its own terms, even as it defends against other issues and where there is pressure for complex transference/countertransference dynamics, is shown in the case of Erica. Although it was important to help Sarit look at her wish to wire her jaw and to eventually, if necessary, try to forestall it, it was impossible to stop Erica from fasting for a full 6 months, with the entirely predictable outcome of her losing approximately 100 pounds, only to gain them back plus more.

Erica grew up as the daughter of parents who were top-level editors of fashion magazines. Their lives were devoted to glamour and looking "right." Erica was always considered to be too fat, and she was obsessed with finding "forbidden" food on which to binge. Erica's father was overtly tyrannical with his daughter, her mother covertly so; and her culture represented an unacknowledged but symbolically violating tyranny. In her psychic life she saved herself from absolute tyrannical engulfment by becoming the ultimate, undaunted rebel. She lived in a fight. It was enacted by the moment-to-moment struggle over food: She wanted to eat all the time and was obsessed with either wanting, procuring, or hiding food—all the while hating herself as the process began anew. She was never at peace. Her life was one of extraordinary torment. Her adaptation, fighting against tyranny, left her quite paranoid, so that any time she so much as questioned her right to eat, she would go into a quiet tantrum and eat all the more. Ruled by the predictable vicissitudes of the diet mentality, she became a very severe bulimic as well as quite obese.

Not surprisingly, there was frequently something to fight about in the treatment, especially in the earlier years of therapy. Erica watched the therapist like a hawk. Certainly, any slip, any "plausible" break in the therapist's stance, any slight boundary violation, any misattunement were all occasions for Erica to feel betrayed and enraged and to go into her "lawyer mode" to describe very brilliantly the therapist's indiscretion. The therapist worked hard at being authentic and flexible with Erica, owning her own mistakes, feeling empathic when Erica was injured, hoping that Erica would experience a new, nontyrannical model of relating. Sometimes, however, the therapist got into the fight, and, as Erica eventually noted with some relief, was a very worthy opponent. Together, they tried to develop a commitment to curiosity about their flareups, and, constructively, they came very far along that path.

It was painful for the therapist to watch her client destroying her digestive tract, developing a hernia, and living on binges interrupted only by whole bottles of Pepto-Bismol or Maalox. At one point Erica fell into such despair about her increasing weight and her inability to control her bingeing that she proposed going on a total fast to lose 100 pounds. She had stopped purging by that time and was facing the terror of fragmentating, as she put it. So it is not surprising that she would turn to the diet to contain her fear. She argued that she knew it wasn't what the therapist wanted for her, that she was deeply appreciative of the therapist for all they had accomplished outside the area of eating (which had indeed been considerable!), and for her flexibility and her being so real, caring, and tough all at once. But she wanted to go on this fast and she felt that the therapist should not be dogmatic. After all maybe it would work for her; maybe she could feel some of the feelings if she could lose weight quickly, maybe, maybe, maybe. She feared for her marriage and her husband's hatred of her fat, she felt she could have absolutely no impulse control although she tried valiantly (which indeed she did). She said she just could not stand being in such a fat body. She could not move, bend, and so on. It is important to note that following the decision of the therapist to support her attempt to fast, before actually beginning to fast, Erica instantly gained 30 pounds by eating pounds and pounds of candy at a time, in anticipation of starvation and deprivation.

The therapist was truly in a dilemma, which she discussed with her patient. She knew it was all but certain that this fast would only increase Erica's weight, cause her to lose a year of treatment, and divert the pain of the moment so that it could not be faced in its own terms. Indeed, Erica would be learning how to starve, not how to eat. There was very little work that could be done on the symptom while Erica was on a "diet high." At the same time the therapist knew that Erica was determined and that she herself was being tested as to whether she would take over with her own philosophy, as Erica's parents and whole culture had done. They discussed all the different meanings this decision might have in their relationship. But finally, the therapist felt it was like another bottle of Pepto-Bismol: She would have to watch it go down. In addition, she wished so much that Erica would get some relief that she hoped against hope that Erica might be the one in a million for whom fasting would work. Together, therapist and client discussed that wish in terms of its implications about their relationship. This example is included because it demonstrates that there are times at which one must entirely give into the diet—if not the diet mentality—in order to preserve the treatment. Only after living through the fast and, unfortunately, the subsequent gaining of more weight than had been lost, could the therapist help Erica see and understand more fully her wish for the instant fix and her conflicts about truly changing her eating behavior. The therapeutic alliance and trust were enhanced by their going through this experience together.

Current Treatment Practices: Some Critical Reflections

There are several standard practices and protocols in the field of eating disorders that we believe are best understood as the institutionalization of cultural countertransferential errors. These protocols are influenced by and predicated on the following three factors: (1) the current ideological prescription for the female body and the intense and very complicated meanings of eating and a "healthy" body have all combined to put pressure on practitioners to reify the desperate importance of "getting eating disorders under control"; (2) these social pressures are supported and intensified by the ideological and institutional hegemony of the 12-step programs in the field of addictions; (3) these two social forces are magnified and justified by the reality that in all too many cases women with eating problems (anorexics or bulimarexics in particular) actually do face death if they do not get their starvation or purging under control. The combination of these three pressures make it quite difficult not to err in the direction of excessive control. However, such mobilization to action and a diet mentality can be punitive or infantilizing to the patient.

Some punitive and infantilizing treatment procedures used in inpatient settings are the forced feeding of a woman in restraints; the humiliating surveillance of her person or room for evidences of bingeing or purging; surveillance of her use of the bathroom; and even forced weighings. These are all particularly thorny techniques or treatment modalities that are commonly practiced in behaviorally oriented hospital-based programs for patients with eating disorders.

A related example, a particularly noxious treatment made famous by Salvadore Minuchin and his associates (1974), involves teaching parents to unite in learning to force-feed—literally stuff the mouth—of their teenage daughters. Without consideration of the social support for anorexic behavior for a possible history of sexual abuse, Minuchin argues that the anorexia is a symptom of the parents' disunity, of their failure to exert executive control of their family and children. Watching a teaching video of this method was horrifying to us and made us feel that parents were being trained to physically abuse their daughters.

Another form of blatant treatment abuse encountered by many patients on inpatient units and in outpatient settings rests on principles of negative behavior reinforcement: actively humiliating clients (one client was told, "You are disgusting, look at yourself, all fat and flabby, and covered with vomit") or scaring them ("Do you know what your fat, starving, or purging is doing to your children?"). Because this is what clients already think and feel about themselves, it is hard to imagine how these doctors think they are helping. In every single case reported personally to us, the eating problems and self-hatred have not improved but, on the contrary, have become more entrenched and intense.

Not only do these sorts of treatment efforts demean, infantilize, and even brutalize, but also they displace the client's struggle from where it rightly belongs: inside herself, between the part of her that wants to get better and the part that still needs to express itself in the form of the eating problem (Orbach, 1986). When the arena of struggle is iatrogenically placed between the treatment team and the woman, it is no wonder that a compliant "recovery" is followed by a terrifyingly high recidivism rate. This sort of treatment colludes with the whole social situation: "she" doesn't have to be in charge of her own body-self; the proverbial "he" of patriarchy will do it for her and for her own good. Unfortunately, even though its dynamics are so destructive, this Pygmalion model of treatment, as Wooley calls it, of anorexia has held great sway in our field for far too long (Levenkron, 1978; Wooley, 1991).

Another standard treatment protocol is, of course, the diet itself, an insidious, more covert treatment revictimization, used widely in inpatient and outpatient treatment. Dieting and food plans are central to contemporary treatments of eating disorders, especially in hospital-based programs. In most such units women are told what to eat, when, and how much. Large women are required to eat less, and underweight women are required, often forced, to eat more. An externally imposed structured "healthy" food plan, often referred to as a non-diet, is at the heart of most eating disorder treatments.* From the standpoint of trying to help the person with eating problems to have an experience of safe structure and reduction of chaos in her eating, this practice is more understandable than some of the others just discussed. But we believe that such an effort ought to be based, however com-

---

*This information was confirmed for the WTCI by an informal phone survey conducted by Tanya Sholsberg, a social work student. Ms. Sholsberg called a large number of inpatient settings. All used a food plan based on restriction, allowances, and requirements. Even in a few cases when physiological hunger was mentioned, the food plan was paramount. Even when programs claimed to be opposed to diets, they eventually used diets and were characterized by the diet mentality.

plicated and bureaucratically difficult it would be, in teaching patients to respond to their hunger and satiation in a safe environment.

In addition, many hospital programs and private therapists alike uncritically rely on Overeaters Anonymous (OA), which teaches a lifelong distrust of self and food as the actual cure. Although on the one hand OA gives marvelous social support for the undoing of eating problems, on the other, it actually supports the obsession about food by arguing that food and eating are addicting and that eating problems, like all addictions, can never be healed. In this way the OA philosophy and practice support the mystification of food and body. According to OA, people with eating disorders will always need to be "abstinent" in relation to food and should strictly plan what they will eat, how much, and when.

Overeaters Anonymous has become central to most treatment programs for a complex variety of reasons. It is enormously supportive to clients feeling shamed and out of control and to overextended professionals trying to help them. It is a free and communal self-help service. These reflect its very admirable strengths. Moreover, OA-based solutions of food-addiction problems are very popular with the insurance industry, and the 12-step programs have a large professional lobbying program; these are less honorable, less patient-focused reasons for OA's hegemony in the field.

In very well-meaning and respectful ways, current treatment philosophies also respond to a felt sense of emergency. Too often, people's lives are in acute danger, and beginning treatment in such an emergency condition presents clinicians with a very complicated problem. In such circumstances, forced-feeding and similar protocols may be necessary and unavoidable for a time. But it is imperative, at the very least, to address the emotional issues that this invasive treatment itself brings to the fore. For survivors of sexual abuse, for example, force-feeding will be experienced as an abuse reenactment in one way or another. Some clinicians are becoming clearer about this problem (Herman, 1992; Putnam, 1989). We do not claim to know how to solve it, but each case requires very individualized thinking and treatment planning, as well as thorough processing of the meaning of the invasive procedure for the patient. Even if because of starvation the brain is not fully functioning, the patient should be engaged in discussion. The sexually abused patient, however compromised, must especially be helped to engage in distinguishing being physically coerced "then" from "now." (See chapter 11.)

Although there are times when invasive procedures are clearly necessary, it is equally critical to reflect on how the mental health field defines what is meant by an "acute emergency," so that the field as a whole will not become rationalized around an emergency mentality that justifies the routine employment of invasive treatment protocol in less-than-emergency situations. This would be an institutionalization of cultural countertransference. The great majority of eating problems, although certainly detrimental to health, are not acute emergencies. Too many clients have been victimized by intrusive treatment procedures. These clients may appear to their doctors quite successful for the length of their inpatient programs. When they leave, however, their problems return, often in a more intense form than previously. Practitioners are familiar with the stories of women who drank gallons of water before their forced weigh-in, women who stuffed their bras with quarters to falsely tip the scales up, women who have found bathrooms or bushes in which to purge, despite the locked bathrooms of their units. Most of these women committed themselves to the hospital programs and were at first motivated to explore their internal conflicts with food and their bodies. In almost all the cases they ended up in conflict with their doctors and losing the focus on their own internal pain and struggle. In other cases we have been approached by mothers who have just discovered that their teenage daughters have been purging. The mothers, horrified and frightened, wanting to nip the problem in the bud, have sometimes chosen to put their daughters into inpatient treatment programs. Our experience is that such young women come to feel stigmatized and pathologized; as a result they focus on fighting against institutional controls rather than on healing their eating habits, bodies, and body images.

CHAPTER 10

Eating Problems and Sexual Abuse: Theoretical Considerations

SUSAN GUTWILL AND ANDREA GITTER

THIS CHAPTER explores from a feminist perspective (1) why and how the problems of sexual abuse and eating disorders so frequently converge, and (2) what the answer to that question suggests about good treatment.

Recent studies and evidence show that there is a large convergence of eating problems with sexual abuse. Research validates that this subgroup is significantly large, although estimates vary (Goodwin & Attias, 1993). Investigations indicate a significant correlation between the two phenomena (Calam & Slade, 1989; Goldfarb, 1987; Smolak et al., 1990). Some studies suggest that fully two-thirds of patients with eating disorders have experienced sexual abuse (Oppenheimer et al., 1985). Other researchers show samples in which approximately one-third of patients with eating disorders have been sexually abused (Crisp, 1984; Nash & West, 1985; Palmer et al., 1990; Sloan & Leichner, 1986). Studies focusing on patients suffering from incest-related dissociative disorders (Coons, Bowman, & Milstein, 1988; Kluft, 1990b) also demonstrate a high frequency of eating disorders (Demitrack et al., 1990). Collin Ross (1989) argues that if one looks carefully, anywhere between 50% to 75% of multiple personality disorder cases reveal eating disorders. In general these studies narrowly define eating disorders as anorexia or bulimia. Moshe Torem (1990, 1993) significantly expands these typical definitions of eating disorders to include some of the more normative problems, such as compulsive eating, excessive dieting or exercising, and distorted body image. Without this expanded definition studies underrepresent the population of trauma survivors who experience eating problems.

However, although many studies emphasize the convergence of sexual abuse and eating problems, few address this phenomenon from a feminist theoretical and clinical perspective (Kearney-Cooke, 1988; Wooley, 1992, 1994; Wooley & Kearney-Cooke, 1986; Zehner, 1992a, 1992b). The next three chapters offer a contribution to the theory and the practice of working with this population.

One answer to the question about why posttraumatic stress and eating problems converge is that both are fundamentally structured into our social life by patriarchy. Sexual abuse is so common that it has been said that it is not incest and sexual assault that are secret but the telling or knowing about it that is taboo, and that rape is more appropriately understood as regulated rather than prohibited (Herman, 1993a; Rush, 1980). Patriarchal social organization makes the high frequency of sexual assault against women and children inevitable (Brownmiller, 1975; Herman, 1981, 1992; Rush, 1980; Russell, 1986). Surveying numerous investigations shows a range of findings. Some studies show that 1 in 4 women has been battered, 1 in 3 women has been abused in childhood, and that at least 1 in 4 women has been raped. Before the age of 10, 1 in 4 girls has been sexually abused and 1 in 5 boys (Russell, 1986; Zehner, 1992a). Diana Russell (1986), in her groundbreaking study of incest based on extensive interviewing and an excellent large sample found that 16% of her sample had experienced at least one incestuous event and that 5% of these had experienced incest with their biological father. In another study, Wyatt (1985) showed findings consistent with those of Russell. Herman (1981, 1990) and Russell (1986) have shown conclusively that not only has a significant percentage of women been abused, but also that the results of incest and sexual abuse are deeply noxious and long-lasting. In clinical studies Goodwin (1982) shows the extensive problems that follow an incest history, as does Christine Courtois (1988) in her comprehensive text, *Healing the Incest Wound*. Most women who have not personally been sexually assaulted live with the constant knowledge and fear that at any time they, too, may join the ranks of victims (Brown, 1991). Herman (1993a) has argued that for women in our culture, sexual abuse, the majority of which occurs in adolescence, is a kind of cultural initiation rite into the violence toward women that is a cornerstone of patriarchal culture.

Unfortunately violations of women in patriarchal culture do not stop with actual interpersonal sexualized violence. Women are routinely assaulted by the symbolic landscape of our consumer culture as well. Although violations carried out by the word and the symbol are not the same as physical and sexual violence, they are homologous violations that do seriously violate and constrain women. Sexual assault controls and terrorizes by overt physical and sexual means. It is usually accompanied by some kind of mind control in which the victim comes to treat herself over time as an object; she colonizes herself and, in the words of Frantz Fanon (1968), comes to be her own jailer. Sexual violence is a tyranny allowed in the private sphere of the family, whereas in the public sphere, which is supposedly based on democracy, violation is symbolic and more subtle (Herman, 1993b). This chapter on the convergence of eating problems and body image disturbance with posttraumatic stress disorder (PTSD) focuses on how these two widespread and homologous forms of violation against women resonate and interact with each other. Recall for a moment some of the outcomes of the consumer culture symbolic landscape, for example, the encouragement to diet and to be slender so central to it. The 80% of American women who diet and live with a fear of food, the 78% of American women who feel wrong and ugly in their bodies or too fat, the many young girls who are obsessed with their weight are all victims of symbolic violations that lead to a chronic kind of insidious traumatization (Brown, 1989). Like Herman (1993b) in regard to sexual abuse, Kim Chernin (1981) argues that the cultural assault on women's bodies and appetites through learning to diet and fearing food is a major initiation rite of women in Western culture. Young girls live with an intense fear of being fat or of even being identified with a fat person. To live in fear and dread of food and with hatred of one's body creates an everyday experience of pernicious fear and assaulting self-criticism that too often parallels the outcomes of sexual violence.

Although many have acknowledged the terrible damage of sexual abuse, only some feminists recognize that the beauty myth, although more subtle, also kills, even if it does so in the name of "health" (Wolf, 1991). Consumer culture is an environment that elevates beauty to such heights that smoking has commonly been promoted in the public at large to keep weight down; chronic dieting is a major institution not only creating the everyday variety of eating problems but also causing thousands of deaths from anorexia and bulimia each year (Brumberg, 1989). All of this is created by a deadly and misogynist culture, where compulsive exercising can stunt growth and lead to anemia; breast implants leak, causing horrifying and often life-threatening complications; liposuction can maim and kill and was accepted into the United States and deemed a success after it had killed "only" nine French women (Wolf, 1991). In the land of the beauty myth, when you are maimed you are improved in health and self-esteem. When you are killed it is likely to go relatively unnoticed.

It is relevant to reconsider these outcomes of the symbolic assaults against women in light of trauma theory, because the beauty myth, especially as it expresses itself in a fat-phobic diet ethos, is a homologous form of violation against women that resonates with the assaults to self deriving from sexual abuse. Chronic dieting and the conditions it causes—even slow-killing anorexia—are not the equivalent of interpersonal sexualized violence, but the cumulative effect of the diet culture and the consumer ethic in elevating beauty shares many factors with trauma in terms of its effects on women, especially on their body/self integration. Moreover, these differing forms of violation reinforce each other's toxic effects as they resonate within each individual's psyche and within the culture as a whole. Understanding the nature of these commonalities in depth can help to establish basic guidelines for effective and respectful treatment of those suffering from both eating problems and posttraumatic stress.

Posttraumatic Stress

The basic tenets of the developing theory of traumatic stress begin with a definition of incest. According to Goodwin (1982), incest means "the sexual exploitation of a child by an older person in a parental role." Russell (1986) defines incest as unwanted sexual contact or attempted contact between relatives, including siblings, no matter how distant, before the victim is 18 years old. (For a fuller discussion of sexual abuse and PTSD, see Briere, 1992; Browne & Finkelhor, 1986; Courtois, 1988; Davies & Frawley, 1992a, 1994; Herman, 1981, 1992; Kluft, 1990a; Putnam, 1989; and van der Kolk, 1987.) Trauma theory studies the effects of war, natural disasters, accidents, torture and imprisonment, and violence against women and children in the "private" sphere of life. This work demonstrates the nature and operation of deep and profound trauma.

Incestuous child abuse begins with perhaps its worst aspect—the absolute betrayal of the child's trust by the adult whom the child loves and counts on for protection and nurturance. This betrayal, inhibiting a sense of basic trust in the safety of the nurturing environment, is as profound as is the horror of the abuse itself. Because the abuse is so violating of the self and its nurturing environment, the ego cannot endure and continue normal development of its symbolic and organizational functions. Indeed, to survive the child must split his or her ego and body-self, so as to find a creative and, paradoxically, adaptive way, to both hide from and know the truth of what he or she has endured and its psychic effects. Dissociation is understood by contemporary thinkers to be the first form of defense called forth by real-life traumatic events that threaten to dissolve the integrity of the ego.

Dissociation begins as a response of the psychological self to horrific events in real life over which one has no control. This escape is accomplished by the focusing of intense attention in two ways. First, a part of the self focuses on the event, and that event imprints itself on the traumatized person. Second, however, that very imprint is denied through the process of dissociation in which the event is disremembered, often by being psychically fragmented. It is as if the self concentrates, focuses attention elsewhere, in order not to see the trauma. This is done so that the memory of the event, feelings, and sensations are all known and seen and yet locked away and frozen in time, amnestically protected through dissociation. As Davies and Frawley describe this process (1992a), a child victim of sexual abuse uses dissociation to split the real experience from the family myth. (For several discussions of the difference between dissociation and repression, see W. Young [1988], R. J. Loewenstein and D. R. Ross [1992], and J. Briere and C. Courtois [1992]. Dissociation is generally thought of as defense against the trauma of real-life events, whereas repression usually refers to defenses against frightening feelings and impulses.) As Davies and Frawley (1992a) say, at least two selves develop: (1) a "daytime" self who functions as if no violation has occurred, a self who keeps the family's secret, who acts as if all were well; and (2) a "nighttime" self who stores the truth of her traumatic violation, and whose ego and self-development are severely inhibited. It is quite typical that a victim of abuse will present in therapy both as a very capable, organized, and highly functioning adult and as a child stuck in time, immensely insecure, incapable of running her life, and disorganized. Both these disparate selves come for treatment, and often there are many other associated and adaptive splits—of body from mind, knowledge from sensation, affect from behavior (Braun, 1990). Some fragments of self hold knowledge of truth, whereas others attempt to live in the world "as if" all were well. The self cannot continue as an integrated whole; or if any of that had been achieved, its development is slowed and affected by the many parts into which its experience is now distorted, pulled, and stored.

Traumatic experiences cannot be metabolized and integrated by a self so divided to cope with that trauma. Thus, the traumatic violation actually lives on inside as if it were always in the present. For example, when a client named Lily sees a portable toilet on the street, the shape of it triggers a dissociated memory, and she believes she is near the outhouse where she was abused as a child. Dissociated memory lives on, not in clear language telling its story, but frozen and split up into various sorts of encoded body sensations, intrusive images, unconscious behavioral reenactments, and cognitive distortions, all of which are typical of posttraumatic stress.

This living trauma, fragmented as it is, demands three particular kinds of adaptation from its victim-survivors. First, it demands that the victim remain in a state of hyperarousal (Herman, 1992; Horowitz, 1986; van der Kolk, 1987). A state of fight or flight, with all its physiological, emotional, and cognitive aspects, burdens the victim, who becomes, for example, given to startled responses, easily triggered into highly terrified and stimulated states, frightened of noise, and unable to sleep restfully.

Second, adapting to trauma leads the survivor to experience a constant oscillation between feeling states that (1) intrusively recall the truth, the trauma, and the terror of the abuse even if in a fragmented way; and (2) call forth the numbing responses that push that trauma away at the expense of feeling and consciousness. Intrusive feeling states are typically reported as flashbacks, nightmares, frequent somatic symptoms, intensely terrifying, vivid sensations (e.g., someone is choking me, watching me, about to jump at me) that although not clearly recalling the memory of an incident, repetitively reproduce aspects of traumatic incidents in the form of fragmented feelings and reenactments thrusting their way into present-day life and relationships. Although the trauma disappeared from conscious knowledge, it stayed encoded in sensory experience. Thus, a smell, a holiday, a season, a song, a sight, a sense of body size or shape or presence, sex itself could all trigger a sensate memory, state-dependent and dissociated, an abstract but terrible pain, or a rash, fear, dread, phobia—all feeling states.

Jeanette, for example, a client who was molested and fondled by her stepfather, often becomes frightened when she sees a chair near a large picture window. Her stepfather typically sat in such a chair and threateningly watched her comings and goings. Triggered by this sight Jeanette has an unconscious state-dependent (in this case, visually induced) experience from which she dissociates. One of the ways in which Jeanette has coped with these intrusive experiences of fear and self-blame has been to transform them into a distorted body image experience. Making use of the cultural fear of and disgust of fat, Jeanette, through complex psychic maneuvers, transformed the unacceptable reality and affects of incest into the bitter-tasting but tolerable and familiar hatred of fat. The incest intrudes into her life, therefore, as a feeling of fatness around the buttocks and hips and a generalized feeling of danger and self-hatred.

Understandably running from knowledge of the frightening world and from the inconsistent and unreliable divided self, an incest victim tries consciously and unconsciously to numb herself. This wish to numb, to shut down feeling, alternates with the unconscious intrusive experiences just described. Herman (1992) calls it the numbing response of the prisoner's surrender. In order to avoid intrusive experiences she withdraws, detaches from life. Eventually she feels that she is not really there and things are not real. Depersonalized and derealized in this way, she may lose time in amnestic episodes. For example, she may fully remember what happened but dull her affect with dissociative adaptions such as trances, drugs, food, self-mutilation, or alcohol. She may have partial and fragmented memories or none at all. Christine was a bulimic client who used food in order to obliterate the intense feelings associated with being sexually abused. She often ate enough to numb all sensations with fullness and then was amnestic to the entire binge as well as to the sexual trauma that caused it.

It is important to note that this defensive posture of dissociation, both the intrusive and the numbing, is accomplished by a self-induced trance (Bliss, 1986; Spiegel, 1990). The typical adaptation to traumatic events is to go into a state of trance—much like an animal does when its eyes are blinded at night by the headlights of an oncoming car. In this heightened state of trance, the traumatized individual's attention is similarly frozen. The person focuses her attention, for example, on the ceiling, dissociates from the feelings in her body, and looks down on her own rape as if it were someone else to whom it was occurring. The goal of this kind of trance is to create amnestic and analgesic barriers. Although at first adaptive, with habit these responses to all stressors become pathogenic and inhibit mastery in life. In intrusive symptomatology, for example, some internal or external experience produces a state-dependent intrusive recall of earlier trauma, which triggers a dissociated trance state in which the victim experiences herself as she did in the original trauma. In this state of being she is frozen, she cannot use new information, she cannot develop new coping mechanisms, she cannot respond accurately and self-protectively to her present situation.

Third, because of her traumatized condition, the victim of sexual abuse is more and more isolated from other people and from feeling a part of the life that they seem to live. Her disconnection and desperation erode what may have been earlier won struggles for intimacy, autonomy, initiative. Instead, she often despairs and feels generally inadequate to live as others seem to do. Her body, too, containing so much that it cannot speak about, often becomes increasingly burdened, separated from psyche; and this very loss of body/self integrity continues the experiences of a body being invaded and defiled. In this way present-day life experience thus confirms the experience of the trauma, as with disordered eating, body image distortion, and fear of fat. Here, the body-self, which should be developing into an important aspect of an internalized caring matrix, becomes instead a source of ongoing betrayal and abuse. What is adaptive on the one hand—forgetting the incest and hating the hips—is pathological on the other. Thus, we interchange the terms survivor and victim, connoting both the strength and the pathogenic cost.

Weakened and broken down in all these ways, the victim is more and more easily held a captive and lives at risk of revictimization. She is disconnected from the world and love and remains in the double bind of having to find a relationship in which she is assaulted and betrayed. Herman (1992) speaks of the experiences of captivity in which the willing victim hates and loves, needs and fears the perpetrator. In this debased state it is not by chains alone but by despair, depression, and self-blame during and long after the trauma has ended that the victim is imprisoned and feels hopeless about any future. This dilemma is clearly demonstrated in the notorious case of Hedda Nussbaum and Joel Steinberg, where Hedda, dehumanized, broken, and isolated by years of torture, clung to her abusive husband so desperately she could not prevent his killing their daughter.

To understand more fully this very painful process Fairbairn's (1952) notions within object-relations theory are particularly helpful and match Sandor Ferenczi's (1992) observations on the effects of child abuse. Fairbairn asserts that in the face of serious frustration, the child, whose most basic need is to remain attached to the caregiving "objects," has a very unpleasant but inevitable task. According to Fairbairnian theory (1952), the dependent child cannot bear to imagine that the caregiver will neither love nor protect him or her. To manage this double bind, the child internalizes outer reality in an attempt to have control over and thereby transform it. The child does this by identifying with a mental representation of the abusive caregiver. Once this object representation is internalized, the child splits the internal image into two objects (reflective of early experiences, which were felt either as good or bad), because conflict is intolerable. One is seen as all good, something that tantalizes but eventually fails her. The other, seen as all bad, rejects her entirely. The tantalizing internal representation tauntingly explains that daddy or mommy would not hurt their daughter if the child were better, thinner, stronger, did not cry, were blonde and short or just different. The child makes an internal relationship with this seductive object representation, splitting off part of her ego to maintain a constant state of attachment. The rejecting object, too, demands a relationship with a piece of the ego-self; it argues that the child is inherently bad, has reason to be ashamed, is evil, and as such is understandably abused again and again. In this way, in service of the absolute need to be in relationship, the child develops an internal world of "object-representational" relationships that form a large part of her internal life experience. This theory empathically demonstrates that the compulsion to repeat is inevitable because the internal ego and object relationship ensures that life will be seen in a way very similar to its original occurrence.

Treatment must address these abuse dynamics as they live on in the victim. David Calof (1988), capturing these dynamics vividly, argues that to cope and remain attached, the abused child internalizes the "whole family," as if a family snapshot were reproduced inside and made part of the child's ego and self state. Thus, internally the abused child is not only the victim but also the other family roles—the abuser and the betraying, unprotecting parent. These roles once inside and part of the child's internal world, remain in an ongoing, incessant conflict that Calof calls an internal "trialogue." In this conflict-laden trialogue the family fight, which usually remains unconscious and silenced in real life, is loud and clear. Internally, victim, perpetrator, and betrayer conflict, leaving the survivor in a state of constant and unbearable tension. Again and again, she needs a release just to let the pressure die down. Many reenactments that are self-injurious—verbally, interpersonally, and physically, including self-mutilation or violent bingeing and purging—are ways to let the trialogue blow up in order to get some release of tension among the inner parts (Harkaway, 1992).

The victim's emotional life is structured by these intrapsychic abuse dynamics, which also characterize and mark treatment. In the field of multiple personality and other dissociative disorders, there is a growing literature on the concept of traumatic transference that is inevitable in work with survivors of sexual abuse (Courtois, 1988; Kluft, 1992c; Loewenstein, 1993). Jody Davies and Mary Gail Frawley (1992a, 1994) have written one of the most thorough analyses of how the internal object world lives on in the survivor and how it profoundly marks treatment experiences with victim-survivors. These authors and Gabbard, Shengold, and Grotstein (1992) in dialogue with them, describe the inevitable and "maddening cycles" of the transference/ countertransference configurations that occur in therapy, attesting to the power with which abuse marks the inner emotional life of its victims. They argue that the major transference/countertransference paradigms that cycle through most treatments contain enactments of the roles of victim, perpetrator, betrayer, and rescuer. Therapist and patient enact these roles in many combinations. These roles appear not only in the therapy relationship but also in a survivor's own relationship to eating and to her body. The conflict, for example, between the "eater" self and the self who berates for eating or for being "fat" reproduces the roles of victim and perpetrator or rescuer and perpetrator, for example. Indeed, the clinician may find that her client's relationship to food is primarily a way to express and to keep alive internalized family conflicts. Thus, what may be important is not only the experience of the eater and of the fat berater but also the essence of their sadistic and masochistic connection.

Why Do Eating Problems Follow from Sexual Abuse?

Returning to the original question of the chapter, why do so many trauma survivors also suffer from eating problems and body image distortions?

Eating problems and body image distortions follow trauma for many reasons. Somewhat artificially, but for conceptual purposes, we have divided these reasons into three major contributing categories: (1) family dynamics, passing along the family experience around food and body; (2) intrapsychic adaptations, the defensive role of body/self dissociation; and (3) the revictimizing impact of consumer culture on body/self integrity. These categories provide a tool with which to think about the varied and complicated kinds of meanings that eating problems can have for the survivor of trauma. They offer the therapist hypotheses and help her to conceptualize areas about which she must make detailed inquiry and to create understanding about the messages of the symptom. They offer a way for the therapist to help a patient speak about and know her upset instead of pursuing those symptoms that in large part silence what she is desperately trying to express. These categories point out fantasied and real-life sources of difficulty that are both important for victim/survivors to know about.

FAMILY DYNAMICS

First, eating problems may follow from sexual abuse because on the concrete level, most abusive families are disorganized or so strictly controlled that in all likelihood, victims of abuse had poor experiences around feeding. In most abusive homes children are neglected in one way or another and, in the absence of good-enough experiences with food, they simply do not learn how to feed themselves properly. Lily, the client we mentioned, was severely neglected and was often not fed. In this light it is not surprising that as often as she could Lily would make mayonnaise sandwiches for herself and her younger siblings that came to represent an expression of love and care.

The use of food as reward, punishment, discipline, and control is common to many families; however in the abusive home, food is often linked to these ends in direct relationship to the traumatic ritual itself. For example, Lily, a woman in her mid-thirties, was the daughter of a prostitute. Her father's family was in a fundamentalist sect in the Midwest. To them she represented sin from the day of her birth. First abandoned by her mother and then abused by her father, she was later taken in by her mother only to be set up for family ritual abuse as well as for child prostitution to profit her mother. As she recalls, there was sadistic systematic abuse acted out in groups very early in her life. When she was placed in a foster residence for girls at the age of 13, after she had finally run away from the scenes of violence, abuse, drugs, and alcohol, she was abused by a religious cult. Because there was no place in society where Lily had been safe, having been abused by parents, family, and the church, it was not surprising that she entered a battering marriage at age 18. Lily has a multitude of eating and body symptoms, not the least of which is chronic pain. It was, however, her eating behavior and body size history that brought her into therapy. At first she did not feel the abuse was important enough to talk about. Her alcohol history, her history of bulimia, and her sense of being fat, however, entitled her to think about getting treatment. After being used or sold by her mother, she was often taken to breakfast and allowed to have pancakes. There, she experienced a moment of maternal nurturance, which she felt to be an expression of her mother's caring, of her mother's regret and remorse. Pancakes continue to hold hope of maternal care for her.

Many clients report other such examples: that specific foods were used to tantalize them into compliance with the sex act, typically ice cream or candy. Thus, Christine was enticed into sexually abusive situations with candy, which was otherwise off limits. Bingeing on candy and then purging can represent her confusion about being enticed toward and repulsed by the sexual act. Women sometimes simply associate being starved or being fed with being violated. In these cases and other similar ones, specific foods or the ab-

sence of food, through the process of state-dependent memory, are directly
linked both emotionally and cognitively with memories of family care or betrayal.

In relation to body image, the dynamics of abusive homes are often characterized by the fact that disowned family feelings of shame, "badness," and
guilt are typically projected on to the victim's body and sexuality. Clients repeatedly tell us, for example, that an abusive father or stepfather would
shame the growing girl's body. In this case the father, mother, or sibling, unconsciously overwhelmed by their obsession with her sexually maturing
body, project on to the victim their own feelings of temptation and longing
for her. Many traumatized clients, in this way, are told that they "asked for
it." Essentially, the process is a form of projective identification in which the
perpetrator's disowned idea about his or her own "badness" or desire is disavowed and unconsciously projected on to the victim. For her part the victim, eager to maintain her important relationship with the perpetrator and
often identifying with him or her as well, is left vulnerable to the projection
(Davies & Frawley, 1992c). She comes to believe that the "badness" is her
own and often acts accordingly. A product of this process is a woman's enactment of it in her aggressive and hostile devaluation of her own body-self.
Carrying this level of projection, a survivor's body image cannot and does
not fare well. The badness of the family deposited in her body is something
that she must reckon with at every moment. Both Christine and Jeanette introjected their families' guilt and shame about their abuse, which the families had projected on to the girls' bodies. Both feel fat when each is indeed
quite thin. The power of projective identification in Christine's case was such
that it was further somaticized, so that, for example, her body actually enlarged when she was filled with these bad feelings. On occasion, prior to a
therapy session her pants would not fasten, whereas after the session the
same pants would fit comfortably.

INTRAPSYCHIC ADAPTATIONS

The second reason eating problems so often converge with a history of sexual abuse follows directly from what we have been arguing throughout the
book: All women, defined by their bodies and so vulnerable in body/self integrity, use eating and body image as metaphors and as an arena for both the
expression of their pain and a way of hiding from their pain. The body, food,
self, and other all easily become transforms of each other in women's unconscious experience. These transformations affecting body/self integrity and
body-self dissociation, emotional well-being, or defensive and pathological
adaptation are pronounced in those who have been sexually abused.

Recall Winnicott's (1989) notion of "indwelling" (see chapter 3), meaning
the achievement of a congruent and integrated sense of a "good-enough"

imaginative self and body-self. Other students of this critical human developmental achievement or failure call indwelling "body/self integration" or "unity." We argued that the experience of body-self occurs first for the baby through the manner in which it is held, handled, fed, mirrored, and recognized by mother, father, and family. Thus, in early life an infant develops a view of itself from what it takes in, what it sees, what it hears, what it feels, and from the way to which it is emotionally related. Visual, aural, tactile, olfactory, kinesthetic, imaginal, and emotional experience all contribute to the development of a sense of self and of self in relation to its world, to others. Later in life, using the processes of symbolization, people are reflected in analogous ways by the culture at large.

These concepts remind us that physical and emotional relating merge, just as in reality body and self are unified at base. As human capacity to symbolize grows, however, and the use of the imaginal, symbolic selves increases, a sense of body-me, separate from feeling-me, separate even from the cognitive, rational thinking mind-me all develop. This ability to imaginatively dissociate aspects of self is paradoxical precisely because, in a fundamental way, these parts are really all interactive and, in many ways, barely distinguishable. The imaginal capacity to separate body-self from psychological self is the very foundation of the dissociative adaptation to trauma.

One application of human symbolic and dissociative ability is the capacity that women have to transform self, body, and need into particular experiences with food, eating, or body image. Women's difficulty in negotiating their place in the world, in owning and having their own desire and subjectivity, in living in the female body, which is filled with culturally derived meanings all find expression in how they feed themselves and see their own bodies. A self that is socially inhibited but cannot dissolve or dismiss itself, transforms its desire and fear from the prohibited emotional realm into another, more culturally syntonic one: the female terrain of food and body. In other words, women first dissociate themselves from their socially prohibited needs and feelings and then reassociate them in the distorted, secret, and unconscious language of their bodies and food.

When this transformation is accomplished again and again, however, it leaves the realm of metaphor and becomes an actual, repeated experience a woman has with her body-self, with her body boundaries, and with her body image in the world. These body, food, self, and other transforms become the experience that ensures a constant intensification of body/self distortion and adaptation. In these structured experiences, then, women come to define and to know *themselves,* just as they first did in their lived experiences with early caregivers. In other words, these dissociations and reassociations, these transforms, become the structures through which women fundamentally create their lives. As the feminist philosopher Susan Bordo might say, as one "does" her body, she becomes it; as she uses the body in time and space, she becomes the product of that experience (Barsky, 1990; Bordo, 1993).

The female victim of sexual abuse will almost always use what society offers her—conflict associated with eating and her body—as a way to express her unbearable pain, hate, fear, rage, and despair. It is understandable that the survivor of sexual abuse, who can neither speak of nor forget what has so fundamentally shaped her life, will use her body experience, body image, and eating both to hide and express the secrets of what happened to her and of how what happened affected her physically, psychologically, and cognitively. For the abused woman, the transforms of food, body, and self tell a great deal about the story of the abuse and its aftermath, about real events and fantasied object relationships.

Starving the abused body, for example, can be a survivor's attempt to make her abuse itself disappear. Purging and severe dieting often feel as if they could eject the shameful experience and finally purify the suffering victim. Getting larger or smaller are typical ways in which the victim can imagine controlling those body boundaries that were violated. Changing sizes can be an effort to create boundaries safe from assault and from state-dependent memories that threaten to intrude on consciousness. On the other hand, a large body size may represent the opposite of safety; it may be a sadistic reenactment in which the survivor continues the hatred inflicted on her from others, a way the internalized self-hater stays alive and busy.

For its part chronic eating for emotional reasons, without regard to physical hunger or satiation, also expresses significant aspects of the trauma and its effects. Eating can soothe. It can modulate intense anxiety by literally changing the psychosomatic state. It can create the state-dependent memory of care that was long ago betrayed but once existed, as pancakes did for Lily. In all these ways and more eating can help to contain needs, fears, conflicts, anxieties, and other "intolerable" feelings. But eating can also be a form of traumatic reenactment, as for example the client who stuffs dry crackers down her throat in large enough quantity to actually scratch herself. Eating like this is a violent way not only to stuff down unacceptable feelings but also to reenact abusive early feeding, relational experiences, and internal fantasy life.*

---

*The reader will see in these contrasting uses of food—for soothing or sadistic reenactments—similarities to current thinking about self-mutilation or other self-injurious behavior frequently seen in PTSD and multiple personality disorder. There are many ways in which to think about self-injurious behavior. John Briere (1992, 1993) sees it primarily as tension-releasing behavior. Richard Kluft (Kluft, 1992a; Kluft & Fine, 1993) thinks of it as entirely noxious and unacceptable. Frank Putnam (1989) speaks of trying to contract to reduce it, substituting nondangerous symbolic behaviors in its place. David Calof (1992) emphasizes the importance of assessing the function before choosing an intervention. We tend to agree with Calof, learning from all the others. Certainly, with self-injurious eating behavior, purging, laxative abuse, and symbolic assault to body image, we usually have to witness and withstand the symptoms for a while before the client can voluntarily end them.

All these meanings and more may exist within the same person, as they do in the case of Lily. Lily's fat is quite complicated. Through it she has rebelled against what was demanded of her: the perfect size of the highly paid prostitute. Her fat also represents a safety zone, a way she could protect the body that experienced such torture. In her thin stages she found herself, dissociated, ending up in sex scenes that she did not remember entering. In yet another way her fat represents her ubiquitously felt sense of essential badness, her shame. She believes that the fat screams out to the world that she is worthless, that she deserves no better than what she got. The fat sings many different and contradictory songs. Lily's weight and its symbols must be accepted into treatment, just as she herself must be, to help her to articulate these meanings.

Her eating, like her fat, works in her unconscious in myriad ways. It soothes her. The child parts of her personality associate the ability to have chocolate ice cream with hope for care and life. At other times her bingeing and violent purging have been literal internal reenactments of being stuffed with noxious substances and made ill, and are often followed by her physically beating herself. Her anorexia is both a memory of and defense against having been starved.

As this example demonstrates, survivors of sexual abuse can unconsciously attribute to food and their bodies a variety of meanings. Indeed, food and the body are culturally created containers for the projection of hated or dangerous thoughts and feelings. In this society, women make psychological use of their bodies to express and contain the indigestible experience of their trauma.

CONSUMER CULTURE AND SYMBOLIC REVICTIMIZATION

There is yet a third way to understand the convergence of eating problems and body image distortion, a perspective that is somewhat different and unexplored in the field. In this conception the eating problem is understood, in essence, as a socially constructed continuation of trauma. As the traumatized woman enters the world outside the abusive experience or home, she is greeted by a social mirror that confirms and consolidates her already well-developed sense of badness. Instead of offering a new set of possible object relationships, which could heal and stand in contrast to those of the family, the culture recapitulates the original abuse.

When facing "the wall of culture" (Gilligan & Brown, 1992) the abused woman finds the general objectification and commodification of the female body especially stinging. She has already learned that she is defined by her body, that her body has been the object simultaneously of desire and of denigration, an ideal representing the height of passion and the most debased and humiliating of human conditions. Her body has already been forced into a separation from self. As she enters the womb of culture, these messages echo loudly. She looks around and sees images and hears messages about how her body should work and how it should look; she cannot help but be reaffirmed in the knowledge that her body is an object to be sculpted, a machine to be tuned and used for maximum mileage. She has already been forced to dissociate from her body and, to a greater or lesser extent, to comply with punitive norms. Christine, for example, a highly paid advertising executive, was in a social environment where any woman larger than a size 8 was considered a disgrace. She was retraumatized not only by the culture at large but by her subculture. This environment provided fertile ground for the development of further abuse by inducing her to exercise vigorously and carelessly for four hours a day, often causing injury to various body parts.

Jeanette, who was not in the world of fashion or advertising, nonetheless received a similar message. Any extra weight would prove her to be as shameful as she actually felt. Her reading of the larger culture was not inaccurate. She could be revictimized easily via her body.

Thus, the messages that the trauma supplied through psychological processes are repeated in the social processes of living in consumer culture at large. The culture itself promotes dissociation; it suggests in its narratives that the body is discrete, separate from self, forever perfectible, forever proof of self-worth. Not only a psychological maneuver, dissociation is also a cultural demand. Both psychological and sociological experience actually encourage delusional transference on to the body (Little, 1957, 1986).

Recall that from the perspective of intrapsychic adaptations discussed, women psychologically make use of the body to handle, hide, and express traumatic stress. In other words, the client with eating problems unconsciously reenacts or expresses the sequelae of the sexual abuse in her eating and body image. The emphasis is on the unconscious of the survivor, who needs to repeat the traumatic assault either because she is obsessively stuck, because she is trying to gain mastery, or both. Using the cultural lens gives us yet another way of envisioning the convergence of eating problems and sexual abuse. From this perspective the sexually abused woman is being subjected to a new but related violation in the symbolic sphere of culture, a violation that itself reenacts her earlier trauma. This social perspective looks at the role of the diet-obsessed, fat-phobic culture in retraumatization. Here the emphasis is on the active violation of women through cultural symbols and institutions, resulting in women's chronic, albeit normative, dieting, fear of food, and hatred of their bodies.

Thus, the third reason that eating problems converge with sexual abuse has to do with the form of trauma perpetrated by the culture at large and engineered in the symbolic landscape of consumer culture. This globally abusive experience targets the female body. Because this abusive experience and its relationship to sexual trauma has not been explored in psychoanalysis, it requires further development.

HOW THE SYMBOLIC LANDSCAPE VIOLATES

The violation experienced by women in the symbolic landscape relates to, parallels, and eventually extends the trauma of sexual abuse. Five aspects of symbolic violation demonstrate how it is homologous with sexual violation.

As argued in chapter 1, symbolic violation begins with the fact that people, as Fairbairn (1952) theorized, are object seeking. However, the objects they seek in postmodern mass society include those of the symbolic transitional realm. In mass consumer culture, women use their capacity for symbolization to look for mirroring and transitional objects in an ongoing effort to negotiate their sense of self, their inner fantasy life, and their relationships to others. (See chapter 1.) Moreover, although individuals are object seeking, even in their symbolic environments, the symbols of consumer culture are subject seeking. Thus, the first element in understanding how the symbolic landscape can violate is to be aware of the intense fantasy relationships made by women to the symbols of their culture, their transitional realm.

The second element is the particular quality of the relationship between women and the symbols of their bodies and appetites. This relationship is in large part determined by the fact that these advertised symbols portraying the female body and appetite are meant to capture and manipulate personal insecurity for the purpose of higher sales and control of the social status quo. Although manipulation is their goal, the symbols and images are presented as if they were both authoritative and nurturing, as if they knew what their subject needed and really cared to help her to meet these needs. As would happen with a frustrating parent, women internalize the hurt in libidinal and antilibidinal object relationships.

Consider the case of Jody, incestuously abused by her father and despised and blamed by her mother. Jody came to hate her trim body. Her thighs, in no way large, her breasts, in no way small, became the socially determined loci of her distorted self-image. Although of modest means and frightened of further bodily intrusions, she felt compelled to pursue cosmetic surgery for her breasts as well as her shapely thighs. She received tremendous social and medical approval for her breast implants and liposuction on what she called her "saddlebags." By buying into the notion of cosmetic surgery, Jody exposed her internal object relationship to the symbols of surgery and to the images of idealized female thighs and breasts. In this relationship Jody's body was judged to be inadequate and in need of improvement, which could be achieved through elective surgery. The cosmetic surgery echoed and joined Jody's internal self-haters, the antilibidinal ego and objects that already claimed that Jody was to blame for her abuse. Consumer culture's exploitation of Jody, as is the case with most women, intensified and strengthened the internal schizoid object relations.

Through her relationship with cosmetic surgery and its message, Jody hoped to feel better about herself but, instead, entered an abusive relationship where the surgical knife invaded "for her own good." Jody was actually revictimized. There are a few cases where specific surgery helps a woman's self-esteem, as argued by Cathy Davis (1991). For most women, however, the surgeries do not make significant changes. Moreover, as a cultural phenomenon, the growth of cosmetic surgery in general suggests to all women that they are in need of improvement and that by violating their bodies, help can be obtained.

The symbolic communication of cosmetic surgery is, "without me you are unacceptable." In the psychological realm the surgery taunts either by rejecting ("you are inadequate") or tantalizing ("if you let me cut you, you can improve"). This taunt, devised to sell the product, resonates with an already existing "deep, psychological structure" (Ogden, 1990) born of a universal adaptation to frustration but also, in Jody's case, of the abusive relationship to her father.

In this way consumer culture fosters extensive ego involvement in the isolated world of internal, addictive object relations, far removed from the potentially healing effect of interpersonal relations. So, for example, no matter how often a thin woman incest survivor with a distorted "fat" body image is told by friends, family, or lover that she looks "just fine," she cannot let go of her culturally reinforced, object-relationally determined body image. Her ego involvement with her internal object is more powerful than her interpersonal relations. This inner object relation is not only derived from early life experiences and their fantasy extensions, but also it is sustained in adult life by an exploitative culture.

The daily reactivation in the symbolic landscape of this assault prevents old psychic wounds from healing, just as physical healing is prevented by reinjury. By inciting the victim to poke at old wounds, with symbolic implements, consumer culture revictimizes by its taunts of fat, greedy, and ugly.

The third aspect of symbolic violation homologous with sexual trauma is its secretive nature. Most people do not see themselves in actual relationships to the symbols of consumer culture. There are no codependency groups for a troubled and compulsive relationship to commercial images of women. The ideology of consumer culture subliminally insists that the products are what consumers need and want, that the advertising message is purely educational, an accurate and concerned response to consumer interest. No product advertises itself as being sold to profit Revlon or whether or not there exists an inherent consumer need. No advertised message overtly admits to being purposely manipulative. To this extent their assault constitutes an unacknowledged, abusive relationship, which is then endured in a kind of se-crecy that aggravates the original violation. Although it may be common knowledge to many that consumer culture is damaging to women, exactly how the culture gets inside and exactly how and what it damages have not been theorized by most schools of psychoanalysis. Without that understand-ing, cultural violation remains hidden. To the extent that the impact of the "toxic culture" is unacknowledged by object-relations theory and remains unconscious, cultural wounds and cultural abuse are hidden and secret.

Object-relationally oriented psychoanalysis privileges early fantasy and family experience and development so thoroughly that it has failed to de-velop a language with which to explore the workings and impact of the cul-tural environment. The psychoanalytic terms "mother" and "father" have only been understood as the actual mother and father, not as metaphors for necessary environmental provision required throughout the life cycle.

In contemporary Western culture, psychoanalysis informs how the gen-eral public think about themselves and their lives, feelings, and situations. People who have never set foot in a psychotherapy office today buy self-help books, join meetings and conversations in which they perceive their situa-tion through the ideas of a popularized version of object-relational theory. "Toxic parents" and "wounded children" are major explanatory notions, used widely to conceptualize personal pain. Object-relation theory's empha-sis on the importance of the quality of mothering and the nurturing environ-ment has captured popular imagination. John Bradshaw, for example, is a charismatic leader whose popularity is staggering. He enjoins everyone to heal their inner child, the child who has suffered from parental failure. Although Bradshaw (1988a, 1988b) and similar popular psychologists may give lip service to the pain that consumer culture causes, it remains superfi-cial. For without in-depth theory about exactly how people are affected by this culture, its values and symbols, lip service is precisely where the analy-sis stops.

Thus, because in the Western world people generally use psychoanalysis to tell the story of emotional life, they are unable to tell themselves a com-plete story. So not only are people deeply marked by relationships with the symbols and artifacts of this culture, but also they have no effective narrative to help them to know and dignify the resultant pain. When a woman stands in front of the mirror crying out, "I'm fat, I'm ugly," she has, in effect, re-gressed to the situation of the baby who cries but whose need is not labeled, symbolized, or understood. She does not really understand what is happen-ing.

Jeanette finds that as Thanksgiving approaches, her hips and buttocks feel huge. Analyzing the first layer of secrets contained in feeling fat, Jeanette sees that she fears facing her brother at the family holiday gathering. He sits silent and still, so traumatized was he by the early beatings inflicted on him by his father who is her incestuous stepfather. She also fears experiencing her conflicted feelings toward her mother who did not stop the abuse. Analysis of the second layer of secrets reveals that Jeanette has an internal image, provided by the media, of what a good woman looks like. Jeanette reasons, and always has, that if she were "better," if she were good, if she met the requirements of this internalized image, she could have stopped the beatings and molestations and she would not have been a betrayed little girl. To the extent that all this is personally and socially unconscious, it is a secret—to herself and many others.

This cultural secret has direct implications for the analytic encounter, the clinical moment. Because the therapy profession has difficulty consciously articulating socially caused trauma, psychotherapists barely know how to ask clients what they feel in relation to their symbols of fatness and thinness, or in relation to the ribs, waist, lips, arms, or buttocks pictured all around them. The relationship to cultural symbols is usually unexplored in the clinical setting. Clinicians may ask about the emotions stirred up by early instincts, fantasies, or experiences, for example, but not about the fear, envy, and hate aroused by these cultural images of the female body. They do not ask about the relationship of incest to the cultural violation. Unfortunately, when clients talk of their needs to starve, of their fear of food, or of their hatred of their bodies, mental health practitioners too often understand these symptoms to be the result of maternal, sometimes paternal, deprivation or frustration, or of sexual abuse.

Such an interpretation is not so much wrong as reductionist. In the absence of a developed language for object relationships with the cultural home, therapist and clients are inevitably reduced to seeing everything in terms of the actual family home and its violations. Although feminists have shown the significant ways in which the culture affects early family relationships, there are also profound, ongoing, usually primitive object relationships made with the symbols of the adult culture. Without personal or professional language, the social assault remains a secret assault, the fundamental hallmark of an abusive relationship.

The symbolic landscape also violates by leading to a regressive use of the body, to regression in body/self integrity. The images of women in consumer culture "collapse" in the "potential" of the transitional realm, as argued in chapter 1 (Ogden, 1990). In this key element of their transitional realm, women are assaulted by intrusive cultural symbols, by the lived experience, and by the patterned interactions dictated by these symbols. For many women this collapse causes an actual developmental regression, a dissolution of ego, and an encouragement to use the body as the mode of expression for psychic pain. For example, when a young woman begins severe dieting leading to anorexia, she may lose knowledge and memory of how to feed herself.

The alteration of Christine's body size we described is another example of a regressive use of the body. Such is also the case of Jeanette, who regressed and, unable to express her anger and ·fear directly with her family at Thanksgiving dinner, instead used her body image to attack herself. In these instances, their bodies spoke when they could not verbalize what was happening to them.

Thus, the internalization of the particular symbols of the beauty myth and the intrapsychic and interpersonal demands implied in these symbols can cause adult women to regress in terms of what psychoanalysis understands as the capacity to symbolize. Because of the assaulting nature of the relationship between self and symbol and because of the atmosphere of silence, minimalization, and outright ideological repression of this assault, the pain is never adequately understood, symbolized, put into words, heard—not even in the analytic setting. Unable to symbolize the pain fully, women must then express their nonmentalized pain in the nonsymbolic, concrete sphere of the body. It is ironic that the sociological use of the symbol causes regression of the psychological capacity to symbolize. In other words, it is not only prementalized, preoedipal pain that seeks expression through somatic expression (Dimen & Harris, 1992) but also adult experience in the cultural realm that actually undoes or undermines the capacity to symbolize, infantilizing women, in this case by causing them to use their bodies in regressive ways. This argument stands in contrast to those of Ogden (1990), Stolorow and Atwood (1991), and Krueger (1989), who all emphasize the preoedipal origins of psychosomatic pathology and do not elaborate on contributions of adult life to such symptomatology.

A further irony is that the regression necessitated by this use of the body is usually accomplished in ways that are generally considered emblematic of social maturity. For example, a woman will typically attempt to contain psychically disorganizing affects of the cultural assault and personal history with culturally offered notions such as: "you aren't good enough, thin enough, shapely enough, young enough, firm enough, self-disciplined enough—go on a diet." By going on a diet, by overriding her internal signals of hunger and satiation, and by developing a self-hating, critical body image, she does not only what is socially sanctioned but also what is revered.

Violation in the symbolic landscape is also homologous to sexual violence in that the victim is blamed for her pain. Victim blaming in sexual trauma is perpetuated in the symbolic sphere. Women share their worries about eating, size, and shape all the time. Women commonly agree about how much they hate their bodies, how much they need to diet, how much they distrust themselves around food, how jealous they are of other women who look better, and so on. It is totally normative to hate one's body, to fear food, and to be involved in intricate plans for self-discipline. Female solidarity around these norms can even sometimes reduce some of the shame they cause. But this solidarity is deceptive, because although women feel sympathy for one another to some extent and these norms condone complaining about their mutual "failures," the norms do not validate pain and shame around food or the body that exist at the deepest and most profound level. For example, therapy groups for large women easily develop solidarity around "successes or failures" in the job of making oneself a "better woman," a thinner, more disciplined, "healthier" woman. But it is difficult for the members to admit to themselves and one another, for example, how a member's extreme obesity traumatically affected her life; and it is almost impossible to speak about the agony of having always felt like a true freak, a social outcast, an ugly woman always visible in these ways. These painful issues may be alluded to, skirted around, offered the nod of unspoken sympathy, solidarity, and recognition. But very rarely do women share, admit, and articulate the full extent of their suffering. Women's solidarity around perfecting the body is usually not like the solidarity of a consciousness-raising group or a survivors' therapy group, where social arrangements are related to personal pain. Instead women largely keep the pain and social arrangements secret, unacknowledged and unspoken, and thereby tend instead to blame one another and themselves as they are all disciplined into the art of womanhood.

CHAPTER 11

Eating Problems and Sexual Abuse: Treatment Considerations

SUSAN GUTWILL AND ANDREA GITTER

Diagnosis and Identification

THE FIRST steps in the treatment of sexual abuse survivors are to work to establish a therapeutic alliance and to evaluate the problem. In the case of sexual abuse, where an inherent part of the abuse consists of grave warnings never to tell, identifying the problem can be quite complicated. Clinicians must read a language that is simultaneously about telling secrets and keeping them. The trauma of sexual abuse, central to all self organization because it cannot be integrated, is enjoined by secrecy. It stays present in both intrusive and numbing configurations. Therefore, the trauma is most often expressed in symptoms such as secret, often somatic metaphors; fantastic dreamlike experiences; deep anxiety and depression; major inhibitions to self-esteem; a huge array of seemingly unconnected intrapsychic and interpersonal suffering; and a number of self-destructive behaviors. Consequently, every guide to the treatment of incest and sexual abuse offers the clinician extensive lists of possible presenting symptoms (Bass & Davis, 1988; Courtois, 1988; Dinsmore, 1991; Herman, 1992; Putnam, 1992a; Ross, 1989; van der Kolk, 1987; Weisberg & Herzog, 1992; Zehner, 1992a). These lists can be quite helpful, given the fact that for all too many years when clients, especially women, presented with many of these symptoms, they were dismissed as hysterical and their connection to the trauma was undetected or overlooked. On the other hand, it would be a mistake to err in the opposite direction today by assuming that if clients present with some of these symptoms it clearly means they were abused but are still un-

aware of it. Just such a mistake would be to assume that a serious eating disorder almost always implies an earlier experience of incest. This is absolutely
untrue, just as is the idea that deep anxiety or depression belongs only to
those who have been sexually abused.

Yet, the very wide range of possible symptoms victims present with are
very important because so often a survivor does not clearly remember abuse
but instead has dissociated from it. Nonetheless, the clinician should ask
about whether there is a conscious history of abuse: Does the patient remember in her childhood any sexual contact with an adult. It has been shown that
clients are more likely to disclose trauma when asked. In addition, asking
implies that the clinician is open to hearing what the client has probably
been warned no one would believe. Just as in the case of eating behavior, it is
important for the clinician to be open about the possibility without in any
way leading a client. Because many clients cannot remember or are afraid to
admit their memories, it is useful to think about other expressive signals.
There may be impairments in physical, behavioral, cognitive, and relational
(intrapsychic as well as interpersonal) functioning, any of which may be a
method of coping with the unmetabolized trauma still living and operative
inside.

Physically, there may be a variety of somatic complaints such as insomnia, body pain, especially in the genital, anal, and urinary areas, or a history
of unexplained and persistent physical illnesses involving various other
body parts. Behaviorally, victims frequently report feeling hypervigilant and
supercautious on the one hand, or counterphobic and risk-taking on the
other. Clients frequently report the abuse of food, drugs, or alcohol, perhaps
in an attempt to self-medicate, or at other times as an internally organized
reenactment of abuse. For these reasons as well as others, self-injurious behavior, such as mutilation, is often an important sign of early abuse and possible multiplicity. Seriously accident-prone behavior is important to note, as
are difficulty sitting still, pacing, going into the fetal position, hair-pulling,
sitting unnaturally still, an inability to make eye contact, and extremely sexualized behavior. Cognitive functioning can be impaired in many different
ways, one of the most important being the inability to remember, to keep
track of time, to know what happens in time and in what order. A form of
cognitive distortion typical of trauma is a confusion between past and present. This is sometimes called a flashback—something in the present that has
an element reminiscent of past trauma triggers a full-blown reexperience of
that past trauma. In this way the unmetabolized trauma reasserts itself in the
present as an experience of terror, a startled response, hallucinations, or a
delusional transference (called traumatic transference) response to the therapist (Courtois, 1988; Herman, 1992; Kluft, 1992c; Loewenstein, 1993).
Obviously, this cognitive impairment is closely allied to and inseparable
from emotional and relational difficulties.

Victim-survivors are certainly not alone in their experience of deep and abiding problems of self-esteem, self-hatred, and shame. Nor are they alone in the experience of profound anxiety and inability to modulate feelings and to self-soothe. But these are ubiquitous and profound presenting problems among survivors. They often report finding themselves repeatedly victimized, trusting themselves in the hands of quite hurtful people, and without boundaries or a sense of entitlement to self-protection. Lack of self-esteem makes victims easy prey to those who seductively offer the promise of love. Alternatively, the survivor, so distrustful of herself and frightened of her history, will disconnect herself from others and suffer the tortures of longing for connection while restricted by intense distrust and fear. The daytime self referred to in chapter 10 often manages life, but the nighttime self, holding so much unintegrated truth, cannot rest and feels that her competence and achievements are both unsafe and fraudulent. Although these intrapsychic and interpersonal relational difficulties certainly are not the province of survivors alone, it is rare not to find them in a virulent form among those who have been abused.

Basic Principles for Treating Incest Survivors

Although evaluation is always ongoing and shifting and the clinician is always reading and rereading symptomatology, one may come to believe quite surely that a client has suffered sexual trauma. Clinicians have now agreed on a number of central and imperative principles of treatment for the "healing of the incest wound" (Courtois, 1988).

Foremost among these principles is the importance for many clients of recovering memories. It is important to note that up until very recently, the emphasis in trauma theory, correcting for traditional treatment that minimized the real trauma and emphasized problems at the fantasy level, has been on the importance of a client's knowing the basic outlines of her story. The argument is not that each detail must be remembered, abreacted, and felt but, rather, that the general picture be known in some detail and its effects mourned. Correcting for the correction, some clinicians have recently warned against a new bias that now overvalues remembering (Comstock, 1992; personal communication with Dr. Karen Hoppenwasser, 1993) and could cause survivors unnecessary retraumatization. It is certainly a good thing for therapists to think carefully about how much each of their clients want and need to remember and not to become rigid or overzealous in believing in the importance of memory. Clients differ markedly in how much memory is required for healing. However, most psychoanalytic thinkers in the tradition of Sandor Ferenczi and his more modern followers (e.g., Davies & Frawley, 1992a, 1994) as well as those working in the area of trauma theory (e.g., Courtois, 1988; Herman, 1992) agree that memories must at least move out of their state of dissociated symptomatology into the formation of the story of what actually happened (Bass & Davis, 1988). As the story emerges it needs to be reassociated to the feelings, behaviors, sensations, and thoughts that were dissociated from it. The events and the horrific consequences must be witnessed and mourned so that they can become integrated as conscious memory and not remain a set of intrusive or numbing symptoms.

Therapists can ask what happened, with whom, and when, about the beginning and the end of the abuse, and about which developmental level the client was at when the abuse started. Carefully, with great respect for the importance of pacing of affect, the therapist helps the client to come to understand those feelings, thoughts, physical sensations, behaviors, and relational habits that marked the ways she adapted to the trauma. This process has been called "debriefing" by Renée Frederickson (1990).

In the case of severe trauma it is imperative for the therapist to hold a position of belief, not in every detail, for there are certainly screen memories and fantasized elaborations inevitably produced by trauma, but more generally of the reality of trauma. In this way she is a witness standing in opposition to the abusers who required the victim to disbelieve her own experience, who routinely admonished "don't tell anyone or I'll kill you—You asked for this. You love this. You enjoy it." "No one will believe you if you tell; and I will cut out your tongue." The therapist represents the belief that knowing the truth is both deeply courageous and the authentic way to secure safety. The therapist does not take over as her own the client's conflicts over belief. She needs to frame the client's struggles with belief and disbelief and hold the client in this conflict. It is not up to the therapist to believe what the client cannot, although she may well do so. Once again there is an issue of correction and adjustment. Historically, after Freud's renunciation of the seduction theory in favor of the overvaluation of infantile sexual fantasies, clinicians working in the recent period have needed to correct for the kind of clinical disbelief that has routinely revictimized clients. Alice Miller's *Thou Shalt Not Be Aware* (1986) is an impassioned account of the retraumatizing effect of therapists disbelieving their clients' tales of abuse and blaming them for sexualized fantasies instead (see also Courtois, 1988; Hainer, 1993; Herman, 1981; Wooley, 1994). This is an especially delicate issue in cases of sadistic systematic group abuse, and the reader is referred to Sakheim and Devine (1992a) for further discussion and bibliography.

The principle of therapeutic safety is accomplished by treating the client with respect; honoring the therapy situation with respect to its real boundaries; working to establish physical safety for client and therapist alike; being aware not to emotionally overload the client with the memory work (Fine,

1991); and reconnecting the BASK components: *B*ehavior, *A*ffect, *S*ensation, and *K*nowledge (Braun, 1992). This point, which will be discussed in more detail in chapter 12, must be considered very carefully. Because the physical and emotional boundaries of trauma survivors have been so cruelly assaulted, victim-survivors often need help in learning how not to overwhelm themselves. Moreover, in severe abuse, spontaneous abreactions are typical ways of reenacting the trauma itself (Fine, 1991; Kluft, 1991b). Especially in the literature on multiple personality disorder, clinicians are coming to respect the importance of titration of affect, dilution, distancing, and planning memory work. These techniques are required to make remembering an experience of empowerment for the survivor, not an even more overwhelming revictimization (Hammond, 1992; Kluft, 1991b; Peterson, 1992a; Ross, 1989). Self-care is something that must be taught, and the therapist is the teacher, advocate, and staunch supporter of this effort.

When someone has been brutally betrayed at the most developmentally vulnerable of times, it is not easy for her to learn to reconnect to others, to trust herself, others, and the world, to grieve and mourn for all that was lost and all that never was provided, and to maintain a relationship with a truly helpful, if fallible, object. The treatment of victim-survivors is long term, intense, and demanding; it can also be very rewarding. Being aware of and capable of working quite deeply in the inevitable and difficult transference-countertransference configurations is a foundational part of this work from an analytic perspective (Davies & Frawley, 1992b, 1994; Harkaway, 1992). Victim, betrayer/bystander, perpetrator, and rescuer all find their way into role reenactments in different combinations. Trauma theory has enriched the contribution of the analytic perspective with its emphasis on the physiological and cognitive sequelae of trauma (Ross, 1989; van der Kolk, 1987). Hypnotherapy, for example, calls for rethinking the impact of dissociation as a form of trance (Bliss, 1986; Liner, 1993; Spiegel, 1990). Successful analytic work, aiming to help the survivor to make new relationships to herself and others requires attention to all these sources of clinical knowledge and theory (Liner, 1993; Davies & Frawley, 1994).

The Feminist Psychoanalytic Contribution to the Treatment of Combined Trauma and Eating Problems

A feminist, socially informed theory and treatment of the convergence of sexual abuse with eating problems must reverse the hidden imperatives shared by sexual abuse and symbolic violation. Both these forms of violation admonish a woman: (1) not to like herself but, instead, to see herself as inadequate and shameful; (2) not to trust herself and her inner truth; (3) not to give a full, curious, and empathic hearing to her symptoms but to eradicate them, sometimes by any means necessary; and (4) not to dignify her pain by knowing her whole story. Therapists need to create a safe, respectful analytic relationship, a holding environment in which a woman can tolerate her feelings about what happened and put her story into words. Only as she does so can she mourn her past and continue her development despite her trauma. As Jody Davies has put it, the victim's story is about what happened to her; about the ideas she developed about herself as a result of her trauma; and about her fantasied elaborations of those events. Knowing this, her story includes coming to perceive and integrate her dissociated self and object relations (Davies & Frawley, 1992c, 1994). The analytic space is the arena in which to do all this work, so that the survivor can finally reconnect self to others in intersubjectively fulfilling ways and let go of her symptoms and compensatory relationships to food and body.

THE IMPORTANCE OF EATING WITH HUNGER FOR THE VICTIM OF TRAUMA

The first treatment principle is the absolute importance of reconnecting the trauma survivor to her own physical signals of hunger and satiation and of clarifying with her the ways in which chronic dieting is damaging. Survivors of trauma are hurt on three basic levels of experience and self development: the physical, the cognitive, and the relational. This subsection addresses the impact on the survivor at each of these three levels of experience of the simple act of eating or not eating according to the basic organizing principle of physiological hunger.

Physical Level

When the body is ready to eat, the digestive tract secretes enzymes that allow the efficient and comfortable digestion of food. This bodily action is readily appreciable as a feeling of hunger, and living with it, for the most part, puts one in synchronicity with basic biological rhythms.

Eating without hunger with regularity and frequency burdens the body. When these basic biological rhythms are overridden, a constant state of confusion is created that perpetuates a chasm between mind and body. On the contrary, attunement to biological and emotional need that includes an appropriate and concerned response of feeding hunger integrates mind and body and creates a state of safe cooperation. The word "safe" is critical here, for heeding hunger goes quite a long way toward establishing the body literally and metaphorically as a safe, nurturing, and attuned environment rather than the old violating, neglectful, and dangerous environment of trauma.

Cognitive Level

Cognitive knowledge of biological functioning, coming to know and recognize how the body works, is an important part of feeling safe and having an experience of mastery in life. Without this very basic knowledge, not only hunger but many other internal signals are not only easily misread but also often actually frightening and ego-disorganizing. Thus, for example, the traumatized person who experiences hunger may not know what her feeling of terrible need and vulnerability is really about. She may experience low blood sugar as if it were the return of the danger or the depression of trauma. To many survivors, signals of hunger do not mean that it is time to eat and be satisfied but, instead, a state of hopeless despair that becomes generalized, an experience of undifferentiated need. For the trauma victim all vulnerabilities may resonate with and even seem equal to the severity of the original trauma. In this unfortunate situation suffering is caused and perpetuated by the inhibition of cognitive development around the basic physical and emotional needs and processes of the body-self.

Effective treatment helps the client to make meaning of her undifferentiated bodily sensations and to feel entitled to pay attention to them. Responding to hunger appropriately builds cognitive ability, including the ability of the ego to discern, and therefore to regulate and to manage intense bodily feelings. In this sense, knowledge is a crucial part of self-soothing. Traumatized clients, typically plagued by symptoms of hyperarousal, need to know what gives rise to their feelings, that their feelings will not kill or revictimize them, and also that food finally cannot rescue them from painful feelings that must be endured and coped with. Building cognitive structure contributes to the capacity of the survivor's internal environment to hold her pain and anxiety.

It is obvious that these cognitive abilities are inseparable from the relational components of experience and development. Knowledge can act as a good mother who knows what to say to soothe a child's distress.

Relational Level

Nowhere is the curative role of learning to eat with hunger more clear than in regard to the relational needs of self. Relationships to food and eating express and contain many of life's developmental and relational issues. The developmental scars and inhibitions caused by trauma often show up as the fear of hunger or the need to modulate feeling by compulsive behavior around food. Therefore learning both to feed oneself in attunement to hunger and how to endure and cope with feeling states without resorting to food when one is not hungry have profound effects on the wounds of the traumatized woman. When she can respond appropriately to her body signals and empathically tolerate her many feeling states, instead of attempting to alter them by means of compulsive food or body behavior, she is essentially treating and healing a part of the incest wound.

Consider some of the key relational meanings that experiencing and eating with hunger may have for the survivor of sexual trauma:

1. Hunger means that her body has spoken. Her body has many tales to tell. She has been carefully trained not to speak, not to express these tales and thus may experience any trace of body expression as a potential betrayal that threatens her. It may feel as if her very life is in danger.

2. Her hunger announces that she has both physical and relational needs; for eating represents the need to survive, to be attached and cared for. Hunger announces that she needs and wants care and comfort. The simple act of feeding her hunger is a profound act of self-care and healing. It heralds a new possibility of being in control of and committed to the meeting of her needy states. It is a profound and healing experience for a woman who has been sexually abused to eat with hunger. The self-respect this entails flies in the face of the degrading experiences she has endured. She is able to act as a true survivor, not a victim yet again of that other form of domination, the chronic diet mentality. Strong enough to take matters into her own hands, she is deciding what will or will not go into her body. Again and again, in meeting her hunger and satiation, the survivor has a chance to draw her boundaries—I want this, I have had enough of that, I don't want that, my body can take no more, my body has a need now. Each time she exercises judgment and responds to her body in an attuned way she heals a broken bit of boundary denied to her. Eating with hunger and stopping with satiation show her time and again her real needs and her real limits. She may be needy; but she can digest only so much. Knowing this reality is boundary-mending.

3. Responding to hunger means that she can finally welcome something basic that comes from inside her without contempt, guilt, shame, or danger. Learning to do this, to know what to eat, when and how much, tells her far more about herself than simply what she is like as an eater. It is a knowledge that affirms her uniqueness and totality—something that has been assaulted all the way along the continuum of violence. When she learns how very much or how very little it takes to fill her and how differently she responds from day to day to different foods, she learns a lot about how her needs actually feel to her. In attuned experiences of hunger and satiation she affirms her right for care in the basic experiences of dependency, neediness, separation, and individuation. She affirms her basic and essential preferences, passions, dislikes, inclinations, capacities, and limits. All of this amounts to a deep experience of individual self-knowledge and her entitlement to be a person in simple but basic ways. Eating in response to hunger offers multidi-

mensional knowledge: It has physical, cognitive, and emotional aspects, all of which are symbolic. It is the kind of experience that is specifically denied by the particular type of adaptation that trauma and symbolic violence requires. It reasserts and develops the body/self integration that was arrested or torn asunder.

4. When eating with hunger, the sexually abused woman is forming a new relationship to herself. She is the nondepriving, nonintrusive, truly interested giver of care. She is willing to know and to respond to herself on an intimate level that lets her be in touch with the truth at each moment. This commitment also opens her to the knowledge of the truth of her past. Only as she is open to this knowledge can she integrate it, removing it from its repressed or dissociated place.

In all these ways, learning to eat with hunger and satiation is both ego-building and renurturing. It is healing to many of the ego and relational wounds of the incest trauma. It makes the repeated practice of a new internal caretaking capacity possible and reestablishes a foundational component of the experience of basic trust that the world is a safe, concerned place in which body/self needs and integrity get a new start.

DIETING AND THE TRAUMA SURVIVOR

Another way to understand the importance of this first treatment principle—reconnecting the trauma survivor to her own physical signals of hunger and satiation—is to examine the consequences of ignoring or bypassing hunger, particularly as they affect the survivor of sexual abuse both in infancy and adulthood. What happens when the hunger signals of an infant are consistently ignored or when the infant is starved? Such gross misattunement insults and traumatizes the infant's sense of well-being, body/self integrity, and the possibility of a comfortable sense of indwelling. Krueger, in *Body-Self and Psychological Self* (1989), reports that infants who were fed intravenously (thus bypassing their hunger and satiation signals by either ignoring them or intruding past their limits) could not learn to eat and feel satisfied, to recognize and to affirm internal body signals. As a result of this foundational deficit, these infants were unable to experience a sense of vitality, motivation, intentionality, or personal mastery. In other words, the infants were developmentally deprived. Like sexually traumatized children, their development of the necessary sense of trust and safety in their environment was inhibited.

While the mother who starves a child is called depriving, neglectful, or even sadistic, this basic knowledge about infants appears very different when one considers adolescents or adults. Then the very prescription of this diet-oriented, food-, and fat-phobic culture is precisely to distrust and by-pass the signals of hunger and satiation. Chronic diets, over the long term, tamper with something basic to the well-being and stability of adults.

Focusing now on simply feeling and believing that one ought to diet, ought to be restricted, ought to be on a food plan, ought not to trust one's self as an eater, and instead ought to find a good diet program or plan and adhere to it, consider how these general effects of the diet mentality dovetail with those of trauma. Chronic dieting, bypassing hunger, creates an internal environment of deprivation and a lack of safety. It also creates the notion that fears, needs, and desires will not be accepted and that self-soothing can-not be achieved. Chronically bypassing hunger, even in adolescent or adult life, disorganizes body boundaries and assaults body/self integration. Over time the diet actually teaches and reinforces a lived pattern of body/self dis-integration. This pattern itself breeds further body/self distortion. Psychoanalysis, just as in the case of the violation caused in the cultural landscape, needs a better language to perceive and discuss this body/self pattern once it is entrenched.

For the survivor of trauma all of this is, at the very least, unfortunate, but it can be tragic. The kind of disorganization, chaos, self-denial, and overrid-ing of body boundaries of the diet mentality and of dieting exaggerates the survivor's already intense experience of lack of safety. When a trauma sur-vivor ignores hunger, the fear and vulnerability associated with the original trauma are reenacted, thus underlining the lessons of the trauma itself. The survivor who chronically diets is taught again and again to repeat aspects of her trauma by disconfirming her inner needs and distorting the knowledge she has of those needs. The diet mentality constantly contradicts and discon-firms her inner experience, her inner truth, her notions of good and bad, right and wrong. All this inhibits her overall mastery in life.

The diet mentality as an ideology is an internalized form of social domi-nation. The diet becomes, as described in chapter 2, an internal jailor whose watchful eyes judge each move with a suspicious glare. This gaze further de-grades and undermines the trauma victim, who has already been trained to distrust, fear, and hide her own impulses, often feeling that they are the di-rect causes of danger to her. For the incest survivor chronic dieting is in the language of Judith Herman (1992), an experience analogous to that of "cap-tivity," which contains the "shadow of the perpetrator." Herman describes captivity, one aspect of trauma, in which the victim's will and independence are deliberately broken by the perpetrators. This is a widespread practice called "seasoning" in the world of prostitution and pornography. The perpe-trator attempts—usually quite successfully—to break the will of the victim by controlling her body functions, eating, sleeping, elimination, and touch. This control and deprivation create a victim desperate enough to carry out the will of the perpetrator. In chronic dieting the cultural need to control the female body is introjected, and the victim then actually looks for someone whom she can enlist or even pay to control her basic body functions. Moreover, in another direct analogy to abuse, because dieting has always created bingeing, it becomes a culturally sanctioned mode of alternating sensory deprivation with sensory overload. The experience of chronic dieting, understood as the shadow of the perpetrator, represents itself as that which is "controlling you for your own good," because on your own you would "fail terribly, bringing great shame upon yourself." As the trauma victim who feels either out of control or constricted, so does the dieter who lives in a constantly oscillating rhythm of bingeing and fasting. As the diet is not a safe environment because it creates bingeing, blaming, and self-hatred, the trauma survivor finds herself in an all too familiar place. The persecutors and seducers who inhabit her internal object-relational world are, in fact, fortified by diets and fat-phobic fears of women's appetites and bodies in the cultural world.

At 10 years old, when Jeanette was first molested by her stepfather, she immediately and compulsively began to diet. First, it was a way to merge with her mother, who was always on a diet. Second, it was a way to try to gain control of her life. Third, it was a new arena in which she could enact and express the self-hatred and shame caused by her abuse and betrayal. She became bulimarexic. As she dieted she blamed herself for her fat stomach and the last binge, Jeanette's internal persecutors, born of her trauma and ready to blame her for her stepfather's abuse, were joined and strengthened by diet and fat-phobic culture. She and her culture express hatred of hips. She and her culture were suspicious of eating as little as would maintain her thin body. The world of the diet, its mentality and rules, offered her false, seductive hope that if she ate little enough, bypassing her natural hunger, she could transform the body that lured him to her. The seducers are clear, the diet is clear. Once again, they gave her the message that she was not capable or worthy of self-care, that her very body functions were best organized by "big daddy," the diet mentality. In the face of this mentality, her needs for food and comfort became ever more suspect, proving to her again and again that she was better off overriding her internal signals and opting instead for external control—4 ounces of meat, one vegetable. But she reduced even that, so eager was she to feel like a better person. In other words because both sexual trauma and bypassing hunger are foundational organizing experiences for the body-self and its internalized relationships, each has tremendous ramifications that practitioners must carefully explore and that resonate profoundly with one another.

Finkelhor and Browne (1985) propose a schema of four major traumagenic dynamics. Using it we can see the homologous relationship of dieting and the diet mentality with the outcome of abuse. According to their model, the first consequence of trauma is traumatic sexualization, which refers to the inappropriate development of sexuality, shaped by abusive sexual relationships. As a result of sexual abuse the child tends to use her body and sexuality for attaining love, care, and other developmentally appropriate needs. One major purpose of dieting is to create a sexually desirable body, one that is to be used as an object for others. Clients who chronically diet in an effort to create the perfectly reified sexual body continue the "traumatic sexualization" of the abuse. The persistent demand for the sexualized body, the self-sacrifice required for chronic dieting, and the constant willingness to manipulate body size, all mimic the dynamic of abuse.

The second dynamic following abuse is the betrayal of basic trust. Inherent in the diet mentality is the betrayal of one's own body. Diets teach one to fail to respond to internal signals and to seriously betray basic needs.

The third major dynamic is powerlessness in which a child's desires and sense of efficacy are continually contravened. Chronic dieting implies powerlessness, a reliance on the "powerful" external rules of the diet in order to know what and when to feed ourselves. In fact, a basic tenet of Overeaters Anonymous (OA) is that one is forever powerless over food. Powerlessness before food parallels Finkelhor and Browne's category of traumatically induced powerlessness.

Stigmatization is the fourth and last dynamic that Finkelhor and Browne describe. Stigma adds insult to injury. When the survivor feels like a marked person, who must forever be guilty and shamed, she comes to feel that her problems are her fault, not the fault of the perpetrator of the original trauma or of its effects on her development. Apart from its manic phase, the diet mentality creates shame and humiliation in chronic dieters who gain back more weight than they lose. The symptoms of chronic trauma and chronic dieting have each been pathologized, and the consequences of each have been dissociated from the original and foundational assaults. Trauma survivors have been ridiculed as irrational hysterics, and chronic dieters have been seen as lazy, willful, manipulative, or impossible to treat. All these attributions are examples of a parallel to Finkelhor and Browne's dynamic of stigmatization.

Finally, the diet mentality closes off therapeutic possibilities. Eating by regulation instead of according to the felt needs of hunger and satiation inhibits self-knowledge not only about hunger but also about all the needs and feelings of the body-self. When clients learn to wait for and to respond to hunger and satiation, they are implicitly ready to know and to hear about their experiences of need, fear, difficulty with containment, vulnerability, and being nurtured. All these feelings will come up in the course of learning, slowly, to wait for and to feel hunger as well as to meet it with food. Chronic dieting also inhibits treatment possibilities because a client who is always on or planning a diet puts forward a compliant self. Offering clients sincere interest in knowing about noncompliant feeling states implicitly fosters an ability to tolerate trauma, memories, and self states.

The Capacity to Permit Food Choice

The survivor of abuse was told that she liked what she hated and what hurt, that she wanted what she was deeply conflicted about, that she mustn't do what feels good to her, and that she must ingest things that are abhorrent. By learning to feel exactly what, how much, and when she wants to eat, she is redrawing her body boundaries so as to develop her sense of body/self integration. As she learns that she can eat what she wants, she learns that her desires are safe. As she finds out what foods feel good in her body and in what quantity, she learns a healthy, nonabusive, self-determined, nonpunitive self-regulation.

"Legalizing" all foods, learning to feel entitled to all foods, removing the labels of "good" and "bad" food taught by the world of dieting, are all indispensable parts of learning to eat with and respond to body hunger and satiation as well as to let go of compulsive emotional eating or starving. As long as some foods remain forbidden and "dangerous," those will be the very foods that are used as magic, imagined as able to change painful internal self states. An anti-diet approach would be quite hollow if it meant that fattening foods must be restricted by regulation rather than true choice. The diet mentality in relation to food choice prevents really healthful food choices and instead promotes uncontrollable bingeing on "forbidden" foods. For the survivor of sexual abuse, learning to trust her desires has special meaning.

However, becoming attuned to the body and its nutritional needs is not an easy task. The victim of abuse has adaptively learned to ignore, repress, and dissociate from her bodily desires. Therefore, it may be difficult to decide exactly what foods will be the right ones to meet her hunger each time it arises. For example, one client, Elaine, wanted to eat only potato chips and ice cream, and she experienced these cravings as her real food needs. Elaine's situation represents a commonly found phenomenon in treatment among survivors as well as nonsurvivors. In the same way that Elaine's masochistic sexual urges left her in danger, her food "choices" leave her undernourished. In a culture that aggressively sells high-fat, high-sugar fast foods Elaine is at risk. She feels guilty and fearful of fat, but the fast foods beckon to her, and she is not able to be in close enough touch with her body-self to ignore their lure. One of the biggest challenges in the work is how to help such clients to learn to know and experience their bodies and nutritional needs as real without imposing or reinforcing a diet mentality. Although information can be offered from external sources, this information should not create compliant behavior. Therapists help clients to use nutritional information in a self-determined, nurturing way. This takes some time, effort, and creativity and is a very individualized process.

When a victim-survivor comes to feel that she can and should allow herself—body and soul—to feel and choose exactly the food that's right for her, she has truly left the scene and dynamics of her abuse. When she believes that she can determine what she wants, what actually feels good to and in her body, what she desires in her mouth, throat, and stomach, she is truly healing the wound of incest and abuse. Several times a day through her ability to choose food and feed herself with her physical hunger, which includes an attuned nutritional match (eating not only what will taste good but what her body can actually utilize) she can learn that a self has wants that are knowable and meetable. When this is accomplished, she has learned something that turns her earlier experience on its head.

SOME IMPLICATIONS OF SIZE ACCEPTANCE FOR TRAUMA SURVIVORS

All too many women are ashamed of their bodies. They want to be thinner, a different shape, younger, and so on. For survivors of abuse body hatred is often very severe. The body can contain a large number of possible meanings; it can represent many different experiences for the trauma survivor living in this culture. In working with anorexics and bulimics, women who are thin but feel fat, therapists are usually clear that their job is to encourage the examination of distorted body image. It is less self-evident to many therapists how to work with large, even very large women in regard to their body image. This approach would be false if the goal was to make certain that patients conform to the culturally acceptable size and shape. Although concerned with the healthy nurture of the body, this approach is also mindful and respectful of the experience of body image and size. The goal is to help all clients to accept their bodies and reclaim the meanings of their bodies and their body images as well as to care for their bodies as they are. Only when some body acceptance is present can women live at peace in their present size or willingly change their size according to hunger and satiation.

When people eat in accordance with their hunger and satiation, they eventually reach a size that is within their natural weight range. This may or may not conform to their ideals for size. However, the process of eating with hunger is so gratifying as well as self-organizing that most people find greatly increased physical and psychological comfort in their body, whatever their size. At the same time, long after eating has stabilized and organized, there is hard work to do, because the cultural landscape and its internal representations, a landscape that hardly mirrors women's glorious variety, is always assaulting. Size acceptance is an important and hard-won achievement for everyone. It has particular meaning, however, for the survivor of sexual trauma, for whom accepting and owning her body means recognizing the site of abuse, humiliation, and pain without dissociating or clinging to internal persecutory objects.

This approach constantly differentiates itself from the demanding, stereotypical, and injurious standards of the present cultural aesthetic. Fat is not bad, and thin and shapely is not necessarily good. However, both the fat body and the socially acceptable thin and young body, will carry important information about clients' selves and lives. The survivor's ability to accept herself at whatever size means that a profound shift had occurred in her internal object relations. At this point she can disidentify with her actual perpetrators and her internal persecutors and instead accept herself without shame, guilt, or punishment. Her body has become a safe place. The stance of holding the possibility of size acceptance creates a transitional space within which patients can have this experience.*

The Importance of Detailed Inquiry

Compulsive eating, restricting of food, and a distorted sense of body image are among the most important avenues of expression for survivors of abuse. They are the normative terrain of women; they are and always have been containers for the expression of relational pain and aspiration; they exist as the center of self experience. Because these containers are far, far too small to contain a full expression of the client's feelings and her present and past experience, it is especially important in dealing with survivors of abuse that the therapist examine the details of all eating incidents and moments of body image distortion.

The repetitive, ritualistic presentation of the incident can induce a countertransference response in which the therapist comes to feel disgust for this "out-of-control" woman who may seem to carefully control and manage the treatment, using her food and body obsessions and compulsions to avoid talking about the more "real" and underlying problems. In working with survivors of trauma, clinicians commonly find themselves irritated or frightened that, in the midst of the memory and grief work about the trauma, the client develops or restarts an eating problem, thereby seeming to create a crisis or at least a diversion in the treatment. Therapeutic success, however, comes precisely by working with that obsession (which may sometimes include deemphasizing it) and by understanding how the obsession itself is both defensive and adaptive as well as self-injurious and thus traumatic.

Traumatic sexual assault becomes a core organizer and disorganizer of ego and self experience, as does the ability or the incapacity to feed oneself and to live in one's body. Both are foundational aspects of life that affect intrapsychic object relations, cognitive development, and interpersonal relations. Because of the injunction against fully exposing sexual trauma, it is often converted into culturally syntonic food and body symptomatology.

---

*For an excellent discussion about helping large women learn to care for the bodies they have, see Burgard and Lyons (1994).

For example, a compulsive or unattuned eating episode could mean, and could be an attempt to cope with, any of the following possibilities at a given time:

She is feeling aggressive, potentially a perpetrator, when she usually allows herself to know only the victim component of her family-induced experience. She eats in guilt and in an effort to stuff in the unwanted parts.

On the contrary, she cannot tolerate the experience of the internalized victim and would prefer to identify with the aggressor aspect of self experience and eats or purges or starves when she feels vulnerable.

She is longing for a rescuer and fears being let down. The food meets the longing, and when it lets her down she is in control of it. She may binge, purge, or starve.

She is feeling any other of the ego-dystonic aspects of her internalized experience, including perpetrator, victim, rescuer, betrayer, or denier.

She eats and then hates herself, expressing the sadistic-masochistic relationship between her inner representation of victim and betrayer and/or perpetrator.

She feels sad, too sad to bear. Food soothes her.

She wants to cry and was told not to cry or she would be further hurt. Again she can soothe herself with eating, purging, or starving.

She revealed a secret in the last session and fears she will be punished by her real as well as her inner perpetrator. Her anxiety is allayed by eating.

She hates herself and believes she caused all her pain with her badness. She proves this to herself with a huge binge, a purge, or more starving.

She felt desire for food/love and wants to squelch it before she is disappointed. She can manage the desire and the squelching by eating and then berating herself.

She has a generalized feeling of shame that at times feels overwhelming. Food covers this up and quiets her anxiety about feeling stigmatized.

She eats to create the illusion of internal parents, not to feel the real betrayal. Food is so reminiscent of early care that it works very well.

She eats to create a real transitional and grounding experience, an experience of some mastery and control. Food, having always been able to transform her sense of self, can still serve in that capacity even if it is finally just metaphoric.

She starves to gain control over the fear of toxic nurturance.

She binges but is reminded of controlling and abusive family relationships and thus purges the food to be cleansed. But the inner conflict between the need for attachment and the dangers of attachment does not go away, and she cannot get out of the binge/purge cycle.

She eats and then cuts herself, representing her need for care and comfort and the vicious internalized assault on her need and wish.

She eats chocolate to cover her abusive associations to the taste of beer, although she can only see herself as a chocaholic.

She eats compulsively because she is terrified she will not have food; and this fear, furthered and anchored by a society that teaches chronic dieting, reenacts earlier deprivation of food related to sexual assault and the betraying, neglectful family that allowed it.

She eats to transform her size from that of the abused body to a size that does not remind her of the abuse.

A distorted body experience could also represent a myriad of possibilities, including a response to any of the aforementioned or of the following:

She must see herself as large to give herself an understandable reason why she has been so hurt. She needs some sense of reason and predictability in the world.

She starves to create a body that she imagines no one would want and is therefore safe from further assault.

She sees an awful, hateful fat and ugly body when she is in the grip of the "return of the rejecting or tantalizing object," an internal reenactment of her earlier relationship with her abuser (Fairbairn, 1986).

In one way or another her life experience creates the idea that what is wrong with her life is caused by what is wrong with her body. Her family blamed her for being both fat and provocative, a double-bind message that is reiterated in her adult life in consumer culture.

She finds it easier to talk about how she hates her body than how much she hates her perpetrator. The hate is directed at the self.

All these and many other meanings come up in the form of eating incidents and moments of body image distortion that may at first all sound alike. With investigation, however, the therapist will quite quickly be able to find the dominant meaning an eating or body image incident carries for the particular moment in life and therapy in which it arises.

Each time the therapist honors and inquires about the details of an eating or body image incident, she has a new opportunity to act both in her archaeological (finding out what happened) and relational (knowing the effects of what happened) roles, as Frawley has expressed it (Davies & Frawley, 1992a). In the archaeological role the therapist can truly comprehend her client's crucial body enactments. Eating and body image are avenues of nonverbal expression, the kind of expression that is required when speech and verbal disclosure are prohibited. By following the details about the organization of inner object relations, traumatically induced or limited cognition and traumatogenic physiological responses are exposed.

In the therapist's relational role, asking about the many different incidents offers a chance to join the client in her dissociated and isolated state. It is especially important for a trauma survivor to carefully attend to her many attempts to express herself in relation to food or body image and not to ignore the only language in which she is able to speak of her trauma and its consequences. Each time the therapist is open to the significance of a particular binge, purge, or starving incident, she demonstrates her ability to meet her client in the pain, shame, and terror stored inside. Understanding that the client is afraid of decoding her experience, terrified of reexperiencing and being overwhelmed by the trauma, requires that the therapist be willing to enter the experience in order to act as a holding environment, a container for the terror, so that the client can manage to see what happened to her and what her responses have been. Again and again the therapist and client must have this ego-building and -healing experience. Not a few times, but again and again, over years, the client must feel her therapist join her experience with an empathic and curious voice.

This may seem self-evident. After all, psychoanalysis is built on deconstructing the meaning of these sorts of details. The interpersonal analysts, following Harry Stack Sullivan, place special emphasis on "detailed inquiry" as a core principle and technique of treatment. Edgar Levenson is known for his insistence that therapists actually find out what happens and has happened (Hirsch, 1993) and argues that mistakes and blunders in therapy are frequently caused by not paying attention to detail, letting theory predetermine what will be selectively attended or unattended instead.

Yet, even interpersonally oriented analysts who specialize in eating disorders speak very little about the actual and different moments and meanings of their clients' experiences with food or their bodies (see, for example, S. Stern, 1992). Perhaps this is because in relation to food, as it has been until recently in relation to sexual trauma, psychoanalysis has been inhibited by cultural biases embedded within it. These biases derive from two contradictory but powerful social tendencies. First, food behavior, the importance of eating, the role of eating have all been trivialized. They are associated with the work of nurturance and as such they have been devalued; hence psychoanalytic theory has been significantly underdeveloped in making food and body image experience a central interest of inquiry. In the absence of theory to hold and codify an interest in eating and body image, the therapist can more easily be prey to the second social tendency in regard to food, which is the desperate wish to control it in the name of health and "virtue." Hence, even while it is trivialized, eating behavior is also the subject of obsessive, almost phobic interest. The social imperative is that the female body and appetite must be brought under control. This contradictory set of social injunctions explains why it is that the trivialization of female concerns about eating and body image can coexist with an imperious, self-righteous or desperately anxious attitude toward a woman who cannot control her eating behavior.

We do not propose reducing anyone to their eating problem or "buying" the obsession and letting it stop our inquiry. Instead, we propose joining our clients in paying detailed attention, in an experience-near way, to their relationships with food and their bodies, and in helping them to understand eating to represent a myriad of possible core experiences. It is wise to minimize theoretical presuppositions that might lead to selective inattention to the real variety of what various incidents may mean (Levenson, 1992).

SOMATOPSYCHIC, NONVERBAL, AND EXPERIENTIAL TECHNIQUES IN A RELATIONAL PSYCHOANALYTIC FRAME

Just as our theory incorporates an analysis of the influence of culture on human experience and psychic structure, so it incorporates an analysis of the details of bodily experience, the realms of the nonverbal, kinesthetic, and sensory into a feminist treatment model. Working with the many details encoded in clients' bodies is essential given that the body is a common vehicle through which eating problems and sexual abuse are experienced. The sexually abused patient has frequently been rendered unable to speak about or may not even know about her traumatic experience. Likewise, the client with an eating problem often cannot articulate her experience, because of the normative nature of the fear of food and fat. In both cases the body can be used as a container for unarticulated but powerful experience.

Somatopsychic, nonverbal, or experiential methods allow clients to bypass social and familial prohibitions against telling their secrets and their stories. These techniques can serve as a way to "tell" without risking threatened punishment for speaking. They allow therapists to meet patients where they are, in the unformed, unknown body/self state, in order to create a form, put words to this undifferentiated experience, and make it conscious. Such techniques include guided imagery, journal writing, art, dance/movement, music, hypnosis, and touch as well as the therapist's use of self as an observer of nonverbal reactions and interactions, such as gesture, posture, breathing, muscle tension, aches, and pains (Hornyak & Baker, 1989; Pruzinsky, 1990; Rabinor, 1991).

Some clinicians and theoreticians have objected to these techniques. Psychoanalysis can be contradictory, and even though Freud's notions emphasized the primacy of bodily experience, contemporary psychoanalysis, the "talking cure," has paid relatively little attention to bodily phenomena. Moreover, nonverbal techniques have sometimes been minimized, marginalized, or idealized. They have been depreciated as "touchy-feely," which, in this culture, refers especially to the "feminine." Verbal, rational, linear modes of expression are seen as higher level functioning, whereas nonverbal expression is seen as primitive. It is presumed that once higher level, symbolic functioning is reached, the need for other kinds of expression may be regressive. In a developmental sense it is true that symbolic functioning is a later development than somatic functioning. However, it is precisely the ability to relinquish symbolic functioning that enables great artists to paint, dance, or create music. The point is to have access to both modes of functioning in order to be fully human. Nonverbal techniques have been marginalized as the purview of "fringe" groups within the therapeutic community, such as creative arts and body work therapists, and have rarely been integrated into more traditional training programs. Sue Shapiro (1993) states, "Today working with the body is relegated to 'outlaw' analysts" (see also Aron, 1992c). This phenomenon is a general result of Western culture's mind-body split and of ideological struggles in the history of psychoanalysis (Shapiro, 1993).

On the other hand, nonverbal techniques are sometimes idealized by those who practice in these modes as being the only road to the early, deep, and most profound of human experience. An objection of analysts has been that nonverbal material is so potent that it so impacts on the transference and countertransference as to make it impossible to track what is happening in the treatment. In fact, difficulties can arise when nonverbal and experiential techniques are implemented. They are powerful tools that can easily become weapons in unskilled, irresponsible, or incautious hands. They can, for example, trigger uncontrolled abreaction, as happened in the case of Francine. While Francine was having a flashback of her mother's invasive use of her fingers into her vagina, her therapist asked her to draw a picture of her feelings and handed her a pen. Francine immediately froze, experiencing the pen as her mother's finger that was uncontrollably being forced upon her. She became more agitated and disorganized and less able to communicate to her therapist.

This suggestion worked to disempower rather than empower the patient, as if the therapist had used the technique to coerce or control Francine without adequate preparation and negotiation. An unfortunate example of this kind of phenomenon has been alleged recently in stories of therapists putting clients into trances and then questioning in leading ways so as to suggest dissociated memories of abuse, the truthfulness of which the therapist then insists on out of trance and later in treatment. In every way, this scenario represents a heinous abuse of professional power and, of course, of the power of trance work.*

---

*The recent emphasis on this phenomenon of therapists' suggestion by the False Memory Foundation (FMF) and associates is complicated, however, because this group seeks to exaggerate how many therapists are biased and severely minimizes and silences the survivors coming forward in treatment. The FMF in our opinion is political and reactive and unfairly dismisses 20 years and more of research on dissociation and trauma. See for example, DeMause (1994) and *Journal of Psychohistory*, 21, 4 (Spring 1994) entire issue.

Defenses that manifest themselves nonverbally on a body level as well as verbally can be bypassed too quickly, disregarding the adaptive functions of defense. It is imperative to be aware of these dangers, because the mere act of engaging the nonverbal realm of experience automatically requires, if only for a moment, the patient to relinquish a layer of defense and conscious control that is inherent in verbalization.

On the other hand, if used carefully, these techniques are a means to several particular ends. A goal of therapy is to integrate verbal, cognitive experience with psyche and soma so that the patient can recognize, accept, and find relief in her body and be able to verbalize her experience. This process furthers the integration of thoughts and feelings, a central analytic goal. Using these techniques, the body can become a site of healing, not just a site of abuse. An example is Sally's experience with guided imagery. Sally eats when she is not hungry much of the time. She has found it difficult to wait for hunger ever since childhood. Sally's therapist asks her if she can try to relax, breathe deeply, close her eyes, and imagine a scenario in which she does wait for hunger. After allowing Sally a few moments to visualize this scene, her therapist asks her to notice what she is feeling as it unfolds. Sally discovers that her experience of hunger is anxiety-provoking, and is very familiar. She opens her eyes and begins to tell her therapist that the anxiety is much like her experience of terror when, as a child, she heard her father's footsteps each night approaching her room, where he would sexually abuse her. In this way Sally is able to contact part of herself, in the safety of the therapy relationship, that she could not reach on her own. This technique enabled her to further cope with the effects of sexual trauma as well as with her eating problem.

Linda is 14 years old and chronically complains about her fat thighs, but she cannot quite articulate her feelings any further. However, when her therapist offers her paper, pens, and crayons and asks if she can draw a self-portrait, Linda draws an elaborate self-portrait, crossing out her genitals with black ink. Her therapist asks her to talk about the drawing and what feelings the drawing projects. This leads to a discussion of Linda's feelings about certain parts of her body, to her first disclosure of being sexually molested and therefore, to another level of inquiry. In contrast to Francine, Linda was able to use the nonverbal technique to facilitate her treatment. Linda's therapist asked her exactly how she experienced this intervention so that she could keep track of its impact on their relationship.

These techniques require the analyst to expand her role as participant-observer, to use Sullivan's (1940, 1953) term. To remain true to the analytic endeavor, where a goal is to always remain open to understanding the relationship itself, requires the therapist to track carefully the impact of these techniques within the transference/countertransference paradigm. The analyst, using these techniques, needs to be vigilant and cognizant of ways in which they affect the relationship. The fact that the analyst introduces and therefore directs the experience may affect the dynamic. The therapist actually being present with her client when the content of an experience emerges, her ability and willingness to be that close, may also have an effect on the treatment that can be analyzed. Here the therapist may ask, for example, how it felt "that I was with you in this experience." It is important that the frame of the analysis remains intact when using these techniques. The boundaries of time, location, and shared intention of the analyst and client to do what is best for the client should not be sacrificed or disturbed. The therapy relationship remains both bounded and analyzable.

CHAPTER 12

Eating Problems in Patients with Multiple Personality Disorder

Susan Gutwill

Identification, Diagnosis, and Treatment of Multiple Personality Disorder

ULTIPLE PERSONALITY DISORDER (MPD) is at the far end of the continuum of dissociative adaptations to trauma. Although MPD may include other forms of dissociation, such as amnesia, fugue, depersonalization, derealization, somnambulism, hypnoid states, and general features of posttraumatic stress disorder (PTSD) such as profound anxiety and dysphoria, it is uniquely characterized by the presence of separate and alternating identities or ego states called alter personalities (Braun, 1990; Fine, 1993; Fine & Kluft, 1992; Kluft, 1986a; Loewenstein & Ross, 1992; McWilliams & Rutstein, 1992; Putnam, 1989; Ross, 1989; Spiegel, 1993). Richard Kluft, a major theorist and clinician in MPD, argues that a better name for the syndrome would be multiple reality disorder, because the real problem is that the subjective sense of reality differs from personality to personality, making life very difficult. Alter ego states originally develop as a response to overwhelming, chronic trauma, usually physical, sexual, and emotional in nature and beginning very early in life at the hands of trusted caregivers (Kluft, 1985c, 1990b; Putnam, 1989). Traumatic experience threatens to overwhelm the ego, and, therefore, the victim begins the journey of survival by dissociating from the horrible reality (Briere & Courtois, 1992; Loewenstein & Ross, 1992; Young, 1988). (*Dissociation* is generally understood as a defense against real-life conditions that threaten psychic unity. *Repression,* on the other hand, is generally understood as a defense against terrifying or unwanted impulses and feelings deriving within the inner world of self and other object representations.)

In MPD, different personalities remember and respond to different aspects of the traumas. In this way, the personalities may be understood as alternate strategies a child creatively develops to cope with profound trauma. These strategies become persistent, and thus alter personalities are usually relatively stable and enduring over time. Although originally adaptive to horrific conditions and, in that sense, truly life preserving, alter personality development becomes a maladaptive, generalized way of responding to subsequent, nonabusive life events. For example, when Jane sees a dark, heavyset man who looks like her abusing father, a protector personality, and/or a terrified-child personality may come out to handle her alarm. The child personality might be triggered into such panic that she spontaneously throws up or urinates in her clothes and whimpers, slumping into a corner. A protector personality may do any number of things, including becoming seductive, as a way to feel powerful rather than powerless. It may attack the self in identification with the abuser, another way to fantasize being proactive rather than powerless. Or it may become anorexic, insisting on starving the body in a magical wish that a thin body would ensure a better person and, therefore, a person safe from harm.

Without appropriate treatment, MPD patients are at risk of great panic, sadness, suffering, and even danger, because they respond to all life events by dissociating from the present. Patients with this disorder return to their pasts and interpret current events as if they were as threatening as was the original abuse. Untreated, MPD can lead to more and more discontinuity of memory, behavior, and sense of self, because each part is coping on its own, often quite self-destructively and without full knowledge of how the other parts operate, think, and feel.

Alter ego states hold traumatic memories and affects and provide functions for the host. Thus, different alters will remember a particular trauma whereas others will not. Certain alters will be able to experience some feelings, such as sadness or anger whereas others will not. Some alters can drive, others can work, others can be social, and still others can be punishing and ultimately self-injurious. Alter personalities can thus be conceived of as highly styled enactments of inner conflicts, drives, feelings, and memory states (Ross, 1989). They have "defensive, representational, symbolic and being-in-the-world aspects" (Loewenstein & Ross, 1992).

Typically, the clinician will encounter the following types of alter personalities: the host, children, persecutors who both identify with the aggressor and attempt to protect the host from further abuse, internal self-helpers, demons, administrators, special function parts representing promiscuous, handicapped, autistic, mute, and cross-gender aspects of the personality, and memory trace fragments. There can be many elaborations in this list and a myriad of ways in which each group combines to form its unique personality system. In cases of ritualized sadistic cult abuse there may also be alters who are the product of mind control torture, instructed and trained to perform specific cult-determined tasks ("Cult Abuse of Children," 1994; Hammond, 1992; Peterson, 1992b; Sakheim & Devine, 1992a, 1992b). These different types of general alter egos have very different body images and feelings about food and eating. Moreover, the extent to which any particular alter personality expresses itself in the metaphor of food and the body varies. Practitioners should be sensitive to the very individualized communications alter egos express when they binge, purge, starve, overexercise, or berate the body for its size or shape or when some foods are repellent and create nausea whereas others are sought out energetically and sometimes even desperately.

Learning to identify and diagnose MPD is extremely important because most patients have been in the mental health system for more than 7 years before being appropriately treated (Kluft, 1991a; Putnam, 1989). Because MPD requires a specialized as well as a general psychotherapy treatment, a patient misdiagnosed is one who is treated for secondary symptoms at best and may be further victimized at worst. The symptoms of MPD are multiple and severe, but the presentation of multiplicity is, unfortunately for the diagnostician, rarely the sort of florid presentation that is dramatized in *Three Faces of Eve* or *Sybil* (Kluft, 1991a).

Identifying characteristics of MPD provide the clinician with not only clues for diagnosis but also a sense of what may require attention in treatment. Such a list includes the following characteristics (Kluft, 1991a; Putnam, 1989; Ross, 1989): time loss (the single most common symptom), depression; anxiety, phobias; substance abuse and eating disorders; auditory and visual hallucinations, which appear to come from inside the head (rather than outside the head as is more common with schizophrenia); out-of-body experiences; suicidality; self-mutilation; intrusive images; unclear memories; disturbed sleep; seizurelike behavior; sensory disturbances (such as blindness, respiratory, reproductive system, and gastrointestinal problems that are organically unexplained and unrelieved by treatment); incongruity in nonverbal presentation (for example, not one characteristic walk or recognizable hand gesture, but several different postural and gestural profiles); and terrible headaches (the single most common symptom associated with visual disturbance).

In addition, the clinician may suspect MPD when no clear chronological life story emerges or when the client refers to herself as "she," "they," or "we" instead of "I." Clients frequently report being called liars, unexpectedly wearing strange clothing, finding strange and unrecognizable articles in the house, being lost or unable to explain how they act. The clinician should check for gaps in memory in regard to general life events. More specifically, the eating-disorder therapist can ask for a chronological food, weight, and body image history in order to further identify possible amnesia. The final confirmation of MPD will be the subjective experience of self as divided into relatively separate, distinct, and enduring personalities.

Understanding Eating Problems in Patients with Multiple Personality Disorder

Current figures about how many MPD patients suffer from eating problems vary. Kluft (1991a) reports that 16% to 40% of clients with MPD have eating disorders, but Ross (1989) argues that the figure is as much as 50% to 75%. Moshe Torem (1993) has done the most careful and thoughtful study to date and reports that 92% of his sample of 84 had eating disorder symptoms and that of the patients with an eating disorder 44% had a previous eating disorder diagnosis and 59% had active eating disorder symptoms at the time of the study. He defines eating disorders as including bingeing, vomiting, laxative abuse, starvation, or excessive exercising. Torem's results reflect a wider, more accurate definition of eating problems. In fact, his definition still may underrepresent eating problems because it does not include constant, long-term obsessions with eating, size, and dieting. In any event, there is no doubt that many—probably a majority—of MPD patients suffer from eating problems.

How do we understand the role of an eating problem in the personality system of a patient with MPD? Some of the literature suggests that one or more alters tend to carry the eating problem (Levin & Spauster, 1992). Diverging from this notion, Torem's latest study (1993) confirms our theoretical expectation and clinical experience. His MPD patients with eating problems had an average of three symptoms per person, and although 38% of those who binged and purged did so in a single alter ego, 35% did so in more than one ego state. Goodwin and Attias (1993) also believe that eating problems have a very complicated role in multiple personality. For example, does an eating problem and body image disturbance exist within the experience of one or two alters, or are they more generally expressive throughout the system? Women's eating problems are complex modes of expression that cut across most aspects of the self. They express intrapsychic difficulties as well as conflicts about women's social role and the diet culture. Therefore eating problems necessarily take many different forms, both among patients with MPD in general and within any one personality system (Goodwin & Attias, 1993). The eating problem requires that the practitioner see it, address it, and even use it for healing in a multitude of ways. As the eating problem permeates the whole person, it provides the practitioner a roadmap, not only to the eating problem itself but also to the secrets, needs, and conflicts of the person as a whole. By following the many discrete details of eating and body image expression, the clinician honors this painful but important guide to the self, its distortions, adaptations, wishes, and fears. Thus, a therapist should inquire about and attend to binges, fasts, chronic dieting, bouts of nausea and vomiting, purges, and even "simple" undramatic sequential eating without physiological hunger—all of which can easily manifest in one personality system.

The eating problem often represents an intermingling of the effects of the original horrific traumas with later, more socially normative experiences described throughout this book—experiences in consumer culture that judge the female body and set impossible standards for it. These experiences all teach dissociation of the body-self. Our definition of an eating problem includes the normative but chronic compulsions to diet, the fear of food, the terror of having eaten too much, and the hatred of the body. This definition encourages the therapist to address the full range of eating problems in the patient with MPD as well as the role of the culture in creating and supporting "normal" eating problems. The relationship between cultural violations and family or other interpersonally induced trauma is complex, as are the relative roles and impact of dissociation and repression in eating disorders and MPD.

Moshe Torem (1993) and others have proposed that we distinguish "dissociatively based eating disorders" from more "typical eating disorders" (Levin & Spauster, 1992). For example, Torem suggests that statements such as the following might indicate a dissociative, abuse-created eating disorder:

> I don't know why I do it. I am so confused. It is not like me.
>
> When I binge, it feels so strange, as if I am in a daze. I don't know what comes over me.
>
> It feels like a part of me wants to binge and a part of me hates it.
>
> Whenever food is put in front of me, I become scared. I know I need to eat, but I am scared, like the Devil gets into me. I don't know what it is. (Torem, 1986, 1992b)

Because clients with eating problems often express various unintegrated ego states that are not induced by sexual trauma, these comments would not, in our estimation, necessarily signal profound dissociation. In fact, therapists routinely hear these very comments and similar ones from a great majority of women in treatment, whether they have been sexually abused or not. Comments such as these would denote MPD only when combined with other serious indicators of underlying traumatically induced dissociation. Indeed, patients who eventually disclose MPD frequently present for treatment in very unremarkable ways: "I need to lose 10 pounds"; "I hate my body—help!"; "I want to stop bingeing and purging"; "I was anorexic at one point in my teenage years, and I still feel afraid to eat." All these are typical presenting complaints heard from clients with MPD; they do not sound different from these coming from the majority of patients with eating problems.

Just as it is not easy to identify MPD on the basis of an eating disorder, understanding the role of the eating problem in the patient with MPD is also complicated. Because nurturing the self and learning to live in the body are, in and of themselves, such complex and central developmental achievements, they have a similarly complex role in the psychology of the client with MPD.

A Case Study: Lily

Lily provides a rich example of the complex way in which a patient with MPD attempts to express herself and to cope with her circumstances, by manipulating her eating and body image. Not one or two alters but a large part of the personality system sends its message with the aid of food and body image metaphors.

When Lily originally entered treatment for severe bulimia, she did not identify herself as having multiple personalities; nor did her therapist suspect MPD. The bulimia was cured after several years of intensive treatment, often focusing on specific binges and purges. The detailed exploration of the binges and purges that so troubled her stimulated Lily to remember and disclose a great deal about her abuse and its traumatic sequelae. Her memory came back in a fragmented way. Certain incidents were remembered, forgotten, then reremembered, shocking her again and again. Eventually, as she stopped both bingeing and purging, she began to identify and to respond to hunger and satiation with some regularity; she stopped her addiction to dieting and, with it, her characteristic yo-yoing up and down the scale. She began to learn to feed herself. While she continued to eat when she was not physically hungry, she was much more in control of her eating. Moreover, her body was not racked by the violent purging that had previously characterized her behavior. She even gained weight lost by fasting in a very slow and stable way. Although she still hated her fat, the vehemence of the self-attacks was diminished, and for the first time in years, there was room in her conscious mind for other subjects, and she could talk and think about more than food and her weight.

The treatment became increasingly focused on those elements that shaped her life in the present and her concepts of self and others: her dysphoria and her vague and foggy or piecemeal memory fragments, with related fantasized elaborations. It was not until almost 10 years into treatment that she expressed her multiplicity, and the treatment changed to accommodate the new diagnosis. About a year after revealing her multiplicity, Lily began to look at body image and eating issues again. A close examination of a session with this focus demonstrates our thesis: If an eating problem and body image distortion is present, it will more often than not reflect myriad issues and open many therapeutic avenues throughout the personality system.

This session occurred after Lily engaged in a difficult exploration of her images of watching animals being sacrificed. She was horrified and deeply pained by these images. She was ashamed of having stood by these events and by the recollections of related torture that she had endured, the purpose of which seemed to be to break her independent will and to make her feel voluntarily a part of the ritual. In the weekend following this session, Lily called the therapist in great confusion and pain, reporting that she had purged for the first time in over 5 years. The therapist asked her if there was an alter, perhaps one who had not been around for a long while, who might be responsible for the purge. The therapist asked her to write from the part of her which had purged and was currently wanting to purge.

In the following session Lily arrived with very complex journal entries. First, she had written from an anorexic alter named Polly, who had previously been mentioned but was still quite unknown. Polly wrote that because she had been starved so often, she preferred to teach herself not to want food, to overcome the fear of hunger, to go beyond it, and, therefore, to be free of it and its control over her. She wanted a thin, controlled body that did not leave a strained silence among people as did Lily's large body. Eventually, the handwriting changed, and Madalyn, a prostitute alter who wanted to attract men, spoke of her hatred of the body. Madalyn said she felt a little less hateful of the body than she used to, but still felt that if she could get rid of it, she could have so much more fun. Then, the handwriting changed to the printing of some of the child alters, who said that the last thing on this earth that they would want was to be without food again, which was like being punished. Finally, Delores, an alter personality who is—even today—very organized and rational, expressed her wish that Lily would go on a diet. Delores wanted the therapist to side with her as she reminded Lily of the principle of portion control learned in OA. Lily reported that there was great conflict inside, that Delores, Madalyn, and Polly were all thin, and that "even though they all feel very convicted that I should diet, the children are the strongest force of all."

At this point the therapist asked if any part had noticed that they said "convicted," when they ostensibly meant to say convinced. Lily was confused. The therapist called out Bruce, hoping that he could look at the meaning of the slip. Bruce is a male alter who acts as an internal helper and who likes to think things over very carefully. At this point the therapist was only thinking of Bruce in his capacity to play with concepts; she was not anticipating that he might have a different view because of his subjective experience of being a male. His first response was not from his intellectual grasp of the "slip" but from his own internal experience: he said he really didn't see what all the fuss was about, the body was just fine the way it was. After this, however, he did discuss with the therapist the possible meaning of being "convicted." Together, they agreed that criminals are convicted for crimes and then put behind bars to be punished. They realized that Delores, Madalyn, and Polly, all women, were mortified by the fat and felt it kept them from freedom in the world generally as well as free from food. Each woman saw the body as fat but herself as significantly thinner. Polly saw herself as very thin, Madalyn felt she weighed 145 pounds (at a height of 5'7"), and Dolores felt she was full, not fat, at 160 pounds. Each of these parts also felt like a criminal for having witnessed the sacrifices of animals without being able to stop them. Shame for being a witness was expressed in the shame of being fat.

Throughout the session, several other relevant issues repeatedly arose. The child personalities continued to reiterate that they refused to be deprived. Lily spoke again and again of her wish to go and feed the starving children in Somalia; she felt she knew them personally and owed them something, that she had no right to complain, because other people had worse trouble. She also said she was seeing her body more clearly than she had ever previously been able to do. She was seeing how large she was and was shocked.

Before going on to some of the work that might be done, consider some of the themes that are on the surface of Lily's food and body concerns in this session:

Guilt for witnessing torture is expressed as guilt for a fat body.

The female alters want to look at least as if they are in control, even though they are part of an abused person who was the object of control by sadistic others.

The child alters want soothing and freedom from the fear of starvation. They think eating will do this for them.

Polly wants to exert control over the body's hunger so that the needy body-self will not be disappointed by those who neglect and abuse her. Anorexia seems like an excellent solution.

The alters who feel guilty for watching the sacrifice want repair, and feeding others who are hungry is one way to repair.

The male alter feels a bit easier about the body; it is not his main concern.

The fat exposes and represents humiliation, even though at other times fat has also meant protection.

No alter clearly knew the actual size of the body.

The different sizes—a very thin Polly "was on the streets," Madalyn at 145 "is just perfect," Delores at 160 "is fuller"—each represent different ego states as well as possible memories.

How complicated it is for different ego states to share one body, like a conflicted family stuck in one room! Lily's relationship to food, eating, and body image shows some of the complexity and power of work that is possible and necessary for the patient suffering with both eating problems and MPD. The goals of treatment for both disorders are, first, to heal the symptoms—eating problem/body image distortion, and a profoundly dissociated and disintegrated experience of self—but beyond that, to address the whole person, the one whose traumatic experiences and ongoing internal fantasies have led her to these originally adaptive but currently maladaptive symptoms. In more client-centered terms the goal is for the client to see her problem, to empathically understand why it is there, and to develop more adaptive ways to cope with her conflicts and pain. These goals are pursued first through the detailed inquiry into the various experiences with food, eating, and the body that the client brings into treatment. The analytic relationship is both expressed and furthered through this repeated process of exploring the combined metaphor of (1) food, eating, and body image experiences in (2) the context of the various alter ego states. Over time, this kind of inquiry can lead to important and healing work.

Working with any self-injurious behavior first requires understanding its function. Although it may be possible to make a contract with a client to stop violent behavior such as cutting oneself or intensive purging, eventually client and therapist together must empathically appreciate the meaning of the metaphor (Briere, 1993; Calof, 1992). The more "normative" a particular destructive behavior, such as compulsive eating, chronic dieting, or unending body hatred, the more likely it is that it can only be changed as the meaning of the symptom is understood. In the example of Lily, a major piece of the hurtful behavior is her berating herself for being fat, out of control, ugly, and undesirable. Lily's slip—that Polly, Madalyn, and Delores were all "convicted," was an important starting place in this work of reading the "fat" metaphor. When Lily saw in session that three of her oldest female alter egos felt that they were worthy of being convicted for their fat, she realized they felt guilty for witnessing the sacrifice. When she felt the impact of the word "convicted," she made another significant association. Lily connected the severity of her body hatred to a foggy image and possible memory of having hoped for protection by the police but instead of having being arrested and actually put behind bars, "convicted" as it were. She believes she was raped and abandoned while in police custody, thus extending even farther the violation of her body and soul. In the world of intrapsychic object relationships, Lily came to feel that she was rightfully put behind bars. She felt she deserved the betrayal and violence that she remembered. It is possible that fragments of two experiences or screen memories merged—being forced to witness animal sacrifices and therefore feeling complicit, and being hurt and jailed by the police—and that together these images attached to and fueled the hatred of her body fat. In other words, the cultural preoccupation with fat offered her an avenue of expression for the shame and self-hate she felt at the hands of perpetrators. This "avenue of expression," hatred of her body, however, continued violating Lily in every moment of her present life. Once some of the connections were made and she could understand that these parts of her felt they should be punished, because they were forced to witness hurting animals, she could now more fully appreciate some of the suffering she was enduring. She could then reconsider whether it was fair to blame herself for what she believed she had been forced to watch; she could assess whether a tortured child really had a choice about whether to assent to the infliction of pain on another living being or whether indeed being forced to watch was one of the worst parts of her own abuse. She could think more rationally and question her prior assumption that as a young teenager she had deserved to be raped and locked up because she was so fat.

The fact that Bruce, from a male position, did not obsess about the body fat also provided therapeutic possibilities: Lily could identify a part of herself that did not evaluate herself so exclusively on the basis of how well the body fit social standards. Perhaps Bruce's role could be strengthened. Bruce's position is a useful contrast, the basis of a new choice about self-image. Examining the slip was an experience-near way of paying attention to Lily's eating problem and body image pain that gave her access to understanding her history and inner compensatory objects and how the societal fear of fat was revictimizing to her. Through the examination of this body image experience, Lily could integrate feelings and knowledge to a greater extent than ever before.

This example shows that by taking each "fat thought" seriously, by not using clients' size as a form of "reality as a defense," by staying close to experience and curious about details, a great many analytical goals are achieved. For example, Lily increased the empathy she had for herself, strengthened her observing ego, and was able to think and feel differently toward herself. In this process the analytic relationship is a tool of healing. The introduction of the analyst into the experience of self-hate and shame as it reverberates throughout the personality system, offers an opportunity for a shift in that body-based shame. The analytic situation afforded the opportunity for Lily's experience of her body to be less hurtful. The analyst's more compassionate ego may even be borrowed and brought into the relationship a patient has with herself and her body.

Detailed inquiry about food and body experiences can also aid in the attainment of the goals of therapy specific to MPD. By reassociating knowledge to feelings, personalities develop knowledge about and empathy for one another. In the case of Lily, for example, the work with food and fat thoughts deepen the knowledge that both she and her therapist had about the map of the system. Learning how different parts eat—how they feel about eating, how they deal with fat, who eats for self-soothing and who leads the self-berating, who protects by expressing need (eating) and who by annihilating it in hopes that Lily would not be further disappointed (self-berating or anorexic behavior)—tells us about internal hierarchies and their role within the personality system and subsystems.

Once the map is more filled in, specific work with Madalyn, Polly, Delores, and the kids around their needs, fears, and characteristic coping mechanisms are all possible. Here the work is both of a general psychodynamic nature and organized around the goals of cognitive reframing. Techniques may include straightforward talking and somatopsychic, experiential, and nonverbal methods such as guided visualizations, hypnosis, or artwork.

Madalyn needs to explore her shame, as she expresses it in regard to the fat. She can be helped to understand and better assess her goal, which is to feel in charge when she flirts and initiates sexual contacts, especially when it is under clearly dangerous conditions. She can explore her hatred of the kids who express dependency needs and fears for the system as a whole. She needs to be encouraged to strive for power, control, and some fun—but in ways that do not threaten her. All of this is made available by investigating her rage at the fat body and the hungry kids. She needs to understand too that when the body actually was the size she still experiences herself to be (146 pounds), she was triggered into traumatic reenactments in the form of various illicit and dangerous sex scenarios. How can she be helped to have a choice to be that size without triggering such reenactments?

The kids and all the other parts need to learn what hunger and satiation feel like and how much food it takes to reach satiation. They need to know that the system is able to unite in making a promise never to deprive and neglect genuine physical hunger again. They need to learn that waiting for hunger is not the same kind of deprivation as that caused by neglect and starvation, that stopping with satiation is not the old thing, and that any momentary feeling of deprivation can be soothed and will pass.

The work with Delores gives entrée into the very important but unexamined theme of culturally induced revictimization. Delores carries a good deal of shame about having eventually failed on all the hundreds of diets Lily attempted. She is humiliated and furious that Lily couldn't keep the weight off whenever she lost it, that she gained back the lost weight and more, that she can't stick to a diet as they were taught in OA, Nutrisystem, and all the rest. She doesn't understand why they can't just simply practice portion control! After all, the concept is clear enough. Lily, as the host, shares many of these feelings and judgments, but in her they are tempered by years of feminist analytic anti-deprivation treatment and exposure to different ideas. Delores, the alter trying to manage life and the demands of this world, this culture, has not yet learned that dieting and its mentality revictimized and retraumatized her. She doesn't yet know, but she can be helped to see, that the bingeing and purging were in part the inevitable reaction throughout the personality system to the trauma of chronic dieting and fasting. It is not only her wish to rid herself of intrusive memories (e.g., swallowing semen) and compensatory object relationships (e.g., spitting up an abusive mother)—the binge/purge cycle is also diet induced. Just as PTSD and MPD are consequences of sexual, physical, and emotional trauma, so is the eating disorder a response not only to that trauma but to the years of dieting, the diet mentality, and the fat-hating culture that is "culture home" to this personality system. Understanding this reality is an important and necessary cognitive-educational achievement. Grieving the effects of this reality is a necessary part of the therapy in general.

This point cannot be overemphasized, so little has it been understood. No one in Lily's life understood that a great deal of the compulsion to eat is the inevitable partner of the compulsion to diet. Instead she was coached into another diet. No one helped her to understand that her body weight will continue to go up as she eats less because of the set point response subsequent to chronic starvation. No one told her that she is entitled to medical care even though she is overweight. She has been to innumerable doctors who have blamed her physical symptoms on her weight. For example, she had terrible back pain for a long time. More than one doctor and chiropractor admonished her for her weight, although none of them took a weight history, nor did even one of them discover that she had finally stopped purging and *then* was having back problems! She never received positive reinforcement for stopping this intense violation to her body; instead, she was blamed for her fat. Not one of the doctors inquired whether she even ate compulsively. Most offered more diets—a kind of disinformation. Delores needs help with her shame about having failed. She also needs the cognitive reframing to teach her that the origin of her fat is in part the diet world itself. Delores needs to understand that if she promises the children they will be fed when hungry, then they may forgo some of their excessive demands for food. She needs to help them to feel their own hunger and satiation in order for the system to develop a notion of "portion control" that is internally cued.

The more that Delores and the others can understand this, the more they are cooperating and learning to live at peace and with clarity in the body that they actually do share. As the personality system comes to understand how Lily was revictimized by the diet culture, the group can withdraw and separate from that culture. The personality system can then take charge and obtain a position from which the eating problem can be solved. The personality system can communicate about when the body is hungry. Enhancing internal conferencing is an important goal in the treatment of MPD. Coming to feel the shared body, to notice its hunger and its satiation can enhance communication and cooperation. Conferring about what foods are desired at a given time also aids overall healing. Not only does this kind of work enhance cognitive treatment goals, but it also furthers goals that can be seen as more relational and psychodynamic. For in identifying the agents of cultural revictimization, the therapist provides the model for a method of analyzing further abuse so that the client can work on choosing to change abusive relationships. Just as a therapist highlights and makes visible family abuse and alternatives to it, so should she make cultural damages visible so that alternatives in this domain are possible too.

Another therapeutic issue is raised in Delores's request that the therapist support her desire to teach the entire personality system the rules of eating that were learned in OA, Nutrisystem, and so forth. The request may have as much to do with the transference experience as it does with eating. She may be using the eating to express her disappointment in the therapy, to say that something is not working, to say she needs or wants something else from the therapist. She may be feeling frightened: If the therapist's ideas about how to eat are not working, how good can the therapist's ideas be about anything? She may be angry. She may feel that the therapist is betraying her and wish to be rescued. It is important to hear her concrete request about eating in light of the therapy relationship and the transference/countertransference configuration.

More generally, as an understanding of the impulse to starve or binge is explored, it is inevitable that many painful memories and feelings will be exposed. Some may require a paced and careful abreaction to be released, known, and integrated. For example, Polly is in touch with periods of having been starved. These periods were connected to other times of horrible torture. She may need to reassociate memory to other feelings and sensations, to own her experience and share it with some parts of the system. She certainly needs to grieve and mourn her past experience. She needs to be helped to feel entitled to the range of her reactions. The clinician will need to know if, when, and how to facilitate such abreactions, how to manage them so that they are helpful and not so overwhelming that they do not contribute to the integration of the past with the present. Madalyn too may need to do some memory recovery and abreactive work with regard to the sexual encounters in which she was involved. Whenever Lily has reduced to the weight that Madalyn subjectively feels herself to be, she has found herself drinking and involved in compulsive sexual scenarios.

Learning to feed the self and live in the body are foundations of a core sense of self. Conversely, tampering with body signals of hunger and satiation and exploiting body image in a desperate effort to maintain a sense of psychological safety, weaken this core sense of self. Thus, it is not surprising that occupational therapists on one MPD treatment team report that patients improve immeasurably when they are taught and learn how to use food to nurture themselves, to notice hunger, to find and prepare food, to notice how much they feel is an appropriate portion (Kanigsberg & Oke, 1992). All this generally makes patients feel more secure, competent, and safe in their worlds. It is not only learning to perform what occupational therapists call "the activities of daily living" that causes improvement in the case of learning to feed oneself but also becoming competent in this first activity of daily living, this symbol of life and relationship—eating—that carries such a profound and organizing potential for psychic life and healing.

SATIATION AND FOOD CHOICE IN THE TREATMENT OF MULTIPLE PERSONALITY DISORDER

The ultimate treatment goal for MPD is the reduction and erosion of amnestic barriers between parts of the self, so that the patient develops an integrated and rich sense of one relatively continuous self, aware of its varied aspects, memories, and abilities, acting with reference to the present rather than only to the traumatic past. (For a full discussion of treatment goals in MPD, see Bliss, 1986; Fine & Kluft, 1992; Kluft & Fine, 1993; Loewenstein & Ross, 1992; Putnam, 1989; Ross, 1989; Spiegel, 1990.) To achieve this overarching goal, the clinician must first work to develop a treatment alliance and to "actively elicit all parts of the mind" (Loewenstein & Ross, 1992) and then to teach all parts to communicate with empathy, tolerance, and cooperation. The clinician will help each part (1) to recognize how, when, and why it developed, and (2) to reframe its traumatogenic thinking, to understand its part in the system as a whole, and to be less and less the victim of spontaneous trance, which isolates it from the system as a whole and from the present. Each MPD patient must learn to know and negotiate her own personality system. Techniques that enhance empathic internal communications are helpful, such as internal conferencing, negotiating, and making contracts about limits and goals.

Helping the MPD client to become attuned to hunger and satiation and to develop the ability to make food choices furthers these therapeutic aims by diminishing rigid ego-state boundaries through working toward a goal that is held very dear by the client. The goal is close to experience, and therefore the patient is motivated to pursue it. Many MPD patients come in with a desperate wish simply to lose 10 pounds. Although weight loss is always a very complicated issue, the wish to eat both with pleasure and in response to actual body signals is an uncontested and client-centered goal. To feed oneself with hunger and stop eating with satiation require many parts of the personality to confer on whether a certain experience in the body is hunger, perhaps indigestion, fear, satiation, or some other sensation. This kind of negotiation is not only stabilizing and a foundation for eventual integration, but it also helps the personalities to leave behind their dissociative delusions of living in separate bodies. It promotes respect for the body rather than the desperately cavalier, even abusive attitude toward it so characteristic of MPD.

Another therapeutic goal in the treatment of MPD, mapping, is also enhanced by the pursuit of detailed inquiry into food and body image experiences. As is clear in the example of Lily, it is important to learn how different personalities approach eating, and what story is told by each of their respective body image experiences, tells an important tale. It contributes to the ability of clinician and client to create a map of the inner landscape: Who is there, what moves each of the members of the system, and what is their internal relationship.

This map, showing what the inner parts of the mind feel and fear and how to reach them, is useful and important in planning whatever abreactions are necessary in such a way as not to overwhelm and unnecessarily retraumatize the survivor. Although not every traumatic memory needs to be abreacted, the patient may need to abreact enough of them so that they can be integrated as memory instead of running her life in the form of intrusive, numbing, unmetabolized, traumatic stress states. Abreaction must be managed in a way that is mindful of the need to titrate and dilute affect and to prevent revictimizing (Fine, 1991; Fine & Kluft, 1992; Kluft, 1989b, 1991b). The philosophy and management of abreaction are major areas in the new MPD literature.

The feminist principle of not overriding internal signals and of opposing a chronic diet mentality helps to prevent revictimization by the culture at large; this is true for all survivors of abuse. Helping the MPD client, in particular, to notice when she is berating herself (for eating, for her size, or for her shape) and to challenge the self-attack, offers her an opportunity to explore the inner dissociative personality system and the object-relational world. Therapist and client learn which parts most hate the body and which are more accepting of it, even if they do want eventually to change it. Each part is encouraged to respect and understand the others.

Working to diminish sadistic inner relationships is naturally paralleled by work in the transference and countertransference. Besides the typical transference/countertransference configurations discussed in chapters 8 and 9, there are tremendous stresses on the therapist in work with MPD patients. Therapists often want to break typical boundaries of therapy to provide extra care for the tremendous pain, grief, and sense of confusion of the MPD patient. In an experience of projective identification, therapists often feel desperate to improve things, as desperate as alter egos feel to survive and avoid their terror and pain. On the other hand, therapists are also sometimes overwhelmed by feelings of fury and rage at their MPD clients. How can they expect so much? Why don't they get better? Why do they feel so entitled? Understanding the vicissitudes of the transference/countertransference configuration is demanding but essential in working with the traumatic material, cognitions, behavior, and affects of such severely dissociated and traumatized clients (Courtois, 1988; Chu, 1992; Davies & Frawley, 1992b;

Herman, 1992; Kluft, 1992c; Loewenstein, 1993; Putnam, 1989; Sakheim & Devine, 1992b). Clients' behavior with food and experiences of their bodies may reflect feelings about the therapist or the therapeutic relationship. Delores, for example, an alter in the case of Lily, may be quite despairing that the system is not making sufficient progress. She may represent Lily's feeling of rage, of being betrayed, of not being helped, or of being a narcissistic object of the therapist's philosophy. All these hypotheses should be explored. The therapist in her own countertransference experience may feel that the therapy is failing, as is proved by Lily's high weight. She may then feel helpless or angry at her own lack of power to change Lily's size. These possibilities may be countertransference clues about intrapsychic and relational configurations and repetitions.

Despair, helplessness, terror, rage, dread, love, sexual desire, tenderness, and longing will all surely surface in the transference and countertransference. The configurations elaborated by Davies and Frawley (1992b, 1994) and by Caloff (1992), including the roles of victim, perpetrator, rescuer, betrayer, and bystander, will surface and play a part. It is likely that these will all be expressed in food and body image terms. In MPD, which is almost always caused by systematic and brutal sadism, the clinician must contain—and help the client to contain and process—sadistic products, experiences, and relational modes all inevitably stored inside (Harvey Schwartz, 1993, personal communication). It becomes especially important to keep this in mind in assessing the meaning of compulsive eating, starving, or purging as well as compulsive hatred of body needs, size, or shape.

Epilogue

IN THE PRECEDING PAGES we have exposed and analyzed the pervasive, insidious aspects of consumer culture as they interact with intrapsychic and interpersonal phenomena to create food, eating, and body image problems. We have presented a detailed relational/cultural model for the treatment of those problems. Interweaving strands of political, psychological, social, historical, and economic analysis suggests an approach for the prevention of eating problems. This approach underscores the power of connection and understanding in relationships as well as the power and necessity of thinking critically about the world in which we live and understanding the complicated and ambiguous way that world resides within us.

We see our work as part of a larger effort to create a world that reflects, respects, and celebrates difference—thus strengthening individuals' and communities' feelings of worth. Heeding Martin Luther King's eloquent plea that we be judged solely on the "content of our character," we must learn to approach difference and diversity with acceptance and vitality. To create a more benign transitional space, we need to think critically about the power given to appearance and to the widely projected symbols that deny diversity. We must challenge very powerful forces in consumer society, forces that foster and profit from the perpetuation of body/self insecurity. We can begin this task in our roles as parents, educators, therapists, and medical professionals by helping adults, and especially the children of these adults, the next generation, to eat in accordance with physiological hunger and to be connected to their bodies and normal bodily concerns without the torment currently engendered about appetite and body size.

The concepts in this book do not exist within a social vacuum. They need to be viewed as confluent with and inseparable from a variety of other complicated societal issues that affect how people feel about themselves and about others (race, class, sexual orientation, gender identity, employment, the environment, aging, family support systems, etc.). This larger weave of social and economic forces shapes family life and interpersonal relations and gives form to the threads of daily life. To be at ease with food, to live comfortably in our bodies whether or not they conform to a rigid ideal, to be able to critique this ideal, and to pass all these abilities on to future generations— these goals are the very heart of our approach. We hope this work will join with other efforts to open up possibilities for a more fluid and expansive notion of self.

Women's Therapy Centre Institute Resources

Compulsive Eating and Body Image Groups for the Public: Six-week, theme-centered groups on eating and body image problems from our anti-deprivation perspective. These groups are didactic and experiential, providing a taste of this approach. Participants then can choose to continue with longer term individual or group treatment.

Compulsive Eating and Body Image Groups for Practitioners: Short-term groups where therapists can work on their own eating and body image issues as well as receive supervision in our approach.

Training Program: Three-year, post-graduate program in psychoanalytic psychotherapy. Unique in its attention to the significance of gender in psychoanalysis and to the theory and treatment of eating and body image problems, our program enlists the work of the British Independent School of object relations, the American interpersonalists, and contemporary feminist theorists to create a framework for understanding psychic life in its developmental, social, and gendered dimensions.

Workshops for Practitioners: Feminist psychoanalytic perspectives on a variety of theoretical and clinical issues such as transference/countertransference, boundaries and policies, sexual abuse, clinical issues of working with lesbians, women and anxiety, therapist and patient fears of intimacy and dependency in the therapy relationship, etc.

Supervision: Individual and group supervision for general treatment issues as well as theme-centered supervision for therapists working with people suffering with eating problems and/or sexual abuse.

Referrals: Local and national referral service for individual and group treatment and self-help information.

In-Service Training: Training and staff development for mental health, educational, and medical institutions on a variety of theoretical and clinical issues from our perspective.

Books and Articles: Written by the faculty of the Women's Therapy Centre Institute are available by contacting:

THE WOMEN'S THERAPY CENTRE INSTITUTE
562 West End Avenue, 1A
New York, N.Y. 10024
Tel. (212) 721-7005
Fax. (212) 721-5554

References

AHERN, R., KIELY, L., & BOHUN, E. (1992). *The use of therapeutic touch with dissociative clients*. Paper presented at the Ninth International Conference on Multiple Personality/Dissociative States, November, Chicago. Available on tape through Audio Transcripts, Ltd., Alexandria, VA.

ANZIEU, D. (1989). *The skin ego*. New Haven: Yale University Press.

ARIES, P. (1962). *Centuries of childhood: A social history of family life*. New York: Vintage.

ARON, L. (1991). The patient's experience of the analyst's subjectivity. *Psychoanalytic Dialogues, 1*(1), 29–51.

ARON, L. (1992a). From Ferenczi to Searles and contemporary relational approaches. *Psychoanalytic Dialogues, 2*(2), 181–190.

ARON, L. (1992b). Interpretation as expression of the analyst's subjectivity. *Psychoanalytic Dialogues, 2*(4), 475–508.

ARON, L. (1992c). *The legacy of Sandor Ferenczi: Discovery and rediscovery*. Paper presented at the Twelfth Annual Spring Meeting of the American Psychological Association Division of Psychoanalysis (39)—Discovery and Rediscovery, April, Philadelphia. Available on tape through Audio Transcripts, Ltd., Alexandria, VA.

BARKER, F. (1984). *The tremulous private body: Essays on subjection*. New York: Methuen.

BARSKY, S. L. (1988). Foucault, femininity, and the modernization of patriarchal power. In I. Diamond & L. Quinby (Eds.), *Feminism and Foucault: Reflections on resistance*. Boston: Northeastern University Press.

BARSKY, S. L. (1990). *Femininity and domination: Studies in the phenomenology of oppression*. New York: Routledge.

BARTHEL, D. (1988). *Putting on appearances: Gender and advertising*. Philadelphia: Temple University Press.

BASS, E., & DAVIS, L. (1988). *The courage to heal: A guide for women survivors of child sexual abuse*. New York: Harper & Row.

BASS, E., & THORNTON, L. (Eds.). (1983). *I never told anyone, writings by women sur-vivors of child sexual abuse*. New York: Harper & Row.

BASSIN, D. (1992). *Representations of motherhood*. Paper presented at the Twelfth Annual Spring Meeting of the American Psychological Association Division of Psychoanalysis (39)—Discovery and Rediscovery, April, Philadelphia. Available on tape through Audio Transcripts, Ltd., Alexandria, VA.

BASSIN, D. (1993). Maternal subjectivity in the culture of nostalgia: Mourning memory. In D. Bassin, M. Honey, and M. Kaplan (Eds.), *Representations of motherhood*. New Haven: Yale University Press.

BATHRICK, S. K. (1991). How mothers quit resisting and managed to love TV. In P. Wexler (Ed.), *Critical theory now*. New York: The Falmer Press.

BEGELMAN, A. (1992). *The devil and the inquisition: Satanic cult abuse in the Basque*. Paper presented at the Ninth International Conference on Multiple Personality/Dissociative States, November, Chicago. Available on tape through Audio Transcripts, Ltd., Alexandria, VA.

BELENKY, M. F., CLINCHY, B. M., GOLDBERGER, N. R., & TARULE, J. M. (1986). *Women's ways of knowing: The development of self, voice, and mind*. New York: Basic Books.

BELL, R. M. (1985). *Holy anorexia*. Chicago: University of Chicago Press.

BELOTTI, E. G. (1975). *Little girls*. London: Writers and Readers Publishers Cooperative.

BENJAMIN, J. (1988). *The bonds of love: Psychoanalysis, feminism and the problem of domination*. New York: Pantheon.

BENJAMIN, J. (1991). Father and daughter: Identification with difference—A con-tribution to gender heterodoxy. *Psychoanalytic Dialogues, 1*(3), 277–300.

BENJAMIN, J. (1993). The omnipotent mother: A psychoanalytic study of fantasy and reality. In D. Bassin, M. Honey, and M. Kaplan (Eds.), *Representations of motherhood*. New Haven: Yale University Press.

BENNETT, W., & GURIN, J. (1982). *The dieter's dilemma: Eating less and weighing more*. New York: Basic Books.

BERGER, J. (1972). *Ways of seeing*. London: BBC/Penguin.

BINDER, R. L. (1981). Why don't women report sexual assault? *Clinical Psychiatry, 42*, 437–438.

BION, W. R. (1967). *Second thoughts*. London: H. Karnac.

BLISS, E. L. (1986). *Multiple personality, allied disorders and hypnosis*. New York: Oxford University Press.

BLOOM, C. (1976). Training manual for the treatment of compulsive eating and body image problems. Master's thesis, State Univ. of NY at Stony Brook.

BLOOM, C. (1987). Bulimia: A feminist psychoanalytic understanding. In M. Lawrence (Ed.), *Fed up and hungry*. London: The Women's Press.

BLOOM, C. (1992). *Cultural countertransference: A consultation with Darya*. Paper presented at the Women's Therapy Centre Institute Lecture Series, April.

BOLLAS, C. (1987). *The shadow of the object*. New York: Columbia University Press.

BOLLAS, C. (1989). *Forces of destiny: Psychoanalysis and human idiom*. London: Free Association Books.

BORDO, S. (1988). Anorexia nervosa: Psychopathology as the crystallization of culture. In I. Diamond and L. Quinby (Eds.), *Feminism and Foucault: Reflections on resistance*. Boston: Northeastern University Press.

BORDO, S. (1990a). The body and the reproduction of femininity: A feminist appropriation of Foucault. In A. Jaggar and S. Bordo (Eds.), *Gender/body/knowledge: Feminist reconstruction of being and knowing*. New Brunswick: Rutgers University Press.

BORDO, S. (1990b). Reading the slender body. In M. Jacobus, E. F. Keller, & S. Suttleworth (Eds.). *Body-politics: Women and the discourses of science*. New York: Routledge, Chapman & Hall.

BORDO, S. (1993). *Unbearable weight: Feminism, western culture and the body*. Los Angeles: University of California Press.

BOSKIND-WHITE, M., & WHITE, W. C., Jr. (1987). *Bulimarexia: The binge/purge cycle*. New York: Norton.

BRADSHAW, J. (1988a). *Bradshaw on the family*. Deerfield, FL: Health Communications.

BRADSHAW, J. (1988b). *Healing the shame that binds you*. Deerfield, FL: Health Communications.

BRAUN, B. G. (1986a). Issues in the psychotherapy of multiple personality disorder. In B. G. Braun (Ed)., *Treatment of multiple personality disorder*. Washington, DC: American Psychiatric Press.

BRAUN, B. G. (Ed.). (1986b). *Treatment of multiple personality disorder*. Washington, DC: American Psychiatric Press.

BRAUN, B. G. (1988). The BASK model of dissociation. *Dissociation, 1*(1), 4–23.

BRAUN, B. G. (1990). Dissociative disorders as sequelae to incest. In R. P. Kluft (Ed.), *Incest-related syndromes of adult psychopathology*. Washington, DC: American Psychiatric Press.

BRAUN, B. G. (1992). *The BASK model of dissociation: Theory and practice*. Paper presented at the Fourth Annual Eastern Regional Conference on Abuse and Multiple Personality, June, Alexandria, VA. Available on tape through Audio Transcripts, Ltd., Alexandria, VA.

BRAUN, B. G., & SACHS, R. G. (1985). The development of multiple personality disorder: Predisposing, precipitating, and perpetuating factors. In R. P. Kluft (Ed.), *Childhood antecedents of multiple personality*. Washington, DC: American Psychiatric Press.

BRIERE, J. N. (1992). *Child abuse trauma: Theory and treatment of the lasting effects*. Newbury Park, CA: Sage.

BRIERE, J. N. (1993). *Tension reducing behavior*. Paper presented at the Fifth Annual Eastern Regional Conference on Abuse and Multiple Personality, June, Alexandria, VA. Available on tape through Audio Transcripts, Ltd., Alexandria, VA.

BRIERE, J., & COURTOIS, C. A. (1992). *The return of the repressed: Memory retrieval*. Paper presented at the Fourth Annual Eastern Regional Conference on Abuse and Multiple Personality, June, Alexandria, VA. Available on tape through Audio Transcripts, Ltd., Alexandria, VA.

BROWN, L. S. (1989). Fat-oppressive attitudes and the feminist therapist: Directions for change. *Women & Therapy*, 19–30.

BROWN, L. S. (1991). Not outside the range: One feminist perspective on psychic trauma. *American Image, 48*(1), 119–133.

BROWN, L. M. (1990). When is a moral problem not a moral problem? Morality, identity, and female adolescence. In C. Gilligan, N. P. Lyons, and T. J. Hammer (Eds.), *Making connections: The relational worlds of adolescent girls' at Emma Willard School.* Cambridge: Harvard University Press.

BROWN, L. M. & GILLIGAN, C. (1992). *Meeting at the crossroads: Women's psychology and girls' development.* Cambridge: Harvard University Press.

BROWNE, A., & FINKELHOR, D. (1986). Impact of child sexual abuse; a review of the research. *Psychological Bulletin, 99,* 66–67.

BROWNMILLER, S. (1975). *Against our will: Men, women, and rape.* New York: Simon & Schuster.

BRUCH, H. (1973). *Eating disorders: Obesity, anorexia nervosa, and the person within.* New York: Basic Books.

BRUMBERG, J. J. (1989). *Fasting girls: The history of anorexia nervosa.* New York: Penguin.

BURGARD, D., & LYONS, P. (1994). Alternatives in obesity treatment: Focusing on health for fat women. In P. Fallon, M. Katzman, & S. Wooley (Eds.), *Feminist perspectives on eating disorders.* New York: Guilford Press.

BURGESS, A. W., GANAWAY, G. K., KLUFT, R. P., LOEWENSTEIN, R. J., & COURTOIS, C. A. (1993). *Town meeting: Delayed memory controversy in abuse recovery.* Paper presented at the Fifth Annual Eastern Regional Conference on Abuse and Multiple Personality, June, Alexandria, VA. Available on tape through Audio Transcripts, Ltd., Alexandria, VA.

BURKE, W. F. (1992). Countertransference disclosure and the asymmetry/mutuality dilemma. *Psychoanalytic Dialogues, 2*(2), 241–271.

BURKE, W. F., & TANSEY, M. J. (1991). Countertransference disclosure and models of therapeutic action. *Contemporary Psychoanalysis, 27*(2), 351–384.

BYNUM, C. W. (1987). *Holy feast and holy fast: The religious significance of food to medieval women.* Berkeley: University of California Press.

CALAM, R. M., & SLADE, P. D. (1989). Sexual experiences and eating problems in female undergraduates. *International Journal of Eating Disorders, 8,* 391–397.

CALOF, D. L. (1988). *Presentation on abuse and dissociation.* Paper presented at the annual conference sponsored by Family Networker, Washington, DC.

CALOF, D. L. (1992). *Self-injurious behavior: Treatment strategies.* Paper presented at the Fourth Annual Eastern Regional Conference on Abuse and Multiple Personality, June, Alexandria, VA. Available on tape through Audio Transcripts, Ltd., Alexandria, VA.

CARLSON, E. B. & PUTNAM, F. W. (1989). Integrating research on dissociation and hypnotizability: Are there two pathways to hypnotizability? *Dissociation, 2,* 32–38.

CHAPKIS, W. (1986). *Beauty secrets: Women and the politics of appearance.* Boston: South End Press.

CHEFETZ, R. A., & COURTOIS, C. A. (1993). *The erotic and traumatic transference-countertransference matrices.* Paper presented at the Fifth Annual Eastern Regional Conference on Abuse and Multiple Personality, June, Alexandria, VA. Available on tape through Audio Transcripts, Ltd., Alexandria, VA.

CHERNIN, K. (1981). *The obsession: Reflections on the tyranny of slenderness.* New York: Harper & Row.

CHERNIN, K. (1985). *The hungry self: Women, eating, and identity.* New York: Random House.

CHODOROW, N. J. (1978). *The reproduction of mothering.* Berkeley: University of California Press.

CHODOROW, N. J. (1989). *Feminism and psychoanalytic theory.* New Haven: Yale University Press.

CHODOROW, N., & CONTRATTO, S. (1989). The fantasy of the perfect mother. In N. Chodorow (Ed.), *Feminism and psychoanalytic theory.* New Haven: Yale University Press.

CHOMSKY, N. (1968). *Language and the mind.* New York: Harcourt, Brace & World.

CHU, J. A. (1992). *Working through impasses in the therapy of MPD.* Paper presented at the Fourth Annual Eastern Regional Conference on Abuse and Multiple Personality, June, Alexandria, VA. Available on tape through Audio Transcripts, Ltd., Alexandria, VA.

COHEN, B. M., GILLER, E., & LYNN W. (Eds.). (1991). *Multiple personality disorder from the inside out.* Baltimore: The Sidran Press.

COLE, C. H., & BARNEY, E. E. (1987). Safeguards and the therapeutic window: A group treatment strategy for adult incest survivors. *American Journal of Orthopsychiatry, 57*(4), 601–609.

COLRAIN, J., & STEELE, K. (1992). *Psychotherapy with survivors of ritualized abuse: Strategy, technique and perspective.* Paper presented at the Fourth Annual Eastern Regional Conference on Abuse and Multiple Personality, June, Alexandria, VA. Available on tape through Audio Transcripts, Ltd., Alexandria, VA.

COMSTOCK, C. (1992). *Abreactions: Past and present.* Paper presented at the Ninth International Conference on Multiple Personality/Dissociative States, November, Chicago. Available on tape through Audio Transcripts, Ltd., Alexandria, VA.

CONNORS, K. J. (1992). Memory, trauma and meaning: Treating ritualistically abused clients. Paper presented at the Ninth International Conference on Multiple Personality/Dissociative States, November, Chicago. Available on tape through Audio Transcripts, Ltd., Alexandria, VA.

Consumer Reports. (1993a). Losing weight: What works. What doesn't. *Consumer Reports, 58*(6), 347–352.

Consumer Reports. (1993b). Rating the diets. *Consumer Reports, 58*(6), 353–357.

COONS, P. M., BOWMAN, E. S., & MILSTEIN, V. (1988). Multiple personality disorder: A clinical investigation of 50 cases. *Journal of Nervous Mental Disorders, 176,* 519–527.

COONS, P. M., BOWMAN, E. S., PELLOW, T. A., et al. (1989). Posttraumatic aspects of the treatment of victims of sexual abuse and incest. *Psychiatric Clinics of North America, 12,* 325–335.

COONS, P. M., COLE, C., PELLOW, T. A., & MILSTEIN, V. (1990). Symptoms of posttraumatic stress and dissociation in women victims of abuse. In R. P. Kluft (Ed.), *Incest-related syndromes of adult psychopathology.* Washington, DC: American Psychiatric Press.

COONTZ, S. (1988). *The social origins of private life: A history of American families, 1600–1900.* New York: Verso.

COURTOIS, C. A. (1988). *Healing the incest wound: Adult survivors in therapy.* New York: Norton.

COWAN, A. (1989). Women's gains on the job not without a heavy toll. *New York Times,* August 21, A14.

CRAIG, I. (1990). *Psychoanalysis and social theory.* Amherst: University of Massachusetts Press.

CRISP, A. H. (1984). The psychopathology of anorexia nervosa: Getting the "heat" out of the system. In A. J. Stunkard & E. Stellar (Eds.), *Eating and its disorders.* New York: Raven.

Cult abuse of children: Witch hunt or reality. (1994). *Journal of Psychohistory, 21(4),* (Spring 1994) entire issue.

DAMLOUJI, N. J., & FERGUSON, J. M. (1985). Three cases of posttraumatic anorexia nervosa. *American Journal of Psychiatry, 142.*

DAVIES, J. M., & FRAWLEY, M. G. (1992a). *Discovery and treatment of childhood sexual abuse in psychoanalysis.* Paper presented at the Twelfth Annual Spring Meeting of the American Psychological Association Division of Psychoanalysis (39)— Discovery and Rediscovery, April, Philadelphia. Available on tape through Audio Transcripts, Ltd., Alexandria, VA.

DAVIES, J. M., & FRAWLEY, M. G. (1992b). Dissociative processes and transference-countertransference paradigms in the psychoanalytically oriented treatment of adult survivors of childhood sexual abuse. *Psychoanalytic Dialogues, 2(1),* 5–36.

DAVIES, J. M., & FRAWLEY, M. G. (1992c). Reply to Gabbard, Shengold, Grotstein. *Psychoanalytic Dialogues, 2(1),* 77–96.

DAVIES, J. M., & FRAWLEY, M. G. (1994). *Treating the adult survivor of childhood sexual abuse.* New York: Basic Books.

DAVIS, C. (1991). Remaking the she devil: A critical look at feminist approaches to beauty. *Hypatia, 6(2),* 21–43.

DAVIS, M., & WALLBRIDGE, D. (1981). *Boundary and space: An introduction to the work of D. W. Winnicott.* New York: Brunner/Mazel.

DE MAUSE, L. (Ed.). (1988). *The history of childhood: The untold story of child abuse.* New York: Peter Bedrick Books.

DE MAUSE, L. (1994). Why cults terrorize and kill children. *Journal of Psychohistory, 21(4),* (Spring 1994), 505–518.

DEMITRACK, M. A., PUTNAM, F. W., BREWERTON, T. D., BRANDT, H. A., & GOLD, P. W. (1990). Relation of clinical variables to dissociative phenomena in eating disorders. *American Journal of Psychiatry, 147,* 1184–1188.

DIAMOND, I., & QUINBY, L. (Eds.). (1988). *Feminism and Foucault: Reflections on resistance.* Boston,: Northeastern University Press.

DIMEN, M. (1990). Power, sexuality, and intimacy. In A. M. Jaggar & S. Bordo (Eds.), *Gender/body/knowledge: Feminist reconstruction of being and knowing.* New Brunswick: Rutgers University Press.

DIMEN, M. (1991). Deconstructing difference: Gender, splitting, and transitional space. *Psychoanalytic Dialogues, 1(3),* 335–352.

DIMEN, M., & HARRIS, A. (1992). An interview with Joyce McDougall. *Psychoanalytic Dialogues, 2(1)*, 97–116.

DINNERSTEIN, D. (1963). *The mermaid and the minotaur: Sexual arrangements and human malaise.* New York: Harper Colophon Books.

DINSMORE, C. (1991). *From surviving to thriving: Incest, feminism, and recovery.* New York: State University of New York Press.

DISALVO, J. (1983). *War of titans: Blake's critique of Milton and the politics of religion.* Pittsburgh: University of Pittsburgh Press.

DOANE, M. A. (1990). Technophilia: Technology, representation, and the feminine. In M. Jacobus, E. F. Keller, & S. Suttleworth (Eds.), *Body/politics: Women and the discourses of science.* New York: Routledge, Chapman & Hall.

DOSAMANTES-ALPERSON, E. (1981). Experiencing in movement psychotherapy. *American Journal of Dance Therapy,* 4(2), 33–44.

EHRENBERG, D. B. (1982). Psychoanalytic engagement. *Contemporary Psychoanalysis, 18*(4), 535–555.

EHRENBERG, D. B. (1984). Psychoanalytic engagement, II. *Contemporary Psychoanalysis, 20,* 560–583.

EHRENREICH, B. (1989). *Fear of falling: The inner life of the middle class.* New York: Pantheon.

EICHENBAUM, L., & ORBACH, S. (1983a). *Understanding women: A feminist psychoanalytic approach.* New York: Basic Books.

EICHENBAUM, L., & ORBACH, S. (1983b). *What do women want?* New York: Coward-McCann.

EWEN, S. (1976). *Captains of consciousness: Advertising and the social roots of the consumer culture.* New York: McGraw-Hill.

EWEN, S. (1988). *All consuming images: The politics of style in contemporary culture.* New York: Basic Books.

EWEN, S., & EWEN, E. (1979). *Channels of desire: Mass images and the shaping of American consciousness.* New York: McGraw-Hill.

FAIRBAIRN, W. (1952). *An object relations theory of the personality.* New York: Basic Books.

FAIRBAIRN, W. (1986). *Psychoanalytic studies of the personality.* New York: Routledge & Kegan Paul.

FAIRBURN, C. G. (1985). Cognitive-behavioral treatment for bulimia. In D. M. Garner & P. E. Garfinkel (Eds.), *Handbook of psychotherapy for anorexia nervosa and bulimia.* New York: Guilford Press.

FALLON, P., KATZMAN, M. A., & WOOLEY, S. C. (Eds.), (1994). *Feminist perspectives on eating disorders.* New York: Guilford Press.

FALUDI, S. (1991). *Backlash.* New York: Crown.

FANON, F. (1968). *The wretched of the earth.* New York: Grove Press.

FAST, I. (1991). Commentary on "Father and daughter: Identification with difference—A contribution to gender heterodoxy." *Psychoanalytic Dialogues, 1*(3), 301–304.

FAST, I. (1992). The embodied mind: Toward a relational perspective. *Psychoanalytic Dialogues, 2*(3), 389–410.

FERENCZI, S. (1992). Confusion of tongues between adults and the child: The language of tenderness and the language of [sexual] passion. In J. M. Masson (Ed.), *The assault on truth: Freud's suppression of the seduction theory*. New York: Harper Perennial.

FINE, C. G. (1990). The cognitive sequelae of incest. In R. P. Kluft (Ed.), *Incest-related syndromes of adult psychopathology*. Washington, DC: American Psychiatric Press.

FINE, C. G. (1991). Treatment stabilization and crisis prevention: Pacing the therapy of the multiple personality disorder patient. *The Psychiatric Clinics of North America, 14*(3), 661–767.

FINE, C. G. (1993). A tactical integrationist perspective on the treatment of multiple personality disorder. In R. P. Kluft & C. G. Fine (Eds.), *Clinical perspectives on multiple personality disorder*. Washington, DC: American Psychiatric Press.

FINE, C. G., & KLUFT, R. P. (1992). *The psychotherapy of MPD: Crucial concepts and critical incidents*. Paper presented at the Fourth Annual Eastern Regional Conference on Abuse and Multiple Personality, June, Alexandra, VA. Available on tape through Audio Transcripts, Ltd., Alexandria, VA.

FINKELHOR, D. (1979). *Sexually victimized children*. New York: Free Press.

FINKELHOR, D., & BROWNE, A. (1985). The traumatic impact of child sexual abuse: A conceptualization. *American Journal of Orthopsychiatry, 55*(4), 530–541.

FINLAY, M. (1989). Post-modernizing psychoanalysis/psychoanalyzing postmodernity. *Free Association, 26,* 43–80.

FISHMAN, C. (1990). Presentation at Carrier Clinic, Spring, Belle Mead, NJ. Sponsored by the American Association for the Study of Anorexia and Bulimia.

FLAX, J. (1990). *Thinking fragments: Psychoanalysis, feminism and postmodernism in the contemporary west*. Berkeley: University of California Press.

FOLSOM, V. L., KRAHN, D. D., CANUM, K., et al. (1989). Sex abuse: Role in eating disorders. In *New research program and abstracts, 142nd Annual Meeting of the American Psychiatric Association*. Washington, DC: APA.

FORWARD, S. (1989). *Toxic parents*. New York: Bantam.

FOUCAULT, M. (1979). *Discipline and punish*. Trans. Alan Sheridan. New York: Vintage Books.

FRAAD, H. (1990). Anorexia nervosa: The female body as a site of gender and class transition. *Rethinking Marxism, 3*(3–4), 79–100.

FRAWLEY, G. (1993). *Incest and sexual abuse in childhood*. Paper presented at the Thirteenth Annual Spring Meeting of the American Psychological Association Division of Psychoanalysis (39)—Discovery and Rediscovery, April, New York. Available on tape through Audio Transcripts, Ltd., Alexandria, VA.

FREDRICKSON, R. (1990). Workshop—Advanced Clinical Skills. In *The treatment of sexual abuse*. St. Paul, MN: Fredrickson and Associates.

FREUD, A. (1965). *Normality and pathology in childhood*. New York: International Universities Press.

FREUD, S. (1961). *The ego and the id*. Standard Edition, trans. James Strachey. London: Hogarth Press.

FRISCHHOLZ, E. J. (1985). The relationship among dissociation, hypnosis, and child abuse in the development of multiple personality disorder. In R. P. Kluft

(Ed.), *Childhood antecedents of multiple personality.* Washington, DC: American Psychiatric Press.

FROSH, S. (1989). Melting into air: Psychoanalysis and social experience. *Free Associations, 16, 7–30.*

GABBARD, G. O., Schengold, L., & Grotstein, J. S. (1992). Commentary on "Dissociative processes and transference-countertransference paradigms in the psychoanalytically oriented treatment of adult survivors of childhood sexual abuse." *Psychoanalytic Dialogues, 2*(1), 37–76.

GAGNON, J. H. (1965). Female child victims of sex offenses. *Social Problems, 13,* 176–192.

GAINER, M. J., & TOREM, M. S. (1992). *Progress versus regression: Strategies for the successful use of abreaction with multiple personality disorder.* Paper presented at the Ninth International Conference on Multiple Personality/Dissociative States, November, Chicago. Available on tape through Audio Transcripts, Ltd., Alexandria, VA.

GANZARAIN, R. (1990). *Object relations group psychotherapy.* Madison, CT: International Universities Press.

GARNER, D. M., & BEMIS, K. M. (1985). Cognitive therapy for anorexia nervosa. In D. M. Garner & P. E. Garfinkel (Eds.), *Handbook of psychotherapy for anorexia nervosa and bulimia.* New York: Guilford Press.

GARNER, D. M., & GARFINKEL, P. E. (Eds.). (1985). *Handbook of psychotherapy for anorexia nervosa and bulimia.* New York: Guilford Press.

GARNER, D. M., ROCKERT, W., OLMSTED, M. P., JOHNSON, C., & COSCINA, D. V. (1985). Psychoeducational principles in the treatment of bulimia and anorexia nervosa. In D. M. Garner and P. E. Garfinkel (Eds.), *Handbook of psychotherapy for anorexia nervosa and bulimia.* New York: Guilford Press.

GHENT, E. (1990). Masochism, submission, surrender: Masochism as a perversion of surrender. *Contemporary Psychoanalysis, 26*(1), 108–136.

GHENT, E. (1992). Paradox and process. *Psychoanalytic Dialogues, 2*(2), 135–160.

GILL, M. (1982). *Analysis of transference* (Vol. I). Madison, CT: International Universities Press.

GILL, M., & HOFFMAN, I. Z. (1982). *Analysis of transference* (Vol. II). Madison, CT: International Universities Press.

GILLIGAN, C. (1983). *In a different voice.* Cambridge: Harvard University Press.

GILLIGAN, C., & BROWN, L. M. (1992). *Meeting at the crossroads. Women's psychology and girls' development.* Cambridge: Harvard University Press.

GILLIGAN, C., LYONS, N. P., & HAMMER, T. J. (Eds.). (1990a). *Making connections: The relational worlds of adolescent girls at Emma Willard School.* Cambridge: Harvard University Press.

GILLIGAN, C., ROGERS, A., & BROWN, L. M. (1990b). Epilogue: Soundings into development. In C. Gilligan, N. P. Lyons, & T. J. Hammer (Eds.), *Making connections: The relational worlds of adolescent girls at Emma Willard School.* Cambridge: Harvard University Press.

GITTER, A. (1986). *The structure and process of compulsive eating groups.* Paper presented at the Women's Therapy Centre Institute Lecture Series, April.

GOLDFARB, L. A. (1987). Sexual abuse antecedent to anorexia nervosa, bulimia, and compulsive overeating: Three case reports. *International Journal of Eating Disorders, 6,* 675–680.

GOLDNER, V. (1991). Toward a critical relational theory of gender. *Psychoanalytic Dialogues, 1*(3), 249–272.

GOODWIN, J. (1982). *Sexual abuse: Incest victims and their families.* Boston: Wright/PSG.

GOODWIN, J. M., & ATTIAS, R. (1993). Eating disorders in survivors of multimodal childhood abuse. In R. P. Kluft & C. G. Fine (Eds.), *Clinical perspectives on multiple personality disorder.* Washington, DC: American Psychiatric Press.

GOULD, C. (1992). Diagnosis and treatment of ritually abused children. In D. K. Sakheim & S. E. Devine (Eds.), *Out of darkness: Exploring satanism and ritual abuse.* New York: Lexington Books.

GRANT-HALL, R., & PEARLMAN, L. A. (1992). *A theoretical framework for the treatment of ritual abuse.* Paper presented at the Ninth International Conference on Multiple Personality/Dissociative States, November, Chicago. Available on tape through Audio Transcripts, Ltd., Alexandria, VA.

GREAVES, G. B. (1992). Alternative hypotheses regarding claims of satanic cult activity: A critical analysis. In D. K. Sakheim & S. E. Devine (Eds.), *Out of darkness: Exploring satanism and ritual abuse.* New York: Lexington Books.

GREENBERG, J. R. (1991). Countertransference and reality. In *Psychoanalytic Dialogues, 1*(1), 52–73.

GREENBERG, J. R., & MITCHELL, S. A. (1983). *Object relations in psychoanalytic theory.* Cambridge: Harvard University Press.

GROLNICK, S. (1990). *The work and play of Winnicott.* Northvale, NJ: Jason Aronson.

GUNTRIP, H. (1973). *Psychoanalytic theory, therapy, and the self.* New York: Basic Books.

GUNTRIP, H. (1980). *Schizoid phenomena, object-relations and the self.* London: The Hogarth Press.

GUTWILL, S. (1992). Countertransference, consumer culture, and eating problems. Presentation at Women's Therapy Centre Institute Lecture Series, April.

HAINER, M. (1993). *On the danger of therapists doubt about reports of childhood sexual abuse.* Unpublished manuscript.

HALL, R. C. W., TICE, L., BERESFORD, T. P., WOOLEY, B., & HALL, A. K. (1989). Sexual abuse in patients with anorexia nervosa and bulimia. *Psychosomatics, 30,* 75–79.

HAMILTON, D. (1992). *Cults in court-forensic implications of ritualistic and satanic abuse.* Paper presented at the Ninth International Conference on Multiple Personality/Dissociative States, November, Chicago. Available on tape through Audio Transcripts, Ltd., Alexandria, VA.

HAMMOND, D. C. (1992). *Clinical hypnosis in the treatment of multiple personality disorder.* Paper presented at the Fourth Annual Eastern Regional Conference on Abuse and Multiple Personality, June, Alexandra, VA. Available on tape through Audio Transcripts, Ltd., Alexandria, VA.

HARKAWAY, J. (1992). *Panel discussion—Hurting women.* Paper presented at Renfrew Foundation Conference: Women: secrets, self and eating disorders, April, Philadelphia, PA. Available on tape through Convention Seminar Cassettes, Simi Valley, CA.

HARRIS, A. (1991a). Gender as contradiction. *Psychoanalytic Dialogues, 1,* 2, 197–225.

HARRIS, A. (1991b). Introduction to symposium on gender. *Psychoanalytic Dialogues, 1*(3), 243–248.

HERMAN, J. L. (1981). *Father-daughter incest.* Cambridge: Harvard University Press.

HERMAN, J. L. (1990). Discussion. In R. P. Kluft (Ed.), *Incest-related syndromes of adult psychopathology.* Washington, DC: American Psychiatric Press.

HERMAN, J. L. (1992). *Trauma and recovery.* New York: Basic Books.

HERMAN, J. L. (1993a). *The secrets of women.* Paper presented at the Fifth Annual Eastern Regional Conference on Abuse and Multiple Personality, June, Alexandria, VA. Available on tape through Audio Transcripts, Ltd., Alexandria, VA.

HERMAN, J. L. (1993b). *Trauma of sexual victimization: Feminist contributions.* Paper presented at the Fifth Annual Eastern Regional Conference on Abuse and Multiple Personality, June, Alexandria, VA. Available on tape through Audio Transcripts, Ltd., Alexandria, VA.

HIRSCH, I. (1993). Countertransference enactments and some issues related to external factors in the analyst's life. *Psychoanalytic Dialogues, 3*(3), 343–366.

HIRSCHMANN, J. R., & MUNTER, C. H. (1988). *Overcoming overeating: Living free in a world of food.* Reading, MA: Addison-Wesley.

HIRSCHMANN, J. R., & ZAPHIROPOULOS, L. (1993). *Preventing childhood eating problems.* Carlsbad, CA: Gurze Books. (Originally titled *Are you hungry.*)

HOFFMAN, I. Z. (1984). The patient as interpreter of the analyst's experience. *Contemporary Psychoanalysis, 19,* 389–422.

HOFFMAN, I. Z. (1991). Discussion: Toward a social-constructivist view of the psychoanalytic situation. *Psychoanalytic Dialogues, 1*(1), 74–105.

HOOKS, B. (1990). *Yearning: Race, gender and cultural politics.* Boston: South End Press.

HOOKS, B. (1992). *Black looks: Race and representation.* Boston: South End Press.

HOOKS, B. (1993). *Sisters of the yam: Black women and self-recovery.* Boston: South End Press.

HOPPMANN, W. H. (1992). *The place of body therapy in the treatment of dissociative disorders.* Paper presented at the Ninth International Conference on Multiple Personality/Dissociative States, November Chicago. Available on tape through Audio Transcripts, Ltd., Alexandria, VA.

HORNYAK, L. M., and BAKER, E. K. (Eds.). (1989). *Experiential therapies for eating disorders.* New York: Guilford Press.

HOROWITZ, M. J. (1986). *Stress response syndromes.* Northvale, NJ: Jason Aronson.

HUTCHINSON, M. (1985). *Transforming body image.* Freedom, CA: The Crossing Press.

ISAACS, S. (1952). The nature and function of phantasy. In M. Klein, P. Heimann, S. Isaacs, & J. Riviere (Eds.), *Developments in Psychoanalysis* (pp 67–121). London: Hogarth Press.

JACOBUS, M., KELLER, E. F., & SUTTLEWORTH, S. (Eds.) (1990). *Body/politics: Women and the discourses of science.* New York: Routledge, Chapman & Hall.

JACOBY, S. (1990). The body image blues. In *Family Circle,* February, 41–47.

KLUFT, R. P. (1986b). Personality unification in multiple personality disorder: A follow-up study. In B. G. Braun (Ed.), *Treatment of multiple personality disorder*. Washington, DC: American Psychiatric Press.

KLUFT, R. P. (1986c). Preliminary observations on age regression in multiple personality disorder patients before and after integration. *American Journal of Clinical Hypnosis, 28*(3), 147–156.

KLUFT, R. P. (1988a). Autohypnotic resolution of an incipient relapse in an integrated multiple personality disorder patient: A clinical note. *American Journal of Clinical Hypnosis, 31*(2), 91–98.

KLUFT, R. P. (1988b). The postunification treatment of multiple personality disorder: First findings. *American Journal of Psychotherapy, 42*(2), 212–228.

KLUFT, R. P. (1989a). Playing for time: Temporizing techniques in the treatment of multiple personality disorder. *American Journal of Clinical Hypnosis, 32*, 90–98.

KLUFT, R. P. (1989b). Treating the patient who has been sexually exploited by a previous therapist. *Psychiatric Clinics of North America, 12*(2), 483–500.

KLUFT, R. P. (1990a). Incest and subsequent revictimizaiton: The case of therapist-patient sexual exploitation, with a description of the sitting duck syndrome. In R. P. Kluft (Ed)., *Incest-related syndromes of adult psychopathology*. Washington, DC: American Psychiatric Press.

KLUFT, R. P. (Ed.). (1990b). *Incest-related syndromes of adult psychopathology*. Washington, DC: American Psychiatric Press.

KLUFT, R. P. (1991a). Clinical presentations of multiple personality disorder. *The Psychiatric Clinics of North America, 14*(3), 605–630.

KLUFT, R. P. (1991b). *The management of abreaction*. Paper presented at the Third Annual Eastern Regional Conference on Abuse and Multiple Personality, June, Alexandria, VA. Available on tape through Audio Transcripts, Ltd., Alexandria, VA.

KLUFT, R. P. (1992a). Advanced treatment of personality disorder. Westwood Institute, California.

KLUFT, R. P. (1992b). Discussion: A specialist's perspective on multiple personality disorder. *Psychoanalytic Inquiry, 12*(1), 139–171.

KLUFT, R. P. (1992c). *Five completed suicides in multiple personality disorder patients: Clinical observations and perspectives*. Paper presented at the Ninth International Conference on Multiple Personality/Dissociative States, November, Chicago. Available on tape through Audio Transcripts, Ltd., Alexandria, VA.

KLUFT, R. P. (1992d). *Transference and countertransference phenomena with MPD*. Paper presented at the Fourth Annual Eastern Regional Conference on Abuse and Multiple Personality, June, Alexandria, VA. Available on tape through Audio Transcripts, Ltd., Alexandria, VA.

KLUFT, R. P. (1993). Basic principles in conducting the psychotherapy of multiple personality disorder. In R. P. Kluft & C. G. Fine (Eds.), *Clinical perspectives on multiple personality disorder*. Washington, DC: American Psychiatric Press.

KLUFT, R. P. (1993b). Clinical approaches to the integration of personalities. In R. P. Kluft & C. G. Fine (Eds.), *Clinical perspectives on multiple personality disorder*. Washington, DC: American Psychiatric Press.

KLUFT, R. P., and FINE, C. G. (Eds.). (1993). *Clinical perspectives on multiple personality disorder.* Washington, DC: American Psychiatric Press.

KLUFT, R. P., ROSS, C. A., & TURKUS, J. A. (1992). *Town meeting: The ritual abuse controversy.* Paper presented at the Fourth Annual Eastern Regional Conference on Abuse and Multiple Personality, June, Alexandria, VA. Available on tape through Audio Transcripts, Ltd., Alexandria, VA.

KOGEL, L., & MUNTER, C. (1986). *Starting with the symptom.* Paper presented at the Women's Therapy Centre Institute Lecture Series, April, New York.

KOHUT, H. (1971). *The analysis of self.* New York: International Universities Press.

KOLATA, G. (1992). The burdens of being overweight: Mistreatment and misconceptions. *New York Times,* November 22, A1.

KOVEL, J. (1981). *The age of desire: Reflections of a radical psychoanalyst.* New York: Pantheon.

KOVEL, J. (1984). Rationalization and the family. In B. Richards (Ed.), *Capitalism and infancy: Essays on psychoanalysis and politics.* Atlantic Highlands, NJ: Humanities Press.

KRUEGER, D. W. (1989). *Body self and psychological self.* New York: Brunner/Mazel.

LACALLE, T. M. (1987). *Voices.* New York: Dodd, Mead.

LANNING, K. V. (1992). A law-enforcement perspective on allegations of ritual abuse. In D. K. Sakheim and S. E. Devine (Eds.), *Out of darkness: Exploring satanism and ritual abuse.* New York: Lexington Books.

LEPISTO, B. L. (1992). *Special considerations in the use of empathy with the multiple personality disorder patient.* Paper presented at the Ninth International Conference on Multiple Personality/Dissociative States, November, Chicago. Available on tape through Audio Transcripts, Ltd., Alexandria, VA.

LEVIN, A. P., & SPAUSTER, E. (1992). Inpatient cognitive-behavioral treatment of eating disorder patients with dissociative disorders. Paper presented at the Ninth International Conference on Multiple Personality/Dissociative States, November, Chicago. Available on tape through Audio Transcripts, Ltd., Alexandria, VA.

LEVENKRON, S. (1978). *The best little girl in the world.* New York: Warner.

LEVENKRON, S. (1982). *Treating and overcoming anorexia nervosa.* New York: Warner.

LEVENSON, E. A. (1983). *The ambiguity of change.* New York: Basic Books.

LEVENSON, E. A. (1992). Mistakes, errors and oversights. *Contemporary Psychoanalysis, 28*(4), 555–571.

LEVINE, H. B. (Ed.). (1990). *Adult analysis and childhood sexual abuse.* Hillsdale, NJ: The Analytic Press.

LICHTMAN, R. (1982). *The production of desire: The integration of psychoanalysis into Marxist theory.* New York: Macmillan.

LINER, D. (1993). *An integrated approach to treating incest survivors.* Paper presented at the Women's Therapy Centre Institute Lecture Series, April, New York.

LITTLE, M. (1957). *Towards basic unity.* London: Free Association Books.

LITTLE, M. (1986). On basic unity (primary total undifferentiatedness). In G. Kohon (Ed.), *The British school of psychoanalysis: The independent tradition.* London: Free Association Books.

LOEWENSTEIN, R. J. (1992). *The Dissociative Spectrum—An Update.* Paper presented at the Fourth Annual Eastern Regional Conference on Abuse and Multiple Personality, June, Alexandria, VA. Available on tape through Audio Transcripts, Ltd., Alexandria, VA.

LOEWENSTEIN, R. J. (1993). Posttraumatic and dissociative aspects of transference and countertransference in the treatment of multiple personality disorder. In R. P. Kluft & C. G. Fine (Eds.), *Clinical perspectives on multiple personality disorder.* Washington, DC: American Psychiatric Press.

LOEWENSTEIN, R. J. & ROSS, D. R. (1992). Multiple personality and psychoanalysis: An introduction. *Psychoanalytic Inquiry, 12*(1), 3–48.

Los Angeles County Commission for Women (1991). *Report of the ritual abuse task force.* Los Angeles: Los Angeles County Commission for Women.

LUEPNITZ, D. A. (1988). *The family interpreted: Feminist theory in clinical practice.* New York: Basic Books.

MACLEOD, S. (1981). *The art of starvation.* London: Virago.

MAGY, T. F. (1992). *Ethical issues in the treatment of MPD: Protecting the welfare of both patient and therapist.* Paper presented at the Ninth International Conference on Multiple Personality/Dissociative States, November, Chicago. Available on tape through Audio Transcripts, Ltd., Alexandria, VA.

MARMER, S. S. (1991). Multiple personality disorder: A psychoanalytic perspective. *The Psychiatric Clinics of North America, 14*(3), 677–694.

MARTIN, B. (1988). Feminism, criticism, and Foucault. In I. Diamond & L. Quinby (Eds.), *Feminism and Foucault: Reflections on resistance.* Boston, Northeastern University Press.

MAYER, R. S. (1991). *Satan's children.* New York: Avon.

McDOUGALL, J. (1989). *Theaters of the body: A psychoanalytic approach to psychosomatic illness.* New York: Norton.

McWILLIAMS, N. & RUTSTEIN, J. (1992). *Multiple personality and dissociation: Psychoanalytic therapy for dissociative patients.* Paper presented at the Twelfth Annual Spring Meeting of the American Psychological Association Division of Psychoanalysis (39)—Discovery and Rediscovery, April, Philadelphia. Available on tape through Audio Transcripts, Ltd., Alexandria, VA.

MICHIE, H. (1987). *The flesh made word: Female figures and women's bodies.* New York: Oxford University Press.

MILLER, A. (1983). *For your own good: Hidden cruelty in child-rearing and the roots of violence.* New York: Farrar, Straus, Giroux.

MILLER, A. (1986). *Thou shalt not be aware.* New York: Meridian Books.

MILLER, J. B. (1976). *Toward a new psychology of women.* Boston: Beacon Press.

MILLMAN, M. (1980). *Such a pretty face: Being fat in America.* New York: Norton.

MINUCHIN, S. (1974). *Families and family therapy.* Cambridge: Harvard University Press.

MITCHELL, S. A. (1988). *Relational concepts in psychoanalysis—An integration.* Cambridge: Harvard University Press.

MORRISON, T. (1972). *The bluest eye.* New York: Washington Square Press.

MUGADZE, J. (1992). *Scripts and screen memories in victims of ritual abuse: Etiological and treatment implications.* Paper presented at the Ninth International

Conference on Multiple Personality/Dissociative States, November, Chicago. Available on tape through Audio Transcripts, Ltd., Alexandria, VA.

NASH, C. L., & WEST, D. J. (1985). Sexual molestation of young girls: A retrospective survey. In D. J. West (Ed.), *Sexual victimization*. Aldershot, Eng.: Gower.

NATHANSON, D. L., & TURKUS, J. A. (1992). *Shame and self-esteem in sexual abuse survivors*. Paper presented at the Fourth Annual Eastern Regional Conference on Abuse and Multiple Personality, June, Alexandria, VA. Available on tape through Audio Transcripts, Ltd., Alexandria, VA.

NESWALD, D. W., & GOULD, C. (1992). *Basic treatment and program neutralization strategies for adult MPD survivors of satanic ritual abuse*. Paper presented at the Ninth International Conference on Multiple Personality/Dissociative States. Available on tape through Audio Transcripts, Ltd., Alexandria, VA.

Newsweek. (1989). Diets incorporated. *Newsweek*, September 11, 56–60.

New York Times. (1991). Study says mothers may pass on eating disorders, May 5, p. 37.

O'Conner, N., & Ryan, J. (1993). *Wild desires and mistaken identities*. London: Virago.

OGDEN, T. H. (1982). *Projective identification and psychotherapeutic technique*. Northvale, NJ: Jason Aronson.

OGDEN, T. H. (1990). *The matrix of the mind*. Northvale, NJ: Jason Aronson.

O'NEILL, M. (1990). Congress looking into the diet business. *New York Times*, March 28.

OPPENHEIMER, R., HOWELLS, K., PALMER, R. L., & CHALONER, D. A. (1985). Adverse sexual experience in childhood and clinical eating disorders: A preliminary description. *Journal of Psychiatric Research, 19*, 357–361.

ORBACH, S. (1978). *Fat is a feminist issue*. New York: Paddington Press.

ORBACH, S. (1982). *Fat is a feminist issue II*. New York: Berkeley Books.

ORBACH, S. (1985a). Accepting the symptom: A feminist psychoanalytic treatment of anorexia nervosa. In D. M. Garner, & P. E. Garfinkel (Eds.), *Handbook of psychotherapy for anorexia nervosa and bulimia*. New York: Guilford Press.

ORBACH, S. (1986). *Hunger strike*. New York: Norton.

ORBACH, S. (1994). Working with the false body. In A. Erstein and D. Judd (Eds.), *The imaginative body*. London: Whurr Publishers.

ORBACH, S. Countertransference and the false body. *Squiggle*, in press.

PALAZZOLI, M. S. (1986). *Self-starvation*, 2nd ed. Northvale, NJ: Jason Aronson.

PALMER, R. L., OPPENHEIMER, R., DIGNON, A., CHALONER, D. A., & HOWELLS, K. (1990). Childhood sexual experiences with adults reported by women with eating disorders—An extended series. *British Journal of Psychiatry, 156*, 699–703.

PERRY, N. E. (1992). *Secondary PTSD in therapists treating MPD patients who report sadistic abuse*. Paper presented at the Ninth International Conference on Multiple Personality/Dissociative States, November, Chicago. Available on tape through Audio Transcripts, Ltd., Alexandria, VA.

PETERSON, J. A. (1992a). *Managing abreactions in the treatment of MPD*. Paper presented at the Fourth Annual Eastern Regional Conference on Abuse and

Multiple Personality, June, Alexandria, VA. Available on tape through Audio Transcripts, Ltd., Alexandria, VA.

PETERSON, J. A. (1992b). *Synthetic/spontaneous multiple personality disorder: The milieu and its treatment frame.* Paper presented at the Ninth International Conference on Multiple Personality/Dissociative States, November, Chicago. Available on tape through Audio Transcripts, Ltd., Alexandria, VA.

PETERSON, J. A. (1993). *Introduction to memory processing techniques.* Paper presented at the Fifth Annual Eastern Regional Conference on Abuse and Multiple Personality, June, Alexandria, VA. Available on tape through Audio Transcripts, Ltd., Alexandria, VA.

PETTINATI, H. M., KOGAN, L. G., MARGOLIS, C., SHRIER, L., & WADE, J. H. (1989). Hypnosis, hypnotizability, and the bulimic patient. In L. M. Hornyak and E. K. Baker (Eds.), *Experiential therapies for eating disorders.* New York: Guilford Press.

PETTINATI, H. M., HORNE, R. J., & STAATS, J. M. (1985). Hypnotizability in patients with anorexia nervosa and bulimia. *Archives of General Psychiatry, 42,* 1014–1016.

PHILLIPS, A. (1988). *Winnicott.* Cambridge: Harvard University Press.

POLIVY, J., & HERMAN, C. P. (1983). *Breaking the diet habit: The natural weight alternative.* New York: Basic Books.

POSTER, M. (1978). *Critical theory of the family.* New York: Seabury Press.

PRUZINSKY, T. (1990). Somatopsychic approaches to psychotherapy and personal growth. In T. S. Cash and T. Pruzinsky (Eds.), *Body images.* New York: Guilford Press.

PUTNAM, F. W. (1985). Dissociation as a response to extreme trauma. In R. P. Kluft (Ed.), *Childhood antecedents of multiple personality.* Washington, DC: American Psychiatric Press.

PUTNAM, F. W. (1986). The treatment of multiple personality: State of the art. In B. G. Braun (Ed.), *Treatment of multiple personality disorder.* Washington, DC: American Psychiatric Press.

PUTNAM, F. W. (1989). *Diagnosis and treatment of multiple personality disorder.* New York: Guilford Press.

PUTNAM, F. W. (1990). Disturbances of "self" in victims of childhood sexual abuse. In R. P. Kluft (Ed.), *Incest-related syndromes of adult psychopathology.* Washington, DC: American Psychiatric Press.

PUTNAM, F. W. (1991). Recent research on multiple personality disorder. *The Psychiatric Clinics of North America, 14*(3), 489–502.

PUTNAM, F. W. (1992a). Discussion: Are alter personalities fragments or figments? *Psychoanalytic Inquiry, 12*(1), 95–111.

PUTNAM, F. W. (1992b). Using hypnosis for therapeutic abreactions. *Psychiatric Medicine, 10,* 51–65.

PUTNAM, F. W., GUROFF, J. J., SILBERMAN, E. K., et al. (1986). The clinical phenomenology of multiple personality disorder: Review of 100 recent cases. *Journal of Clinical Psychiatry, 47,* 285–293.

RABINOR, J. R. (1991). The process of recovery from an eating disorder—The use of journal writing in the initial phase of treatment. *Psychotherapy in Private Practice, 9*(1), 93–106.

RACKER, H. (1968). *Transference and countertransference.* Madison, CT: International Universities Press.

REAGOR, P. A. (1992). *Life, death, and structured MPD: Perspectives for treatment.* Paper presented at the Ninth International Conference on Multiple Personality/Dissociative States. Available on tape through Audio Transcripts, Ltd., Alexandria, VA.

RICHARDS, B. (Ed.). (1984). *Capitalism and infancy: Essays on psychoanalysis and politics.* Atlantic Highlands, NJ: Humanities Press.

ROSS, C. A. (1989). *Multiple personality disorder.* New York: Wiley.

ROSS, C. A. (1991). Epidemiology of multiple personality disorder and dissociation. *The Psychiatric Clinics of North America, 14*(3), 503–518.

ROSS, C. A. (1992). *MPD, mind control, and cognitive distortions.* Paper presented at the Fourth Annual Eastern Regional Conference on Abuse and Multiple Personality, June, Alexandria, VA. Available on tape through Audio Transcripts, Ltd., Alexandria, VA.

ROSS, C. A., NORTON, G. R., & WOZNEY, K. (1989). Multiple personality disorder: A clinical investigation of 236 cases. *Canadian Journal of Psychiatry, 34,* 413–418.

ROTH, G. (1989). *Why weight? A guide to ending compulsive eating.* New York: Penguin.

RUDDICK, S. (1989). *Maternal thinking: Toward a politics of peace.* New York: Ballantine.

RUSH, F. (1980). *The best kept secret: Sexual abuse of children.* Englewood Cliffs, NJ: Prentice-Hall.

RUSSELL, D. E. H. (1986). *The secret trauma: Incest in the lives of girls and women.* New York: Basic Books.

SAKHEIM, D. K., & DEVINE, S. E. (1992a). Bound by the boundaries: Therapy issues in work with individuals exposed to severe trauma. In D. K. Sakheim and S. E. Devine (Eds.), *Out of darkness: Exploring satanism and ritual abuse.* New York: Lexington Books.

SAKHEIM, D. K., & DEVINE, S. E. (Eds.). (1992b). *Out of darkness: Exploring satanism and ritual abuse.* New York: Lexington Books

SANDS, S. (1991). Bulimia, dissociation, and empathy: A self-psychological view. In C. L. Johnson (Ed.), *Psychodynamic treatment of anorexia nervosa and bulimia.* New York: Guilford Press.

SCHECHTER, J. O., SCHWARTZ, H. P., & GREENFELD, D. G. (1987). Sexual assault and anorexia nervosa. *International Journal of Eating Disorders, 6,* 313–316.

SCHWARTZ, H. (1986). *Never satisfied: A cultural history of diets, fantasies and fat.* New York: Macmillan.

SEINFELD, J. (1991). *The empty core: An object relations approach to psychotherapy of the schizoid personality.* Northvale, NJ: Jason Aronson.

SENNETT, R., & COBB, J. (1973). *The hidden injuries of class.* New York: Knopf.

SHAPIRO, S. A. (1993). Gender-role stereotypes and clinical process: Commentary on papers by Gruenthal and Hirsch. *Psychoanalytic Dialogues, 3*(3), 371–388.

SHENGOLD, L. (1989). *Soul murder: The effects of childhood abuse and deprivation.* New York: Fawcett.

SHORTER, E. (1977). *The making of the modern family.* New York: Basic Books.

SILBERMAN-DEIHL, L. J., & KOMISARUK, B. R. (1985). Treating psychogenic somatic disorders through body metaphor. *American Journal of Dance Therapy, 8,* 37–45.

SLAVIN, J. H. (1992a). *The rediscovery of trauma: Implications for psychoanalytic theory and treatment.* Paper presented at the Twelfth Annual Spring Meeting of the American Psychological Association Division of Psychoanalysis (39)—Discovery and rediscovery. Available on tape through Audio Transcripts, Ltd., Alexandria, VA.

SLAVIN, J. H. (1992b). Unintended consequences of psychoanalytic training. *Contemporary psychoanalysis, 28*(4), 616–630.

SLOAN, G., & LEICHNER, P. (1986). Is there a relationship between sexual abuse or incest and eating disorders? *Canadian Journal of Psychiatry, 31,* 665–660.

SMOLAK, L., LEVINE, M. P., & SULLINS, E. (1990). Are childhood sexual experiences related to eating disordered attitudes and behaviors in a college sample? *International Journal of Eating Disorders, 9,* 167–178.

SPENCER, J. (1989). *Suffer the child.* New York: Pocket Books.

SPERLING, M. (1961). Psychosomatic disorders. In S. Lorand & H. I. Schneer (Eds.), *Adolescents: Approach to problems and therapy.* New York: Hoeber.

SPIEGEL, D. (1981). Vietnam grief work using hypnosis. *American Journal of Clinical Hypnosis, 24,* 33–40.

SPIEGEL, D. (1986). Dissociation, double binds, and posttraumatic stress in multiple personality disorder. In B. G. Braun (Ed.), *Treatment of multiple personality disorder.* Washington, DC: American Psychiatric Press.

SPIEGEL, D. (1990). Trauma, dissociation, and hypnosis. In R. P. Kluft (Ed.), *Incest-related syndromes of adult psychopathology.* Washington, DC: American Psychiatric Press.

SPIEGEL, D. (1993). Multiple posttraumatic personality disorder. In R. P. Kluft and C. G. Fine (Eds.), *Clinical perspectives on multiple personality disorder.* Washington, DC: American Psychiatric Press.

SPILLIUS, E. B. (1988). *Melanie Klein today: Developments in theory and practice.* New York: Routledge, Chapman & Hall.

STACEY, J. (1983). Brave new families. Berkeley: University of California Press.

STARK, E., & FLITCRAFT, A. (1983). Social knowledge, social policy and the abuse of women. In D. Finkelhor, R. Gelles, G. Hotaling, & M. Stark (Eds.), *The dark side of families.* Beverly Hills, CA: Sage.

STARK, E., & FLITCRAFT, A. (1988). Personal power and institutional victimization: Treating the dual trauma of woman battering. In F. Ochberg (Ed.), *Post-traumatic therapy and victims of violence.* New York: Brunner/Mazel.

STARK, E., FLITCRAFT, A., & FRAZIER, W. (1979). Medicine and patriarchal violence: The social construction of a "private event." *International Journal of Health Services, 9,* 461–493.

STARK, E., FLITCRAFT, A., ZUCKERMAN, D., GREY, A., ROBISON, J., & FRAZIER, W. (1981). *Wife abuse in the medical setting: An introduction for health personnel.* Monograph #7. Washington DC: Office of Domestic Violence.

STEINEM, G. (1993). *Accidental prophets*. Paper presented at the Fifth Annual Eastern Regional Conference on Abuse and Multiple Personality, June, Alexandria, VA. Available on tape through Audio Transcripts, Ltd., Alexandria, VA.

STEINER-ADAIR, C. (1986). The body politic: Normal female adolescent development and the development of eating disorders. *Journal of American Academy of Psychoanalysis, 14*, 95–114.

STEINER-ADAIR, C. (1991). New maps of development, new models of therapy: The psychology of women and the treatment of eating disorders. In C. L. Johnson (Ed.), *Psychodynamic treatment of anorexia nervosa and bulimia*. New York: Guilford Press.

STERN, D. (1985). *The interpersonal world of the infant*. New York: Basic Books.

STERN, D. (1983). Unformulated experience. *Contemporary Psychoanalysis, 19*(1), 71–99.

STERN, D. (1987). Unformulated experience and transference. *Contemporary Psychoanalysis, 23*, 484–491.

STERN, D. (1989). The analyst's unformulated experience of the patient. *Contemporary Psychoanalysis, 25*, 1–33.

STERN, S. (1992). Opposing currents technique. *Contemporary Psychoanalysis, 28*(4), 594–615.

STOLOROW, R. D., & ATWOOD, G. E. (1991). The mind and the body. *Psychoanalytic Dialogues, 1*(2), 181–196.

The Stone Center. (1991). *Women's growth in connection: Writings from the Stone Center*. New York: Guilford Press.

SUGARMAN, A., & KURASH, C. (1982). *International Journal of Eating Disorders, 1*(4), 51–67.

SULLIVAN, H. S. (1940). *Conceptions of modern psychiatry*. New York: Norton.

SULLIVAN, H. S. (1953). *The interpersonal theory of psychiatry*. New York: Norton.

SZEKELY, E. (1988). *Never too thin*. Lincoln: University of Nebraska Press.

TAX, M. (1982). *Rivington Square*. New York: Morrow.

TAX, M. (1990). *Union Square*. New York: Avon.

TERR, L. C. (1991). Childhood traumas: An outline and overview. *American Journal of Psychiatry, 148*, 10–20.

THOMPSON, B. W. (1992). "A way outa no way": Eating problems among African-American, Latina and white women. *Gender and Society, 6*(4), 546–561.

THOMPSON, B. W. (1994). Food, bodies, and growing up female: Childhood lessons about culture, race, and class. In P. Fallon, M. A. Katzman, & S. C. Wooley (Eds.), *Feminist perspectives on eating disorders*. New York: Guilford Press.

TOREM, M. (1986). Dissociative states presenting as an eating disorder. *American Journal of Clinical Hypnosis, 29*(2), 137–142.

TOREM, M. (1987). Ego-state therapy for eating disorders. *American Journal of Clinical Hypnosis, 30*, 94–102.

TOREM, M. (1990). Covert multiple personality underlying eating disorders. *American Journal of Psychotherapy, 44*, 357–368.

TOREM, M. (1992a). "Back from the future": A powerful age-progression technique. *American Journal of Clinical Hypnosis, 35*(2), 81–88.

TOREM, M. (1992b). *Double jeopardy: Eating disorders and multiple personality.* Paper presented at the Fourth Annual Eastern Regional Conference on Abuse and Multiple Personality, June, Alexandria, VA. Available on tape through Audio Transcripts, Ltd., Alexandria, VA.

TOREM, M. (1993). Eating disorders in patients with multiple personality disorder. In R. P. Kluft & C. G. Fine (Eds.), *Clinical perspectives on multiple personality disorder.* Washington, DC: American Psychiatric Press.

TOREM, M., & CURDUE, K. (1988). PTSD presenting as an eating disorder. *Stress Medicine, 4,* 139–142.

TOREM, M., GILBERTSON, A., & LIGHT, V. (1990). Indications of physical, sexual, and verbal victimization in projective tree drawings. *American Journal of Clinical Psychology, 46*(6), 900–906.

TURKUS, J. A. (1991). Psychotherapy and case management for multiple personality disorder: Synthesis for continuity of care. *The Psychiatric Clinics of North America, 14*(3), 649–660.

U.S. *News & World Report.* (1990). Getting slim. *U.S. News & World Report,* May 14, 56–65.

VAN DER KOLK, B. (Ed.). (1987). *Psychological trauma.* Washington DC: American Psychiatric Press.

VYGOTSKY, L. S. (1978). *Mind in society: The development of higher psychological processes.* Cambridge: Harvard University Press.

WATERBURY, M. (1992). *Back for a future: A case report with 20 years follow-up.* Paper presented at the Ninth International Conference on Multiple Personality/ Dissociative States, November, Chicago. Available on tape through Audio Transcripts, Ltd., Alexandria, VA.

WATKINS, H. H., & WATKINS, J. G. (1993). Ego-state therapy in the treatment of dissociative disorders. In R. P. Kluft & C. G. Fine (Eds.), *Clinical perspectives on multiple personality disorder.* Washington, DC: American Psychiatric Press.

WEISBERG, L., & HERZOG, D. B. (1992). *Sexual abuse in eating disorders: Evaluation and treatment.* Paper presented at the Fifth International Conference on Eating Disorders, April, New York. Available on tape through Conference Copy, Inc., Brooklyn, NY.

WESTKOTT, M. (1986). *The feminist legacy of Karen Horney.* New Haven: Yale University Press.

WILBUR, C. B. (1985). The effect of child abuse on the psyche. In R. P. Kluft (Ed.), *Childhood antecedents of multiple personality.* Washington, DC: American Psychiatric Press.

WILBUR, C. B. (1986). Psychoanalysis and multiple personality disorder. In B. G. Braun (Ed.), *Treatment of multiple personality disorder.* Washington, DC: American Psychiatric Press.

WILLIAMSON, J. (1991). *Consuming passions: The dynamics of popular culture.* New York: Marion Boyars.

WINNICOTT, D. W. (1971a). Mirror-role of mother and family in childhood development. In D. W. Winnicott (Ed.), *Playing and reality.* Harmondsworth, Engl.: Penguin.

WINNICOTT, D. W. (1971b). Transitional objects and transitional phenomena. In

D. W. Winnicott (Ed.), *Playing and reality*. Harmondsworth, Engl.: Penguin.

WINNICOTT, D. W. (1971c). *Playing and reality*. Harmondsworth, Engl.: Penguin.

WINNICOTT, D. W. (1975). *Through paediatrics to psycho-analysis*. New York: Basic Books.

WINNICOTT, D. W. (1980). *The maturational processes and the facilitating environment*. Madison, CT: International Universities Press.

WINNICOTT, D. W. (1981). *The family and individual development*. New York: Tavistock.

WINNICOTT, D. W. (1986). *Home is where we start from: Essays by a psychoanalyst*. New York: Norton.

WINNICOTT, D. W. (1989). On the basis for self in the body. *International Journal of Child Psychotherapy, 1* (1), 7–16.

WOLF, N. (1991). *The beauty myth: How images of beauty are used against women*. New York: Morrow.

WONDERLICH, S. A., & SWIFT, W. J. (1990). The borderline versus other personality disorders in the eating disorders: Clinical description. *International Journal of Eating Disorders, 9*, 629–638.

WOOLF, V. (1929). *A room of one's own*. New York: Harcourt, Brace and World.

WOOLEY, S. C. (1991). Uses of countertransference in the treatment of eating disorders: A gender perspective. In C. L. Johnson (Ed.), *Psychodynamic treatment of anorexia nervosa and bulimia*. New York: Guilford Press.

WOOLEY, S. C. (1992). *Keynote address: Sexual abuse and the legacy of silence*. Paper presented at the Renfrew Foundation Conference: Women: Secrets, self and eating disorders, Philadelphia, PA. Available on tape through Convention Seminar Cassettes, Simi Valley, CA.

WOOLEY, S. C. (1994). Sexual abuse and eating disorders: The concealed debate. In P. Fallon, M. A. Katzman, & S. C. Wooley (Eds.), *Feminist perspectives on eating disorders*. New York: Guilford Press.

WOOLEY, S. C., & KEARNEY-COOKE, A. (1986). Intensive treatment of bulimia and body-image disturbance. In K. D. Brownell & J. P. Foreyt (Eds.), *Physiology, psychology and treatment of eating disorders*. New York: Basic Books.

WYATT, E. (1985). The sexual abuse of Afro-American and white women in childhood. *Childhood Abuse & Neglect, 9*, 507–519.

YOUNG, W. C. (1988). All that switches is not split. *Dissociation, 1*(1), 31–41.

YOUNG, W. C. (1992). Recognition and treatment of survivors reporting ritual abuse. In D. K. Sakheim & S. E. Devine (Eds.), *Out of darkness: Exploring satanism and ritual abuse*. New York: Lexington Books.

YOUNG, W. C., & YOUNG, L. J. (1992). *Manchurian hysteria and therapeutic impasses in treating patients reporting sadistic ritual abuse*. Paper presented at the Ninth International Conference on Multiple Personality/Dissociative States, November, Chicago. Available on tape through Audio Transcripts, Ltd., Alexandria, VA.

YOUNG-BRUEHL, E. (1993). On feminism and psychoanalysis—In the case of anorexia nervosa. *Psychoanalytic Psychology, 10*(3), 317–330.

ZARETSKY, E. (1986). *Capitalism, the family, and personal life*. New York: Harper & Row.

ZEHNER, M. (1992a). *Panel discussion—Hurting women.* Paper presented at the Renfrew Foundation Conference: Women: Secrets, self and eating disorders, Philadelphia, PA. Available on tape through Convention Seminar Cassettes, Simi Valley, CA.

ZEHNER, M. (1992b). *Workshop: When abuse and eating disorders intersect in therapy.* Paper presented at the Renfrew Foundation Conference: Women: Secrets, self and eating disorders, Philadelphia, PA. Available on tape through Convention Seminar Cassettes, Simi Valley, CA.

Index

Abandonment, 58, 62, 77–79, 110; and bulimia, 65; and working towards body/self integration, 129

Abuse, 5, 180–81; and body image, 50–51; and learning to feed oneself, 90; and transference, 163–64, 170. *See also* Alcohol abuse; Battered women; Drug abuse; Ritualized abuse; Sexual abuse

"Action symptoms," 58, 60, 69, 151

Adaptive functions, 71, 74–76, 77, 78

Addictions: and dieting, 30; field of, 12-step programs in, 180, 182. *See also* Twelve-step programs

Adolescence, 51–54, 126, 185. *See also* Puberty

Advertising industry, 9–11, 15, 21–23, 101; and dieting industry, 32; and sexual equality, 133. *See also* Consumer culture

African-Americans, 23–24, 25

Ageism, 125

Agency, 15–16, 17–20, 75; and learning to feed oneself, 103; and working towards body/self integration, 132

Aging, 125, 142, 152

Alcohol abuse, 189, 206

Amnesia, 227, 230. *See also* Memory

Anger, 58, 75, 79, 82; and bulimia, 64–65; and learning to feed oneself, 98, 110; and working towards body/self integration, 124, 140. *See also* Rage

Anorexia, 14, 42, 61–63, 65; and body size acceptance, 218–19; and bulimia, shifting between, 69; and force-feeding, 180–81; and learning to feed oneself, 83, 98–99, 107–8, 110; and medical concerns, 71, 72; and multiple personality disor-

der, 230, 231; and psychosomatic symptoms, 58–59; and sexual abuse, 184, 186, 196, 202; and symptoms, adaptive functions of, 76; and transference, 147, 154; and using scales, 138; and working towards body/self integration, 122, 125, 130–32, 135–36, 138, 140–41, 143

Anxiety, 30, 60, 69, 77; and anorexia, 62; and hunger, 92, 95–96; and learning to feed oneself, 87, 89; and psychosomatic symptoms, 58–59; and transference, 147; and "trashing," 113–14; and working towards body/self integration, 130–31, 134, 140

Asymmetry, 167–71

Attias, R., 230

Atwood, G. E., 203

Auschwitz, 159. *See also* Concentration camps; Holocaust

Authenticity, 21, 48

Autonomy, 45, 56, 79, 92; and learning to feed oneself, 109, 110, 111; and puberty, 52; and sexual abuse, 190; and working towards body/self integration, 141

Barsky, S. L., 106

BASK components, 209

Bathrick, Sarafina, 23

Battered women, 5, 35, 185

Beauty, 6, 10–11, 120, 152; myth, 186, 203. *See also* Objectification

Behavioral theorists, 16

Benjamin, J., 8, 17*n*, 52

Berger, J., 49

Bion, W. R., 69

Bisexuality, 166. *See also* Homosexuality

Bloom, Carol, 40–56, 57–66, 67-82, 83–115, 116–43, 147

Bluest Eye, The (Morrison), 24

Body: during adulthood, 54–56; and anti-diet approach, 73-74; changes, and treatment, 140-43; in childhood, 49–51; as a container of needs and affects, 127–30; as an expression of developmental issues, 130–32; images, and co-motion, 164–71; images, statistics on, 33; images, and transference, 144–71; in infancy, 46–49, 50; in puberty, 51–54; size, acceptance of, 142–43, 218–19; size, as a container of memory, 126–27; and splitting, 99–103. *See also* Body/self integration; Hunger; Medical concerns

Body-Self and Psychological Self (Krueger), 213

Body/self integration, 46–47, 54, 94, 116–43; and dieting, 214; and permitting food choice, 217–18; and sexual abuse, 190, 192, 194–95, 202, 213. *See also* Body

Bollas, Christopher, 146

Bolshevism, 9

Bonding, between women, 53, 84

Bordo, Susan, 24, 54, 195–96

Boundaries, 1, 43; and anorexia, 62; and bulimia, 66; in early development, 47–49; and learning to feed oneself, 111–12; and satiation, 110; and working towards body/self integration, 121, 131, 139. *See also* Separation

Bradshaw, John, 200

Breaking the Diet Habit (Herman and Polivy), 34–35

Brown, L. M., 53

Brown, L. S., 215, 216

Brumberg, Joan, 10, 37

Bulimia, 16, 63–66, 78–79; and anorexia, shifting between, 69; and body size acceptance, 218–19; and learning to feed oneself, 83, 87–91, 109; and multiple personality disorder, 230, 231; and sexual abuse, 186, 189, 191, 193, 197; and symbolic meanings of food, 59; and symptoms, adaptive functions of, 76; and transference, 147, 148; and working towards body/self integration, 119–20, 125, 133–34, 135–36, 142

Burke, W. F., 167

Calmness, fostering, 74–75

Calof, David, 191, 196*n*, 242

Calorie Control Council, 33

Calories, 33, 107; eating fewer, 35; information regarding, and treatment, 72–73; and learning to feed oneself, 101, 106

Calvinism, 10, 23

Cancer, 106

Capitalism, 3, 4, 9

Carcinogens, 33

Case study individuals: Aaron, 44; Amanda, 118–19; Angie, 153; Ann, 169–71; Annie, 80–82, 127–29; Barbara, 166–67; Beth, 93–94; Brenda, 165–68; Carla, 117, 131–32; Cathy, 127; Christine, 189, 193–94, 198, 203; Claire, 162–63, 164, 176–78; Colleen, 161–62; Dana, 98–99; Debbie, 60; Doris, 93, 122–23; Dorothy, 91; Elaine, 217; Erica, 133–35, 178–80; Eve, 133; Faith, 126; Francine, 224; Gene, 136; Gina, 44; Harriet, 124–25; Jackie, 90–91, 142; Jane, 84–86, 91, 139, 228; Jeanette, 189, 194, 197, 200–203, 215; Jeanne, 107-8; Jesse, 44; Joan, 75, 142; Joanna, 86–87, 91; Jody, 199–200; Josie, 89–90; Joyce, 76; Julia, 123–24; Julie, 59–60; Kate, 44; Lily, 193, 196, 197, 232–42; Linda, 225; Lisa, 85–86, 91, 139; Lois, 113; Louise, 44; Marcia, 76; Marge, 133, 136–37; Margo, 126–27; Mark, 158; Melanie, 90–91; Melinda, 64; Nancy, 108–9; Nell, 130–31; Nicky, 44; Paula, 138; Penny, 94–95, 97–98; Rachel, 87–89, 91, 95–97, 119, 133, 138; Ralph, 163–64; Ray, 117; Rebecca, 155–62, 164; Reni, 74-75, 76–77; Robin, 142; Ruby, 110; Sally, 225; Sammy, 44; Sara, 153; Sarah, 44, 91; Sarit, 174–76, 178; Sheila, 98; Sonia, 77; Susie, 133, 135–36; Terry, 165–66, 167–68; Tom, 166, 168

Chaplin, Charlie, 4

Character, social standards for, 6, 10, 23

Chernin, Kim, 53, 186

Childrearing, 4–5, 64

Cholesterol, 106

Chomsky, Noam, 25

Chubbiness, 50

Cigarette smoking, 34

Civil rights, 19

Class, 24–25, 105, 146; mobility, and thinness, ideal of, 11–12; working class, 10, 12, 25, 130–31

Clothing, 33, 132; and body changes, 141, 142; and cultural symbols, integration of, 20–25; and puberty, 53

College attendance, 64, 130–31

Colonization, 6, 185

Commodification, 24, 197

Compassion, 77, 107, 121, 148

Competence, 64

Competition, 56

Compliance, 18, 173, 177

Concentration camps, 72, 155–56, 159, 173

Congress, 32, 33

Consciousness-raising groups, 204

Consumer culture, 2, 5–27, 54, 67, 154, 243; and agency, 17–18; and cultural symbols, integration of, 20–25; and deep psychic structure, 25–27; and producer-selves, 12–13; and sexual abuse, 186, 192, 197–99; and sexual equality, 133; and thinness, ideal of, 11–15

Control, 12–13, 31, 35, 56, 77, 83–84; and anorexia, 62; and bulimia, 66; and learning to feed oneself, 103, 104–5; and "trashing," 114; and working towards body/self integration, 117–19, 126–27, 141

Cookbooks, 101

Cosmetic surgery, 11, 25, 186, 199–200

Countertransference, 144–71, 180–83; and body changes, 142; cultural, 146–47, 150; and diet mentality, 172–83; "error," 150; and multiple personality disorder, 239, 241, 242; and returning to the diet, 90–91; and sexual abuse, 209; totalist view of, 145; and working towards body/self integration, 124–25

Courtois, Christine, 185

Cravings, 95–97

Crisp, A. H., 130

Cult abuse, 229

Curiosity, stance of, 68–70

Davies, J. M., 187–88, 192, 210, 242

Davis, Cathy, 200

Debriefing, 208

Deep psychological structure, 25–27, 38

Democracy, 9, 12, 185

Dependency, 78, 79; and learning to feed oneself, 90, 110; and transference, 154; and working towards body/self integration, 123, 125, 131–32

Depression, 69, 117, 134, 137; and sexual abuse, 205, 206, 211

Desire, 7, 12, 32, 55, 56, 111; and bulimia, 66; and the culture of food, 37; and deep psychological structure, 26; and sexuality, 132–37; and social division of labor, 7–8; and symbolization, 20; and transference, 154. *See also* Sexuality

Detailed inquiry, 68–71

Devine, S. E., 208

Diabetes, 34, 105

Diagnosis, 60, 84, 205–7

Diet, 15, 25, 28–39, 43, 53–55, 61; anti-, approach, 73–74, 83–115; vs. attuned eating, 172–83; during childhood, 50; and food industry, 35–39; and gaining weight, 29;

health risks of, 16, 32, 72; industry, 32–33; mentality, 83–90, 172–83, 213–18; and mother-daughter relationship, 45–46; and personal diet experience, 28–30; pills, 50; psychodynamics of, 31-32; and puberty, 53, 54; publications, 33; returning to, during treatment, 90–91; and sexual abuse, 186, 189–90, 184, 213–18; statistics on, 28, 29, 32; and symbolic meanings of food, 57, 58; and transference/counter-transference, 90–91, 151–52; and "trashing," 114–15; types of, 32–33

Diet Center, 32

Difference, 20

Differentiation, 52, 53, 110

Dinnerstein, Dorothy, 163

Disclosure issues, 167–71

Disintegration, defenses against, 58

Dissociation, 53, 69; and learning to feed oneself, 87–88, 94; and multiple personality disorder, 227, 231, 240, 241; and nonverbal techniques, 224; and sexual abuse, 149*n*, 187–89, 192, 194, 195, 198, 206, 208, 210, 218, 224; and social division of labor, 29

Diverticulitis, 105

Dreams, 118, 132, 141–42

Drug abuse, 75, 189, 206

Education, 9, 19. *See also* Psychoeducational work

Ego, 25–26, 56, 61, 67, 122, 222; and anorexia, 63; and body changes, 142; as a body ego, 47; and bulimia, 64; in childhood, 51; and dieting, 31, 32, 34, 38; and eating with hunger, 213; healthy central, 32; and multiple personality disorder, 227, 228, 234–35, 236; and sexual abuse, 187, 188, 191, 202; and symptoms, adaptive functions of, 74, 75, 78; and "trashing," 113–14; and working towards body/self integration, 138

Ehrenberg, Darlene, 146

Eichenbaum, L., 7, 16

Elimination, need for, 129

Embeddedness, 146

Emergencies, "acute," 182–83

Empathy, 68–70, 79, 119, 175

Enmeshment, 62

Entitlement, sense of, 42, 73, 79

Ethnic groups, 23, 24–25, 36, 44, 146

Ewen, Stuart, 8

Exercise, 50–51, 57, 78, 80, 230; and anorexia, 63; and dieting industry, 33; and symbolic meanings of food, 58

Experiential techniques, 223–26

Fairbairn, W., 18, 25, 31–32, 38, 190–91, 199
False Memory Foundation (FMF), 224
Fanon, Frantz, 6, 185
Fantasies, 30, 72; and body changes, 142; and bulimia, 64; and cultural symbols, 22; about food, and early development, 42; and internalization of culture, 17–18; and learning to feed oneself, 101–2; sexual, 136, 137; and social structure, 25–27; and symptoms, adaptive functions of, 74; and transitional objects, 20; and working towards body/self integration, 116, 143
Fashion industry, 10, 13*n*, 120
Fasting, 109, 128
Fat: as a good caretaker, 122–23; as internal rejecting and traumatized object, 123–25
Fathers, 16, 125; and concerns about body size, 50; in early development, 48; and mirroring, 8; and puberty, 52
Femininity. *See* Gender
Feminism, 10, 132–33, 136, 150, 161, 184–85, 209–19
Ferenczi, Sandor, 190, 207
Fertility, 127
Fight or flight state, 188
Film, 15, 24
Finkelhor, D., 215, 216
Fonda, Jane, 50
Food: allergies, 27; choosing different, 100–103, 217–18, 240–42; in early development, 40–46; and food industry, 35–39; and health concerns, 105–6; legalizing, 103–5; as metaphor for life, 107–9; and multiple personality disorder, 240–42; as object relationship, 97–99; rejecting, and rejecting the mother, 44–45; spending money on, 105; and splitting, 99–100; symbolic meanings of, 57–66
Force-feeding, 180–181, 182
Foucault, Michel, 6, 25*n*
Frawley, Mary Gail, 147, 187–88, 192, 221, 242
Frederickson, Renée, 208
Freud, Anna, 44
Freud, Sigmund, 41, 47, 144, 208, 223

Gaze, "oppositional," 24
Gender, 56, 67, 131; and bulimia, 64; identity, and development, 48–49. *See also* Sexuality
Gilligan, Carol, 53
Gitter, Andrea, 184–204, 205–26
"Good girl" syndrome, 65

Good Housekeeping, 33
Goodwin, Jean, 185, 187, 230
Grazing, 37
Grief, 98, 110, 130, 151, 219, 241
Guilt, 34, 63, 148, 172; and multiple personality disorder, 234; and sexual abuse, 216, 217
Gutwill, Susan, 1–27, 28–39, 144–71, 172–83, 184–204, 205–26, 227–44

Hallucinations, 206, 229
Harper's Bazaar, 33
Harvard Medical School, 106
Harvard Project, 53
Headaches, 94
Healing the Incest Wound (Courtois), 185
Health concerns, 4–5, 34–35, 70–72, 105–6, 171–73; and "acute emergencies," use of term, 182–83; and beauty myth, 186. *See also* Heart conditions
Heart conditions, 34, 70, 72, 106
Hedonism, 37
Hegemony, 15, 16, 24
Heimann, Paula, 145
Herman, Judith Lewis, 34–35, 185, 186, 189, 190, 214
High blood pressure, 34
Holocaust, 155–56, 159. *See also* Concentration camps
Homosexuality, 23, 24–25, 133, 134, 166
Hormones, 53–54, 106
Hospital programs, 180, 181–82, 183
Human rights, 19
Humiliation, 180, 181, 234; acknowledgment of, 58; and learning to feed oneself, 109; and sexual abuse, 218; and social division of labor, 7–8; and thinness, ideal of, 14; and working towards body/self integration, 127, 129, 136
Hunger, 7, 13, 35, 67; and anti-diet approach, 73–74; in early development, 40, 41–49; and food as object relationship, 97–99; importance of eating with, for victims of trauma, 210–13; and learning to feed oneself, 83–86, 88, 91–97, 101–2, 105, 210–13; and multiple personality disorder, 240–42; as a reliable signal, 72; and working towards body/self integration, 129, 138, 143
Hunger Strike (Orbach), 7, 16, 17*n*
Hyperarousal, 188
Hypertension, 34
Hypervigilance, 127
Hypoglycemia, 85
Hysteria, 151

Identification, 6–8, 45, 48–49, 52; and multiple personality disorder, 241; and sexual abuse, 194
Incest. *See* Sexual abuse
Individuality, 4, 25–27
Individuation, 35–36
Industrialization, 3, 8–9
Indwelling, 46–47, 51
Insurance industry, 13n, 34, 182
Introjection, 7, 20–21, 65
Isaacs, S., 25

Jaw wiring, 173, 174–75, 178
Jenny Craig, 32
Jewish tradition, 157
Job security, 19

King, Martin Luther, Jr., 243
Klein, Melanie, 25–26, 145
Kluft, Richard, 196n, 227, 229, 230
Kogel, Laura, 18, 40–56, 57–66, 67–82, 83–115, 116–43
Krueger, D. W., 203, 213
Kurash, A., 130

Labor, division of, 2–8, 25, 26–27, 36, 44
Lacan, Jacques, 21
Ladies Home Journal, 33
Laxative abuse, 57, 63, 66, 72, 88–89, 230
Lesbians, 23, 25, 134
Levenson, Edgar, 146, 222
Lipstick, 25, 26
Little, Margaret, 145
Loneliness, 66, 95, 135
Longevity, 34

McDougall, Joyce, 58–59, 130
Madness, 58
Masculinity. *See* Gender
Masochism, 150
Matriarchy, 53, 37
Medical concerns, 34–35, 72–73, 105–6
Memory, 55, 79, 92; body size as a container of, 126–27; and multiple personality disorder, 228, 229–30, 235, 239, 241; and nonverbal techniques, 224; and sexual abuse, 187–89, 194, 207–9, 219, 224. *See also* Amnesia
Menopause, 72, 127
Menstruation, 52, 72, 127
Metabolism, 35, 72, 142
Middle Ages, 4
Miller, Alice, 208
Minuchin, Salvadore, 180–81

Mirroring, 8, 21, 47, 53–54, 79, 195. *See also* Mirrors
Mirrors, 22, 48–49, 139, 153. *See also* Mirroring
Misogyny, 55–56, 62, 186
Mitchell, Stephan, 18, 146
Modern Times (film), 4
Moral defense, 31, 125
Morality, 114
Morrison, Toni, 24
Mother-child relationship, 14, 36, 47, 60, 154; and the "culture mother," 18; and deep psychological structure, 27; and internalization of culture, 16–17; and meaning and function of food, 40–46; and social division of labor, 2, 8; and symbolization, 18, 19–22. *See also* Mirroring; Mother-daughter relationship; Pregnancy
Mother-daughter relationship: and anorexia, 98–99; in early development, 44–46; and identification, 6–7, 48–49, 52; and internalization of culture, 16; and puberty, 51–52; and social division of labor, 8. *See also* Mother-child relationship
MPD (multiple personality disorder), 191–92, 196, 209, 227–42
Mutuality issues, 167–71

Narcissism, 49–51, 60, 132, 143; and bulimia, 63; and learning to feed oneself, 111; and symbolic meanings of food, 58
Natural food movements, 36
New York Times, 1
Nonverbal techniques, 223–26, 237
Nurturance, labor of, 3–5
Nussbaum, Hedda, 190
Nutrisystem, 32, 237, 239

Objectification, 5–6, 49, 132–37, 197
Object relations theory, 15–16, 31, 67, 84, 146; and diet mentality, 173; and encountering internal objects, 78–82; and fat as internal rejecting and traumatized object, 123–25; and food as object relationship, 97-99; and learning to feed oneself, 104; and multiple personality disorder, 241; and sexual abuse, 190–91, 210; and symptoms, adaptive functions of, 74; and thin as barrier to the rejecting, annihilating object, 125–26; and "toxic culture," 201–2; and transitional objects, 19–20, 21, 61; and "trashing," 115; and working towards body/self integration, 122–39

Obsession, The (Chernin), 53
Oedipal complex, 132, 152–53
Ogden, Thomas, 25–26, 203
Omnipotence, 41, 78, 80
Optifast, 32
Orbach, Susie, 7, 16, 17*n*, 36, 37, 62
Orgasm, myth of vaginal, 132–33
Overeaters Anonymous (OA), 151, 182, 216, 233, 237, 239

Palazzoli, Mara Selvina, 44, 130
Patriarchy, 16, 54, 134, 147, 181; and anorexia, 62; and consumer culture, 10, 11; and racism, 24; and sexual abuse, 185–86; and social division of labor, 2, 6; and thinness, ideal of, 12
Peer group pressures, 27
Perfectionism, 28
Personalization, 46–47
Plastic surgery, 11, 25, 186, 199–200
Plausibility issues, 167–71
Polivy, Janet, 34–35
Pornography, 214
Posttraumatic stress disorder. *See* PTSD (posttraumatic stress disorder)
Poverty, 6, 24–25, 63
Pregnancy, 72
Preoedipal stage, 145, 152–53
Profit, production of, 3, 9, 32
Projection, 7, 20–21, 125, 164, 194
Prostitution, 214
Psychodynamic model, 83–115
Psychoeducational work, 67, 71-73, 86, 140
Psychosis, 94
Psychosomatic symptoms, 58–59
PTSD (posttraumatic stress disorder), 185, 187–92, 196*n*, 227, 238
Puberty, 51–54, 185
Public/private split, 2–7, 12–13, 21–22, 26, 37
Putnam, Frank, 196*n*

Race, 23–25, 146
Racism, 4, 5, 23–24, 63
Racker, Heinrich, 145, 151
Rage: and diet mentality, 172–73; and multiple personality disorder, 241, 242. *See also* Anger
Rape, 5, 8, 11, 185. *See also* Sexual abuse
Rationality, 56, 64
Rebellion, 172–73
Recidivism rates, 181
Regression, 203
Repression, 7, 188, 227–28
Revlon lipstick, 25, 26

Ritualized abuse, 46, 229
Rivalry, between women, 153
Ross, Collin, 184, 230
Russell, D. E. H., 185, 187

Saboteur, internal, 70, 113–15, 122, 162, 170
Saccharine, 33
Sadism, 50–51, 150, 169, 170
Safety, therapeutic, principle of, 208–9
Sakheim, D. K., 208
Sands, S., 130
Scales, 15, 137–39
Schizoid experience, 26, 38
Schwartz, Hillel, 38
Seduction theory, 208
Self-hatred, 7–8, 11, 27, 30–32, 34, 75, 77; and bulimia, 66; and learning to feed oneself, 107; mutual, and bonding between women, 53; and transference, 148, 150, 153, 167, 169; and treatment practices, 181; and working towards body/self integration, 118, 119–20, 122, 124–25, 133–34. *See also* "Trashing"
Selfishness, fears about, 79, 109
Self-mutilation, 189, 191
Separation, 80, 110–11, 195; in early development, 41, 43; and puberty, 53
Set points, 34–35
Sexism, 128
Sexual abuse, 27, 54, 147, 149*n*, 150; and anorexia, 180–82; and consumer culture, 192, 197–99; and experiencing hunger, 94; and family dynamics, 192, 193–194; and force-feedings, 180–181, 182; hypervigilance after, 127; and intrapsychic adaptations, 192, 194–197; and social division of labor, 5; and symbolic landscape, 198, 199–204; theoretical perspective on, 184–204; treatment considerations for, 205–26; and working towards body/self integration, 127
Sexuality, 33, 56, 58–63; and anorexia, 61–62, 63; and bulimia, 63; and cultural symbols, 23–24; and development, 49–51; and learning to feed oneself, 88; and puberty, 52–53; and sexual abuse, 194, 206, 215–16; and sexual objectification, 132–37; and sexual preference, 24–25, 133, 166; and social division of labor, 4, 5; and symbolic meanings of food, 58; and transference, 154; and "trashing," 114; and "traumatic sexualization," 215–16; and working towards body/self integration, 121–22, 127, 128–30, 132–37

Shame, 30, 34, 68, 152–64; and learning to feed oneself, 109; and sexual abuse, 194, 197, 207, 209, 216, 220; and social division of labor, 7–8; and transference, 150, 151, 152; and working towards body/self integration, 129, 137

Shapiro, Susan, 224

Shlosberg, Tanya, 181*n*

Slavery, 24

Slenderella, 33

Smoking, 186

Sociobiology, 2

Somatopsychic techniques, 223–26

Splitting, 58, 62; and learning to feed oneself, 99–103; and sexual abuse, 187–88, 191, 207; and working towards body/self integration, 116, 125, 129–30

Stauffer system, 33

Steinberg, Joel, 190

Steiner-Adair, Catherine, 14, 51, 147, 150–51

Stern, Daniel, 47, 146

Stolorow, R. D., 203

Stomach stapling, 173

Subjectivity, 67; and cultural symbols, integration of, 20–25; in early development, 41–42; and internalization of culture, 15–16; and mother-daughter relation, 52; and object relations theory, 15–16; sexual, 132–37; and social division of labor, 4, 5–6, 8; and symbolization, 18, 19–20

Sugarman, A., 130

Suicide, 143

Sullivan, Harry S., 145, 222, 225

Superego, 113

Superior/inferior schema, 170

Superwoman, 1, 14, 51, 112

Surgery, cosmetic, 11, 25, 186, 199–200

Symbols, 17–25, 41–42, 198, 199–204, 209

Symptoms: adaptive functions of, 74–76, 77, 78; and beginning treatment, 68, 69; as bridge to inner lives, 59; as "pan defense," 74, 78, 89; tenacity of, working through, 78–82

Taboo, 185

Tanny, Vic, 33

Television, 15, 22, 23, 24, 50

Thinness, 24, 36; as barrier to the rejecting, annihilating object, 125–26; and consumer culture, 11–15; and learning to feed oneself, 106, 109, 112; lived experience of, vs. images of, 120–22; and misogyny, 55–56

Thompson, Becky Wangsgaard, 24

Thou Shalt Not Be Aware (Miller), 208

Thyroid problems, 105

Torem, Moshe, 184, 230, 231

Tower, Lydia, 145

Trance states, 189–90. *See also* Dissociation

Transference, 70–71, 78, 144–71, 180–83; and analytic resistance to food and body material, 147–52; and asymmetry, in body image co-motion, 167–71; /countertransference co-motion, 164–67; and diet mentality, 172–83; and disclosure issues, 167–71; and learning to feed oneself, 95; and multiple personality disorder, 239, 241, 242; and mutuality issues, 167–71; and nonverbal techniques, 224, 225–26; and plausibility issues, 167–71; and returning to diets, during treatment, 90–91; and role of body image shame, in treatment, 152–64; and sexual abuse, 192, 206, 209; and working towards body/self integration, 124–25

"Trashing," 61, 113–15

Triggers, identifying, 76–78, 89

Twelve-step programs, 180, 182. *See also* Overeaters Anonymous (OA)

Unconscious, 15, 29, 30, 52, 77, 134; and internalization of culture, 16, 17, 18; and transference, 144, 146; and working towards body/self integration, 141–42

Unions, 8–9, 10

Urination, need for, 129

Valium, 35

Vegetarians, 36

Victim blaming, 203

Vietnam War, 33

Voice, 18; loss of, 53; and "trashing," 61, 114–15

Voting rights, 8, 10

Weaning, 43

Weight, 70–72, 152; and anorexia, 71, 107; changes, and treatment, 139, 140–43; history, disclosing, 68; lack of change in, accepting, 142–43; and learning to feed oneself, 86, 88, 93; and set points, 34–35; and working towards body/self integration, 124, 133–35. *See also* Scales

Weight Watchers, 32, 80, 81, 88–89, 90

Wholeness, 111

Wilson, Phillip C., 130

Winnicott, D. W., 19–22, 41, 48, 145; indwelling in, 46–47, 194–95; true and false selves in, 125–26

Women's Therapy Centre Institute (WTCI), 147, 150, 181*n*, 245–46
Wooley, Susan, 145, 130, 147*n*, 167, 181
Work, 3, 6, 64, 86–87
Working class, 10, 12, 25, 130–31
Working through, the tenacity of symptoms, 78–82
World War II, 72

Wyatt, 185
Wyden, Ron, 32

Young-Bruehl, Elizabeth, 17*n*
Yo-yo syndrome, 35, 72, 232

Zaphiropoulos, Lela, 44, 67–82, 83–115, 116–43, 170